BIOGRAPHICAL RESEARCH IN EASTERN EUROPE

Biographical Research in Eastern Europe

Altered lives and broken biographies

Edited by

ROBIN HUMPHREY
University of Newcastle upon Tyne, UK

ROBERT MILLER
Queen's University, Belfast, UK

ELENA ZDRAVOMYSLOVA
Centre for Independent Social Research and European University, St Petersburg, Russia

LONDON AND NEW YORK

First published 2003 by Ashgate Publishing

Reissued 2018 by Routledge
2 Park Square, Milton Park, Abingdon, Oxon OX14 4RN
711 Third Avenue, New York, NY 10017, USA

Routledge is an imprint of the Taylor & Francis Group, an informa business

A Library of Congress record exists under LC control number: 2002025873

ISBN 13: 978-1-138-72218-7 (hbk)
ISBN 13: 978-1-138-72217-0 (pbk)
ISBN 13: 978-1-315-19374-8 (ebk)

Contents

Acknowledgements viii

Notes on Contributors xi

1 Introduction: Biographical Research and Historical Watersheds 1
Robert Miller – UK, Robin Humphrey – UK, Elena Zdravomyslova – Russia

PART 1 The Potential of Biographical Research

2 Context, Authenticity, Referentiality, Reflexivity: Back to Basics in Autobiography 27
J. P. Roos – Finland

3 The Usefulness of Life Stories for a Realist and Meaningful Sociology 39
Daniel Bertaux – France

4 Three Dimensions of Biographical Narratives 53
Valery Golofast – Russia

PART 2 Communists, Informers and Dissidents

5 Estonian-inclined Communists as Marginals 71
Aili Aarelaid-Tart – Estonia

6 Portrayals of Past and Present Selves in the Life Stories of Former Stasi Informers 101
Barbara Miller – Austria

7 Czech Dissidents: A Classically Modern Community 115
Vladimir Andrle – UK

8 Anti-Soviet Biographies: The Dissident Milieu and its Neighbouring Milieux 129
Sofia Tchouikina – Russia

9 The Café Saigon *Tusovka*: One Segment of the Informal-public Sphere of Late-Soviet Society 141
Elena Zdravomyslova – Russia

PART 3 Exile, Migration and Adapting to Social Change

10 Living the Life: Exile in the Experience of the Polish Intelligentsia 181
John A. Jackson – Ireland

11 Biographical Continuities and Discontinuities in East–West Migration before and after 1989. Two Case Studies of Migration from Romania to West Germany 191
Roswitha Breckner – Austria

12 Trajectories of Coping Strategies in Eastern Germany 211
Olaf Struck – Germany

13 Inequality and Exclusion in the History of Poor Slovak Families 225
Zuzana Kusá – Slovakia

PART 4 Ethnicity and Sexuality

14 Different Generations of Leningrad Jews in the Context of Public/Private Division: Paradoxes of Ethnicity 239
Viktor Voronkov and Elena Chikadze – Russia

15 Shame, Promiscuity and Social Mobility in Russian Autobiographies from Poor Working-class Milieux 263
Anna Rotkirch – Finland

16 The Construction of Sexual Pleasure in Women's Biographies 299
Anna Temkina – Russia

Index 321

Acknowledgements

This book arises out of the work of the Biographical Perspectives on European Societies Research Network of the European Sociological Association (for particulars and contact addresses see *www.valt.helsinkifi/esa/biog.htm*). Under the chairmanship of, first, J. P. Roos of the University of Helsinki and then, more recently, Bob Miller of Queen's University, Belfast, this research network has been responsible for lively and well-attended workshops and conference streams at St Petersburg (1996), Essex (1997), Amsterdam (1999) and Helsinki (2001). One feature of all these meetings has been the contributions from those who had researched aspects of the rapidly changing social context in Eastern Europe and Russia. As we mention in the opening chapter, the coincidence of 'biographical turn' in the social sciences with the dramatic social, economic and political upheavals taking place in the eastern half of Europe at the close of the twentieth century meant that a highly appropriate methodological perspective was employed extensively for the exploration of how people were adapting and realigning their lives in response to a profound historical watershed.

This book brings together the work of many of the most advanced and active biographical researchers working on Eastern Europe, and presents also the work of many authors who have published extensively in their own languages but who have had less opportunity to disseminate their work more widely in English. The authors in this volume come from nine countries across Europe and the research on which the chapters are based was conducted in seven different languages.

Although all the draft chapters were delivered in English, major editorial issues were raised through the translating and copy-editing of the texts. Particularly careful attention has been paid to the translating of quotations, as in sociology these are not simply pieces of text or dialogue, but sequences of data. Great care was taken throughout the editorial process to balance the sometimes competing demands of maintaining authenticity and of presenting the texts in clear and idiomatic English. We acknowledge the immense help we received in this process from Michael Ayton, a long-standing friend of one of the editors and a meticulous professional copy-editor of academic texts. He can be reached through the website of his company, *www.alembic.info*. We recommend him without reservation!

This book also would not have been possible without the new technology that is transforming our working lives and shrinking the world by making communication fast and easy. Email, then, has provided us all with the means by which we have sent drafts back and forth and asked and responded to questions swiftly. Without it, the task of editing this book would have been immeasurably more arduous – probably too arduous to contemplate!

For help with the preparation of the camera-ready copy of this book we thank Richard Nowley, from the Staff Development Unit at Newcastle University, who was always ready to provide the expert support and guidance that were needed regularly towards the end of this project.

We all have personal thanks to make: Robin would like to thank Jane, for her patience, support and understanding, and his daughter Rosie, who interrupted the work on this book many times and who enriched and complicated the editorial process in equal measure! Bob would offer thanks to Jo Campling, who helped find this book a publishing home, and Elena to Marina Badkhen, who translated several Russian chapters.

One final comment: on a wintry night in Durham City, in the North East of England, in the early 1980s, Robin attended a talk given by the radical historian and campaigner E. P. Thompson. He was arguing for European Nuclear Disarmament, and Robin remembers being greatly enthused by his vision of a thawing of the Cold War and a unification of East and West Europe. 'Visionary but a little idealistic', he thought at the time. The fact that now he has collaborated on a book spanning nine European countries from what was both East and West Europe and has edited the contributions with a Russian and a North American, albeit one who lives and works in Northern Ireland, gives him enormous satisfaction and acts, in a small way, as testament to the scope of E. P. Thompson's political imagination and to the courage and determination of all those who have risked so much to bring his vision considerably closer to a reality than it was twenty years previously.

Notes on Contributors

Aili Aarelaid-Tart is an Assistant Professor in the Department of Sociology at Tallinn Pedagogical University, Estonia. She started to take an interest in biographical research in 1996, at first interviewing Estonian intellectuals about their lives and mentalities during the period of Soviet occupation. This fieldwork was concluded in the book *Still Thinking about Culture*, which was published in Estonian in Tallinn in 1998. At the moment she is working on comparing the life stories of Russian inhabitants of Estonia and Estonian exiles in Sweden. The goal of this work is to find out more about the different ways of acculturation of ethnic diasporas under totally opposite political systems. She is a member of the board of the Biographical Perspectives on European Societies Research Network of the European Sociological Association.

E-mail: *aarelaid@iiss.ee*

Vladimir Andrle was, until September 2002, a Lecturer in the Department of Sociology, University of York, UK. He is the author of *Managerial Power in the Soviet Union*, 1976; *Workers in Stalin's Russia*, 1988; and *A Social of History of Twentieth-Century Russia*, 1994. While all these earlier works are based on applying analytical frameworks of qualitative sociology to textual materials that include also biographical data and recollections, life narratives became the focal point of his interests in the mid-1990s. He has done life-story interviewing in the Czech Republic and supervised student projects of this kind in York. His analyses of the Czech life narratives have been published in journals including *Sociology* and

Qualitative Sociology, as well as, in the Czech language, *BIOGRAF*. Further work is in progress.

E-mail: *vladimir@andrle1.vispa.com*

Daniel Bertaux is Directeur de Récherches at the French Centre National de la Récherche Scientifique, Paris, in the Sociology section. His various substantive interests include social classes and social mobility/social reproduction, which he has studied in France and in Soviet Russia; the survival of artisanal forms in France (on the example of artisanal bakery); and, more recently, the relation between welfare regimes and the action of households in precarious situations in six European societies. From the 1970s onwards he has actively participated in the rediscovery of the life-history approach as a sociological research tool, consistently developing it – in a realist and 'ethnosociological' perspective – as a way of studying subsets of sociostructural relationships and dynamics, and enlarging its scope though the collection of case histories of households and families over several generations. He is the author of *Destins personnels et structure de classe*, 1977, *La mobilité sociale*, 1986, *Pathways to Social Class* (with Paul Thompson, 1997) and *Les récits de vie*, 1997, as well as numerous papers published in French or English. He works presently at the Centre d'Étude des Mouvements Sociaux.

E-mail: *Daniel.Bertaux@ehess.fr*

Roswitha Breckner is a Lecturer and researcher at the Institute of General Sociology, Vienna University of Economics and Business Administration. She has been working with the biographical approach since 1982 in different areas of research, recently mainly in studying migration processes from East to West Europe before 1989, life stories and histories of Austrian veterans of World War II, and, in the context of an EU project, biographical strategies in risk societies. She edited, with Devorah Kalekin-Fishman and Ingrid Miethe, the volume *Biographies and the Division of Europe: Experience, Action and Change on the 'Eastern Side'* (Leske & Budrich, 2000).

E-mail: *roswitha.breckner@wu-wien.ac.at*

Elena Chikadze is a researcher at the Centre for Independent Social Research, St Petersburg. Her areas of interest include ethnic identity, qualitative methodology in social sciences and discourse analysis.

E-mail: *chikadze@indepsocres.spb.ru*

Valery Golofast is Senior Researcher as the Sociological Institute, Russian Academy of Sciences, St Petersburg, and Head of the Social and Cultural Changes Section. His areas of specialisation include research methodology, social stratification, and social and cultural change.

E-mail: *golofastvb@newmail.ru*

Robin Humphrey is a Senior Lecturer in the School of Geography, Politics and of Sociology at the University of Newcastle upon Tyne, UK. He first became interested in biographical research in the early 1980s and adopted the approach for his Ph.D. thesis, which focused on the social lives of elderly people in an ex-mining town in the North East of England. He has retained his interest ever since, and is on the board of the Biographical Perspectives on European Societies Research Network of the European Sociological Association.

E-mail: *robin.humphrey@ncl.ac.uk*

John A. Jackson is Emeritus Professor of Sociology at Trinity College, University of Dublin in Ireland. He retired in 1997 after 23 years as Professor and Head of Department. From 1969 to 1974 he was Professor and Head of Department of Social Theory and Institutions at Queen's University, Belfast. He completed postgraduate work at the London School of Economics, where he wrote a thesis on the Irish in London under the supervision of Professor David Glass. He also did postgraduate work at the University of Chicago. He was born in England in 1929 as the only child of an Irish mother and an English father. He is pursuing an active retirement as Chair of the Irish Aid Advisory Committee and has long been interested in intergenerational linkages, biographical research and narratives.

E-mail: *jjackson@eircom.net*

Zuzana Kusá is a Senior Research Fellow at the Institute for Sociology of the Slovak Academy of Sciences, Bratislava. She has been the coordinator of a number of research projects using life stories since 1991, including *The Social History of Poverty in Slovakia: Patterns of Family Behaviour and Reproduction of Poverty*, funded by the SOCO Program of the Institute for Human Sciences, Vienna. She has been a member of the boards of the Biography and Society Research Committee of the International Sociological Association and the Biographical Perspectives on European Societies Research Network of the European Sociological Association. She is also on the editorial board of *BIOGRAF*, the bulletin of the Association for Reflexive Sociology, Prague, Czech Republic.

E-mail: *sukusa@klemens.savba.sk*

Barbara Miller became interested in biographical research while working on her Ph.D. thesis in the mid-1990s. The thesis – which has since been published in book form by Routledge – considers the motivations for working as an informer for the East German State Security Service, the Stasi. She is now working as a broadcast journalist in Vienna, Austria.

E-mail: *barbaramillerbm@hotmail.com*

Robert Miller is Senior Lecturer in Sociology at Queen's University, Belfast and Director of the Centre for Social Research. He came to biographical research through attempts to analyse quantitative life-history survey data and has since moved to the qualitative study of social mobility through biographical methods and the study of family histories/strategies. He is presently Chair of the Biographical Perspectives on European Societies Research Network of the European Sociological Association.

E-mail: *r.miller@qub.ac.uk*

J. P. Roos is Professor in the Department of Social Policy at the University of Helsinki, Finland. He has been working with biographies since the late 1970s and has published several books on Finnish life and generations. He has been chair of the Biographical Perspectives Research Network of the European Sociological Association. He is presently working on generations, and especially baby-boomers, in Finland, in the framework of a comparative research project. For more information see his website: *www.jproos.org*.

E-mail: *jproos@valt.helsinki.fi*

Anna Rotkirch is Docent in Social Policy and Women's Studies at the University of Helsinki, Finland. She is currently working as a Lecturer at the Christina Institute of Women's studies at the University of Helsinki. She has been involved in several research projects using the biographical method, notably 'Social Inertia and Cultural Change in St Petersburg' (1996–9) and 'Models of Selves: Russian Women's Autobiographical Writings' (1998–2000), both financed by the Academy of Finland. Her publications in English include *Moments of Passion: Life Stories of Sex and Love in Three Generations*, with Elina Haavio-Mannila and Osmo Kontula (2001); *The Man Question: Loves and Lives in Late Twentieth-century Russia* (2000); and *Women's Voices in Russia Today*, coedited with Elina Haavio-Mannila (1996).

E-mail: *anna.rotkirch@helsinki.fi*

Olaf Struck is Assistant in the Department of Sociology at the Friedrich Schiller University, Jena, Germany. He has worked with narratives for more than ten years, mostly in the context of employment but also within the perspective focusing on processes of social change.

E-mail: *struck@netware.uni-leipzig.de*

Sofia Tchouikina is a research fellow at the Centre for Independent Social Research, St Petersburg. She became interested in the biographical approach in the beginning of the 1990s and applied it in studies of politically-deprived groups in Soviet society. Her dissertation is devoted to the life-paths of the ex-aristocrats in the 1920s and 1930s after the Russian revolution of 1917. She is also the author of several publications on subculture of the anti-Soviet dissident movement of the 1950s–80s.

E-mail: *sofia@rednet.ru*

Anna Temkina is Associate Professor in the Department of Political Science and Sociology, European University at St Petersburg, and co-director of the MA Gender Study programme. She was awarded a Ph.D. in social sciences in 1997 from the University of Helsinki, and her thesis was focused on the new social movements in Russia. Her study of the women's movement, gender culture and sexuality In Russia led to her interest in biographical research.

E-mail: *temkina@nevsky.net*

Viktor Voronkov is Director of the Centre for Independent Social Research. His areas of interest include qualitative methods, urban ethnic minorities, migration and excluded groups. The biographical approach has become the preferred methodology for researching these subject areas.

E-mail: *voronkov@socres.spb.ru*

Elena Zdravomyslova is Associate Professor in the Department of Political Science and Sociology, European University at St Petersburg, and co-director of the MA Gender Study Programme. She is also a research coordinator at the Centre for Independent Social Research in St Petersburg. Her study of social movements and grass-roots initiatives in contemporary Russia, including counter-cultural groups and women's initiatives, led to her interest in biographical research.

E-mail: *zdrav@eu.spb.ru*

1 Introduction: Biographical Research and Historical Watersheds

ROBERT MILLER,
Department of Sociology,
Queen's University, Belfast, UK

ROBIN HUMPHREY
School of Geography, Politics and Sociology,
University of Newcastle upon Tyne, UK

ELENA ZDRAVOMYSLOVA
Centre for Independent Social Research and European University,
St Petersburg, Russia

Introduction

Biographical research gravitates towards historical watersheds. When one scans the volume of publications employing biographical methods, the period of the Second World War and the Holocaust in Europe stands out.[1] Other versions of the same phenomenon can be seen in the emergence of biographical writings about the transition from apartheid to inclusive democracy in South Africa or writings about the period of the Russian Revolution (Semenova, 2000). This volume reflects that pattern. The period at the end of the 1980s and the beginning of the '90s, the change from socialism to post-socialist societies, marked the greatest transition in eastern Europe since the aftermath of World War II. This transition is being reflected in the emergence of a new blossoming of biographical research.

This blossoming of biographical work is hardly surprising. Or is it? Perhaps we should ask why there is this fascination among biographical researchers with historical fault lines. One of the goals of sociological research is to sensitise the observer to that which is usually unremarked – the taken-for-granted everyday behaviours that 'hide in plain view'.

Biographical research may be guilty of the same laxity. We all know that times of important social transitions receive special attention from biographical researchers, but we have not thought to ask *why* they merit this attention.

In part, this tendency is driven by the way in which respondents react when they are asked to relate their life stories, especially if they are allowed to do so with a minimum of direction. Given their heads, most life-history interviewees will gravitate directly to the times of greatest change in their lives. The life course provides one axis of orientation – a personal axis. Many respondents exhibit a tendency to concentrate upon the period of the greatest transitions in their own life courses. Many of these events are solely personal: leaving the home of origin; marriage; childbirth; a major illness and so forth. However, when people recount the significant points in their lives, one can often note a striking juxtaposition of the personal and the public. The public events that people relate as being of great personal significance tend to be public events that took place around the time of a person's transition to full adulthood. 'Sixty-somethings' will nostalgically recount the first time they heard *Rock around the Clock*, those aged in their fifties will belabour the rest of us with accounts of their political awakening in 1968, while later generations have the misfortune of having to make do with Glam and punk rock. It is as much that one was aged 18–24 when certain historical events were experienced that gives them their personal significance as that these events were significant in themselves.

At the same time, however, some events and historical periods are more important than others. A series of related historical events happening in close sequence[2] can have the effect of fundamentally transforming the social and political life in a society so that the events come to be seen as a 'historical watershed'. For one writing within Northern Ireland, for instance, the events centred on the breakdown of civil order during August 1969 constitute just such a 'watershed'. The events around the transition from socialism in central and eastern Europe centred on 1989 are another such watershed. When genuinely important historical transitions happen to coincide with one's entry into young adulthood, personal and historical significance interact and intensify. The basis is laid for a cohort generation – an aged-based collectivity of individuals with a common identity distinct in comparison to that of those who came before and those who will follow (Miller, 2000, pp. 29–34).

So, one reason for the tendency of biographical research to gravitate towards periods of transition is that the respondents to biographical inquiries – the interviewees themselves – tend to gravitate towards these periods in their accounts. This, however, is only part of the answer. Even if the respondents did not do so spontaneously themselves, biographical inquirers would inquire about the period or periods of major societal transformation that their respondents have experienced. For instance, a researcher interviewing a German born during the early decades of the twentieth century would be remiss if they did not probe someone who neglected to mention the Nazi period or the Second World War and its aftermath.

Some of the reasons for this are obvious. The respondent who skates around the major historical events of their life span paradoxically draws attention to those very events. Either they are exceptional is some way in managing to have lived through seminal events while somehow remaining unaffected by them, or, more probably, they are suppressing or avoiding the significance of these events. Either way, their account is incomplete in areas that may be most central to their life stories and the researcher will want to probe further. Has the biographical interviewee really managed to have been unaffected by the major events of his or her epoch? If so, they are exceptional and worth further attention. If interviewees are avoiding the relation of these events in their interview, again there must be reasons for their doing so.

It would be difficult (if not impossible) to find *any* society in the contemporary world that has not experienced some major socially-transforming event or events at some point across the lifetime of its elder members. The apocryphal Chinese curse 'May your descendants live in interesting times' in fact applies in some degree to everyone's descendants in all times and places. The difference between present-day societies is not one of the presence or absence of socially-transforming events, but rather one of differences in kind between societies in the degree or intensity of the trauma caused by the events to which they have been subject. Biographical researchers in any society have a fund of social watersheds to draw upon.

The Issue of Continuity

While these motives for centring on historically significant periods are important and legitimate, in a way they are peripheral to the core of the biographical approach. Concentrating solely upon the events that form the unique history of a society will produce an atomised corpus of biographical research concerned with each 'case' or society in isolation. Events will be taking over and driving the biographical impetus. Biographical researchers are also drawn to periods of significant social transition because these periods afford the possibility of discovering how informants have maintained and constructed their biographical identities. This is a more universal project that transcends any given society or generation from which information is being drawn.

Continuity of identity is the problem of biographical analysis that periods of profound societal transition offer some opportunity for solving. Anyone who has carried out biographical interviews with older respondents and invited them to reflect on their lifetimes will often hear their informants remark how, while many things have changed drastically over their lives, the core of their identity has remained constant. Remarks such as 'But really, inside I'm still the girl I was at sixteen' are common.[3] Remarks of this ilk are posing an implicit question: 'How is it possible, after all that has happened to me over the years, that inside I'm still the girl I was at sixteen?' Might it not seem more likely that the personal experiences of a normal life course – a working life, marriage and child-rearing, illnesses and so forth, all culminating inevitably in the loss of loved ones and the ageing of one's own body forcing a person to contemplate their mortality – would alone be sufficient to cause one's sense of identity in old age to have little in common with that experienced when one was young?

Counter-arguments also can be made. The same accounts of lives can be interpreted differently, with the discontinuities between youth and age being highlighted. For ill or good, the experiences of a lifetime do change people. The elderly person knows that he or she is not completely the same person as they were when they were young. While the theme of continuity of personal identity between old age and youth is not unusual, it is possible to find respondents who will state emphatically that they have nothing in common with the person they used to be. Furthermore, for those who do claim continuity, this continuity may only be an illusory construction of the present. Real change may have occurred, but it could have been gradual over decades or have taken place so long ago that the point of view of the younger version of the respondent has faded beyond their recollection.

Either situation, however, carries the same implications for the biographical researcher. Continuity of personal identity across the life course – its extent, whether it is real or not, how to deal with it conceptually and the mechanisms and circumstances of its change – is a genuine problem for the biographical researcher. Continuity, whether recognised as such or not, is a central and persisting concern of biographical research and much biographical writing is concerned with how continuity of personal identity persists or is describing the circumstances when personal identity alters.

Habitus

Bourdieu's concept of *habitus,* with its associated theorisation, provides a means for beginning to work with the biographical issues surrounding the problem of the continuity of personal identity. *Habitus* is a janus-faced concept, located between structure and action and affected by, and affecting, both:

> The conditionings associated with a particular class of conditions of existence produce *habitus*, systems of durable, transposable dispositions, structured structures predisposed to function as structuring structures, that is, as principles which generate and organise practices and representations that can be objectively adapted to their outcomes without presupposing a conscious aiming at an end or an express mastery of the operations necessary in order to attain them. (Bourdieu, 1990 [1980])

One of the aspects of *habitus* is a set of dispositions to behaviour which are mainly laid down when the individual is young. These dispositions can be inculcated through explicit instruction or admonition: for example, parents telling their son 'Walk up straight like a man' or their daughter 'Nice girls don't do that'. However, the core of this bedrock of behaviour that will become the *habitus* is laid down without conscious intent on the part of a 'socialiser' through the young child absorbing modes of thinking and ideas of appropriate behaviour while experiencing the social milieu of its social class – the 'all-encompassing field' of structures and interactions around it:

> A product of early childhood experience, particularly of unconscious family socialisation, it is continually modified by the individual's encounters with the world. To the extent that members of different social classes differ in the nature of their primary socialisation … each class has its own characteristic *habitus,* with individual variations. The *habitus*, then, 'brings about a unique integration, dominated by the earliest experiences statistically common to the members of the same class [Bourdieu, 1977]' … (DiMaggio, 1979, p. 1,464)

The young child internalises the world view of its class fraction and gender through its direct experience of the everyday lived world. In this way, the objective social structure and relations of the society are imprinted upon the child, but the view that is imprinted is that which the child experiences directly. It is a view of the complete society, but seen through the lens of the specific social position of one's origin, high, low or intermediate.

So, in one sense *habitus* is passive. A view of social structure is imprinted upon the individual which gives him or her a body of knowledge that includes knowledge about the behaviour appropriate to given situations. This body of knowledge is both enabling and constraining. On the one hand, *habitus* structures the world. It is the systems of categorisation and thinking that are employed to order one's perception of the social environment. Through the *habitus*, the child has an understanding of reality and possesses a repertoire of behaviour. On the other hand, the individual is not aware of the social environment beyond the manner in which his or her *habitus* has ordered it (Schwartz, 1997, pp. 105–7). Hence, the child is constrained, having only the understanding of reality as it is seen from the social class position of its origin and limited in its compass of action to those behaviours understood as appropriate for someone of its origin. Perception of the world and action comes about through *habitus*, but a person's perceptions and their dispositions to action have been determined by their origin. Assuming that the imposition of *habitus* has actually reflected the world view represented by an individual's social class position of origin, that individual is tightly constrained in having to remain within their class fraction.

At the same time, however, the *habitus* is active. 'In Bourdieu's work the concept "habitus" designates those internalised group norms which regulate the practice of individual human agents according to a logic that mediates social structure and willed human action' (Garnham, 1986, p. 424). Even more than a body of knowledge and a view of the world, the *habitus* is also a set of dispositions to behaviour. The ultimate goal of these dispositions to action is to benefit the individual in competition with others for valued or scarce goods – to maximise capital is one of its forms (DiMaggio, 1979, p. 1,463). Some of these dispositions are specific – what a child of their social fraction should do in a specific situation – but the dispositions are also non-specific: modes of behaving that are not bound to any specific situation but are general ways of reacting. The dispositions can be thought of as a 'feel for the game' – 'fuzzy logical'[4] modes of acting brought into play to maximise a person's capital in any given situation or field:

> The concept has broadened in scope over time ... to emphasise inventive as well as habituated forms of action. The variety of designations, nonetheless, all evoke the idea of a set of deeply internalised master dispositions that generate action. They point toward a theory of action that is practical rather than discursive, prereflective rather than conscious, embodied as well as cognitive, durable though adaptive, reproductive though generative and inventive, and the product of particular social conditions though transposable to others. (Schwartz, 1997, p. 101)

To the extent that there were objective constraints on action and exposure to a limited scope of actions when a person's *habitus* was laid down, the dispositions to behaviour in a person's *habitus* will be incomplete and/or inaccurate: *méconnaissance* ('the process whereby power relations are perceived not for what they objectively are but in a form which renders them legitimate in the eye of the beholder': Bourdieu and Passeron, 1979). This feature, which in English is usually translated as *misrecognition*, means that a person's *habitus* will be limited, and will probably fail to include at least some of the dispositions to action that could be beneficial to them.

The academic as social analyst has the potential here to play a radical role by undermining misrecognition. A social group disadvantaged by discrimination based on ethnic origin, gender or disability will be limited by the behavioural dispositions of a *habitus* built up in congruence with a discriminatory social structure. If given the opportunity of becoming aware of this, however, it is capable of evolving a more accurate perception of its position. This can generally be accomplished by recasting previously legitimate but inequitable social relations as *illegitimate*. With reference to social mobility, predispositions can be altered so that previously unrecognised routes of upward mobility or opportunity become recognised.

Misrecognition links to the denial of self-interest, especially material self-interest, by advantaged groups. The naked pursuit of self-interest can be rationalised by attaching a different symbolic meaning which obscures the self-aggrandisement. For instance, the accumulation of wealth by private individuals or corporations can be legitimated by philanthropy or charitable giving (Schwartz, 1997, pp. 89–91). The self-aggrandisement of intellectual and artistic strata can be seen in a much more favourable light if depicted as disinterested artistic endeavour. And, of course, patriarchy or paternalism can be portrayed as protection of the 'weaker sex' or the inferior.

Misrecognition is based upon power. Those with social power, whether it is based in class, gender, ethnicity or anything else, have the capacity to effect misrecognition through a process of *symbolic violence* – imposing evaluative meanings on cultural traits to accentuate the desirability of traits possessed by dominant categories and class fractions while simultaneously belittling traits that are characteristic of the lower classes, the disadvantaged and the less abled (Jenkins, 1992, p. 104; Lash, 1993, p. 198):

> Hierarchies depend on the social arrangements that sustain and reproduce them. The persistence of these arrangements, says Bourdieu, itself depends on the systematic misrecognition of their oppressive nature by both dominators and dominated. This misrecognition is inculcated, in advanced societies, by differential socialisation of children of different social classes; by the rationalisations advanced by institutions and fields about their own processes; and by a continuing work of 'euphemisation', of unconscious self-censorship of communication to render it legitimate according to the structure of the field within which it is to be received. (DiMaggio, 1979, p. 1,462)

A cycle develops, in which limited opportunities and exposure to the social structure from a point of view that allows only a limited repertoire of actions produce a limited *habitus*, which in turn limits the capacity of individuals to change either the structure or their places in it. This in turn feeds into the next cycle of generation – a process of *social reproduction* in which individuals in effect impose their own exploitation. In order to be truly socially mobile, the individual will have to overcome the view of the world imposed by their origin and reconstruct the constraining dispositions of their *habitus*, *only then* becoming able to recognise and exploit potential avenues of upward mobility (Richardson, 1977).

As time passes, the child becomes older and the situations it encounters change. The petty[5] squabbles and conflicts experienced by the small child graduate later to successively larger stages, eventually culminating in adult competitions. The dispositions to actions must be adapted in order to be applied to new circumstances. The *habitus* that was laid down in childhood comes to constitute a repertoire of ways of reacting to new situations. Nevertheless, the individual remains constrained by their *habitus* because the basic repertoire is still that which has been laid down in early life.

However, the *habitus* is malleable. As time goes by and the individual grows older, it is possible for it to evolve. Exposure to new situations or broader parts of the social structure can lead to elaborations or development of the dispositions to action that make up the *habitus*. The most immediate stage at which this is likely to occur for most people is when they enter formal education and for the first time are exposed to social institutions outside those of the family. New social structures will impact upon the *habitus*, new layers of knowledge accumulate, and it is possible that new modes of reacting can develop. However, the initial *habitus* laid down in early childhood retains primacy (Schwartz, 1997, p. 107). Even if dispositions to action are maladaptive in changed circumstances, they are resistant to being replaced. As the individual ages, the possibility of new modes of reacting being laid down which supplant the existing dispositions becomes ever less. A continuity of personal identity develops that has begun to gel by the beginning of adolescence and has set by its end.

There are, however, paradoxes to be observed. The *habitus* is a set of generalised dispositions to action fundamentally set in concordance with the social structure as the individual experiences it in relation to their class fraction at the time of early childhood. Social structures change with time, and the way in which these dispositions play out in the changed circumstances that the adult may experience decades later can be unpredictable. Furthermore, the behavioural dispositions of the *habitus* are largely laid down unconsciously as a product of everyday experience and are themselves not usually perceptible. They make up a set of givens that are so close to a person's centre that they are not easily known. Being unaware of them, the individual normally has little prospect of altering them consciously. At the same time, however, dispositions that may have been maladaptive for a school child or maladaptive in the general society some decades previously may become adaptive in the present, particularly if the society is changing.[6] So, while the behavioural dispositions of the *habitus* are resistant to change, the circumstances and context in which they are expressed can alter, with the effect that the same behavioural dispositions can result in radically new or unanticipated behaviours, with consequences that may be harmful or helpful.

Capitals

An individual's *habitus* can be thought of as the set of dispositions and orientations to action in which the goal of the action is to maximise capital in one of its forms. The core of the idea of 'capital' is that it is 'social goods' in limited supply for which people compete. 'Capital' can take on a variety of forms. Its most obvious state is *material* or *economic capital* – goods, materials or possessions that have a direct monetary value which can be converted relatively straightforwardly into exchangeable finance; obviously cash and stocks and bonds, but also land or other property, valuable possessions with a definite resell value and so forth. But there are other forms of capital that also are valued and capable of exchange.

Cultural capital is the possession of knowledge or skills and the ability to utilise information. The skills needed to carry out specialised tasks and intellectual knowledge, in terms of capacity for working with ideas, makes up part of cultural capital. The idea of cultural capital extends to the individual's own intellectual capacity: '[t]he ensemble of cultivated dispositions that are internalised by the individual through socialisation and that constitute schemes of appreciation and understanding' (Schwartz, 1979, p. 76). Analogous with Bernstein's (1977) ideas about people from higher social strata possessing elaborated language codes, the capacity for working with knowledge can also be extended to the individual's developed capability for dealing effectively with intellectual concepts. This includes possessing a larger vocabulary and more complex modes of using language that facilitate higher mental functioning. The possessors of intellectual capital have a greater capacity for exploiting intellectual material and opportunities effectively and efficiently than those deprived of it. Furthermore, *habitus* includes dispositions to approach problems requiring 'thought work' or intellectual analysis in certain manners that benefit those already advantaged because those coming from upper social strata will unconsciously have absorbed ways of thinking that predispose them to abstract, 'intellectual' thought.

Thirdly, there is *social capital.* This includes networks of friends, acquaintances, colleagues, 'contacts' and the like that an individual may develop. Such networks may be considered resources in themselves because they provide their possessor with real competitive advantages such as access to information, social support, opportunities or even physical protection. Social capital also attaches directly to the individual in that he or she may acquire for good or ill a 'reputation' – an assessment of their virtues (and vices) that they can draw on as a resource. A person's personal social capital can mean that others will react more or less favourably towards them than would be expected on strictly rational grounds – the ability to attract deference, charismatic adoration, fear, support, and so forth.

An overarching concept that draws together all three variants of capital is that of *symbolic capital*. As well as having intrinsic worth, the various capitals that a person may possess also have a value that lies in their estimation or esteem by others. This estimation by others usually, but not necessarily, bears a relation to the actual worth of the capital. It symbolises the intrinsic worth. For instance, an educational certificate such as a university degree represents or symbolises the possession of certain types of cultural capital, but this relationship does not have to be exact. Possession of a university degree of a given classification implies a level of knowledge or competence in a subject as well as implying a set of behavioural competencies and social skills that university graduates are presumed to have.[7] It is quite possible for a person to possess knowledge in an academic subject to the level of a university graduate but not to possess the degree. The lack of the certification of the knowledge through the degree will cost the person. He or she will find it more difficult to realise the value of the cultural capital that they in fact do possess. Similarly, the simple possession of a university degree does not always guarantee that the owner actually has the knowledge and cultural traits that one would expect. Nevertheless, the symbolic value of the degree alone has a real value and can impart advantages, including access to material capital through mechanisms like competition for valued employment positions. Similarly, material possessions have a symbolic worth beyond that of their convertible cash value. The display of expensive possessions or status symbols can be used crudely as signifiers of the material wealth necessary for their acquisition. In turn, as a weapon to negate the strategic advantages of conspicuous consumption 'taste' can be used symbolically to discriminate 'old wealth' from 'new wealth', to the advantage of the former.

Symbolic capital perhaps overlaps most with social capital. Others' estimations of the type of people a given person can include in their networks of friends or business contacts may be of as much importance for determining that person's own social standing as the actual use-value of the network: the 'bubble reputation' is by definition determined by the esteem or lack of esteem in which others hold the person.

The disadvantaged – whether they are distinguished by gender, ethnicity, race, disability or anything else – by definition have, in sum, less access to economic, cultural and social capital. Furthermore, prejudice itself can be seen as a 'pure' manifestation of negative symbolic capital

(Connolly and Keenan, 2000). The negative assessment is at least partially independent of other types of capital and, while individuals may succeed in a given field, the negative assessment of the group cannot be redressed by success.

Watersheds

The *habitus* is a set of dispositions to behaviour whose rationale is the maximisation of capital. Under normal conditions of social stability where societal change is gradual, the set of dispositions to behaviour will remain opaque. While the situations that the person confronts will alter, this is usually due to normal circumstance or to incremental changes as the person moves through their life course. When the *habitus* 'fits' well with the objective reality, behaviour appears spontaneous and uncalculated.[8] Furthermore, since the *habitus* has been laid down through the person's perceptions of the general social environment of their upbringing, the dispositions of the *habitus* can be said to anticipate changes in circumstances as the person grows older. Part of the person's *habitus* will have been set through their experience of the behaviour of older individuals which they observed as a child. The person will 'grow into' the situations they will have seen their elders dealing with in previous decades. This 'invisibility' of the *habitus* poses a problem for the biographical analyst. The *habitus* is part and parcel of a person's identity. If the interviewee is not aware of their *habitus*, how can the researcher hope to access information on it?

A phase of rapid and profound social transformation opens a window of opportunity for collecting information on the working of the *habitus*. If the rules governing how to maximise the various types of capital suddenly change, the dispositions of the *habitus* will no longer operate in the same way and their application will consequently alter. Dispositions that were advantages may suddenly become liabilities and handicaps may become features that facilitate adaptation. When the individual's society is subjected to a sudden radical transformation which is overarching and which affects virtually all aspects of life the routine applications of the *habitus* no longer serve, and the process of adapting dispositions to action will become much more transparent and capable of being perceived. This is not to say that the working of the *habitus* has been supplanted by 'strategic choice and conscious deliberation':

> The lines of action suggested by habitus may very well be accompanied by a strategic calculation of costs and benefits which tends to carry out at a conscious level the operations which habitus carries out in its own way. (Bourdieu in Wacquant, 1989, p. 45)

Nevertheless:

> Times of crises, in which the routine adjustment of subjective and objective structures is brutally disrupted, constitute a class of circumstances when indeed 'rational choice' often appears to take over. But, and this is a crucial proviso, it is habitus itself that commands that option. We can always say that individuals make choices, as long as we do not forget that they do not choose the principle of these choices. (ibid.)

In terms of the various types of capital, what has happened is that the values of the goods that go into making up each type of capital and the mechanisms for converting or realising their values have been changed by altered circumstances. The set of interrelationships between actors centred on a locus of the distribution and control of some category of valued goods – what Bourdieu calls a *field* – loses its stability and goes into a state of flux. 'The field is the crucial mediating context wherein external factors – changing circumstances – are brought to bear upon individual practice' (Jenkins, 1992, p. 86). In a time of transformation or profound social change, the symbolic values attached to the various forms of capital will have altered and the processes of symbolic violence that take place to establish and maintain their values must be reimposed with a vengeance. At such times, the workings of the *habitus* are much less opaque and are more open to conscious perception. This opening for analytical insight, when the old rules no longer apply and new rules must be hammered out, is what draws biographical researchers to periods of profound social transformation.

The Transition to Post-socialism

The transformation from socialism to post-socialism in central and eastern Europe at the beginning of the 1990s was just such a window. The most obvious change was in the rules governing material capital, where the regulations constraining free market economic activity were swept away and replaced with *laissez-faire* economic policies. At the same time, the safety net of cradle-to-grave social support disappeared. The result is that individuals must alter their modes of acting in order to survive: some learn to (re)apply their abilities to great effect in changed circumstances while others find themselves losing out.

Social capitals go through a similar inversion, with some carefully cultivated networks suddenly becoming irrelevant (or, worse, liabilities) and other networks being adapted to convey access to material wealth in a manner analogous to that which they had used to transfer political power in the past. The possession of cultural capital, which has been documented previously as providing some continuity during the transformation *to* socialism (see e.g. Andorka, 1997), seems again to continue to operate relatively untouched after the transformation to post-socialism. The worth of skills and knowledge persists, if not the certification systems that validated them.

Lifestyles and ostentatious consumption serve to discriminate between the new élites and the rest. Possession of material wealth is converted into legal title. The stabilisation of the post-socialist system can be seen as a vast process of symbolic violence at a societal level as the interrelationships of fields undergoing transformation are (re)constructed and new regimes of élites consolidate their new-found status by imposing a social view of reality that confirms and validates their status.

Studies of Transition

The readings that make up this volume all relate in one way or another either to the role of evidence in biographical research or to the maintenance of continuity of identity and the mediation of the *habitus* during the conditions of radical social change that followed the collapse of socialism in Eastern and Central Europe.

The chapters by Roos and Bertaux both present 'neo-realist' perspectives on the conduct of biographical research. They are 'neo-realist' in the sense that each author provides a thoughtful and critical consideration of the issues raised by 'the reflexive turn' in biographical research before arguing for the necessity of relating biographical information to a substantive framework.

A third of the chapters in this volume are concerned directly with the former Soviet Union and arise out of two key components of the context of biographical work in present-day Russia: (1) the revival of a biographical initiative associated with the Russian transition; and (2) the Soviet 'biographical' legacy. Contemporary Russian public discourse in this area is characterised by a biographical 'boom'. This boom takes the form of numerous TV talk shows, the wide publication and discussion of biographies and memoirs in the press, personal notes, biographical competitions stimulated by social scientists, family genealogical searches, and so forth. This of course is part of the transformation of Russian identity which is currently taking place and which has meant that the context in which this discourse is occurring is conducive to biographical research. On the other hand, the same context creates certain research problems: precisely because they are so interested in the study of biography, and personally engaged in constructing it, people are extremely sensitive to interpretation – they are very much 'ethnomethodologists' today.

The Revival of a Biographical Initiative in the Russian Transition

The breakdown of Soviet society, and the emerging opportunities and barriers caused by the reforms that have taken place in the last decade, have brought about a phenomenon which is referred to in Russia as an identity crisis (see e.g. Ionin, 2000). Former Soviet sources of identification often do not work in the current context: the borders of the states, the political configuration, the social stratification of the society are undergoing change. These changes demand active reflexive work from post-Soviet subjects, who are compelled to look for their identities – new ones and old ones. The revival of old sources of identity – class, ethnicity, gender, politics – and the establishment of new ones are a feature of the intellectual climate in Russia during this time of transition. This kind of identity search can, to use the terminology of Fischer-Rosenthal (1995), be labelled as biographical work, and in post-Soviet Russia this has often taken the form of the deliberate construction and recovery of genealogical knowledge. In the course of this intensive biographical work, not only do new emerging social agents – individuals and groups – invent life stories, but biographical work also becomes part of the construction of identities and a pivot of the coping strategies via which individuals clarify those assets that they can use in the structuring of their lives (life-worlds).

This mass biographical work can also be seen as a part of the construction of privacy that is so new to the post-Communist transformation. Biographical informants who were asked about the reasons for the genealogical searches in which they are involved gave diverse answers. One reason which needs little interpretation was just 'interest': the construction of a family genealogy as a hobby. Another reason is the demand of collective memory. One is considered to be a cultured, civilised person if one knows one's background. One more motivation is family pride – having a famous person as an ancestor or being the one with noble origin in the family background. The next reason is looking for new resources for coping with the current situation strategically – resources that will help one find a job, get a child into a school or a summer camp, emigrate, and so forth. One more reason is to consolidate the family as a unit of privacy and an agent of survival. For instance, one informant claimed that she had reconstructed her family's genealogical tree back eight generations because she wanted her granddaughter to understand her family's resources and how important the family is for her life. 'Things could change. Friends come and go, political winds could be good or bad, but actual and virtual relatives will support you.'

The indicators of this popular biographical initiative are numerous. To mention only a few: growth in the publication of life stories, biographies, and the memoirs of leaders of mass opinion and members of élite groups; genealogical searching for families of origin, in which thousands of citizens are involved; formations of oral-history collections spanning different milieux; autobiographical competitions; urban renaming campaigns; and so forth. Biographical social research, with its interest in life stories, is a part of this flow, albeit a small part.

Biographical work as a mass phenomenon gives the biographical research situation in the former Soviet Union a specific flavour and has both a positive and a negative influence on academic biographical research. On the one hand, the interest in self-identity construction, which is replacing the memory-blocking of Soviet-era coping strategies, makes people eager to share their self-understandings and self-constructions. The intellectual atmosphere of voicing identities favours the biographical researcher, who can expect willingness and openness from informants and their emotional involvement in the study. However, the same context can have a negative effect on the study or at least make the research situation more difficult. Cathartic involvement in biographical work, part and parcel of an individual's coping strategy in previous times of social instability, makes the narrator very sensitive to the inquiries of the biographical researcher. The informant may perceive the sociologist as a political intruder into his or her private life who could very well misinterpret it. If informants are carrying out an autobiographical project themselves, they may see themselves as biographical experts. Consequently, they can expect respect for their self-reflections and are ready to oppose the judgements of the academic. Such research situations require specific research designs and techniques of interviewing. Not only should anonymity and confidentiality be guaranteed (which is normal in most studies) but it is important to share with informants the ideology and the concept of research. In post-Soviet Russia, it is important to make the study interactive and to convert an interview into a dialogue of two partners, in certain cases presenting the research results in the presence of the informants and considering their agreements/ disagreements.

The Soviet Biographical Legacy

Soviet 'rules of the game' still influence everyday life in Russia including attitudes and expectations regarding communication, and they continue to impact on professional settings. Their legacy in relation to biographical research is twofold. On the one hand, the Soviet system blocked initial biographical work. A great number of experiences had to be eliminated from individual and collective memory – these blockages were part of the reflective coping strategies of the individuals and groups. People preferred to keep silent or just to forget, not only certain experiences of their own but those of their families of origin as well. Certain memories were not only psychologically harmful – as is always the case with human beings – but could also be dangerous in respect of life-strategies. In the Soviet era people did not engage openly in the search for their roots and certain stories were concealed from the younger generation, just to make their life smoother and less traumatic. People changed their family names so as not to be identified as Jews or Germans or Finns; they forgot or did not know that they were *kulak* or upper-class or had White Guard ancestors. It was safer to live with an anonymous individual biography – to be a Soviet orphan, a *mankurt* (a person without memory), as the Soviet writer Chingiz Aitmatov (1982) put it. This is one part of the Soviet legacy.

The other side of the same coin is the official biographical forms that were designed by the Soviet bureaucracy and filled in by Soviet subjects hundreds of times in their lives. People were obliged to fill in bureaucratic questionnaires that were extremely detailed and covered not only multiple aspects of an individual's public and private life, but also those of his immediate relatives, descendants and ancestors. Soviet subjects provided detailed information on official biographical forms on multiple occasions – in medical offices, in educational institutions, in the workplace, and so forth. These files contained, among other things, such facts as: ethnicity;

the social origin and occupations of parents, wives and husbands; relatives abroad; membership of political and Soviet voluntary organisations; affiliation to the Soviet Army; work histories, with relevant lists of rewards and sanctions; detailed information on children; and so forth. While the types of information were not different in *kind* from those collected in other societies, what was unique was the amount that was collated on individuals. These records were put into archives as personal files, were obtainable from the KGB, and were used in career promotion or prohibition. In the course of dealing with this official biographical work on the part of the Soviet bureaucracy, Soviet citizens did their best to construct politically-correct life histories that fitted the demands of party-state ideology.

These official formulas can be seen as *imposed life stories* which informants used in their self-presentation to official publics. Such self-presentations during official interviewing or interrogations became part and parcel of a person's (multiple) Soviet self-identity. For the inner circle of friends and family individuals had other, 'true' stories, less selective and less politically correct. Secrets – mainly about distant relatives and ancestors, ethnicity and social origin – were an important part of family memory. Even here, however, discretion was a wise strategy and sometimes, for the purposes of self-preservation, people stayed loyal to their official life story even in private. Formal Soviet biographical work was part of a social control and self-censorship system (Voronkov and Chikadze, 1997).

The influence of such a legacy on the contemporary biographical research situation is severe. It forms part of the legacy of Soviet sociology's reputation in present-day society (Voronkov and Zdravomyslova, 1996; Zdravomyslova, 1998). Soviet sociologists, equipped with questionnaires validated by the CPSU departments, were seen as interrogators. People provided them with their imposed life stories that had been developed for official occasions. This means that today the sociologist has to invest a great of energy if he or she wants to get an authentic life story from an informant. Any narrator has at least two (but probably more) stories at his or her disposal for official purposes and for trustworthy people (Voronkov and Chikadze, 1997). To take into account such a legacy, it is extremely important in the current research situation to create basic trust as the ground of interaction between the researcher and the informant.

That it is important to identify the context for biographical discourse is an important methodological assumption for the biographical research one carries out. The type of biographical work in which a society is engaged indicates its reflexive capacity. Knowing how people do their life story telling, we can see the opportunities for qualitative research and its consequences. If we can identify the context (or situation) for biographical discourse we can expect, on the one hand, a certain level of authenticity from the individual life story and, on the other, a certain level of representativeness of the life story in terms of the culture it comes from. Here authenticity does not mean 'truth', but rather the adequacy of a narrative in relation to the frames and categories the informant uses in constructing his or her identity in the life story.

The chapters concerning the former Soviet Union all have in common an interest in the 'quasi-public' or 'public-private' sphere: an area of social life which was lived in open spaces but which was concerned with hidden anti-establishment or dissident themes that could not be expressed openly. The chapter by Valery Golofast sets the stage in a general piece that proposes 'Three Dimensions of Biographical Narratives': (1) a 'Routine' dimension that is concerned with the structural parameters of 'normal' everyday social intercourse at the personal, the family and the group level; (2) an 'Event' dimension that centres on issues of sequencing in time and the life course; and (3) a 'Hidden/Covert' dimension that introduces both the anti-establishment concerns taken up in several subsequent chapters and other subjects, such as sex, that were taboo during Soviet times.

Anna Temkina employs a *habitus*-like conceptual device in her use of the idea of 'scripts' to order how Russian women recount biographies of their sexual experiences. She uses women's accounts of their experiences to construct ideal types of sexual scripts, and in turn uses these scripts to explain the women's differing views of sexual pleasure.

Anna Rotkirch provides two accounts of male sexuality in which the case study accounts are used as devices for comparing the psychological patterns of upward social mobility of an immediate post-World War II cohort with those of a contrasting cohort that came to adulthood at the end of the 1950s. The earlier case makes a psychic journey from 'brute' to 'citizen' while the latter is more opportunistic in his strategy.

Sofia Tchouikina's chapter deals most directly with dissidence in the Soviet Union. She employs the analytical device of the 'career break'. This applies the metaphor of a biographical lifetime as a career in which there is a moment of epiphany when the course of that life diverges from the 'normal' into a dissident life path. In term of *habitus*, the unconscious constructions of strategies are re-formed at the point of epiphany along new lines, the consequence of which is a life transformed on to a radically different pathway. Social structure, in the form of the Soviet establishment, reacts to set the new patterns beyond the possibility of return.

Elena Zdravomyslova continues the focus on 'anti-Soviet' biographies by presenting a retrospective account of the lifestyles centred on Café Saigon. Here, the denizens of Café Saigon occupy a 'quasi-public' niche that parallels political dissidence but can more accurately be termed anti-establishment cultural dissidence. One of the most interesting aspects of this chapter is its follow-up of the habitués of Café Saigon in post-socialist Russia. The effects of the workings of *habitus* that were expressed in Café Saigon appear quite differently in post-socialism. Some of the most successful proponents of the anti-establishment 'Saigon' culture have failed miserably to make the transformation to the open post-Soviet society, while, for others, their previously iconoclast stance pays off big under *laissez-faire* economic conditions.

The division of social life in the Soviet Union into 'public' and 'private' spheres, with a grey 'public-private' area in between in which unsanctioned forms of expression can find a niche, is used most prominently by Viktor Voronkov and Elena Chikadze in their account of the paradoxes of ethnicity experienced by generations of Leningrad Jews. While the common *habitus* of 'Jewishness' persists across the generations, the experience of being Jewish varies depending upon how it can be expressed in ever-changing social conditions. Voronkov and Chikadze posit four distinct generations of Leningrad Jewry: (1) an idealist, immediately post-Revolution 'internationalist' generation for which Jewishness became no longer the major determinant of identity that it had been in Tsarist times; (2) an 'assimilated' generation for which Jewish identity was no longer salient at any level; (3) an 'anti-Semitic' generation in which the majority remained 'assimilated' while a minority revived a Jewish identity, but only at the private and public-private levels; and (4) a contemporary 'transformation' generation in which the split between 'assimilated' and 'revived' persists, but among whom the issue of Jewish identity is now discussed openly in public.

Ethnicity of a different sort forms the centre of Aili Aarelaid-Tart's contribution, 'Estonian-inclined Communists as Marginals'. The 'Estonian-inclined communists' were post-war officials attempting to work within the system of the Soviet empire while professing to uphold the instincts of Estonian culture. Aarelaid-Tart recounts their mixed success in attempting to operate with an Estonian *habitus* while constrained by a Russian Soviet system, and argues for a more favourable historical verdict than the one which has been assigned to them by present-day Estonia.

The life stories of former dissidents are also the topic of Vladimir Andrle's chapter, only he deals with dissidence in the Czech Republic rather than in the Soviet Union. His dissidents from Czechoslovakia can be said to have undergone a 'double transition': first, from political pariahs to positions of authority; and secondly, from political power back to private life, only in the post-socialist Czech Republic. Once thrown into the intense twenty-four-hour exposure afforded by the arena of the politically powerful, Andrle's respondents discovered life to be personally fragmented – they found little from their previous lives that could guide them, and a lack of continuity with their previous existence.

Zuzana Kusá takes a long view and attempts to follow poor Slovak families across three generations. Her responses lead to an exploration of the perceived relevance of major political and historical events for the economically excluded. She does find continuity, but a continuity based upon the 'inclusiveness' of the family. The narratives of Kusá's respondents suborn the egos of individuals to the good of the family, even though the material and structural contexts of the families have altered across the generations.

The problem of biographical continuity is dealt with most explicitly in Roswitha Breckner's chapter 'Biographical Continuities and Discontinuities in East West Migration before and after 1989'. Breckner presents two contrasting case studies of migration across the East–West divide. Both display the common features of a double trauma of transformation. The initial trauma was represented by a flight from eastern Europe to life as an exile and a foreigner in the West, and the second by the abrupt removal of constraints upon travel to the country of origin after the end of the Cold War. One case study represents an example of successful assimilation. The individual's *habitus*, established in his childhood, laid down from the outset a favourable disposition towards assimilation into German society. The end of involuntary exile poses no problems of choice since there is no felt need to return to the country of origin. In the second case, however, the interaction of *habitus*, history and social has created a 'perpetual foreigner'. The false memory of an intellectually-advanced country of origin prevents assimilation into Germany, and then, when return becomes a viable option, the failure of the nation of origin to live up to the fiction means that the individual is left stranded between cultures.

The meaning of exile within European biographies also forms the centre of John Jackson's chapter on members of the Polish intelligentsia who suffered exile. Jackson makes use of Anderson's idea of 'imagined communities' to consider the problems posed by involuntary separation from the homeland and the ironic role that this separation can play in nation-building. As with the latter case study in Breckner's chapter, the maintenance of a false *habitus* can be functional for coping with exile, but only for as long as return to the country of origin is not a viable option.

Olaf Struck's chapter 'Trajectories of Coping Strategies in Eastern Germany' makes the most explicit use of the concept of *habitus*, combining it with Goffman's frame analysis. Employing several kinds of data, both qualitative and quantitative, Struck carries out a genuinely longitudinal study tracing the rise and then the collapse of East German expectations following reunification. He finds evidence in his case study for the consistent expression of the same *habitus* across vastly altered public and personal circumstances.

The extent to which circumstances can invert utterly is displayed in Barbara Miller's chapter about the life stories of former Stasi informers. This chapter can be seen as an account of the changing value of social capital, the imposition of symbolic violence and then its radical transformation. Being an informer, a link to the state establishment which provided access both to considerable social capital and to the agencies that imposed symbolic violence in the German Democratic Republic, became, with reunification, an almost fatal social liability. Miller's respondents recount how they came to realise the adverse implications for them of their participation in the East German state security apparatus as the extent of the revulsion held by the general populace gradually became clear during the post-reunification period. The imposition of a new form of symbolic violence in which the informer becomes a pariah, with its radical symbolic revaluation, means that informants[9] are in danger of having their lives defined solely by one negative aspect, with associated severe consequences. As respondents desperately work to reconstruct their life stories, interesting problems and opportunities of method are created for the biographical researcher. Miller's interviewees are strongly motivated to engage in a process of rationalising their actions and minimising the significance and extent of their involvement in informing. In such circumstances, the mechanisms by which the *habitus* is employed become more visible.

Notes

1 The number of biographical references that could be supplied here is legion. Some of the most significant are those of Schütze (1992) on the life story of a 'typical' German soldier and the Holocaust narratives of the Rosenthals (Rosenthal, 1998).

2 Or perhaps even a single event.

3 Such observations and remarks are hardly confined to biographical research, having many echoes in everyday life. Most of us can think of similar sentiments being voiced in conversations with elderly relatives or acquaintances. (And the older biographical researcher may reflect ruefully that they also are discovering themselves a young person trapped in an ageing body.)

4 Logical, but not consciously worked out. The authors are grateful to Paul Johnson for this insight and for other observations on this chapter.

5 'Petty' from the vantage-point of the adult, not so petty for the child.

6 Or, of course, the other way round. Dispositions that were adaptive in the past may become a liability in a changed present.

7 The actual university which has issued the degree significantly affects the symbolic worth of these latter cultural characteristics. A graduate of an élite university, even if the level of his or her degree is poor, will be assumed to possess more of the latter features, appropriate behaviours and social virtues than higher-level graduates of lesser universities.

8 To both the observer and the actor.

9 If they could not cover their tracks completely and avoid unwelcome attention (of which Miller's research is a comparatively benign, though still threatening, example).

References

Aitmatov, C. (1982), *Burannyi Polustanok* [Burannyi Halt], Sovetskii Pisatel, Moscow.

Andorka, R. (1997), 'Social Mobility in Hungary since the Second World War: Interpretations through Surveys and through Family Histories', in D. Bertaux and P. Thompson (eds), *Pathways to Social Class: A Qualitative Approach to Social Mobility*, Clarendon Press, Oxford.

Bernstein, B. (1977), *Class, Codes and Control*, Routledge & Kegan Paul, London, 3 vols.

Bourdieu, P. (1977), *Outline of a Theory of Practice*, Cambridge University Press, New York.

Bourdieu, P. (1990 [1980]), *The Logic of Practice/La Sens Pratique*, Polity Press, London.

Bourdieu, P. and Passeron, J.-C. (1979), *The Inheritors: French Students and their Relation to Culture*, University of Chicago Press, Chicago, IL.

Connolly, P. and Keenan, M. (2000), 'The Ethnic Career *Habitus*: A Case Study of Chinese People's Career Aspirations and Choices in Northern Ireland', University of Ulster, Jordanstown.

DiMaggio, P. (1979), 'Review Essay: On Pierre Bourdieu', *American Journal of Sociology*, vol. 84, no. 6, pp. 1,460–74.

Fischer-Rosenthal, W. (1995), 'The Problem with Identity: Biography as Solution to Some (Post)modernist Dilemmas', *Comenius*, vol. 15, pp. 250–65.

Garnham, N. (1986), 'Extended Review: Bourdieu's *Distinction*', *Sociological Review*, vol. 34, no. 2, pp. 423–33.

Ionin, L. (2000), *Sotciolologija kultury: put vnovoe tysyacheletie* [The Sociology of Culture: The Path into the New Millennium], Logos, Moscow.

Jenkins, R. (1992), *Pierre Bourdieu*, Routledge, London.

Lash, S. (1993), 'Pierre Bourdieu: Cultural Economy and Social Change', in C. Calhoun, E. Lipuma and M. Postone (eds), *Bourdieu: Critical Perspectives*, Polity Press, London.

Miller, R. (2000), *Researching Life Stories and Family Histories*, Sage, London.

Richardson, C.J. (1977), *Contemporary Social Mobility*, Frances Pinter, London.

Rosenthal, G. (ed.) (1998), *The Holocaust in Three-generation Families*, Cassell, London.

Schütze, F. (1992), 'Pressure and Guilt: War Experiences of a Young German Soldier and their Biographical Implications. Parts 1 and 2', *International Sociology*, vol. 7, nos 2–3, pp. 187–208, 347–68.

Schwartz, D. (1997), *Culture and Power: The Sociology of Pierre Bourdieu*, University of Chicago Press, London.

Semenova, V. (2000), 'The Message from the Past: Experience of Suffering Transmitted through Generations', in R. Breckner, D. Kalekin-Fishman and I. Miethe (eds), *Biographies and the Division of Europe: Experience, Action and Change on the 'Eastern Side'*, Leske & Budrich, Opladen.

Voronkov, V. and Chikadze, E. (1997), 'Leningrad Jews: Ethnicity and Context', in V. Voronkov and E. Zdravomyslova (eds), *Biographical Perspectives on Post-Socialist Societies*, CISR Working Papers No. 5, St Petersburg, pp. 187–91.

Voronkov, V. and Zdravomyslova, E. (1996), 'Emerging Political Sociology in Russia and Russian Transformation', *Current Sociology*, vol. 44, no. 3, Winter, pp. 41–52.

Wacquant, L.J.D. (1989), 'Towards a Reflexive Sociology: A Workshop with Pierre Bourdieu', *Sociological Theory*, vol. 7, pp. 26–63.

Zdravomyslova, E. (1998), 'Becoming of Political Sociology in Russia: The First Steps', in P. Sztompka (ed.), *Building Open Society and Perspectives of Sociology in East-Central Europe*, International Sociological Association.

PART 1

The Potential of Biographical Research

2 Context, Authenticity, Referentiality, Reflexivity: Back to Basics in Autobiography

J. P. ROOS
Department of Social Policy, University of Helsinki, Finland

Introduction

In an earlier article (Roos, 1994), I have discussed the implications of the poststructuralist/postmodern position on autobiography which is – to put it crudely – that there is no Truth, no Reality, not one 'true' way to connect the object world and the spoken or written wor(l)d, but instead many interpretations, all equally possible. Or, as Peter Berger says: 'It is a central thesis of postmodern thought that in our society signs no longer refer to a designatum, but always only to other signs, and that we thus in our discourse no longer arrive at anything resembling meaning, but merely move around within an infinite chain of signifiers (Berger, 1992, p. 95).

As Paul Ricoeur (*www.theology.ie/thinkers/ricoeur.htm*) has noted, the history of thinking has developed through the tension between theories of '*sens*' and theories of the sign, a tension which is currently expressed in the debate between poststructuralist and 'classical modern' thought (see Arditi, 1993; Dosse, 1992; Heiskala, 1993; Heller and Feher, 1988; Taylor, 1990; Toulmin, 1990).

In the article referred to above, I discussed this ambivalence from the point of view of autobiographies, which are, in many ways, exceptionally problematic from both perspectives. I used a 'biblical/dialectic' perspective which contained three stages (actually, in the first version there was a fourth stage, 'Genesis', in which I explained the origins of the poststructuralist approach to auto/biography, i.e. the Genesis not of

Paradise but of Paradise Lost): Paradise Revisited, Paradise Lost and Redemption. The argument was, very briefly, as follows.

The Paradise Revisited

The early sociologists and historians who rediscovered the autobiography as sociological data all approach this wonderful material in this straightforward and euphoric manner: it is the ideal material with which to get to know what really happens or has really happened in a society, as well as to explain what has really happened (see the well-known texts of Bertaux, 1976; Bertaux and Kohli, 1984; Thompson 1978, etc.[1]). This rediscovery provided the initial impetus for everything that was to follow: without this enthusiastic first reaction there would not have been anything else.

The Fall

It was seen (revealed), upon leaving the Paradise of True Autobiographies, that no text is innocent, independent of certain theoretical, conceptual and textual frames. Nothing we describe or see in the world do we just see: it comes to us and through us mediated, always, by the current way of seeing things. In the most extreme versions of this thought, texts are simply written, the author has no significance, and the reader is also just an instance of a more general reader. The 'facts' are not facts but just figures of speech or text. As Eakin (1992) has noted, every element in the simple definition 'autobiographies are texts written by the author, about the life of himself' has become suspect, and many more besides: self, reality, life, culture, etc.

In the most extreme case, then, anything goes (this claim is, of course, firmly denied by the defenders of poststructuralist theorising, but at least in a relative sense it is true, and sometimes even proclaimed). Autobiography becomes simply a text heard by ears of a certain size or form which determine what we hear (Derrida's *Otobiographie*; see Levesque-Christie, 1992), and nothing is as it is said to be. There is no subject, no author, no reader, no reference. I can write whatever I wish, call it autobiography (or even not call it autobiography, but a novel or a text), and autobiography it is (or if it is not, no matter).

The Repentance

But already, in the early 1990s, the end of postmodernism was proclaimed. Writing in *Contemporary Sociology* (1993), Alan Sica and Jorge Arditi seemed to be unanimous that the textual, poststructuralist turn has spent its energy, and, what is most important, has been an interesting critique, but has not given much by way of positive impulses. It is now possible to draw up a balance sheet of what has taken place, and what the effects of poststructuralism have been upon the field of biographical research. In the field of autobiography, the discussion has brought about the following:

1. An awareness of narrativity as a very important factor in the autobiography.
2. An awareness of the often tenuous relationship between *the author*, *the self* and *the 'reality'*.
3. The problem of the identity of the self (continuity, perspectives, multiple identities, etc.).
4. The multiple levels of authors and audiences.
5. The primacy of the text – that it is the text, not the life, with which we are dealing.
6. In the extreme case, autobiography may be seen as determining the life, not vice versa – or in another, more Derridean extreme case, the autobiography and the life may have a totally contingent relationship.

To put it in a nutshell, we know now that is impossible to write an autobiography in the ordinary sense: all aspects of the process are problematic: story, self, life, etc. But as we (I) know from real life, people go on writing their life stories under the assumption that there is a life outside, that they are describing it, that their selves are contiguous not contingent, and that there is a causal narrative connecting the different events, etc.

The Redemption

While it must be admitted that this change of perspective has had many useful consequences (in the best case it is simply a question of increased reflexivity (see Giddens, 1991)) and that the questioning of the different aspects of the process of production of the autobiography has greatly improved our insights into the different aspects of the *autobiographical I* (and precisely in so far as social and cultural codes or narrative strategies have affected the autobiography in the astonishing ways they have), I should like to propose a further change of perspective. Supposing that everything is much more complicated than previously thought, what if the original supposition of an 'I' representing his or her life were still true, or, to put it another way, is an essential aspect for understanding the autobiography?

This is exactly what I wish to propose.[2] The autobiographical project or pact is that of an auto(bio)grapher wanting to tell others about life: how it really was, what has happened, what his or her views of it are. Unless we accept this, we may indeed talk about the end of autobiography, not in the poststructuralist sense, but rather in the sense of having thrown out the baby with the bathwater. But, on the other hand, we cannot revert back to the old perspective: we have lost our innocence; there is no paradise of true autobiography. Things may not be what they look like; they may in fact be drastically different. But still, it is not all interpretation. And most importantly, there is something outside the text, outside the representation, outside the spoken or written wor(l)d. We may have to put our ideas on paper or into words if we want to communicate them, but we are still aware that there is something else, something that we know very well exists but which we cannot (or need not) reach, or express. It eludes us, but it is there. Because I am not a philosopher, *I like to call this reality, or real life.*[3] It need not be extreme, like a concentration camp experience (but it is true that such 'extreme' experiences are more easily perceived as really real if we are sure that they have happened; see Bauman, 1991). With practice, with hard work, with creative insights, flashes, we can advance in our project and 'get closer to the real truth' about a life (objectivity out of subjectivity, as Bertaux, 1995 has noted).

Life stories are serious texts. There is no postmodern frivolity or lightness, play with identities or mere identity-relationships *à la* Gergen, Derrida and Co. For the people who write of their lives, these lives are real, in a very concrete sense, not just situation- or relation- or perspective-bound.

It is much better and more fruitful to go back to the lives themselves, to try to use common sense and experience in deducing more general conclusions coming out of them, using general concepts only when they really are useful and necessary, never theorising unnecessarily. Of course, one should not go too far. There are phenomena which may be or may have to be generalised. But individual lives are unique. They are always a combination of accidents and there are never two similar lives. For a theory of autobiography to be fruitful, it must always be a very concrete generalisation.

In an article which is quite relevant from my perspective (although it refers to fiction!), Abercrombie *et al.* (1992, p. 120) define realism in the following way:

1. The position of the producer is the referent of reality itself.
2. The position of the audience is the perceptual rather than [the] cognitive apparatus.
3. The position of the text is a window, stationed between the observer and the referent; all of which is an excellent description of the classical position of autobiographical writing [only here we should say 'reader' instead of 'observer'].

These realist assumptions govern the writing of popular autobiographies and all the work around and about them. And the punch-line of Abercrombie *et al.* (p. 138), 'Critics of the twenty-first century, then, will be well advised once again to take realism seriously', fits autobiographical theorising like a glove!

One of the arguments against the referential point of view is that texts (or transcriptions of speech) are the only things we can actually have and know about: there is no life outside the text because there is no other way to make statements about life, and thus is it nonsense to speak about real life outside the text or spoken word (see Rahkonen, 1999). I find this implausible and also very positivistic: a simple redefinition of evidence, which an autobiography is definitely not. Of course we mainly use texts, but these texts are nothing at all in an autobiographical context if we do not impute an external reality to them, 'something' out there which they try to describe, more or less adequately. And which we try to understand, and make understandable to others, communicate.

The fundamental questions are these. What is the essence of the autobiographical from the sociological point of view? What are the basic assumptions of research? In what way can one use life stories? That is, when the dust raised by the poststructuralist theory construction has settled.

I thus propose to treat autobiographies (as distinct from biographies) as *essentially reality- and truth-oriented narratives of practices*,[4] where the truth is seen from a unique, concrete viewpoint: that of the author, who simultaneously is the narrator in the story and sees himself as such. Central to the story are life-events, things which have happened in his life, some of which are seen as turning points or definitely important events, while most are ordinary events. But the important thing is that they have happened in the narrator's presence (or were told to him by sources known to and trusted by him). An autobiography which refers only to (say) news in newspapers would not be interesting or believable.

I propose to anchor autobiographical research to four concepts: *context*, *authenticity*, *referentiality* and *reflexivity*. For me, all these concepts are closely interrelated even though they all bring their own contribution to the story. Still, they cannot be separated in a meaningful way.

In what follows, I shall try to discuss the analysis of autobiographies starting from these four concepts. The most important is obviously context. Context means here: concrete conditions and the significance structure of the autobiography, as referred to, explicitly or implicitly, by the author. A good example of context in autobiography is when the story is only understandable in the framework of a given generation and its experiences of a given socio-historical process. For example, when continuous difficulties, deceptions, etc. turn finally into a very positive picture of the whole life, this can be only understood in the context of the war, poverty, the building of the welfare state, new security, social mobility, new possibilities of education, etc.

If one reads any autobiography, the important (but difficult) thing to determine in a sociological analysis is its context. We must discover and construct the context in order to be able to understand and give meaning to the stories. This is particularly obvious if one is doing cross-cultural comparisons of autobiographies, say comparing Russian and Finnish sexual autobiographies. But this is equally important when the analysis is restricted to autobiographies in one cultural context only. The authors are not themselves necessarily aware of the context or able to present it explicitly: this is the work of the analyst/reader, who also 'creates (constructs)' the context. The context may vary enormously: it may be class, a historical situation, an intergenerational family story, etc. The context may be partly created in advance by specification either of the activity (*pratique*) (sexuality, sport, parenting) or of the field (*champ*) of the autobiography (work, family, class, childhood). These are both possible themes for writing the autobiography. When writing a sexual autobiography, for instance, one would in principle write one's whole life, but looking at it from the perspective of sexuality: childhood, relationship to parents, youthful loves, wives, husbands, children, relationships at work, etc. Here the context is transparent, but of course there are more opaque (sub)contexts where a wife may take revenge on her husband by writing a terrible story about him, or where the context may be misery, happiness, justification, etc. In any case, the autobiography must be anchored to social reality through a contextual analysis. In Daniel Bertaux's analysis of bakers (1995) this is very clear: the stories of the different actors – bakers, bakers' apprentices, wives – fall into place only after the context (i.e. the ways in which people move from one position to another, and all the stories are related) is discovered. In this sense, context is especially necessary when one works with a number of autobiographies simultaneously. It is like the society game where at first only certain glimpses of the whole picture are revealed, and then through intelligent questioning more and more pieces fall into place and finally/hopefully the total picture is there.

Authenticity is also problematic, but on a different level (see also Taylor, 1991). It is related to the endeavour of the author to present his life as directly and realistically as possible. This also includes levels of representation or signification, changes of perspective, etc., much as Abercrombie *et al.* do when they attempt to reintroduce realism starting from the observation that it is still the most pervasive regime of 'signification' in popular culture today (1992, p. 115). Typically, autobiographies are relatively 'simple' from the point of view of narrative techniques, perspective, intended meanings. In fact, the discussions about the different levels and appearances of the *I* of ordinary autobiography are more or less meaningless, to tell the truth (no insult intended). The authors do not usually reflect upon the fact that the *I* telling of childhood must be different from the one telling of recent events, or that the present *I* telling of childhood events must be quite different from the *I* who experienced them 20–60 years ago.

The important thing in an autobiography is that the author knows of things (events, relationships) that have happened in his past and wants to tell them. That is the essential difference for the author, as well as for the reader, whatever icing he wants to put on the cake. In fact, I would be prepared to go further than Eakin (1992) and claim that the problematic circular relationship between 'self' and autobiography is actually quite unnecessary: what is needed is simply 'experience of life events': that is, in an autobiography the author tells the story not of 'self' but of his personal life experiences, which belong to him and nobody else (in their totality; many of these experiences may be shared with various other persons).

There is no need to resort to a mythical modern European self to make autobiography possible: all that is needed is referentiality, the fact that I am telling of something that has actually happened to me, that I have experienced. Of course, it helps to have a conception of self, but it is not necessary, at least not historically. And what other way is there of creating a self than by telling an autobiography?

Authenticity is also related to evaluation of the autobiographies. For all the autobiographical competition juries of which I have been a member, this question has been one of the central and most important criteria for evaluating the stories. In principle we are interested in more or less authentic stories, that is, stories perceived (read) as such. The less authentic the story seems to be, the less useful it is from the point of view of analysis. But authenticity is also a dual construct: authenticity on the part of the author and authenticity on the part of the reader. It may be that a superficial, trivial story becomes authentic for the reader from a specific point of view. But this is an exception. Normally, then, the first thing one should do is to find the most authentic stories or the most authentic sections of the stories. There is only one small problem: we cannot be sure whether the story is really authentic, that is, not only constructed as authentic but actually a true reflection of what the author has experienced and lived.

Authenticity also has to do with reflexivity and referentiality. An authentic story is authentic because it refers to something: it stands in an authentic relation to actions, events, social reality. But this is not enough. Authenticity also presupposes reflexivity: a story where the narrator is taking stock of him- or herself, moving on different levels or using different perspectives. This, of course, has also to do with contextuality: the more reflexive the story, the more context is also present.

What I mean here by reflexivity is more or less connected with a multi-layered story: 'If I had known what I now know …', 'In hindsight this was not such a good thing after all', etc. In other words, the author him- or herself is evaluating the story. But it also has to do with motivation: the author tries to explain why he must tell the story in the way he tells it ('This is important for me').

But, in the last analysis, authenticity is all about whether we can believe the story or not. There are, obviously, techniques for making a story believable (to quote the Finnish painter Kimmo Kaivanto, 'As to my own relationship to realism, I can say that I haven't yet made one single realist painting. All I've done is to change the visual reality in order to make it more authentic'), but ordinary authors do not usually resort to any tricks, but create authenticity though their own straightforwardness: this is the story and that is all there is to it. Sometimes the events told in the story are such that one starts to disbelieve the story: a teacher who talks about all kinds of evil things happening to him in a village loses authenticity because he himself believes in impossible events. Or when a Russian autobiographer tells of incest in his life – he meets incest everywhere, all his new women have their own incest stories. These coincidences appear to the reader unbelievable, inauthentic. But of course it is still possible that the story is really true, that is, that there is a context (a milieu) in which such things happen. Only in the case of Soviet society in the 1970s does this seem quite improbable: how could the local community not notice, the circumstances would make it impossible ...

Another example of the problem of referentiality/reality is related to current (Finnish/American) discussion about incest with children, especially the question of recovered memory. There are therapists who think that it is possible for a person to forget an extremely traumatic and difficult event (e.g. the murder of a friend by the subject's father) and then recover the memory much later, often with the help of therapy. Others, on the other hand, believe that such events are so important and momentous that they cannot be forgotten. It is another thing if they happen to children who are so small that they scarcely even know what is happening: even in these cases people have produced memories which have been accepted as true. Here, then, the question of truth and referentiality is really acute: if we think that the memories are completely irrelevant in terms of their referent they could just be interpreted as symbolic, as lacking any kind of truth value. If, on the other hand, we believe in their referentiality, that they reflect the truth in some hazy way, then they are, of course, extremely explosive and terrible memories. In any case, the present knowledge we have about recovered memories indicates clearly that they are constructed fantasies and have nothing to do with reality. They are one aspect of the postmodern mirage which is rapidly disappearing.

Notes

1 A German former specialist in autobiography commented on this text to me, saying that it is all quite correct, but that for him the whole problem has never existed. This is certainly true for several researchers: they are still, so to say, in the Paradise of autobiography, but perhaps feeling a little *ennui* …

2 As an example of the difference in our respective cultural positions, I have formulated this much more 'softly' than Bertaux, who does not experience the same contextual pressure.

3 I readily admit the point of Willke (1993, p. 98): 'Es ist allerdings zu befürchten, daß diese Ironie der Erkenntnis Sozialwissenschäftler, insbesondere ihre Theoretiker, überfordert und deshalb Philosophie bleibt'.

4 In the previous version I did not mention the concept of practice (pratique), which comes from Bertaux, but leaving it out made the whole thing very misleading, as I am not primarily interested in narratives without a referent.

References

Abercrombie, N., Lash, S. and Longhurst, B. (1992), 'Popular Representation: Recasting Realism', in S. Lash and J. Friedman, *Modernity and Identity*, Blackwell, Oxford, pp. 115–40.

Arditi, J. (1993), 'Out of the Maze? Twists and Riddles of Postmodern Thinking', *Contemporary Sociology*, vol. 1, pp. 19–23.

Bauman, Z. (1991), *Modernity and the Holocaust*, Routledge, London.

Berger, P. (1992), 'The Disappearance of Meaning', in S. Lash and J. Friedman, *Modernity and Identity*, Blackwell, Oxford, pp. 94–112.

Bertaux, D. (1976), *Histoires de vie – ou récits de pratiques? Methodologie de l'approche biographique en sociologie.* Unpublished Report to CORDES [mimeograph].

Bertaux, D. and Kohli, M. (1984), 'The Life Story Approach: A Continental View', *Annual Review of Sociology*, vol. 10, pp. 215–37.

Bertaux, D. and Bertaux-Wiame, I. (1995), 'Artisanal Bakery in France and Why It Survives', in B. Glaser (ed.), *Grounded Theory 1984–1994*, Sociology Press, Mill Valley, CA, pp. 539–62.

Dosse, F. (1991, 1992), *L'histoire du structuralisme*, Vols 1–2, Éditions la Découverte, Paris.

Eakin, P.J. (1992), *Touching the World: Reference in Autobiography*, Princeton University Press, Princeton, NJ.

Giddens, A. (1991), *Modernity and Self-identity: Self and Society in the Late Modern Age*, Polity Press, Cambridge.

Heiskala, R. (1993), 'Modernity and the Intersemiotic Condition', *Social Science Information*, vol. 32, no. 4, pp. 581–604.

Heller, A. and Feher, F. (1988), *The Postmodern Political Condition*, Columbia University Press, New York.

Levesque-Christie, C.V.M. (1992), *L'Oreille de l'autre. Textes et débats avec Jacques Derrida*, VLB Editeur, Montreal.

Rahkonen, K. (1999), 'Der biographische Fehlschluss', in K. Rahkonen, *Not Class But Struggle: Critical Overtures to Pierre Bourdieu's Sociology*, Department of Social Policy, University of Helsinki.

Ricoeur, P., *www.theology.ie/thinkers/ricoeur.htm*

Roos, J.P. (1994) (also *www.valt.helsinki.fi/staff/jproos/truelife.html*), 'The True Life Revisited: Autobiography and Referentiality after the "Posts"', in *Lives and Works: Auto/Biographical Occasions*, special issue of *Auto/Biography*, vol. 3, nos 1–2, pp. 1–16.

Sica, A. (1993), 'Does PoMo matter?', *Contemporary Sociology*, vol. 1, pp. 16–19.

Taylor, C. (1989), *The Sources of the Self: The Making of Modern Identity*, Harvard University Press, Cambridge, MA.

Taylor, C. (1991), *The Ethics of Authenticity*, Harvard University Press, Cambridge, MA.

Thompson, P. (1978), *The Voice of the Past: Oral History*, Oxford University Press, Oxford.

Toulmin, S. (1990), *Cosmopolis: The Hidden Agenda of Modernity*, Free Press, New York.

Willke, H. (1993), 'Konstruktivismus und Sachaltigkeit soziologischer Erkenntnis: Wirklichkeit als imaginäre Institution', *Sociologia Internationalis*, vol. 31, no. 1, pp. 83–100.

3 The Usefulness of Life Stories for a Realist and Meaningful Sociology

DANIEL BERTAUX
Centre d'Étude des Mouvements Sociaux, Paris, France

Introduction

The biographical approach has come a long way since the 1960s, when it was totally disregarded. I coined the expression '*approche biographique*' in 1976 in order to express all the potentialities of life histories for social research; I had a strong feeling that this 'thing' was much more than just one more technique of data collection. I even wrote a short paper under the title *Comment l'approche biographique peut transformer la pratique sociologique.*

Since that time, twenty years ago, the practice of sociology has indeed been deeply transformed, but still not enough to my mind. Moreover, the biographical approach has not yet reached centre-stage, where, as I think, it really belongs.

I would like to develop my conceptions about the life-story approach in relation to sociological research as a whole, and even to civil society. I shall focus here only on the uses of *life stories,* as collected through interviews, for *sociological* research.

Life Stories as '*récits de pratiques*'

Life stories, as collected within a sociological perspective and purpose, are not about what one person thinks of her or his life; such an orientation would be adequate for a psychological perspective, or perhaps a literary one, but not for a sociological one. Life stories in a sociological perspective are primarily about what people have done, where and when, with whom, in which local contexts, with which results. They are also about *what has been done to those people*, and how they reacted to it.

The sociologist *as sociologist* is not interested primarily in what has happened to a particular person, but in the social *context*, in the background. It is this social context – be it an occupation, a branch of industry, an institution, an informal network – which is the object of the sociologist's intellectual focus and obsession. Her/his task is to understand this social context. This means identifying the main games people are playing in this social context, along with the stakes of these games, their hidden rules, their inner workings and conflicting dynamics, and the power games being played. This is, to my mind, what the biographical approach in sociology is all about.

There is no need to say that, in this perspective, one life story is not enough at all! No amount of textual analysis can allow a non-sociologist, but also even a sociologist, to make explicit the traces of social phenomena and processes that are showing – to the informed eye – on the surface of somebody's life experiences as narrated to the interviewer. It takes not only a sociological mind, but also comparisons between various life experiences of the same social milieu, to be able to perceive, to recognise, to see such traces.

If they are used in this way, as I used them in, for instance, my research on artisanal bakery in France (Bertaux and Bertaux-Wiame, 1981), life-story interviews appear to be a very powerful tool of observation. Why? Because they permit the making visible of these '*lignes de force sociales*' these objective social relationships which are almost impossible to observe with other techniques, except participant observation. These *lignes de force*, like those of our planet's natural magnetic fields, are all important for shaping social processes and the historical meta-process, as well as the courses of individual lives. But they are invisible. How to make them visible? Life stories as stories of practices, in which people can describe how they hit these invisible lines, how these lines prevented them from doing what they wanted to do or, on the contrary, provided them with unexpected resources, provide a methodological answer to the problem.

Life stories, as collected through interviewing, can thus be used by sociologists to collect very useful information, including much objective information, about the structuring forces behind a given set of social phenomena. If this is done properly, through a proper research design and through adequate analysis, it is possible to reach, if not entirely objective descriptions and explanations of such phenomena (I believe this is a hopeless task, given the very nature of social processes), at least high-quality levels of 'thick description' (Geertz, 1973) of social phenomena and of the processes underlying them. Such a research design allows us to develop well-grounded interpretations of such processes; and even to put forward predictions of their oncoming evolutions, on the basis of an inside knowledge of their internal dynamics.

Although life stories are undoubtedly subjective productions, they can be used as stepping stones to the construction of sociological descriptions and interpretations that come as close to objective sociological knowledge as is humanly possible. Moreover, life stories allow us to reintroduce into social research the dimension of time and the multiple temporalities of activities; this in itself is of extraordinary importance. And finally, well-designed sets of life stories lead the researcher to focus on concrete interactions through time, over weeks, months, years and even generations, thus helping sociologists to distance themselves from both abstract speculation and the false concreteness of isolated individual cases.

Life Stories as Treasures of Objective Information

Life stories, as well as autobiographies, are of course thoroughly subjective, in the sense that each is the expression of a particular subjectivity; one could even say that both forms (but in particular autobiographies) are 'subjectivity squared', because they result from the mobilisation of a subject's subjective skills in talking about him- or herself.

This property of life stories has led too many scholars to conclude that, if they are so thoroughly subjective, they cannot be objective at the same time. This is a typical mistake. It is the unfortunate result of decades of hegemony of scientism in social sciences; for the scientistic discourse is indeed wholly built around the objective–subjective opposition.

Let me show you how life stories can bring objective information, using my own professional biography as an example. I will sample the years 1976, 1981, 1986, 1991, 1996 – every five years.

Fact: I first gave a version of this paper in St Petersburg, 14 November 1996.

Fact: twenty years earlier, I published in Paris a research report, entitled *Histoires de view – ou récits de pratiques?*

Fact: that same year, 1976, I wrote a book, *Destins personnels et structure de classe* (published in 1977), which was an attempt at reconstructing the whole theory of social mobility, starting from Marx, and at developing one of his ideas – the idea of the 'production of human beings themselves' – which I had found extremely promising, but which Marxism had completely overlooked.

Fact: in 1981, a volume called *Biography and Society* was published, which was the first of its kind and which put life stories on the sociological agenda worldwide.

Fact: in 1986, our international network of sociologists working with life stories and autobiographies was recognised by the International Sociological Association as one of its Research Committees, and held sessions during its World Congress in New Delhi. Interpretation: the life-story movement had moved from network to institution.

Fact: in 1991 I went to Moscow and convinced two young scholars at the Institute of Sociology, Victoria Semenova and Marina Malysheva, to try to collect family histories through interviewing. They had no experience whatsoever in this kind of work (fact) but they learnt fast (fact again); they recruited other scholars, and we soon had a team of ten Russian scholars collecting case histories of families. The title of my research project, 'One Century of Social Mobility in Russia', gives a rough idea of what we were looking for.

Fact: in 1996, we published the first volume of this research project. It is called *Sudbi Ljudei* – 'People's Destinies'. Please note the use of the word 'Destinies', a title which my Russian colleagues have chosen to convey to the Russian public what the book is about.

All these are facts of my own biography as a sociologist, facts which may be checked, facts which are not only subjectively true, but objectively true. I could have embedded them in a narrative to put them in perspective, instead of sampling every five years. The question I am asking you is: because my comments and interpretations are necessarily subjective, does this mean that they are not objective? Or rather, should one consider that my subjective interpretations, added to the facts themselves, be treated as stepping stones in the quest for an objective history and sociology of the life-history movement?

Life Stories as Much More Objective Forms than Standardised Biographical Questionnaires

At least in the Western world, the old arguments of quantitativists against 'qualitative data' as subjective data have been completely defeated; it is now obvious to everybody that the 'quantitative data' provided by surveys are nothing but the summation of answers to standardised questions, answers which are of course thoroughly subjective themselves, and remain so even if you code them into numbers, mix them all and produce national statistical averages or correlations whose sociological meanings (by the way) remain doubtful. However you cook cats, or even a representative sample of cats, you still cannot make a rabbit stew.

A team of four of my colleagues have reinterviewed, all over France, 50 persons who had previously answered a standardised biographical questionnaire, and compared the results. The conclusion is very clear: both kinds of data are obviously subjective; but the life stories, because they leave room for detailed descriptions and first-order explanations of what happened, yield a picture which is more detailed, 'thicker', more consistent: in a word, more objective (Battagliola *et al.*, 1991).

I do not deny, of course, that surveys have their own, specific properties; the 'representative sample' is a very powerful tool for obtaining relatively accurate statistical descriptions of the morphological features of social phenomena. But this is not the last word in terms of objective knowledge.

Compared with life stories, biographical questionnaires yield very poor information. The power of the survey lies elsewhere, in the principle of the representative sample. By combining the (coded) data yielded by one or two thousand questionnaires, one may reach a good morphological description of a specific type of collective phenomenon, those such as voting or buying consumer goods, which consist of the mere addition of individual behaviours.

My point here, which is based on my own experience, is that if you replace the biographical questionnaire by life-story interviews, if you limit your investigation to a given social phenomenon, and if you know how to combine the life stories thus produced, you can move fast and deep into another cognitive direction; not that of statistical representativity, but that of in-depth description and understanding of how such a phenomenon takes place, and of when, where, why and with whom, according to which mechanisms and processes, norms and conflictual dynamics. The crux of the matter is very simple (once one has understood it ...): life stories are *stories*, that is, they are narratives (*récits*, in French). As long as sociology was trying to imitate Newtonian physics (as economists are still doing nowadays) it had nothing to do with narratives: physicists do not work with narratives, but with experiments. Then sociology reluctantly (re)discovered the centrality of action in social-historical life. But what *is* the discursive form which is adequate for the description of action? What if not the narrative form, as any historian or lay-person knows? So it is only a matter of time before sociology abandons its cherished dream of becoming a 'full science' and discovers the value of the narrative form (Bertaux, forthcoming; Chamberlayne *et al.*, 2000). This form need not be restricted to individual lives. It applies, for instance, quite well to whole families (or to groups, political parties, social movements, corporations and so on; for a set of papers using case histories of families to study processes of social mobility, upward and downward, in various European countries see Bertaux and Thompson, 1997).

The Anti-realist Perspective

During the 1980s, another kind of criticism was developed towards autobiographies and life stories: a kind of friendly, but in the end very destructive criticism. This critique came not from scientistic minds, but from the opposite direction: that is, from such disciplines as literature, linguistics, and psychology, and from such schools within sociology as phenomenology or sociolinguistics. Unfortunately, it has now become all but common sense under the label of 'narrativism'.

It amounts to saying that while autobiographies or life-story interviews are very interesting texts or discursive productions, they inform us only about the present state of mind of the interviewee, and about her or his values, world view, taken-for-granted assumptions, beliefs, sense of identity, as well as about the narrative patterns offered by her or his culture, and about the interview situation itself. But it also states that, as one of our colleagues put it, 'All of us would question the naïve realism which uses the life history as a documentary method to grasp external realities' (Kochuyt, 1996).

Such a statement is, to my mind, completely absurd; but I have to admit that it does not look absurd to many of my colleagues, who have been exposed during the last decade to new and highly fashionable ideas, such as those carried by the discourses of 'deconstruction', narrativism, and other forms of what used to be called 'idealism'. The new idealism is, as a matter of fact, extremely strong in the United States, and pervades the whole intellectual field (one of its favourite statements, often quoted and variously attributed to Nietzsche or Roland Barthes, is that 'there are no facts; there are only interpretations'). In North American analytic philosophy, this position is called 'anti-realism'. The statement of our colleague Kochuyt quoted above is obviously influenced by this perspective.

Now, I find this extremely disturbing. I accept that the social world is also historical, and that the social-historical world, as an ongoing process or rather meta-process, rather than being a 'given' that needs to be studied and deciphered, gets constructed, co-constructed rather, reconstructed and transformed every minute by the activities and actions of people as agents. That is, I can accept a constructivist view as long as it holds, as a double postulate, that there is a reality 'out there' independent of my or your perceptions, and that this reality can be at least partially observed, understood through research, and talked about. I can and will accept that the reality out there is made up of signs and subjective meanings as much as of material or structural realities such as institutions, relations of production, class relationships, entrenched power relations, norms, projects, and the like. I can accept that I am not only an observer, but also a participant in this moving reality. But if you tell me there is no such reality, but only perceptions of it, representations of it, beliefs about it, I, as a sociologist, cannot follow, because it would mean the end of the sociological quest.

I will not, however, use my time here to try to deconstruct the deconstructionist discourse. J. P. Roos, who shares at least some of my realist postulates, has perfectly described the situation in saying that, whatever the consistency of the anti-realist discourse, in the end he will not abide by it. 'We are', he writes, 'still aware that there is something else (than words), something that we know very well exists, but which we cannot (or need not) reach, or express … Because I am not a philosopher, I like to call it reality' (Roos, 1994). He adds further: 'Of course we use mainly texts, but these texts are nothing if we don't impute an external reality to them, something out there which they try to describe' (ibid.). There is, I believe, much wisdom in this position. We sociologists should not be too sensitive to the winds of philosophical fashions, for these winds are based on mere speculations, and turn around as quickly as they come, while the social-historical realities we are studying do not change that fast.

Having fought for a long time against the 'spirits' of anti-realism, I have discovered, by carefully examining the origins of these 'spirits', that they all come initially from disciplines, or 'fields of thought', that are idealist by construction. I mean philosophy, literature, psychology, and linguistics. None of these disciplines needs a clear conception of 'the world out there' to prosper. Philosophy is only concerned with the world of ideas and values. Literature is concerned with works of fiction, and there are no facts in works of fiction. Linguistics has come to believe that it does not need a real world or 'referent' (what we would call 'the world out there'); linguists conceive of the 'referent' as made up of 'extra-linguistic realities', which – if you are a linguist – can be left out of sight without any damage. As for psychologists, whose actual practice is to listen to clients talking about themselves, many have come to believe that what the client believes about what has happened to her or him is what matters, and all that matters; what he or she has been through 'really' is irrelevant.

There are, of course, in each of those fields, scholars who do not share the anti-realist perspective. In linguistics I could refer to the outstanding work of Bakhtin and Volochinov, *Marxism and the Philosophy of Language*, which was developed and published in St Petersburg in 1927 and rediscovered only 50 years later in France, where it came as a great shock. In psychology I could refer to the works of the British-American neurologist Oliver Sacks, whom J. P. Roos helped me to discover, and who considers, in line with Sigmund Freud, that research should proceed through the study of concrete cases, each one being different from all the others because each one has its own history.

And in sociology itself, I am happy to hear that the case for realism has recently been forcefully made by such scholars as Bashkar, Layder, Archer and Giddens (see the review essay by Layder in *Sociology*, Summer 1996). This reaction is healthy; because if some disciplines (such as the ones quoted above) can prosper perfectly well without a conception of the reality out there, sociology, history and anthropology just cannot. For them it would mean suicide.

From Max Weber to C. Wright Mills

The biographical approach might even receive support from a new reading of Max Weber. Here is a founding father of sociology, who unlike Auguste Comte or Durkheim was thoroughly influenced by historians and by the German distinction between natural sciences and '*Kulturwissenschaften*'. This led him to ground all his thinking in the concept of human action. As human action is never fully predetermined, this point of departure protected Weber against the temptation to look at social phenomena as the mere expression of hidden laws.

In the light of an actionalist perspective, causality is seen in a very different light: the role of contingencies comes at the centre of attention.

Causality is not seen as the effects of some variables upon others, as it is in a Newtonian science and in survey research when it mimics Newtonian physics; it is seen as a process embedded in historical time, where former events and actions create the conditions of possibility of later actions and events. These conditions of possibility are not always necessary (i.e. other events could have created similar conditions), and almost never sufficient; between one cause and its effect, there is not only the interplay of many other causes and influences but also the mediation of human action which is always unpredictable to some extent.

If one accepts Weber's perspective, which could be called 'co-constructivist', it seems that the best way to understand a given set of phenomena would be to look for the processes that have produced them and reproduce them in (always slightly changed) forms. At the core of such a conception would lie a keen attention to the meanings alternative courses of actions have for actors. If taken seriously, this view leads to a capturing of the complexity of the real world, because social actions are also and always interactions. There is thus a potential convergence between Weber and interactionism; and what better definition of this potential point of convergence could be given than that provided by C. Wright Mills when he wrote that 'social science should focus on social structure, history and their interplay within biography' (Mills, 1959)?

This conception of social research remains as valid today as it was forty-one years ago when Mills published it. For Mills it was intimately connected to the need for commitment which, to him, was inherent in social research. If sociologists do not help their contemporaries to understand better the world in which they live and which they construct every day, who will do it? Should this task be left to armchair intellectuals, or even worse, to journalists and politicians?

Conclusion

To end this chapter, I would like to turn to a very important issue for sociologists. What should we do? In which direction, in which kind of research, should we invest our intellectual energies, our professional life? This is an old question, to which several answers have been given; but since most of these answers have recently become obsolete, it deserves to be considered again.

The most common answer has long been the scientistic one: sociologists should try to discover the laws of society. This answer now seems obsolete: there are no such laws. Weber knew it, and Elias too. One can discover recurring patterns of activities shaped by norms and/or by interests and values. But what happens in social-historical reality is not predetermined, only conditioned; in the last resort, it is *action* that makes history.

Besides, sociological knowledge is historically-bound; its validity is limited to the cultural context within which it is developed. The illusions of scientism are, so it seems, lost for ever; constructivism, or rather a co-constructivist but realist perspective, seems to be, as of today, the only reasonable perspective. Whatever the approach used, all that sociology can hope to do is to shed some light on a given social-historical process.

But for what purpose? The answer of most of the founding fathers has consistently been: to try to contribute to orienting this overall meta-process, or at least some of its components, in the 'right' direction; to make societies a little better, more free, more equitable, more peaceful and democratic. Both Marx and Durkheim thought and acted in this way, as of course did Proudhon, Fourier, Saint-Simon, and Weber in his own way; and as do today scholars such as Touraine, Bourdieu, Habermas or Giddens. They are all committed to some extent.

What remains unclear, however, is how sociological knowledge could become a social force weighing on the historical course. Here again, old answers have suddenly become obsolete.

For Marx, a clear understanding of the inner workings of political economy, ideologies, political and social struggles should have helped the world proletariat to throw off its chains by itself. (One should remind those who assimilate Marx to Lenin – not to mention Stalin! – that Marx chose, for the First International Association of Workers, the following motto: '*L'émancipation des travailleurs sera l'oeuvre des travailleurs eux mêmes*'.) Nowadays, however, it would seem that the world proletariat invests its energies elsewhere.

For Durkheim, who once said that all sociological research would not be worth one hour of pain if it did not prove useful in practice, the social agent which could effect the transformation of sociological ideas into social forces was the state. But since Durkheim we have learnt not entirely to trust the state.

If not the state, if not the proletariat, should the actor be the revolutionary Party?

Political parties are useful in pluralist democracies; but can one trust them entirely? Whatever their idealist motives, they are bound eventually to become power machineries, to forget ideals and focus on keeping power. Could one substitute, perhaps, for political parties spontaneous, sincere and active social movements? Such has been the answer of Alain Touraine for twenty-five years; but none of the real social movements he studied lived up to his (admittedly very high) expectations.

I believe, however, that there is an answer; that there is a social actor who is positively oriented and who has affinities, structural affinities, with sociology. This actor is a curious one; it is not a social class; it has no well-established status; at times it even disappears into the woods for long periods. This actor is what is usually referred to as *civil society*.

Let me explain why I perceive close links between sociology and civil society. I will start from a recurrent phenomenon in France, and I guess in other Western European countries as well, and perhaps in Russia: the so-called mass media normally do not pay any attention to what sociologists have to say. They invite instead a steady flow of economists to reiterate the same '*pensée unique*' – their beliefs in the wonders of the market economy, which has become the religion of a world without religion.

At election times, the media will also invite political scientists. But sociologists are left out, *except when there is an unexpected strike, some social movement, some rebellion against the established social order*. By the way, they are invited as experts, but the questions addressed to them by journalists quickly make them answer as intellectuals, which means: they are asked, not only to explain the rebellions, but also to *evaluate* them. What does all this mean sociologically?

The ideological status and power of economists cannot be understood without taking into consideration that these colleagues are locked into an alliance with the most powerful force in the contemporary world, that is, big business, for which they work as ideologues and (sometimes) as experts. As for political scientists, their fast-growing status comes from their relation with the '*classe politique*', the political élite.

The paradigm of the contemporary 'free market' world is 'Markets and States', meaning business and the governance of populations; it is fast reshaping the whole world. This explains why economists and political scientists have such a high status, and sociologists such a low one. The latter are of little use to either big business or the political élite.

The status of sociology is stagnating, or perhaps sinking in comparison with those of economics or political science. Nevertheless sociology, good sociology, trickles into collective reflexivity, and eventually gets appropriated by those socially active minorities which struggle for reforms in, for instance, the environment or gender relations and, generally speaking, for the recognition of the rights of such or such a category. These groups, which taken together are the active part of civil society, are the natural allies of sociology; each of both partners needs the other to keep alive and active.

I believe that there is no better name for this fuzzy nebula of groups than 'civil society'. Here I stand in strong opposition to those who go on defining 'civil society', as in the eighteenth century, as made up of entrepreneurs and professionals. Two centuries ago these groups had corporate (class) interests which ran contrary to those of absolutist regimes. They were objectively pitted against state power. But at the beginning of the twenty-first century, they do not stand any more against state power. They *are* the powers; they *are* the ruling class, and not only in the Western world. It makes no sense any more to refer to entrepreneurs as 'civil society'. When they are given free rein, their behaviour is not civil at all.

What civil society needs and wants is full transparency of the social-historical nexus of social relations. What the ruling classes have always wanted is exactly the contrary: power surrounds itself with layer upon layer of secrecy, manipulation and outright lies. The anti-realist stance, which claims that reality cannot be known, is their epistemological ally: it obviously contributes to weakening the project of sociological knowledge, social awareness and the progress of Reason.

What is needed, therefore, is a sociological vector which aims at penetrating the social veils, by focusing on the inner workings of the various parts of the societal whole, and in particular those parts which are most relevant to shaping the historical course of a society. I believe that the life-story approach is a powerful tool to be used in such a perspective. C. Wright Mills understood it. By refusing his legacy, sociology has betrayed its vocation, its collective *Beruf*. But the present rediscovery of Weber may help sociology to find itself at last, after so many decades of erratic search. The biographical approach, through its simultaneous focus on human action, social contexts and historical trends, all embedded within one another and shaping each other, may contribute to this awakening of sociology to itself.

References

Battagliola, F., Bertaux-Wiame, I., Ferrand, M. and Imbert, F. (1993), 'A propos des biographies: regards croisés sur questionnaires et entretiens', *Population*, vol. 2, pp. 325–46.

Bertaux, D. (forthcoming), 'Biography and Society', in P.B. Altes and N. Smesler (eds), *International Encyclopedia of Behavioural and Social Sciences*, Elsevier, Oxford.

Bertaux, D. and Bertaux-Wiame, I. (1981), 'Artisanal Bakery in France: How It Lives and Why It Survives', in F. Bechhofer and B. Elliott (eds), *The Petite Bourgeoisie*, Macmillan, London, pp. 182–200.

Bertaux, D. and Thompson, P. (1997), *Pathways to Social Class: A Qualitative Approach to Social Mobility*, Clarendon Press, Oxford.

Chamberlayne, P., Bornat, J. and Wengraf, T. (2000), *The Turn to Biographical Methods in Social Science: Comparative Issues and Examples*, Routledge, London and New York.

Geertz, C. (1975), *The Interpretation of Cultures*, Fontana, London.

Kochuyt, T. (1996), 'Biographical and Empiricistic Illusions: A Reply to Recent Criticism', *Biography and Society Newsletter* [Research Committee 38 of the International Sociological Association], p. 6.

Mills, C.W. (1959), *The Sociological Imagination*, Oxford University Press/Grove Press, New York.

Roos, J.P. (1994) (also *www.valt.helsinki.fi/staff/jproos/truelife.html*), 'The True Life Revisited: Autobiography and Referentiality after the "Posts"', in *Lives and Works: Auto/Biographical Occasions*, special issue of *Auto/Biography*, vol. 3, nos 1–2, pp. 1–16.

4 Three Dimensions of Biographical Narratives

VALERY GOLOFAST
Institute of Sociology, St Petersburg Branch,
Russian Academy of Sciences, Russia

Autobiographies and Cultural Legacy

Unlike Britain, Germany, France and other European countries, Russia joined in the discussion about the nature and scientific status of biographical narratives, personal and family chronicles, biographical interviews and oral histories only after a considerable delay. This might seem surprising if we consider that the practice of writing and publishing memoirs and, to a lesser extent, autobiographies in Russia is as old and well-established as in the rest of Europe (Wachtel, 1990).

Tolstoy and Aksakov, Dostoevsky, Korolenko, Chekhov and Gorky laid the foundation of modern literary genres by telling the stories of their own and other people's lives, presenting evidence regarding the historic events of their epoch. Modernists at the beginning of the last century, and nationalists and revolutionaries of the 1910s–20s, added further to the social and cultural pith of this genre.

The Russian cultural scene, despite all the upheavals of the twentieth century, has always been open to a variety of European influences. European literature in translation has carried authentic cultural value and has been read in this way alongside the Russian literary classics. The picture will not be complete, however, if we do not mention the high level of literacy among the Russian population, several generations of whom have experienced the effects of a fully-developed system of universal education. Thus, lack of a cultural tradition or a reluctance on the part of the Russian population to follow and develop one cannot explain Russian backwardness in the field of autobiographical studies.

In 1989, when we started to collect autobiographies and other personal texts, it was sufficient to make an announcement in the press and over the radio for an avalanche of narratives to flow in. The materials we received at the Institute of Sociology (at the Russian Academy of Science, St Petersburg) were so numerous that we could hardly find enough space to store them or sufficient hands to process and maintain our Biographical Fund (Golofast, 1995). We also discovered that it was not only our encouragement that had set people in the writing mood. Many of our correspondents had already had some ideas, and had even written texts before. Ordinary Soviet people, it turned out, had been writing autobiographical stories during the first stormy decades of the century, but had really taken to it since the 1960s. Nowadays this sort of activity is perceived as nothing but natural. It might be noted that the first studies in which autobiographical materials were used also date back to the 1920s, and were carried out by educators, psychologists and social workers of that period.

While mastering the life-story method, we also started to run autobiographical competitions, and in recent years have held several of them. We organised a competition for the *shestidesyatniki* (the generation who entered the active period of their lives in the 1960s during the years of the political 'thaw' and Khrushchev's reforms), followed by the competition 'I'm Talking about My Life', a competition involving sexual biographies (focusing on sexual lives both inside and outside wedlock), and a number of others. By the end of the year 2000 we had brought to conclusion 'Living in Times of Transition', a competition devoted to the last fifteen years of the twentieth century. At present, these kinds of life-story competition are being organised by a number of other centres in St Petersburg. The Shelter Fund, for example, has published a voluminous collection of homeless persons' life stories in a book entitled *Tell Us Your Story*. Other Russian cities and former Soviet states (Latvia, Ukraine) also collect biographical texts and run similar competitions. This is not to speak about countless research projects based on biographical interviews (see e.g. Dmitrieva and Sokolov, 1999; Golofast, 2000; Travin and Simpura, 1999; Vitukhnovskaya, 2000). I believe that it is of crucial methodological importance that all the above-mentioned studies, and a large number of other studies, deal with texts written by ordinary people.

By the end of the 1980s we had amassed hundreds of books containing the reminiscences of World War II veterans. Public libraries had special shelves for the memoirs of famous production workers, scientists, sportsmen, actors and writers. But all of these were examples of more or less institutionalised discourse, carefully screened, edited and censored.

Their very existence was encouraged by the rigid constructions of official history and political ideology. The internal value system and moral priorities of these texts seemed to be legitimised by the well-established literary and definitional standards that were in force. Everything that one could find in them was approved and, in some cases, even dictated by anonymous authorities to meet the official requirements for ideological writings. This served to make academically-oriented researchers always rather suspicious about them.

Texts originating from the Biographical Fund were intended to be of a different nature – and different they were (though not entirely in the way that had been expected), as a result of *glasnost*, cultural freedom, democratic thinking, the loosening of prejudices and the unveiling of people's private lives and public events. In fact, the quantity of official discourse has shrunk. Such discourse has withdrawn from the foreground and stays hidden in the shade. Its values have more or less lost their power; they have diminished without having been replaced. Some taboos have been broken for good (as was shown by the sexual biographies competition). The main subject of these texts, however, is personal and family routine, the dimension of everyday life and of small events, including the way people experience these and structure, describe and evaluate them in their narratives. Details such as these were either completely missing or sometimes just vaguely hinted at in the officially-approved texts of the previous years. The main difference is in the scale of life-presentation and not so much in its modality; in the focus of attention and the minuteness of description, not in the boundaries of discourse; and in the loyalty shown towards routine and everyday life, as opposed to public, headline events. Thus, the orientation towards institutional or political and ideological discourse that had been cultivated for decades by the Soviet establishment has lost its predominance.

Clifford Geertz and other socio-cultural anthropologists claim that any textualisation of pre-written cultures results in their codification and generalisation, and that these obscure and eliminate the variety and multi-dimensionality of social practices, the situational freaks of chance, the risk and arbitrariness, the spontaneous aspirations and the confrontations and external interventions which form an inherent part of social interactions. The same is true when speaking about the unifying power of large-scale ideologies and institutional influences. This may be seen as an additional argument for the usefulness of routine descriptions, and as an additional reason for studying autobiographies.

I believe that there are at present two major ways of working with personal texts. Alongside autobiographies (and similar texts), many qualitative researches use free-script interviews, sometimes also called biographical and narrative interviews. The recent publications of our colleagues in St Petersburg belong to this genre. To my mind, however, they should be distinguished from oral history that is oriented towards collecting ordinary evidence. Both of these techniques are subject to a substantial 'thematising' pressure from the researcher. This implies that they are affected by the foreign (for the informants) norms, senses and meanings which may predominate in the professional milieu of the interviewer, or by currently-approved forms of self-expression, or by the vague social myths operating in their immediate environment. The pressure of such thematising can be seen even in the specialised (as opposed to the general) autobiographical competitions.

Why should we cultivate attention to the routine? At present, Russia, along with some other European countries, is facing an important social and cultural choice. Its social institutions and whole sectors of its social life are undergoing vast transformations. New societal myths are being created. But the reproduction processes taking place in the shade of social life, in its foundations – the routine – seem to go on autonomously. The extent to which the routine is influenced by the societal machine of cultural re-evaluation and the rewriting of history is still unclear and must be a matter for further research. What is clear is that, as the pressure imposed by official discourse diminishes, the white spots of personal biography and the black spots of history become further and further developed on the photographic plate of personal texts. There are still substantial gaps and omissions, but the broad palette of life stories is gaining more diversity and colour.

Historical and biographical consciousness, individual and collective memory are inherent parts of cultural legacy. Cultural heritage in its turn never remains unchangeable and frozen. It never becomes stable, fixed in the past, but is continually revealed and reinterpreted. Under certain historical and social conditions it may transform itself, undergo certain mutations, and become a source of social change and personal mobilisation. To describe these processes more fully it might be useful to introduce the concept of 'social book-keeping'. Thus, following the end of the Soviet epoch the process of re-evaluating modern history commenced in all post-Soviet states, but in each of them this re-evaluation took a specific form. In Russia it gave rise to strong restorative forces. Undoubtedly, what brought these about were feelings of deep resentment and revenge, as well as the silence and stigmatisation that had operated in previous historical periods. They were explained, however, in terms of a need to restore historical truth and justice and to balance the ideas of the 'winners' and 'losers', the victims of political repression and its perpetrators. Initially, this kind of scrupulous re-evaluation involved only the most obvious periods of modern history or its pivotal points: the Revolution of 1917, the Civil War, the Stalinist period and the 'thaw', stagnation and the emergence of reforms. This perspective on twentieth-century history might seem politically engaged, its judgements morally biased and its classification of historical periods superficial, but the restructuring of the collective legacy that stemmed from it can be found in almost every biography. In the course of time this restructuring went deeper, developed, and became more complex. The area of historical book-keeping expanded to incorporate events from the mythic past of ethnic groups and their territories, the socio-cultural history of the nineteenth century, the two World Wars, the post-war period, and current political changes. It turned out, for example, that the war in Afghanistan and both Chechen campaigns (strongly-denoted events in current Russian history) became a mirror for the re-evaluation of stable models of more remote history. Whether new historical models will be created or new cultural myths canonised is yet to be seen. One thing, however, is obvious: official discourse has largely lost its influence, and has become one of the components of an established pluralism. At present, nobody can say for sure where this will take us.

Besides, revitalising memories is not always harmless. It can eliminate injustice, cruelty and evil, but can also give rise to them. The same is true of researchers, since authors of personal texts have scant protection from researchers' interpretations (Kozlova, 2000). Thus, in working with a separate personal text we should consider, explicitly or implicitly, the whole cultural context and, if necessary, all its transformations and contradictions. This task seems too large and too complex to accomplish, especially since all research has its problematics. But who has ever said that scientific problems are easy?

Autobiography as the Archaeology of the Socio-cultural World

Autobiographical narratives are good examples of texts possessing a culturally-oriented content. Their personal form rather obscures this fact, by transforming the identity problem (if it ever gets revealed at all) into a series of more or less ideologically-approved attempts to define, state and evaluate the narrator's place in the historical flow of constant reproduction and structural change. The strength of this flow far exceeds, in its diversity and interlacing, the individual potential of any human. Thus any biography, if a researcher manages to discard the mask of biographical illusion, becomes a personalised piece of evidence of the socio-cultural world of an individual of a certain type – and not just of his or her life-world. This implies that in spite of, and sometimes independent of, the subjective position assumed by the narrator any biography is always extremely rich in inter-subjective content. Thus the sociological value of the autobiographical narrative becomes clear when the narrative is viewed from a distance, when this evidence is matched by and synthesised with the social knowledge of the relevant socio-cultural forms. Only in this case a perspective is established for what is normative and deviant, ordinary and unusual, new and habitual or banal, as well as for other socio-cultural points of reference. Naïve confidence in the narrator's perspective and judgement gives way to a more critical vision and comparison made in terms of social knowledge rather than merely in terms of personal experience, intuition, individual empathy and understanding.

To simplify this methodological situation we may define three dimensions of the biographical narrative: (1) *the routine*; (2) *life as a sequence of events*; and (3) *the hidden or covert life aspect*. These are discussed in turn below.

1 The Routine – Personal, Family and Group Life

This is the area of perpetually reproduced actions, thoughts, feelings and circumstances. Sociologists usually focus on family routine as well as on institutional and status-bound daily practices. Note the implicitly normative character of the associated phenomena. It reveals itself in the emotional responses accompanying the inertia of everyday life, or obvious gaps and ruptures in its smooth flow. In one way or another we should define the group of people who preserve, maintain and share a certain everyday practice. The routine rarely becomes the focus of individual, much less of collective, attention. Nor is it honoured with words. It simply exists. It is self-evident. It is always there as the dressing, cooking or eating code, as the unspoken rules regulating any hierarchical structure, any kind of meeting or gathering, or item of folklore. The only difference is that, in the case of the routine, the point is not the rules but rather the essence of what can be regulated by them:

> From early morning till late at night we worked in the fields. Used cows and bulls to plough. Horses were few. And in summer, at harvest-time, children also took part in the work: they gathered ears of corn left after reaping and brought cold water to the reapers – getting one work/day [unit of work on the collective farm]. In spite of the hard work on the collective farm everyone was looking forward to the changes for the better. In the evenings you could often hear people sing. ('Childhood Reminiscences, The Countryside, WWII'. Competition of the 1960s Generation, 1995, Vol. 8, p. 2, Biographical Fund, Institute of Sociology, Russian Academy of Science)

In interpreting the routine, a researcher may encounter two major dangers. The first of these is the uncertainty of generalisation. One should always define the context (or series of contexts, including the period, the place and the social group) in which the specified regularity has come about and currently exists, and is habitual and routine. Without these parameters it is not possible to establish whether the described event falls within the norm and what its social and personal meanings are. The second danger is over-generalisation. Any generalisation requires additional verification, well-grounded argumentation and the establishment of clear boundaries as regards its validity. Here is another comment by the same attentive observer:

> It was quite difficult for my father to support his family – even the highly-skilled workers earned little. Therefore he often changed plants, but it was the same everywhere. Designers and scientists had a considerably higher standard of living. The husband of my sister Lena headed the shipbuilding design office. They lived very well. My father would sarcastically call them *gospoda* [members of the ruling class] – they had their own inner circle of friends, and they were the first to buy a TV set and a 'Moskvich' car in our family. In general, this was a time of considerable social stratification. It was especially true for the agricultural workers, for in that sector the decline in living standards was considerable. There was, however, no antagonism between different social strata. Everyone was assumed to get what they were supposed to. (ibid., post-war period, Leningrad)

Sometimes the routine is seen as an incautious step, an unfavourable event, a failure or an obstacle, or any other kind of intrusion into the ordinary flow of life. But in most cases these events are regarded as samples illustrating the cross-section of the routine, something which stands out in the narrator's memory and arbitrarily arrests the attention of the narrator. These pseudo-incidents most frequently emerge in thematised interviews and are treated as 'occasional' artefacts.

2 Life as a Sequence of Events, or Event Culture

Personal and public events form the usual subject of biographical research. As a rule, events are also routine, but the routine is that of social life – familial, local, urban or societal. Ordinary people rarely get caught up in the thick of social events, usually remaining in the background, but when they do, they are profoundly affected by the experience. In general, however, it is surprising to how small an extent public events are included in ordinary biographies. By using individual, family and group life-cycle theories, we can comparatively easily structure any biographical narration. If, however, silence is kept up about events at the macro level (institutional, sectoral or societal) we are forced to introduce the concept of the individual life horizon. However many news and entertainment programmes we watch on our TV screens, very few of them enter our lives as real events. Perhaps we simply do not know who is pulling the strings, or else the TV generation have not yet written their biographies. Or perhaps the boundary between the virtual and the real is still haunted by the inertia of tradition.

Whatever the case, non-ordinary biographies are not uncommon. They show a high degree of life-course individualisation, and an awareness of a highly personal attitude towards everything meaningful and exceptional. (Incidentally, the narration found in other kinds of personal text (letters, diaries) appears to be more individualised.) Another important point is the critical attitude towards the cult of individuality so common in our culture. It manifests in the amazing matter-of-factness with which people describe their encounters with famous figures (public leaders, cultural heroes) and in the trivial way in which they speak about critical moments in history:

> I remember Stalin's death. For several days, funeral music was played throughout the school. Some people had tears in their eyes. But after the mourning days were over everything went back to normal. (ibid., Sevastopol, p. 3)

> I remember when N. S. Khrushchev came to our regiment. It happened in 1959 after his visit to China. Of course everyone was getting ready to meet him properly. Everything that could be painted was painted. At last the message came: 'He's coming!' He arrived escorted by a group of military and

> local authorities. After he inspected all the equipment my men and I happened to stand closer to him than anybody else. He came up to me, shook my hand and asked a few questions. When I answered Nikita Sergeyevich commented: 'Without an effort one can't even kill a louse.' His escorts smiled unanimously as if on command. As for me, I remember his tired face and his sky-blue necktie. After Khrushchev's visit our *zampolit* [commanding officer in charge of political and ideological issues] plagued the life out of me by asking to share my experience of meeting the First Secretary with the personnel. I firmly refused to take part in all this crap. (ibid., Pacific Navy, p. 4)

Thus, the integration of personal and social (group, institutional, etc.) events is a peculiar aspect of the relation between individual life and social history. It may form the subject for separate study, involving the comparison of biographical narratives belonging to different cultures.

3 The Hidden or Covert Life Aspect

This one might term the *mystery* or *destiny* of a biographical narrative: the obscure and sometimes totally incomprehensible and frightening, with its unexpected coincidences and failures. It would be only natural to associate this aspect of personal texts with the diversity of forms of social control: the taboo issues of sex, physical and mental illness, death, ethnic, social and physical inequality or suffering and humiliation – as well as shame and stigmatisation, violence, and any other manifestation of ethical extremes in general. But the problem seems much broader. According to the established theories, an individual is a point of conflict between socio-cultural determinism and freedom, biological need and social obligation, awareness and delusion, intuition and ignorance. The very idea of social science implies that an individual (and a society) is unable to read and direct an individual life independently and impartially. At the same time, self-awareness may not only intensify existential drama, but may also bring about serenity.

The standard technique applied to clarify the hidden aspects of life in biographical interviews and biographical scenarios is their active thematising. This technique, however, increases dramatically the dialogism of biographical texts, as well as the risk of introducing researcher-stimulated artefacts.

In spontaneous autobiographies, when it is difficult to tell what exactly has motivated their authors to write them, the third dimension becomes obvious as soon as such questions as 'Why?', 'What for?', 'What happened?' and 'What was its cause?' come to our mind. Below is another extract from the biography of the military engineer from which we have already quoted. Most of the turns in his career seem to be rather well-motivated, but still there are many things that remain vague and unclear:

> In 1952 I finished secondary school and entered the Higher Naval School for military engineers. [...] Part of this choice was due to my interest in the profession, and partly it can be explained by the desire to make my parents' life easier. [...] In 1956 our department was moved to Sevastopol, where a new engineering school was founded on the basis of the old school for naval officers. [...] At the beginning of 1958, after graduating, I was sent to the place of my permanent service. This was a naval rocket base of the Pacific Fleet. [...] My service was quite interesting, but I wanted to do something more creative, to design and to study new equipment. My desire accorded with the government decision of 1960 concerning substantial redundancies in the armed forces. I had to make some efforts and in 1960 was transferred to the reserve.
>
> In Leningrad, after a long search for work I joined the State Institute of Applied Chemistry (GIPKH). One of the main directions in the Institute at the time was the research and development of new rocket propellants. My diploma allowed me to work as an engineer and I was admitted as a junior researcher. [...] In 1970 I supported my candidate and in 1991 my doctoral thesis. My whole life was devoted to the enormous, complex and important work. [...] My team (and I personally) have contributed to the successful launching of the 'Energiya' carrier rocket and the 'Buran' spaceship. (ibid., pp. 4–5)

At this point a number of natural questions arise. Why did a young and obviously successful military engineer resign just a couple of years after his graduation? Was it because he valued civil life so highly, or because he had a very strong interest in science, or because he wanted to keep his residential permit in Leningrad, or, perhaps, because he was trying to help his parents to get a new apartment? (This latter fact is mentioned later on in his text in relation to the early 1960s.) Did all these reasons apply, and if so which were the primary ones? Why did it take a talented researcher working in one of the most advanced fields of science as long as ten years to get his candidate degree? Why did it take him twice as long to get his doctorate?

In studying one particular biography we are unlikely to find definite answers to all such questions. It is similarly improbable that if asked directly the author of the biography would give comprehensive answers to all of them. Questions of this kind encourage further research which might involve more materials and new research methods.

Subjective and Socio-cultural Forms of the Routine

One of the unclearest and most disputed issues in biographical studies is the degree to which these texts express the subjective world of the narrator (as against the socio-cultural world). Let us recall our previous thesis that routine comprises the major part or even the essence of everyday life. That means that the role motivation plays in the routine is accidental and optional. Social need for its clarification emerges only when there is some sort of conflict, suspicion or misunderstanding. As a rule, motivation is of no great interest to people. It is usually taken for granted, as if implied by the very course of events. Motives belong to the realm of the internal world of an individual. They are of no interest to others. Actually, in accordance with existing cultural norms individuals are rarely aware of their own motives, and as a rule do not give much thought to the personal and social meaning of their actions. The subjective remains subjective, that is, rather intimate.

This brings us to an important conclusion: a conscious cultural effort is necessary to discover the subjective, to reveal it to the individual and, under certain conditions, to others. Until there is a direct conflict of interests, the routine as a collective practice keeps motivation at the periphery of people's awareness. As soon as there is a conflict people begin to look for ways of resolving or avoiding it, as some unwanted, accidental, unnecessary or intentional obstacle. This 'sorting out' of things brings forward the issue of motives, and they bubble up into the awareness of the parties involved. (It is not unusual for this awareness to be shared only by the 'third party', the witnesses, the impartial judges – which, without any doubt, is the primary role of a researcher.)

In fact, the motivation issue is usually secondary and derivative, the primary being the direction and the intention of actions. Are these actions still within the boundaries of the routine, or do they transcend it? At what are they directed? Who is distorting the routine, or what causes its distortion? What are the interested parties? Whose motives or actions are behind the distortion if it is intentional? If the actions do not violate the routine, no question of selfishness arises. Egoism and calculation of individual actions are socio-historical features, cultivated and directed by and within the routine as its essential components. They are the results of broad systemic changes, consequences of particular situations.

Most of the time, motives are used to make excuses, while insights into other people's motives quite often become instruments for their accusation. In both cases they are inherent elements of the socio-cultural texture of everyday life. They are standard ingredients of the ritual games of politeness, rudeness, impudence, cunning, stupidity, carelessness, etc. Morality is yet another ingredient of this ritual game, in which variants are selected until the context of mutual understanding is restored and all the participants in the routine who have experienced the situation as ambiguous, unbalanced or threatening are satisfied.

Besides, motives are the major part of the status game. The structure of collective actions and relations includes hierarchy, the right of the strong, and the priority of his or her interests. At the same time, motives are part of his or her dialogue with other participants, when they go through the existing set of relational contexts and choose mutually acceptable variants. The rebellion of one of the participants can be accepted, rejected or ignored in the hope that it may fade away or be repressed in the future.

The qualities of acceptable socio-cultural patterns are pre-defined and comprise the necessary condition for the very existence of collective routine. Individual intentions, aspirations and motives remain the internal stuff of the author until he or she makes a special point of presenting them against the background of the existing social and cultural code. But even in these cases the vocabulary of motives is limited. They can easily be deciphered and seen through or accepted both by the partners and by the actor. An insight into a new motive or into an unusual cluster of motives would mean a cultural discovery. This kind of insight is that most likely to cause psychological shock, indignation and protest. To spot a special motive means to pinpoint some deviant behaviour, which implies appealing to the conscience, putting a certain action into moral context, and inviting witnesses for further assessment. In this sense motives are usually a collective product, the result of a dialogue, a search for mutually accepted definitions which are adapted to match the specific context.

In the course of the dialogue, the insights into the motives of the others may be evaluated and further elaborated. But the need for such insights arises only in a limited number of marked situations. The congruence of individual perspectives is already established by the habitual reciprocal collective practice of the routine, by the shared cultural form. When two strangers meet they immediately turn to the familiar repertoires of cultural forms, including different subcultures and even different cultural contexts. The key individual feature involved in this game is the cultural competence of the participants, the set of social contexts to which each of them is affiliated.

In this case, distinguishing words and actions acquires special meaning. If no direct threat is perceived in actions, all the uncertainty, vagueness and contradiction resides in words or in paralingual behavioural elements. It is not unusual for the persons involved to coexist in particular cultural contexts (personal, group) for years, completely ignoring this pluralism and multiculturalism as if shutting their eyes to it. Disciplined indifference, as we know, is a feature of modern mass milieux. The coexistence of different status standards is not much different. (In similar situations, one and the same person can show familiarity and arrogance towards some people and respect, politeness and even flattery towards others.) But these are examples, perhaps, of stable cultural patterns demonstrating the relative moral standards and personal characteristics of the persons involved. These variants are inborn and ritualised in the very status differences. They shape interaction and dialogue tactics under given conditions.

The familiar and the well-known block the analysis and impede the discovery of conditional diversity, rules and regularities. On the other hand, the structural character of the biographical material is its fundamental feature. It allows us to discard unrealistic theory from the very start. At the same time, the multidimensional character and asymmetry of the dialogue, the depth of cultural determinism, is, perhaps, the most difficult theoretical issue.

Personal texts, being the concentrated socio-cultural tissue of the routine, should not be treated only as the signs of individual psychology or as an area for psychoanalysis. They may be regarded as the window into the socio-cultural world, which is much more comprehensible than the world of the psyche or the unconscious. Many of its elements are on the surface; they are part of history and are available for observation. They have a structural character, and knowing some of the structural elements we can rather easily reconstruct the others. By their very definition the elements of this world are more stable and reproducible, and subject to more general and more culturally-pervasive factors, than psychological features.

Personal texts are the real archaeology of the social and cultural world of the routine. They represent a kind of reality that does not so much reflect the individual psyche of a narrator as show the effects of social institutions and culture on a human being. Personal texts render these effects visible in the concrete form of individual biography; they show all the entanglements of social relations and meanings in the way the author reproduces them and presents them to the reader. They are not only a kind of parallel reality redoubling the world of actions and behaviour, imitating, reflecting and reproducing it. They are an inherent part of these very actions, the condition of their repetition and understanding. In many cases, this is a far more important and stable reality than people's physical actions. Personal texts undergo cultural processing, and only in respect of this quality are they perceived, regulated, controlled, and even imbued with sense. Lacking this quality, physical actions drop out of the socio-cultural process. In the rare cases when they do interfere with this process, they are perceived as very special events, as a destructive force of nature or some incomprehensible power. These events do not become a meaningful fact of life until they are interpreted and adapted in terms of the existing socio-cultural reality.

Generally speaking, textual interpretation is equivalent to the production of a new text, which is related to the original text (intertextuality) and can thus be viewed as a new dialogue stage. This raises the question of how the dialogue is organised: it may be organised on one cultural level, on different levels, or within one culture, or it may transcend cultural boundaries. It is assumed that, ideally, the interpretation of the text should be comprehensible to its author. But most of the time, especially in science, this ideal cannot be achieved. Thus there is the problem of how the diversity of interpretations may be limited.

Another important feature typical of biographical texts (in addition to 'common sense' and everyday language) is their close-up view of reality. This quality, not always too helpful to a researcher in search of the essence, makes biographical texts appealing to the ordinary reader. Devoid of any literary excesses, biographies attract their readers by the magic of the possible (possible achievements and possible disasters) – what could have happened to the other can happen to me.

The three-dimensional structure of the biographical narrative is but one resource in the structure of socio-cultural coordinates. In future I intend to look for other possible paths in the complexity of cultural oppositions. We may assume, for example, that any text of sufficient length consists of a number of heterogeneous pieces, each built around a number of separate oppositions or sequences. These pieces differ in their chronological rhythm and the scope of their events (see the above-mentioned difference between the ordinary and the macro routine). This enables us to refer to different institutional discourses and different means of constituting cultural space. Besides, it would be extremely helpful to define what stylistic (language) elements are used in the given culture to mark the zones of hidden, covert, implied content, since it is likely that these zones will have a comparative logic of their own.

References

Dmitrieva, V. and Sokolov, V. (eds) (1999), *Rasskazhi svoju istoriju* [Tell Your Story], Na dne, St Petersburg.

Golofast, V.B. (1995), 'Mnogoobrazie biographicheskikh povestvovanii' [The Diversity of Biographical Narratives], *Sotsiologicheskii zhurnal* [Sociological Journal], vol. 1, pp. 71–89.

Golofast, V.B. (2000), 'Veter peremen v sotsiologii' [The Winds of Change in Sociology], *Zhurnal sotsiologii i antropologii* [Journal of Sociology and Anthropology], vol. 4, pp. 122–39.

Kozlova, N. (2000), 'Opyt sotsiologicheskogo chtenija "chelovecheskikh documentov" ili razmyshlenija o znachimosti metodologicheskoi refleksii' [Experiments in the Sociological Reading of "Human Documents", or Thoughts on the Significance of Methodological Reflection], *Sotsiologicheskie issledovanija* [Sociological Studies], vol. 5, pp. 22–32.

Travin, I. and Simpura, J. (eds) (1999), *Povsednevnost serediny 90–kh glazami peterburzhtstv* [Daily Occurrences of the mid-1990s in the Eyes of St Petersburg Inhabitants], Evropejskii Dom, St Petersburg.

Vitukhnovskaya, M. (ed.) (2000), 'Na korme vremeni. Intervyu c leningradtsami 30–kh godov' [Looking Back in Time: Interviews with Leningrad Inhabitants of the 1930s], *Neva*, St Petersburg.

Wachtel, A.B. (1990), *The Battle for Childhood: Creation of a Russian Myth*, Stanford University Press, Stanford, CA.

and the scope of their events (see the above-mentioned distinction between the ordinary and the extraordinary). This enables us to relate to different institutional discourses and different means of constituting biographical [illegible]. Besides, it would be extremely helpful to define which [illegible] elements are used in the given culture to mark the [illegible] implied content, since it is likely that these can [illegible] logic of their own.

References

Dmitrieva, V. and Sokolova, [illegible] (eds) (1999) [illegible]
Gorshkov, V. [illegible] (1995) [illegible] Biographical Narratives [illegible]
Golofast, V.B. (2000) [illegible] Zhurnal sotsiologii [illegible] vol. 3, pp. [illegible]
Kozlova, N. (2000) [illegible] Sociological Reading of 'Human Documents' [illegible] Methodological Reflections] [illegible] vol. 3, pp. [illegible]
Travin, I. and Simpura, J. (eds) (1999) [illegible] Daily Occurrence of the [illegible] St Petersburg]
[illegible] (ed.) (1996) [illegible]
[illegible] (1996) [illegible] Stanford University Press, Stanford, CA.

PART 2

Communists, Informers and Dissidents

5 Estonian-inclined Communists as Marginals

AILI AARELAID-TART
Institute of International and Social Studies, Tallinn Pedagogical University, Estonia

Historical and Political Background to the Emergence of the Estonian-inclined Communists

In the post-war Stalinist period (1944–56), Estonia became fully integrated into the Soviet Union's ideological and economic system. Estonian industry underwent important changes. Whereas, during the early part of the century, the major emphasis had been on textile and food production, by 1950 a significant shift towards heavy industry had taken place. The Moscow administration started to send abroad large numbers of Russian-speaking workers to be employed in these industries, although the officially-declared aim was to remedy the lack of a sufficiently large workforce caused by heavy losses sustained during the War. Thus, forced industrialisation was closely connected with a specific political policy, aimed at restricting the role of native Estonians in society.

The campaign to reorganise Estonian agriculture was launched in 1947, but in reality began two years later, when a massive deportation of the rural population was undertaken in March 1949 (20,700 people were deported to Siberia) with the aim of scaring the Estonian people into submitting to the *kolkhoz* regime.[1] In 1939 there were approximately 140,000 single farms in Estonia, but by the end of the Stalinist era there were 934 agricultural and 84 fishing *kolkhozes* (collective farms) in the country (Raun, 1991, p. 180). Liquidation of the kulaks[2] as a class was also undertaken on the Stalinist model, with at least 1,200 families deported in 1947.

The main tool of Bolshevik ideology was the Estonian Communist Party (ECP), which had a membership of 2,400 people after World War II and by the end of the Stalinist era had grown approximately tenfold. While at the beginning its members were mainly Estonians (90 per cent), by 1952 the percentage of non-Estonians in the ECP had already grown to 58.5. The russification of the ECP reflected both Moscow's distrust of ethnic Estonians and a reluctance on the part of Estonians themselves to take any part in the administrative regime occupying their homeland (Raun, 1991). A direct leadership coup occurred in March 1950, when a decree was adopted by the eighth plenary session which replaced and pushed aside secretary-general Nikolai Karotamm, who had been born in Estonia and who had defended the Estonians' actions in their country as well as those of other national Communists (the so-called 'June Communists'). Thus the leadership of the ECP was taken over by Estonians born in Communist Russia or by Russian chauvinists. Another decree of the same plenary session launched a campaign of persecution that was termed a 'fight against bourgeois nationalism', during which around 3,000 members of the Estonian intelligentsia were either deported or sacked from creative posts.

The de-Stalinisation and modest liberalisation of Soviet society following the 20th Congress of the Communist Party of the Soviet Union in 1956 ended the so-called 'severe class struggle period' in Estonia and created the environment for a certain social stabilisation. Thousands of deportees returned from Siberia, first contacts with exiled Estonians were established, travelling was allowed to a limited extent, and the creative freedom of the intelligentsia widened to some extent. The impact of a Moscow-centred mentality on Estonian cultural life having been reduced, the new generation of young educated Estonians aimed to restore connections with their pre-war cultural heritage, and opportunities to communicate with people from Socialist Central Europe increased. The creative intelligentsia realised that under the canons of socialist realism they could, in moderation, cultivate both nationally-rooted art and contemporary Western practice.

Thanks to N. S. Khrushchev's campaign to increase the role of the agricultural economy and to minimise the difference between rural and urban regions, agriculture in Estonia, a country with a long tradition of peasant farming, prospered. By the beginning of the 1960s the Estonian farmer had got used to collective land ownership; his living standard was stable, and his income was gradually surpassing that of the industrial worker. Most of the chairmen of the *kolkhozes* were experienced native Estonians for whom protecting the fields and forests of their collective farms as sacred national territory was important.

By the 1960s, an industrial complex had evolved in northern Estonia, led by the capital Tallinn. Since industry had developed largely at the expense of immigrant labour, in these regions there was a strong tendency towards russification. According to the all-Union work distribution scheme, to Estonia fell the processing of electrical energy for the north-west of the USSR on the basis of local oil shale mining; two-thirds of the oil shale was exported to Russia. Also, situated in northern Estonia was the highly secret Sillamäe uranium plant, where half of a number of specific raw materials necessary for the Soviet nuclear industry were processed, which also posed dangers to the environment. By the 1960s, Estonia had become strongly integrated into the economic life of the Soviet Union, but at the same time the region was becoming a site for the all-Union economic experiments owing to its superior results in the area of work efficiency and quality.

Under these conditions of liberalisation and economic progress, the attitudes of native Estonians towards the ECP changed, and the illusion spread that the leadership of the ECP was turning over to native-born Estonians. In 1966 the membership of the ECP stood at 59,000, of whom 52 per cent were native Estonians, the majority of whom were either leading agricultural and industrial administrators or else members of the intelligentsia, who up until then had defied bolshevism. Since 1950, the leader of the ECP had been Johannes Käbin (1905–99), who though educated in Soviet Russia had been born in Estonia and had turned his face firmly towards the Estonians during those years and had become decidedly tolerant towards manifestations of nationalism. But events in Czechoslovakia in 1968 destroyed Estonians' liberal illusions about the possibility of communism in their home country having a human face.

In the 1970s, the Estonian economy was secretly taken over by the all-Union economic monopolies. At the same time, liberalism in cultural life gradually receded. By 1978 the ECP was led by the so-called 'Estonian-inclined' Communists who had managed to soften the ideological pressure and economic directives emanating from Moscow. But in 1978 another 'palace revolution' took place in the ECP and power was again seized by Russian-born Estonians extremely loyal to the Kremlin powerholders.

Problems Faced by National Leaders amid Circumstances of Turbulent Change

Nations coming under occupation inevitably face leadership problems. There will always be people who appear to be drifters who are eager to make a career and who will be ready to collaborate with the occupying power, and there will also be those who become known as terrorist-like dissidents in their resistance to the occupying regime (Voronkov and Zdravomyslova, 1997, p. 125). In order to adapt to the new circumstances, however, such nations require a certain kind of passionate individual, who through their powerful charisma try to create a certain common dimension between their own people and the occupying administration. As a by-product of World War II, Estonian people experienced two occupations (German and Russian), the second of which may be treated as an annexation that lasted slightly less than 50 years (1944–91). The rapid alternation of occupations at the beginning of the 1940s demonstrated the janus-facedness of local leaders, and was followed by a deep alienation of people from the political leadership.

The leaders of the independence era had been physically expelled from the scene, primarily as a result of the Stalinist repressions and the 1944 emigrations to Sweden, where a government-in-exile was established. During the first post-war decade of the Soviet regime, Estonia was governed by Moscow via Russian-born Estonian governors, mockingly known as *Istlased* (from the erroneous pronunciation of the Russian noun for Estonians). Born into the families of native Estonians in Russia, the latter had obtained their Red education in the Soviet Union during the Stalinist repressions at the end of the 1930s. Many of them had fought in the Red Army (in the Estonian Rifle Corps); few of them had mastered the Estonian language, and as a rule they were ardent supporters of 'strong-handed' Stalinism. They usually had rough manners, wore a special military style of clothing, and had the self-assurance of being 'superior': they were true solders of class struggle. Naturally, Estonian-born Estonians could not accept them as leaders, and labelled them 'aliens' and stooges of the occupying power. After the massive deportations of 1949 and the Eighth Plenary Session of the ECP in 1950, during the campaign of 'bourgeois nationalism',[3] significant public figures, who had grown up in Estonia and who favoured social-democratic ideas, were removed from office. Moreover, the finest of the intellectual élite were condemned to internal emigration. Isolated by the Iron Curtain from the Western world, native Estonians felt themselves under the command of 'Red overseers' whom they viewed as traitors to the national ideals.

In post-war Estonia too resistance occurred. There were hiding in the forests a moderate number of armed 'forest brethren', who were indeed supported by the people but who could not grow into popular leaders because of the extremes of their living conditions and their outsider status. The majority of these forest fighters were liquidated by KGB troops before Stalin's death in 1953. During the 1950s, the Estonians did not possess any leaders, either in the intellectual or the administrative sphere, who would have been accepted by the native people.

Nikita Khrushchev's rise to power brought about a limited democratisation of Soviet society: the direct terror ceased, the gates of the Siberian prison camps fell open, and so on. The Estonian community also breathed a sigh of relief. In addition, *kolkhoz*-based agriculture got to its feet surprisingly well; opportunities appeared for young people to obtain an education, and they started to 'hear out' the new ideology. Thereafter, the nationalist movement for the most part took the form of cultural preservation and small measures to promote political and economic autonomy within the Soviet system. By the beginning of the 1960s the time was ripe for a compromise, as public opinion had changed and it was now felt that it was better that the political leaders in Estonia were native Estonians, rather than immigrant Russians who would be more likely to represent Russian national interests emanating from Moscow.

Which social groups were interested in appearing in the political arena of the janus-faced new leaders? First, there were a large number of chairmen of and specialists in well-run collective (*kolkhoz*) and state (*sovkhoz*) farms. This rural intelligentsia needed more space for independent economic development without direct intervention from Moscow, and they looked for more liberal mediators. The second group were the rebellious students of the 1960s, who were inspired by the ideas of New Left philosophers such as Herbert Marcuse, Theodor Adorno and Louis Althusser. They could seldom read these authors in the original but instead read them from secondary sources (the French Communist newspaper *l'Humanité*, translations or reviews in Russian journals, etc.). These avant-garde students were motivated by the Euro-Communist ideas and by the criticisms of USSR-style socialism put forward by French and German analysts. The radical student movement was ready to sweep away the clique of Russian-born Estonian party leaders (the *Istlased*). The third group were younger professionals – teachers, journalists, and creative intellectuals such as scientists, writers and artists – whose everyday work was deeply connected with ideological regulation. They were not so afraid of the games of the totalitarian regime as their older colleagues had been, and sought every opportunity to crack the system.

Thus, the leadership of the Estonian-inclined Communists was formed out of the moderate readiness of native Estonians to accept 'double' persons as the real local administrators of the Moscow paradigm of power. Events in Poland, Hungary and Czechoslovakia had taught Estonians the uselessness of armed struggle against Soviet occupation. There might be another, peaceful but quite radical, way of carrying protest forward in a manner more acceptable to the Estonian nation. Thus a beautiful myth about the 'Lithuanian way' spread among Estonian intellectuals. This was the myth of nationalist forces taking over power from the Reds by using the same corridors of power as the Communist Party. In other words, many Estonian intellectuals (like Lithuanian ones) felt that if they really had to live under the socialist regime, it would be better to oust the occupying Russians from their ECP positions and rule the Republic by themselves. The 'Lithuanian way' might be interpreted as a national compromise with the occupying power: if the Estonians (i.e. all Baltic peoples) could not change socio-historical circumstances, then they might be ready to play these 'compulsory' games with some of the decisive cards in their own hands. Twenty years had passed since the beginning of Soviet-enforced rule; contestation and cooperation between Estonia and Moscow were more or less balanced, and most native people were sure that the Communist regime would continue for ever. When the self-reliant, home-grown brotherhood of nationally-inclined Communists appeared on the stage of history, Estonian society was ready to draw upon their skills to moderate Kremlin rules for the benefit of local people. The late 1960s and early 1970s were the 'right' time for this kind of social experience. On the one hand, commemorations of the independent Republic were played down, a brutal break with democratic norms came about, real contacts with the Western world were impossible for the majority of citizens, and the only undisputed all-powerful centre was Moscow. On the other hand, the era of the *Istlased*, or Russian Estonians patterning themselves on strong Stalinism, was coming to an end, since the next generation of Kremlin loyalists did not have enough back-up from their patrons. Thirdly, in the huge territory that was the USSR there were small 'spots' of dissidence, but Estonia as a whole was a famous site of creative persons (writers, artists, musicians) of a 'different' opinion. True, most Russian dissidents acted as underground heroes and 'voices from the prisons', while the Estonian intellectuals attained their 'otherness' in restricted but legal ways. There was an excellent young generation of poets and novelists who were experienced masters of 'hide-and-seek' – that is, of situating their anti-

Soviet messages between the lines. There was a huge legal folk-song and folk-dance movement, demonstrating to Party comrades the real feeling of a forcefully subordinated nation. This meant that, during the above-mentioned decade, Estonian society was not ready to support any group of radical political dissidents, but neither did it want to be led politically by 'Russian Estonians', who were thought of as people who had betrayed the national interest.

Estonian-inclined Communists developed mainly as nurselings of the *komsomol*[4] as a training ground for future Communist Party members. The analogous creation of 'buffer-persons' for temperate Communist acculturation occurred also among other nations that had fallen into the sphere of socialism. But there were obvious differences in timing: in Hungary, protest took the shape of Imre Naggy's reforms, which ended with the bloody revolt of 1956; in Finland it was called the Paasikivi-Kekkonen line, established in the 1950s. Nevertheless, the term 'Estonian-inclined (national) Communists' was not coined at the grass-roots level: it did not have currency as an affectionately-regarded name. Quite the opposite: the term 'national Communists' (*'natsionaljnõe kommunistõ'*) originated from the Moscow Central Committee. Initially, it had a clearly pejorative tone, comparable to that label indicating severe Party condemnation 'bourgeois nationalists'. Since the end of the 1960s the term had been used in a positive way by Estonian farmer-Communists, that is, the *kolkhoz* chairmen. Judging from memoirs, it appears that the circles in question themselves used this term as a form of self-identification, and they see themselves as a brotherhood even today. More generally, people simply said 'This or that man appears to be surprisingly reasonable and tries to defend his people against Moscow', or, 'He does not act like a Communist but as an Estonian'.

The group of truly nationalist-minded leading Communists was not large (around thirty people), but because of their very high placement in the Soviet-Estonian official hierarchy (they included ministers of education and agriculture, the ideology secretary and the head of the department of culture at the Central Committee, the chairman of the Planning Committee, etc.) their hands were less tied, and their decisions had a greater effect on Estonian society in general. One central figure, Vaino Väljas, the ideology secretary of the ECP, characterised the nationalist-minded Communists by the term 'cork fender': that is, a buffer between a ship and the dock, which, being itself constantly kicked about, lessens the pressure on the dock while the ship runs ashore. The mission of the national Communists was to relieve the pressure on the approximately one million Estonians – the political and economical pressure, often ineffective and mirroring Russian chauvinist ambitions, exercised by the Moscow bureaucrats (Aarelaid, 1998, p. 214). Their activities created good outcomes, since from the second half of the 1970s Estonia (and the Baltics in general) was referred to as *Sovetskii Zapad* (the Soviet West), that is, a region that is economically and culturally well-developed (i.e. as developed as the West).

Double-mindedness and Marginalisation

The totalitarian system created a deep discrepancy between public and private spheres, which in turn brought about the phenomenon of double-mindedness. Nationalist feeling, and the collective memory of lost independence and the terrible Stalinist past, belonged to the neighbourhood- and home-centred private sphere: this was opposed to the public sphere, which was dominated by the doctrine of the flourishing and united Soviet nations. It was precisely this split which provided the circumstances for the creation of a body of Estonian-inclined leading Communists. These ambivalently-inclined persons were imprinted simultaneously by the ideals and norms of two totally different cultural configurations. In fact, they were marginals in terms of both ideological systems, but that marginality and double-mindedness gave them the opportunity to cherish the values of the oppressed private sphere and act accordingly in the firmly-restricted public sphere, thus moderately diminishing the influence of chauvinist Moscow rule.

Let us briefly describe these two oppositional but complementary mental configurations determining the minds of Estonian people under post-war conditions. The first was Estonianness, which was characterised by a value-cluster which included a will to continue as before the style of life that had been interrupted in 1940. It upheld a turned-in lifestyle within the farmstead or workshop along with correct working practices, priority for the Estonian language on every level of social interaction, and protection of national territory as a guarantor of social stability. The keywords marking this configuration were pastorality, individualism and localism, as well as national feelings associated with the mother tongue and glorification of a lost independent past. The second configuration may be called Sovietness, with a value-cluster consisting of: (1) an orientation towards Communist internationalism, which aimed at loosening ties with a past that had contained many national enemies; (2) deep class distinction and, following it, forced collectivisation, powerful industrialisation and urbanisation as the main means of building up Communism; and (3) a forceful prioritising of the Russian language as a tool of imperialism. Whereas, in the Orthodox and collectivist tradition of Russian culture, there is no place for the 'primacy of the law of Man' (Lazari, 1995, p. 50), the new socialist society was restratified through violent political campaigns. The key concepts in this reconfiguration were large-scale 'heroic' collectivism, a never-before-seen 'happy future', and empire building; in addition, priority was given to Russians as 'elder and more experienced brothers'.

Amalgamation of these controversial double discourses was one of the main characteristics of the Sovietisation of cultural life in Estonia. In the first Soviet decade, after the Second World War, this took the form of a dialogue between the past, which seemed ever more beautiful as it drifted further away, and the bloody present. People were psychologically not ready to lose their memories of the independent nation-state; at the same time, they did not want to remain losers in abruptly altered social circumstances. In the post-war years, this double-facedness sought to make a special accommodation with the new regime as a response to the problem of survival. This was the period of the 'death troikas', and nobody was free to express what they thought about the Soviet system. In the following decades, 'double-mindedness' appeared more as a domestication of the ghost of Communism. Most people, in other words, did not strive any longer to place their hopes in the restitution of the pre-War independent republic, but looked for milder ways of accustoming themselves to the Communist dispensation. For many older intellectuals this represented a freely-chosen 'inner immigration' and inaction in the public sphere. They regarded themselves as civilised Europeans who would never be placed under the brutal 'Asiatic' yoke. For many career-minded young people, their public manipulation of Soviet ideology conferred on them powerful kudos whereby they could build up a comfortable lifestyle and then boast to their very small private social network of family and close friends about how skilled they were in cheating the Reds. Several methods existed for operating double-mindedness, but only a few of them made a bridge between two opposing and isolated cultural configurations. The mentality of the Estonian-inclined Communist was one such.

In characterising the Estonian-inclined Communists as marginals, we would define marginality as the state of being part-insider and part-outsider in respect of a social group. Such people represented so-called cultural hybrids, who shared the life and traditions of two distinct groups. Usually, this kind of cultural hybridism, involving mixed or contradictory identities, resulted from immigration or occupation and was located on the borders of a certain cultural landscape. Such persons' 'doubleness' is recognised only in a very limited way by each distinct group, and this is a source of long-term personal suffering and alienation (Brooker, p. 128).

This, however, was not the case with the Estonian-inclined Communists, who, as persons with a compound identity, employed the new 'mixed' discourse in order to govern the whole of Estonian society from the mid-1960s to the mid-1970s. As masters of a (then highly-valued) *bricolage* located not on the border but in the centre of the socio-cultural environment, they played fascinating political games of liminality, moving between the categories of national feeling and command-economy vocabulary. Their marginality reflected superbly the double-consciousness of the majority of homeland Estonians, which gave them a chance to acquire a central position in the contemporary social hierarchy. This small group of nationally-minded Communists did not ignore the norms of 'good behaviour' of each distinct group, but rather, reconstituted the social norms whereby they could live permanently 'in-between'. Their newly-fashioned discourse represented a commingling of ideas that permitted the continuous, creative making and unmaking, mixing and remixing, of unstable identities.

The Interviews, and the Interconnections between the Cohorts

Such rapid changes may also be seen both in post-Communist societies and elsewhere in Europe, especially where entire peoples – as in the Baltic States – produce new and varied historiographies. These new versions of history are often based on the trauma inflicted on the population by, for example, Soviet military occupation: the trauma and the heroic struggle thus become constituents of a new mythology and form the core of a new type of nationalism (Thompson, 1981, p. 16).

During the three years 1996–8, 73 semi-structured interviews were conducted with Estonia's most famous cultural and political activists. Most of the respondents were 'winners', persons with strong inner powers of adaptation to changing social circumstances. Inside the Soviet system they not only survived the alien mental conditions, but even acquired notable positions in the cultural landscape or in the political hierarchy of Soviet Estonia. Today, more than half of these respondents speak of the traumatic effects of Soviet power on their personal life courses. Twenty, 30 or 40 years ago, these same traumatic effects were interpreted as greater or smaller victories over the foolish system-makers and dull Soviet bureaucrats.

Thus, the restitution of an independent Estonian state has, for our respondents, resulted in self-clarification and self-purification. It must be stressed that our database represents a collection of the life experiences of individual Estonian men and women living under Soviet rule; every story is unique and full of elements of self-defence and self-delusion. The researcher must be very careful in interpreting these records, because there is a large difference between lives lived and lives remembered (Josselson, 1996, p. 54). In the mid-1990s these respondents did not tell us their real biographies, but a renewed version of the myth about their 'real lives' lived at least 25 years ago. Following the restoration of an independent Republic they presented themselves either as heroes in a long-fought struggle against Soviet reality, or as victims of inhuman and traumatic historical circumstances. This very clear polarisation of life-myths is itself a new reincarnation of the ambivalent phenomenon of double-consciousness belonging to the Soviet period.

In order to present a more systematic overview of the several cohorts that are treated in this account, it is necessary to provide an outline of their chronological ordering as well as of the interconnections between different cohorts (Bertaux, 1981, p. 34). Historically, the first group in power in Soviet Estonia were the so-called 'June Communists' – ideologically-committed, native-born and educated Estonians who participated in the first Moscow-imposed takeover in 1940–41 and continued to abet Moscow in 1944–50 when the Nazi occupation had ended. During the second half of the 1940s there existed permanent conflict between them and the first-generation cohort of Russian-born Estonians who returned to Estonia after 1941/4 (the *Istased*), which concluded with the latter group taking over. During our fieldwork nobody from these two cohorts was interviewed, since they had all died.

Our central focus of interest was the Estonian-inclined Communists who were young *komsomol* leaders in the post-war period and who became the 'first echelon' in the years 1965–78. Their distinguishing biographical feature is their experience of the pre-war Estonian Republic and of the ravages of the first Russian occupation (1940–41) and the German occupation (1941–4). They were persons who were clearly committed to socialist ideas, but who sought an 'Estonian way'. Five of my interviewees may be categorised as authentic former leading national Communists. They included the minister of education for the years 1960–78, the ideology secretary of the ECP from 1971 to 1978, the director of the Institute of History 1971–8, the rector of the Institute of Fine Arts 1959–89, and the ideology secretary of the *komsomol* 1957–62 (later, the dissident chair of Scientific Communism at Tallinn Polytechnic Institute). In the 1990s these people were, inevitably, too old and 'tainted' to occupy positions of power, but they told their life stories with great humour and analytical depth.

There were other intellectuals among the respondents who had entered the Communist Party in the 1960s and 1970s with the aim of changing this organisation to a pro-Estonian one from within. Among them were one academic, two cinema critics, four *komsomol* leaders, two writers, one journalist and one ethnologist. Were I to have had a larger database, I could have posed the question of whether the life courses of the Estonian-inclined Communists (especially the formative period of their childhood and youth) can be distinguished from those of other socially-prominent people who reflected their time. But it must be stressed again that only a very restricted group of people may be considered as forming the brotherhood of Estonian-inclined Communists: the larger part of my respondents may be characterised only as Estonian-born members of the ECP.

Ideologically speaking, the group who stood in contrast to the Estonian-inclined Communists were the powerfully anti-Soviet dissidents who began their political careers as teenagers in the 1950s but were soon sent to the Gulag Archipelago. Born just a few years later than our central group of interest, they had different early life experiences, since they had no memories of an independent national state and had experience only of permanent conflict with KGB officials. Among my respondents only one person, who was arrested as 17-year-old schoolboy and who was later a long-time prisoner of conscience, represented this micro-group. Most of the members of this dissident cohort were slightly younger peers of the Estonian-inclined Communists who began their political activities not in the 1950s but in the 1970s as small-scale anti-occupation-movement leaders. Their long-standing opposition to socialism meant that many of them gained leading positions in the post-1990 hierarchy, but lost them soon afterwards owing to their ignorance of everyday practical politics (Aarelaid, 2000, p. 116). Nevertheless, two of our respondents were working in 2001 as members of the Estonian parliament: one is the above-mentioned former prisoner of conscience, and the other the author in the 1970s of several Appeals to the UN, who put up his candidacy for the post of president in autumn 2001. It was extremely interesting to compare the life stories of leading Communists and well-known dissidents, of whom I interviewed four.

The other contrasting cohort as regards our main group of interest is the second generation of Russian-born Estonians who returned to Estonia in the late 1950s and did not gain senior positions of power until 1978, when they were at long last successful in taking over leadership of the Estonian Communist Party. The restoration of the independent Republic of Estonia in 1991 led to their escaping back to Russia. For understandable reasons I have not conducted any interviews with representatives of this generational cohort.

Among my respondents there were two small groups of previous *komsomol* leaders who had connections with the Estonian-inclined Communists. The first such cohort (4 interviewees) was made up of *komsomol* leaders born in the post-war period who became political leaders in the mid-1960s. In terms of our main group of interest they functioned as younger, but very critical (sometimes even rival) colleagues, who gradually lost their opportunity to gain real power following their rebellious behaviour during the 'Prague Spring and Autumn' of 1968. In terms of today this cohort represents, first of all, the newly financially rich groups of people who are mostly very cynical regarding their youth and their various connections with the national Communists. The second cohort is younger than all the other groups, although they had time to take up their initial positions in the early 1980s, which meant that they do not have direct ties with the Estonian-inclined Communists. Their careers in the *komsomol* were of no importance because they functioned not as ideologues but as managers of practical concerns such as the Students Building Company. Today, they either continue as a managerial élite or participate in right-wing politics. Our sample contained three members from this cohort, whose attitude towards the Estonian-inclined Communists was negative.

Reconstruction of the Life Courses of the Estonian-inclined Communists

'The history of the individual is never anything other than a certain specification of the collective history of his group or class' (Bourdieu,

p. 86). My collection of the life stories of that distinct brotherhood who called themselves 'Estonian-inclined Communists' may be seen as a quintessence of the discourse of 'betweenness' that was virtually inevitable for the majority of creative persons living profitable lives under the totalitarian regime.

These Estonian-inclined Communists were born before 1935, which means that they had had to pass at least their early childhood (and usually a few of their school years) under the conditions of the first Estonian Republic. They frequently belonged to patriotic boy-scout organisations such as the Young Eagles. The attitude they adopted at home towards the independent state was positive: the Estonian state was sacred, and as a matter of course one had to respect one's own state. The stability they had experienced in society and in culture-loving homes and home surroundings had created for them feelings of a secure childhood.

The dissidents, on the other hand, had been born 3–5 years later, and their childhoods had born the impress of morbid war recollections and existential fear; their homes had been filled with the distress caused by the loss of the independent state. Respondents emphasised the contrast between the safety of their very early childhood and later horrors. One respondent recounted that, as a seven-year-old child, he was, in June 1940, separated from his grandparents for four days because Russian troops would not let his family cross the Tallinn–Narva road to return to home from church. 'I was frightened by those events for a long time!' he reported.

The national Communists came from poor regions like the islands and south-eastern Estonia, although in their own homes daily bread had not been the main problem. The important factor is that people who come from less prosperous rural regions always tend to be better prepared for mobilisation into voluntary organisations, and from their own early childhood remember their parents' and relatives' common social activities (e.g. the founding of shipping or dairy cooperatives or cultural associations). These children certainly joined their parents in taking part in the local singing or drama activities or adult education societies. The eldest of the respondents (b. 1914) had already, in his twenties, founded on his own a voluntary cultural association in his village. At home, the respondents had encountered the moderate, intellectually-inclined social-democratic mentality that was widespread in Estonia in the 1930s. Two of them stressed the role played by the feeling of justice common among the village people as an important element in their personal development. As an example, let me present a story about small fish. The village men who formed a boat crew always left part of their catch – the small fish that dropped through the mesh of their net – to be distributed among those households where there were no men to go to sea or where there were a large number of children and never enough food. The respondents claimed that it was just that kind of responsibility for the whole village which had, in their later years, impelled them to reflect on their own personal responsibility for the fate of their people.

Dissident-minded persons, by contrast, often came from urban, more culturally-inclined and sometimes religious families. Their parents and other close relatives were frequently strong anti-Communists. Among the dissidents interviewed, it was typical for family background to have limited their mobility within the Soviet system. One respondent's father was executed by the Russians because he was a prosperous farmer. Others were as children exiled to Siberia with their entire families. One respondent described how he escaped from a Siberian village and returned clandestinely to Tallinn to live with his elder brother.

Thus, during the years 1940–45 tragic events took place in the lives of both the national Communists and the dissidents: the loss of their native home, the violent deaths of their parents or close relatives, and so on. The only dissimilarities are the different executants. Thus, in one case the father had been killed by the Germans as being a Red education official, in another case by the Russians as being a White-minded prosperous farmer. In their future life the mentality of the sons was set firmly against the killers of their fathers, against those who had destroyed their homes.

But there was one significant difference. Estonian-inclined Communists were the older cohort, and they saw with their own eyes the vandalism of the destruction battalions established by Stalin to carry out his 'scorched earth' policy in the areas to be abandoned, as well as the brutal retreat of Nazi troops in 1944, when houses, roads and bridges were demolished in their wake. They had no illusions about one side in the War being better than the other. Dissidents looked at wartime events from a very childlike point of view; their reactions were emotional and were inspired by boyish revenge. Revenge directed against the builders of the socialist system became the most important motivating force of their adult lives.

Among my respondents the Estonian-inclined Communists have, as a rule, shown themselves to be more talented at school and more eager to learn – students who have inspired other young people. It is quite conceivable that, if Estonia had remained independent, they would sooner or later have risen to leading office. But when they reached the age when they wanted to make their mark, they had to face nothing but the rather one-sided *komsomol* organisation. They were undoubtedly young people who wished to achieve something in life, but their further career paths led them through the hierarchy provided by the *komsomol*. Before reaching the age of 25 they became recognised as youth leaders, but in the Red gown that was the only option at that moment in history. Inside the *komsomol* a real shift in these young persons' mindsets must have occurred, and they became enthusiastic agitators for the new Communist world view. They understood very well why several of their classmates or teachers had disappeared, and sometimes they even tried to defend friends against the Red terror. At the same time, however, they were eager believers in the happy Communist future of mankind. They struggled resolutely against 'bourgeois survivals' such as marriage rings, preparations for confirmation, etc. Working inside the Soviet ideological system opened up for them good life-perspectives, and because of these opportunities they were ready to collaborate with the regime.

The dissident-minded young people – little younger agewise – tried to found secret anti-Soviet organisations of schoolchildren, but they were either imprisoned or else could not find an adequate number of sympathisers. Their social depression was accentuated also by the fact that they did not have the 'right' parents, which might cause them not to be accepted by the universities they aspired to enter. Some of them, for example, instead of acquiring the education they desired in the fields of linguistics or art, had to enrol at the Tallinn Polytechnic Institute.

The lives of the Estonian-inclined Communists continued to follow a similar pattern. Their career paths took them to the over-ideological party-élite higher education institutions in Moscow or Leningrad, which represented the highest educational level in the CPSU Academy of Social Sciences. Although these institutions were supposed to produce ultra-orthodox senior officials loyal to the system, life itself proposed and produced an unexpected variation. At these institutions they tended to meet young people from various countries under the dictatorship of Moscow, and being intelligent individuals they started to compare the different versions of socialism. A new empirical truth appeared out of these student discussions: the doctrine of Moscow was far from being unselfish, and one had to defend the people of one's native country against Russia's uncaring chauvinist mentality. At the beginning of the 1960s these people, in possession of a higher Party education and in their thirties, turned back to Estonia. They preserved their student friendships with the rising leaders of other socialist countries, and they soon began to communicate with their comrades abroad at the level of university rectors, ideology secretaries, etc. Compared with that of ordinary Estonians, their social networks were much wider and their knowledge about the essence of real socialism much deeper. They had been trained as solders in the field of ideological work, but as talented persons their capacity to analyse social phenomena was broader.

By that time, they had been shaped to be the carriers of two cultural configurations. To be more exact, as skilled people they had learnt to master perfectly two 'languages', and yet they could not identify themselves completely with either of them. This perfect 'bilingualism' was, of course, the élite version of the same double-consciousness that was spreading at the grass-roots level. Nevertheless, the majority of Estonians considered mere membership of the Party to be the original sin; at that time holding a senior position in the *nomenklatura* was destined to cause alienation. 'Party member' was an insulting expression among many Estonians for a long period of time; in most circles, holding any post in the Soviet *aparat* was considered treason towards one's people. This meant that a member of this later brotherhood of Estonian-inclined Communists could not be recognised by the ordinary people as one of them. At the same time, the same men remained 'outsiders' also in the eyes of the Kremlin, because in Moscow they constantly stressed the priority of national interests. They faced two options: either to make a conscious choice in favour of one cultural space, or to confirm a psychologically-burdening marginality as the central core of their personality. They chose the more difficult path. But why? Why it was essential for them to continue as 'bilinguals'?

By the 1960s, Estonian society had developed to the stage were there appeared to be a necessity for 'ombudsmen' – experts who could, to a certain degree, manage to reconcile national distress, along with the painful loss of freedom, with Communist ideals. It was impossible to produce such leaders under artificial circumstances, either in Tallinn or in Moscow. Such a leader – one capable of maintaining that kind of enormous social compromise – could only evolve on his own from among a limited circle of men whose life courses had up to that moment provided certain inevitable preconditions. The strongest requirements were a positive attitude towards an independent Estonian state and, secondly, a completely opposite component – a deep loyalty to the Communist world view. Such a person needed to have been born at the right period; that is, their recollections of independence needed to be not too deep, but yet sufficient for maintaining nationalism. Their life course had to include a negative encounter with those who hated the Communists, yet at the same time they must not have been turned into blind executants of Communist terror.

The historic mission of the nationalist-inclined Communists was to create the conditions for Estonia to survive as a nation in the Soviet melting pot. In trying to square the circle, they could not themselves become conformists or selfish career-Communists, but rather, needed to remain charismatic persons holding certain ideals. Besides, they were in actuality authentically double-minded people who frantically strove to adapt the value system essential for the preservation of the Estonian nation to the repressive game-rules dictated by Moscow. Among their achievements we should mention the maintenance of an education system in the Estonian language at all levels, the support for nationalist-inclined voluntary organisations, the establishing of a relatively open range of activities for the creative intelligentsia, and the development of the *kolkhoz* system into a prosperous national agricultural industry.

Already at the stage of late Brezhnevism, the socialist system showed signs of the coming collapse. Initiated by a survival instinct, a campaign of ideological repression was launched, expressed by the new wave of russification. There was a Party coup in Estonia in 1978 and the Estonian-inclined Communists were forced to resign. One of those whom Moscow considered among the most dangerous received a commission for a diplomatic post in Latin America. Some were forced to retire; others were demoted to posts with magnificent names where they were actually deprived of all power. In rendering their life stories, my respondents mentioned 1978 as having been the gloomiest year in their life. But this career break was not associated with a tumbling of ideals: on the contrary, they continued to uphold both nationalist and socialist ideals.

During the new era of the fight for national independence which began in 1988, the Estonian community once again required the favours of these men. In the West, these years were characterised by 'Gorbo-mania', when most people believed in the miracle-worker Gorbachev and saw in Mikhail Sergeyevich the super-reformer of Russia. In Estonia, people did not yet dare to formulate the idea of restoring independence, but everybody was ready to criticise the centralised governing style and monopolism of Moscow. By degrees Estonia moved to the forefront of the destroyers of state socialism, and the danger of such resistance being crushed by Russian tanks grew continuously. Day after day one had to do 'translation work' in order to interpret for Moscow as a harmless process growing Estonian aspirations towards freedom. Moscow no longer believed that Estonia would stay under its rule, but the only couriers it could accept were the Estonian-inclined Communists who had partly regained their power – the more so, as one of them happened to be a personal friend and confidant of Mikhail Gorbachev.

On the other hand, it was precisely during that same so-called 'singing revolution' period that the Estonian-inclined Communists began to lose their previous 'double-cultured' identity. Neither socialist ideology nor Estonian-mindedness was the same any longer as it had been twenty years previously, and the language skills of the 'interpreters' dwindled very quickly. Two of my respondents worked in administrative posts also after the restoration of independence, but they soon withdrew from leading positions. By way of comparison let me point out that, at the same time, three interviewees with dissident pasts worked in Parliament, two of whom are still there today.

Who Were They Really?

'The collection of life histories brings the question of time to the fore that has been obscured or neglected by more conventional research' (Miller, 2000, p. ix). The effects of the passage of time may be seen in a variety of areas: historical background, ageing, generational or cohort experience. A correct identification of true historical trends is central to an understanding of the life courses of certain cohorts, including the Estonian-inclined Communists. As Miller points out:

> When a person's lifetime is viewed as a whole, the idea of their 'history' can be apprehended at two levels. First, the individual has their own history of personal development and change as they 'process' along their life course. Second, a considerable amount of time passes as they move along their life course. In this respect, historical events and social change at the societal level impinge upon the individual's own unique life history. (Miller, p. 9)

There may be a large discrepancy between the evaluation of life courses from a personal and from a social point of view.

In telling the researcher their stories the respondents from the closed 'brotherhood' of Estonian-inclined Communists had explicit explanations for every meaningful solution or important participation that took place over their life courses. Everything was very logical and in its right place: their joining of the *komsomol* and the Communist Party, their studies in the CPSU Academy of Social Sciences, their acceptance of very senior positions of power inside the occupying regime, the balance they struck between Estonianness and Sovietness. Respondents agreed that their choices had sometimes required them to put aside their youthful memories of the Estonian Republic and the Stalinist terror in order to navigate a career path in the Communist Party. In their own eyes, however, they were torn by their opposing commitments as Communists and as Estonians.

But this role of Kremlin mediator was not recognised by the broad population of Estonia as one deserving sympathy. A great many people saw these people as legitimators of the Soviet regime, who enjoyed the benefits of the *nomenklatura* such as shops with a special supply, better apartments, state-owned summer cottages, and so on. How can one evaluate who these people really were?

It should be mentioned that the Estonian-inclined Communists had predecessors – the June Communists. The term refers to those home-grown Estonian Communists who came to take up positions in the Party and state after the Soviets occupied Estonia in June in 1940, but who in reality were simply puppets. *De-facto* power resided in the hands of the military and the Russian leadership sent from Moscow. Most of this cohort were true believers in orthodox Marxism-Leninism and the proletarian revolution; indeed, many had been imprisoned following the attempted Communist *coup d'état* of 1924. As long-term prisoners they did not have a full picture of what went on in the Soviet Union in the 1930s. Yet the 'Redness' of this cohort was partly mitigated by its Estonianness. Such people were often characterised as 'radishes' by Estonians: Red on the outside, but White (nationalist) on the inside. They soon came to understand the brutal game that Moscow was playing, but too late to do anything except soften and deflect Moscow's harshest policies whenever possible. It has been argued that between 1945 and 1950 the first secretary of the ECP, and many of the lesser Party members following his lead, had tried to soften the impact of the collectivisation campaigns and the 'liquidation of the kulaks' (landowners with more than 100 hectares of land) by helping uprooted farmers remain in Estonia rather than consigning them to Siberian exile. These attempts were 'evaluated' by the Eighth Plenary Session of the ECP as 'ignoring the principle of collegiality in leadership, not fighting "bourgeois nationalism" with sufficient vigour, and providing mistaken guidance in ideological work' (Raun, 1991, p. 171). They were forced by the Russian-born Estonians to leave the political arena.

If the June Communists were born at the beginning of the twentieth century, the Estonian-inclined Communists were born in the 1930s – the life courses of these two cohorts had different historical backgrounds. The latter cohort remembered very well the sad story of their predecessors and hoped to avoid it. At the end of the first Soviet decade, the June Communists who were rendered political outsiders were disappointed by the termination of their careers and to some extent turned against Stalinism and the system itself. This cost them their senior positions, and some of them became political prisoners. At the same time, both cohorts had a common enemy: the Russian Estonians (*Istlased*), whom they saw as entirely ignorant of Estonian affairs and ardent combatants purely for Moscow's interests.

Members of the younger cohort are distinguished by having risen to senior positions within the Soviet system: in other words, they were 'insiders' from the very beginning of their careers. But the mental climate in Stalinist Estonia during the period of their shaping as persons was complex and ambivalent. Many parents, wishing to spare their offspring, simply stayed silent about what had happened in earlier times. By the second half of the 1950s it had become evident that Soviet power would not come to an end immediately or even soon, and thus it made no sense to intimidate the new post-war generation with dissident stories. Besides, people harboured fears in connection with children's naïve habit of prattling: they might start to explain matters that were dangerous to the welfare of the home or the family in some unsuitable place or to an alien person. Thus, this 'double-minded' cohort of young leading Communists did not have good contacts either with the generation before or the generation after them, even though they had experienced times of independence as well as of war and Stalinist terror. In reality, they were situated between two different life-perspectives not only in terms of their mentality but in a historical sense too: in the 1950s one era in Estonia was basically closed, and the other barely in its formative phase. Indeed, the split between the private sphere of family and friends, which was Estonian, and the public sphere of Party discourse and of managing relations with Moscow was unavoidable, but not so deep as it may have been earlier or later. In the 1950s, the whole of Estonian society existed in a liminary situation; double-mindedness was common, and there is nothing surprising in the fact that the youth vanguard was patterned in terms of 'doubleness'.

It represents more the rule than the exception that the meteoric flight of this cohort towards the highest-level political careers following the mid-1960s was characterised by their balancing and alternating between the demands of Soviet reality and Estonian national identity. In terms of their personal character these young people began under late Stalinism as universally adaptable 'winners'. At the time, while their peers in the 1950s learnt a 'science of small lies' and were permanently afraid of KGB agents, the *komsomol* leaders were just pushing through. They felt themselves to be the masters of a new history, which was full of beneficial compromises and the art of conducting dialogues.

Double-mindedness was a frame for the social actions of thousands of Estonians, but usually they did not recognise this clearly. One historian in her late seventies commented:

> It is our mistake now to over-estimate public consciousness during the Soviet period. Usually people lived their everyday lives – fell in love, took care of their children, obtained something, worried about their relatives. From time to time they wished to express their opinion in some way: sang ribald songs about 'our lovely Stalin', told toothless anecdotes about Lenin or Nikita Sergejevitš – they demonstrated resignation regarding their political position and claimed their actions were not purely political. (quoted in Aarelaid, 1998, p. 157)

In other words, when a large number of people were used to living inside this double-minded social discourse, only a small group of comrades recognised the situation clearly and used that recognition to maintain power. 'To help the nation within the Soviet system' was a phrase older respondents often used to characterise the Estonian-inclined Communists. Others might point out that those who operated behind this slogan of 'in-betweenness' also benefited from their position inside the system, but this should not serve to obscure the concrete ways in which living conditions in Estonia were improved. One literary critic, born in 1928, commented on the situation as follows:

> Some friends who had joined the Party said in the sixties, in a half-mocking way, 'Please, come with us and let's turn the Party messy from inside'. Really they themselves banged their heads against the wall, but nevertheless they did not leave the Party for those reasons. Opportunities inside the Party were used for themselves and sometimes 'the Estonian ideal' was achieved too. (quoted in Aarelaid, 1998, p. 168)

One respondent, a popular media figure and a CP member from the 1960s, compared himself with a member of the dissident cohort: 'Every movement should have its resistance fighters ... but I am not personally self-destructive', he said. 'We all lived a double life and tried to widen the [political] territory allowed.' This gradual impinging upon restrictive alien borders was the common language that was forged between native people and their leaders from the second generation of Estonian-born Communists.

In the mid-1990s, in conditions of restored independence, all respondents stressed how strong their desire had been during the 1960s and 1970s to help the Estonian nation survive the pressure from Moscow. But did they, 25–35 years ago, really act so unselfishly? Yes, they had a clear mission and a large enough circle of native-born local CP and municipal administrators, *kolkoz* chairmen and industrial élites to support them. But this game between two opposite configurations was both dangerous in personal terms and exhausting. It might have been psychologically easier to relinquish this 'double' game completely or to show greater loyalty towards Moscow, thereby avoiding permanent difficulties in defending national positions. What, we may ask, was the strong inner motivation for that stable 'in-betweenness'? It could not be the benefits enjoyed by the *nomenklatura* or the gratitude of ordinary Estonian people.

Maybe they were idealists – believers, first of all, in radical left-wing Euro-Communism, which was popular enough in Central and Western Europe. The first secretary of Party ideology in the ECP in the 1970s (b. 1931) appeared to think so:

> From the mid-1960s, Euro-Communist ideas were spreading in Estonia. To those clever people who taught the history of philosophy, historical and dialectical materialism, the idea of socialism cannot have been unfamiliar. The thing was, the pattern placed upon the outcome did not match it. In other words, everyone understood that the pattern and the idea are one thing but the Soviet reality another. The word 'Euro-Communism' was in widespread use in Estonia. Without doubt it contained a desire for a lost Europe, a nostalgic search for our Western identity. At the same time, it was the pattern of the protest, because it was not our will that had brought us where we were, and really we required something else. (quoted in Aarelaid, 1998, p. 168)

On the other hand, a discussion with a *komsomol* leader (b. 1946) of rebellious university students in the late 1960s suggests a precisely opposite estimation:

> Since history has shown that people who are governed democratically have never voluntarily voted for Communists as their leaders, Euro-Communism was a huge branch of idealism. The first ECP ideologist, up to the time of his being chased from Estonia in 1978, was in no way a Euro-Communist. He was an honest servant of the system, maybe a victim too. But as the son of a fisherman from the island of Hiiumaa he had a more realistic and sober understanding of Estonian life than Russian-born Estonians. (quoted in Aarelaid, 1998, p. 169)

This modest ideological shift in Estonia from the Moscow paradigm was brought about through the personal contribution of the first secretary of the ECP, who held that post for 28 years. After the Eighth Plenary Session of 1950, Käbin began his career as an orthodox Marxist-Stalinist, but in time he 'gained the reputation of [being] a pragmatic and rational leader whose role as a buffer against inordinate demands from Moscow was appreciated' (Raun, 1991, p. 192).

Over the years, Käbin became relatively Estonianised, and no doubt this was primarily due to the influence of a number of people within the brotherhood of Estonian-inclined Communists. This does not mean he was the first person to have retrenched from Moscow-derived modes of thinking: he was, all the time, loyal to the mainstream instructions of the Communist Party, carrying them out with only small variations. Another respondent (b. 1943), who belonged to the cohort of radically-minded *komsomol* enthusiasts of the 1960s, described the mentality of the Estonian-inclined higher ECP echelon quite critically:

> V. Väljas was hardly a Euro-Communist in the 1960s: he was a hard maker [ruled with an iron fist] as a leader of the Communists in Tallinn. Both he and the creative intelligentsia got along with Käbin tolerably well, but such that when they met, smiles were brief. Both sides put on a face that everything was OK ... but [they] never fell into embraces – distance was always maintained. Central Committee men were gods, artists or writers in other words simple mortals, and the gods knew of their elevated status. (quoted in Aarelaid, 1998, pp. 169–70)

Thus, if the brotherhood of Estonian-inclined Communists did not follow the path of the Western reformers of Communism, perhaps they were highly talented adapters to changing circumstances? In reality, Estonian culture had begun to revive, and even flower, within the frame of Soviet ideology by the early 1960s. From the mid-1960s on, the window to the West was progressively opened: the Helsinki–Tallinn shipping route caused an influx of Finnish tourists into Tallinn, which represented a consequent source of capital, while the availability of Finnish television in the northern third of Estonia showed up the contrast between Western and Soviet lifestyles. The centennial of the first Pan-Estonian Song Festival in 1969 proved to be the occasion of a powerful but peaceful national demonstration of anti-Soviet feeling, while members of the artistic unions sharply criticised the realities of life under the Soviet regime in their regular congresses. During the same period ethnic unrest increased, owing to new flows of Russian-speaking *gastarbeiter*, who were sent into large Estonian towns on the instructions of all-Union administrators.

During the era of cultural and national renewal the position of Russian-born Estonians weakened. The first secretary of the ECP recognised clearly that 'would-be Estonians' could not continue to command Estonians because of the danger of a large-scale confrontation with the native people. The time was ripe for better moderators between Moscow and Tallinn to come forward. 'The native Estonians' role in the ECP increased considerably, and the hope of an eventual re-Estonianisation of the Party leadership emerged' (Raun, 1991, p. 219). The Estonian-born, highly-principled Communists were connected via an Estonian-disposed network involving family ties, morality, manners and cultural traditions. They were more flexible as regards alignment with local aspirations and could not avoid appreciating the basic interests of native people. Käbin was a clever politician in initiating a newly-fashioned cadre-politics from the top.

The permanent veiled contest between Estonian- and Russian-born Estonians (the *Istlased*) entered a fresh phase: that of competition for the support of local networks. The period of class struggle was over and new methods of managing the people were required. The brotherhood of Estonian-inclined Communists were ready to exploit the moderately liberalised circumstances and play their power games using the card of growing nationalism. As serious and acute analysts of the socialist system, they understood clearly that the key to holding the institutions of power in their hands was the postulate of Estonianness. Russian-born Estonians (of both generations) who were Kremlin loyalists were, throughout the whole Soviet period, in the majority inside the ECP Bureau, but this did not of itself enable them to succeed in the concrete conditions that applied in Estonia as the least-Sovietised region of the USSR. The Estonian-inclined Communists realised that the secret of holding power lay in the keeping up of excellent contacts with nationally-inclined local groups such as countryside specialists, key workers in the cultural and educational fields (e.g. teachers of folk culture and organisers of local social clubs), creative people, and so on. The Russians and Russian-Estonians, being entirely infused with the Party ethos and ignorant of national problems, had not been able to build up loyal administrative networks among the native people. The Estonian-inclined Communists had better ears for listening to the public voice. The national Communists secured their senior positions by establishing good contacts with a number of people who were very popular at the grass-roots level, such as the chief conductor of the Estonian Song Festival, the head of the Society for the Conservation of Estonian Nature and the chairmen of the Writers and Painters Unions. Through their own industry they built up a new native set of first secretaries of regional party committees and leaders of the Estonian Young Communist League. To Moscow, they stressed the importance of the well-being of Estonian agriculture and industry, which might, they argued, serve as the best example of these things to hold up in peaceful competition with the capitalist world. They asked the Moscow ideologues to decide what was better from the point of view of this competition with Western countries: to introduce in Estonia a regime of 'Red corner' political education, or to establish a system of native-language practical advice regarding the achievement of high productivity? – to raise to the highest plane ideological purity, or to increase economic efficiency?

During my interviews with the distinct cohort of national Communists, I was interested in how the clash of two fundamentally different cultural configurations determined so many of the respondents' life-events, and sometimes the whole course of their lives. I asked this question indirectly, in asking in which way these respondents recognised this intellectual clash and the double-mindedness consequent upon it, and in asking how they tried to overcome their inner alienation. The answer was quite surprising. For the Estonian-inclined Communists there appeared to be no discrepancy between these two mental configurations. Evidence is lacking as to whether or not they believed the rationales they offered for their behaviour. Could it be possible that the inner disharmony of a double-minded nation temporarily created a leadership with a harmonious 'double' consciousness?

Epilogue

Nowadays, the official Estonian line is to hate our Communist past, because most currently economically and politically mobile persons have been born, or as a minimum educated, within the Soviet system. Right-wing power-holders prefer to interpret these 50 years in the history of the Estonian nation only as a dark period of oppression and violence, when our country was enclosed within the KGB network and suffered under command-economy directives. This, however, is not the case, which explains why Estonia, as a western Soviet state, was better placed to evolve a liberal market economy and develop political pluralism than most other regions of the former USSR. Succeeding political generations have denied the importance of those narrow passages between Estonianness and Sovietness which the Estonian-inclined Communists established in order to protect their people and national territory, thus differentiating themselves from the mainstream Communists who brought about such political chaos.

In conclusion, I might add that, during the years when full power was exercised by the so-called 'first generation', there grew up alongside them a second generation of cultured Party officials of Estonian descent (the two above-mentioned cohorts of *komsomol* leaders). I have conducted interviews with them also, and have therefore been able to observe certain dissimilarities in lifestyle. The restless student *komsomol* of the 1960s drew their leaders from among the graduates of prominent city schools, who had had no chance of getting to know Estonian village solidarity, and who lacked the straightforward rural ethics. Naturally, these young people who grew up during the Soviet period did not have direct experience of the mentality operating during the first Republic. The historical memory appeared to them as vague and mystical, and the one-time independent state had lost its sacred glory. They perceived the 'bilingualism' of their senior colleagues mainly as a means for making a successful career and gaining a share of the privileges accorded to the Party *nomenklatura*. There was no longer the sense that such marginality had developed authentically, as a result of a particular combination of circumstances, including a charismatic sense of having a mission. The second-generation national Communists were epigones, for whom double-mindedness was no longer a natural thing, but rather a consciously cultivated state of mind that could be observed from the outside and discarded at any given moment if personal interest required it. It was an irony of fate that owing to the launch of the russification campaign these young people never reached the corridors of Soviet power. Instead they seized power in 1991, and have held their posts with changing fortunes up until the present. They discarded their Red mentality, along with the membership card of the Communist Party of the Soviet Union, in 1990. To date, several have become the leaders of right-wing-inclined political parties. Moreover, nationalist-mindedness has been replaced by the cult of money. My interviews with first-generation national Communists have left me with the impression that they are deeply disappointed by the treacherous conduct of their followers, and they ask a grave question, namely, why does none of them wish to restore an authentic national social-democratic political mentality?

Notes

1 *Kolkhoz*: in Russian *kollektivnoje hozjaistvo*, or Soviet-type collective farm.

2 *Kulak* is a Russian word meaning prosperous landowner. The kulaks, along with factory-owners, became the state enemies of workers and the peasantry.

3 This Soviet campaign sought to 'eliminate intellectuals' bourgeois mentality' (Aarelaid-Tart, 2000). Many were imprisoned or lost their jobs, while others 'in-emigrated' (i.e. emigrated internally so as not to participate in Soviet activities).

4 Komsomol: the Young Communist League.

References

Aarelaid, A. (1998), *Ikka kultuurile mõeldes* [Still Thinking about Culture], Virgela, Tallinn.

Aarelaid-Tart, A. (2000), 'Political Generations in Estonia: Historical Background To Form the Contemporary Political Scenery', in J.F. Zagórska and J. Wassilevski (eds), *The Second Generation of Democratic Élites in Central and Eastern Europe*, Warsaw, pp. 112–38.

Bertaux, D. (1981), 'From the Life-history Approach to the Transformation of Sociological Practice', in D. Bertaux (ed.), *Biography and Society: The Life History Approach*, Sage, London, pp. 29–45.

Bourdieu, P. (1977), *Outline of a Theory of Practice*, Cambridge University Press, Cambridge.

Brooker, P. (1999), *A Concise Glossary of Cultural Theory*, Édward Arnold, London. 'Hybridity', p.105; 'Marginality', p. 128.

Josselson, R. (ed.) (1996), *Ethics and Process in the Narrative Study of Lives: The Narrative Study of Lives*, Vol. 4, Sage, London.

Lazari, A. (ed.) (1995), *The Russian Mentality: Lexicon*, Śląsk, Katowice.

'Marginality' (1991), in D. and J. Jary (eds), *The HarperCollins Dictionary of Sociology*, HarperCollins, London, p. 288.

Miller, R. (2000), *Researching Life Stories and Family Histories*, Sage, London.

Raun, T. (1991), *Estonia and Estonians*, Hoover Institution Press, Stanford University, Stanford, CA.

Thompson, P. (1981), 'Trauma and the Long-term Life Story', in D. Bertaux (ed.), *Biography and Society: The Life History Approach*, Sage, London, pp. 232–40.

Voronkov, V. and Zdravomyslova, E. (eds) (1997), *Biographical Perspectives on Post-Socialist Societies*. Proceedings of the seminar held in St Petersburg, November 1996.

6 Portrayals of Past and Present Selves in the Life Stories of Former Stasi Informers

BARBARA MILLER
Vienna, Austria

Introduction

For many citizens of the former East Germany, the fall of the Berlin Wall in November 1989, and the subsequent amalgamation of the GDR with the FRG less than one year later, led to a fundamental re-evaluation of their personal history. Whereas, according to Fischer-Rosenthal, for a 40-year-old West German woman decisive biographical markers centred on family life and were incorporated into a continuous and permanent present, for her East German counterpart all that had taken place before the demise of the GDR now belonged to the realm of the past, and was viewed and evaluated from the post-1989–90 'present' (Fischer-Rosenthal, 1995, p. 54). In other words, a past–present threshold was set at 1989–90 in the biographical perceptions of many East Germans as a result of the phenomenal impact of the social and political change that had come about.

In some cases, this past life became the subject of much internal and external scrutiny. This was particularly the case for those former East Germans who had acted as informers for the GDR's State Security Service, the Stasi. The implementation of the *Stasi-Unterlagen-Gesetz*, the Stasi-Document-Law, in December 1991 meant that many of the approximately 174,000 informers who had been registered as active in 1989, and the many more who had collaborated at some point during the GDR's 40-year life span, could now be identified as such. The introduction of the law therefore meant that theoretically an end was in sight to the widespread speculation about who had or had not been involved in the Stasi's wide-scale surveillance and control measures. There has been a huge response to the Stasi-Document-Law, and by summer 1999, when the fourth report of the *BStU*, the government authority in charge of the files, went to press, over 4.2 million applications to view files had been lodged.[1] The majority of these requests have come from employers in the public sector, but over 1.5 million are applications from ordinary citizens wishing to discover exactly what role the Stasi played in shaping their past lives. The answers these individuals receive can have a marked impact on their understanding of self, and thus on the individual and collective reconstruction of auto/biography.

Some former Stasi operatives are only with great reluctance prepared to admit publicly (and sometimes, it seems, even privately) that they belong to the group of former *Inoffizielle Mitarbeiter* (*IM*), literally 'unofficial employees', the Stasi's term for informers. As the law stands, one-time informers active in the public service face possible dismissal and may also face social stigmatisation if word of their collaboration gets out, with the result that many feel they are defined solely in terms of this aspect of their biography. The mere label '*IM*' may thus potentially define the self-perception and public image of a former Stasi collaborator. The well-known writer Christa Wolf said, after the debate surrounding her Stasi connections, that she felt that her biography been reduced to the two letters 'I.M.'.[2]

Other one-time informers are also keen to emphasise that it is unreasonable that they should be judged only on this one aspect of their past life. A woman who worked under the cover name 'Sonnenblume', and whose period of collaboration encompassed just over a year, argued: 'After all, it was really only a small part of my life, just a tiny part.'[3] 'Theodor', too, feels that no one understands that his collaboration with the Stasi was 'only one small fragment in the mosaic of life'.[4] Since most people were previously unfamiliar with Stasi terminology, some, although well aware that they had met with a Stasi officer on a regular basis, were unaware that they had been classified as an *IM* and that they belonged to a larger group of *IM* whom the Stasi had extremely precise guidelines for dealing with. The post-1989 discovery that this was the case led in some cases to a re-interpretation of personal history to incorporate this knowledge. The former *IM* discovers retrospectively that he or she previously belonged to an apparently definable and distinct group, membership of which may have far-reaching repercussions for the interpretation both of the present and of the past.

Defining Conformity

Since 1989, many attempts have been made to define the behaviour of the average GDR citizen under Communist rule. Schröder (1990, p. 166) divides former East Germans into three groups: standard conformists; non- or anti-conformists; and opportunistic conformists. Standard conformists were individuals who, at least initially, believed in the system and sought justification for their actions in seeing themselves as representatives of it. The number of such individuals decreased during the GDR's existence, but some who had become disillusioned worked hard to continue to convince themselves of their stance, motivated as they were by their previous commitment and by their desire to preserve the way of life to which they had become accustomed. Only a small percentage of East Germans belonged to the second group of non- or rather anti-conformists. These were individuals who spoke out or acted against the status quo.

Most East Germans fell into the third group, of opportunistic conformists, that is, those who were very much aware of the frequent disharmony between private conviction and public behaviour, but who had learnt to live with the existing power structures and to use them to their own advantage wherever possible. This group may periodically have engaged in acts of opposition, but were probably not under active Stasi observation.[5] This range of behaviour patterns can be found throughout East German society and, of course, within the group of former Stasi informers. In applying Schröder's classification to the cases of the three former Stasi informers, 'Wolfgang', 'Theodor' and 'Stephana', this chapter demonstrates how distinctly varied past lives are now in some respects categorised and defined principally in terms of membership of the group of Stasi collaborators.

Standard Conformity

'Wolfgang' stated emphatically at the beginning of our conversation that he considered it vital to impart a great deal of detailed biographical information in order that his story could be fully understood: 'I was a part of the GDR. I was convinced that the way things were meant to be there was the right way.'[6] His loyalty to the GDR was a recurring theme throughout our conversation, and he became periodically quite animated when talking enthusiastically of certain positive aspects of life there and of how terrible things are now under the current political system.

'Wolfgang' was born in the midst of economic crisis in the late 1920s and was brought up in a small village in Saxony. His family was very poor, and he was fortunate that the local teacher was keen to see someone from the village obtain a secondary education. He was the only working-class child at the secondary school, and was conscious of how poorly dressed he was in comparison to the other children there. He was called up in 1944 but never saw active service. Those young men who had been born a year before him were involved in the battles during the last days of the war, and many were killed in action. After finishing school, 'Wolfgang' began work as a civil servant, in a post which involved close contact with Soviet troops. During this time he made the acquaintance of many Russian officers, with whom he says he had a good working relationship. Later, he studied economics and took up a managerial post. He told me that he had begun working for the Stasi in the early 1960s. This work involved travelling undercover to West Berlin and meeting a man there who gave him what he said were seemingly harmless pieces of information to pass back to his Stasi handler.

I was able to view the Stasi files of eight of the ten former informers I interviewed. 'Wolfgang' was one of the two men for whom the *BStU* did not uncover or release any information. It is possible that he worked for the Stasi's foreign espionage department (the *HVA*) and that his files were destroyed along with many others which the *HVA* was allowed to destroy in 1989–90. It is also possible that the relevant material was still to be catalogued at the time this research was undertaken.

'Wolfgang' seems to belong to the first of the three categories defined by Schröder, that of the standard conformist. Coming from what he describes as a poor and working-class background, he sees himself in many respects as a true child of the GDR. He identified with the state from a young age and says now that he was prepared to suffer hardship on behalf of the collective good. His depiction of his life story revolves around this key construct of being a fervent patriot, and he says he experienced the workers' uprising of June 1953 not as a revolution but as a counter-revolution. Indeed, his belief in the GDR did not waver in the final days of its existence. When he heard, during a holiday in the summer of 1989, that GDR citizens were escaping to the West via Hungary he considered returning home in case the *Kampfgruppe*, the combat group to which he belonged, was called into action: this from a man who at that time was over 60. 'Wolfgang' is still, and given his age will probably remain, bitterly opposed to the current political-economical situation. It is, however, not always easy for him to escape some pangs of guilt about what he did, and he frequently says that the work he did for the Stasi could not possibly have done anyone any harm. Yet he seems to need an additional justification, above and beyond being a convinced socialist, as to why he agreed to work for the organisation when approached, saying he is someone who 'could just never say no'.[7] He also told me how it shocked him to discover that his daughter had nightmares that she was being followed and observed by the Stasi, even though it seems that this was not the case. He says he had never previously considered the indirect harm which the Stasi's surveillance measures could potentially do. He also tells me that he has not told his family yet of his past collaboration with the Stasi. He says he wants to wait until he has viewed any files which might still be available from this time. He is thus to some extent waiting for the files to re-create a part of his biography, the details of which, despite his insistence, he can no longer be sure of. He is unwilling to tell his family of the collaboration until the files allow him to judge the extent of his compliance, and ultimately perhaps of his guilt.

Opportunistic Conformity

When we first speak on the phone, 'Theodor' seems somewhat confused and nervous. It is then quite a surprise to meet the composed, polite and articulate man behind the voice. He periodically becomes quite excited when talking, but seems to remain ultimately in control, carefully selecting his words and never, I imagine, giving away more than he intends to.

In contrast to 'Wolfgang', 'Theodor' was born into a professional and wealthy family. His mother's family were titled landowners and his father served as an officer in both the First and the Second World War. The end of World War II signalled, he says, the second great defeat in his father's life. Once again the system he had actively supported had crumbled and its failings been brought to light. Viewing his own situation in the united Germany of today, 'Theodor' feels that he can now empathise with his father. Born in the 1930s, he says that as a young boy he was deeply shocked by and ashamed of Germany's war crimes, and so embraced life in the GDR as a true alternative to fascism. He describes himself as someone who displayed a 'more than average deference to authority' and joined the Army after leaving school.[8] He talks of how he initially loathed military life but, since he had committed himself to ten years' service, would have been unable to stand the humiliation of leaving before this time elapsed. When he became a communications officer, life for him improved immensely. From 1975 to 1985 he was active as an informer after having been relatively easily recruited. In his first letter to me, he writes that his contact with the Stasi in this form spanned the period from approximately 1972 to 1986. Since he could derive no advantage from claiming to have been active as an informer for longer than was the case, it would seem that this miscalculation is evidence that individuals do have trouble remembering the exact details of their contact with the Stasi, if not its general tenor. It is also a sign that, before the '*IM*' terminology and the structures of the informers' recruitment and subsequent handling became more widely known, the informer did not see becoming an informer as a significant life step or biographical marker. The Stasi's sometimes subtle recruitment techniques, and the way in which, in the initial days of their collaboration, informers were often given only minor tasks to complete, means that informers were not always aware of a definite point in time at which they commenced membership of what they now know to have been a strictly-defined group of individuals.

'Theodor's' biography, although superficially that of a standard conformist, is perhaps more accurately described as that of an opportunistic conformist. Whereas 'Wolfgang' sees himself as someone whose behaviour was determined by his unfailing belief in one specific ideological system, 'Theodor', although loyal, regards himself as someone who was keen to establish himself in a position of power regardless of the specifics of the regime he was living under, someone whose biography was characterised by a respect and a desire for authority. He says that when he was asked to collaborate with the Stasi he considered it 'a great honour'.[9] Indeed, in his Stasi file the recruiting officer notes that he was quick to agree to work as an unofficial employee:

> The candidate immediately declared his willingness to work with us, but tried to impose some restrictions concerning personal details and information on people close to him. It was explained to him, however, that such a stance was contradictory to the nature of our work, which the candidate recognised before immediately providing some information about himself and his family.[10]

Ultimately, it seems 'Theodor' was a fervent supporter of the Communist doctrine only because it was the one he lived under. He says he truly believed that socialism was the necessary consequence of the failure of capitalism, stating 'I would defend this belief structure in front of anyone', but adding, 'if reality hadn't proved it invalid'.[11] It is these last words which indicate that this socialist ideology, in contrast to that of 'Wolfgang', belongs for 'Theodor' very much to his past life in the GDR and has not crossed the past–present threshold of the events of 1989–90. In addition, he recognises that those who have not crossed that threshold, or feel that their past lives are being negated to too great an extent, tend to idealise the past:

> As a result of the speed with which unification was realised, we've really been put on the defensive, and we have to defend things – I catch myself at it sometimes – defending things which I used to curse at – simply because the amount of ignorance around makes me furious. That's a really dangerous tendency.[12]

Perhaps because 'Theodor' has now distanced himself from the ideology of his 'past' life, he experiences more of a sense of guilt when looking back on what he did. He explains, for example, how he told a friend of his involvement with the Stasi:

> I hoped that he would ask me some questions, but he didn't and I still remember how disappointed I was. Perhaps it was just simply too much for him. [...] You see, no one wanted to know how I had ended up doing what I did – I had to do all the analysis on my own. The results didn't exactly make me feel good about myself.[13]

Now, 'Theodor', like many former collaborators, feels he has become one of the new Germany's scapegoats in its reckoning with the GDR past. He sees himself as a victim twice over of the unification process, first as an East German and second as a former Stasi collaborator. In response to this real or potential marginalisation, informers often experience an intense feeling of self-pity, primarily as a result of their immediate social and material plight, but also, as seems to be the case with 'Theodor', out of a sense of shame at the unveiling of their support for a power which has been defeated and whose weaknesses have since been exposed. He sums up these varying and conflicting emotions in the following words:

> You know, since 1990 [...] you've had to live with the stigma of having been an informer. You can justify it to yourself if you want, but you're still stuck with it. And ... and it turns out that it was all so pointless. [...] I regret not having taken a more critical stance towards our senile leaders. [...] We certainly spoke about the problems, yeah, [...] made all these typical GDR

> jokes. We made these openly, even with the Stasi officers. But in the end we were in charge of the system, and that means that we weren't true to our ethos to be revolutionaries and to change the world. I regret that we all became so horribly petty bourgeois. And my time as an unofficial employee or as an informer or whatever you want to call it is, of course, a part of that.[14]

Non-conformity

Before our first meeting, I had the feeling that 'Stephana' did not want to go through with the interview after all. During our conversation, however, she was always very engaged and seemed to have a real need to analyse her past. This is perhaps partly explained by the fact that she has spent many years becoming involved with a variety of spiritually-oriented groups and engages in much self-reflection. Her biography is also one which is characterised by periods of emotional disharmony and vulnerability. Her active interest in various ideological systems, in addition to what seems to be a continuing search for stability, perhaps goes some way towards explaining how someone who was regarded by the GDR authorities with suspicion could become so bound to the Stasi after having been recruited only under considerable duress.

'Stephana' was born in the 1960s in a small town situated in the north of the GDR. Her parents were Catholics, and theirs was one of only a few Catholic families in the area. 'Stephana' says she feels she grew up in a diaspora, and stresses the fact that her life was characterised by inner and outer conflict.[15] She did well at school, but difficulties arose when, because of her beliefs, she did not take part in the *Jugendweihe* ceremony, the ritual celebration of entrance into adulthood widely practised in the GDR. As a result, she was not allowed to complete her school leaving certificate and trained instead as a construction worker. She found this work frustrating, because she felt that she was getting nowhere, and also because she had married someone who was doing well in a more stimulating job and who was disappointed that she had taken on, as he saw it, such menial work. She decided to take a job in a post office since it offered good childcare facilities. The marriage did not fare well, and she and her husband separated when she was 20. The child remained in the custody of her ex-husband. 'Stephana' met someone else, had a second child and changed job again. Prior to being recruited as an informer, she had applied on two occasions to leave the GDR, once to marry an Algerian man, and once to pursue her religious interests in a Buddhist centre in the West. She then began a new relationship and changed her mind about wanting to leave.

In May 1985, 'Stephana' was picked up and interrogated by the Stasi. She had remained in contact with a former colleague with whom she had at one time discussed leaving the GDR. This man still intended to do so, and had told her of his plan to escape by entering the American embassy and seeking asylum. They agreed that if he did not reappear within two days of his planned entering of the embassy, she would phone a number in West Berlin he had given her and relate the story to the person who answered. After her friend did not return within the agreed time, she phoned the number, which turned out to be that of a newspaper, which printed the story. Either the Stasi found out about her role in the attempted escape because the story appeared in the West German newspaper, or else the telephone she used was perhaps bugged. It is also possible that her friend was already working as an informer himself and had set up the situation in order to give the Stasi grounds to detain her and exert pressure on her to work as an informer.

Whatever the background to this was, it resulted in her being picked up from her home on 22 May 1985 and taken for questioning about the role she had played in the man's real or fictitious escape attempt. At the end of the interrogation she signed an initial commitment to the Stasi, which was worded as follows: 'In order to avoid further legal action being taken against me, I hereby agree to work for the Ministry for State Security in order to atone for my actions.'[16] 'Stephana' was subsequently sent home, and she says she found the following days and weeks highly distressing. She describes her feelings as a form of paranoia, and says she was unable to shake off the feeling that she was constantly being observed and followed. Regular meetings soon began to be set up between 'Stephana' and Stasi officers, during which she was asked to give information about the principles and the members of the various religious groups with which she was involved. Just over four months after the initial interrogation, she signed the final statement of commitment. The Stasi documents relating to the signing recount how it was she herself who wanted the word 'continue' to be included in this written statement, which read: 'I hereby agree to *continue* to work for the Ministry for State Security and have chosen "Stephana" as my cover name.'[17] 'Stephana' was clearly keen to understand the future contact with the Stasi as a continuation of what had gone before. It seems to have been important to her to emphasise that her collaboration was a direct consequence of her interrogation and of the threats made against her at that time, namely that she could collaborate, go to the West for good and without her daughter, or face the legal consequences of trying to help someone escape from the GDR. Later, she tried to find a purpose in the collaboration with the Stasi:

> I sort of gradually had the feeling that I was acting as a kind of mediator, ensuring that these events [the meetings of the religious groups] could take place, you know. And of course I didn't always tell it exactly as it was, but portrayed the meetings as a lot less oppositional than they actually were.[18]

The word 'gradually' in 'Stephana's' statement is significant as it indicates that she developed this personal justification argument over time. Again, it is evident that statements such as these are not merely justifications which informers employ now in a public forum, but ones which they developed and used at the time of their collaboration as a means of privately rationalising their behaviour.

'Stephana' was one of only a small minority of informers who were actually put under direct pressure to collaborate. She was interesting to the Stasi because of the connections she had already established with various religious groups, whose activities were considered suspect. Once recruited, she was encouraged by her Stasi handler to become involved with more such groups, whose activities the state was keen to monitor:

> I have to say that I would have done it anyway. It wasn't something I wouldn't have done. They just sometimes put the idea in my head – you know, 'Do that, why don't you?' – or reinforced an idea of mine to go here or there – you know, it was never anything that went against the grain. And when I took part in something I did so because I really wanted to and I played an active role. I guess you could say that was schizophrenic, but I didn't even think about the fact that I had been sent there, because it was what I did anyway.[19]

'Stephana' was not actively involved in overt opposition activities, but certainly had connections with fringe groups. Indeed, her biography in the GDR can be characterised in terms of an identification with various minority groups. 'Stephana's' life then was in many respects that of, in Schröder's terms, a non-conformist, if not quite an active anti-conformist. Partly for this reason, she found it very difficult after 1989 to come to terms with the fact that she had been an *IM*, a person who is sometimes classified as a faithful servant of the system. She was, of course, aware that by 1989 she had been working with the Stasi for approximately four years, but she did not suspect how commonplace and regulated such contact was. She says it took her quite some time to realise that she too belonged to the group of 'unofficial employees' suddenly being given so much media attention, since previously she had considered her situation to be a 'one-off'.[20] She describes how she constantly asked herself 'Am I one of them or am I not?' as she gradually faced the truth about her past. When I ask 'Stephana' whether she feels guilty about having been an informer she replies: 'Yes, yes ... let's say guilty, furious-disappointed.'[21] Perhaps a part of the disappointment she feels is realising that she was not quite so special as once she thought.

Just as she must recognise that there were many informers, 'Stephana' must also face the possibility that her Stasi handler was not perhaps the 'good friend' she once considered him to be, but simply a man carrying out contact with her in a routine and regulated manner, as he did with other informers on his caseload. This reality perturbs her, as she says that at the time of her contact with the Stasi she felt her conversations with her handler were divided clearly into an official part and a part where they talked as friends. With hindsight she realises that the information she in effect imparted in what she considered to be the unofficial part of the meetings was probably just as likely to be recorded in the standard reports compiled after the meetings.

Later, 'Stephana' forgets her frustration and disappointment and not only becomes curious about the way in which her Stasi contacts have been recorded, but also seems to be willing to be judged according to the Stasi's perspective on her past. After she learns that I have viewed her Stasi file, she asks me on the telephone, in what seems to be a state of great excitement, 'What kind of person am I then?'

Conclusions

For many, daily life in the GDR involved a delicate balance between conformity and resistance, resulting in a wide spectrum of individual behaviour patterns, loosely categorised by Schröder into the three types discussed above: that is, the standard conformist, the non- or anti-conformist and the opportunistic conformist. Although the pre-1989 lives of 'Wolfgang', 'Theodor' and 'Stephana' represent a range of possible GDR life histories, all now find themselves belonging to the group of former Stasi collaborators. This former collaboration, although in some cases merely a small fragment of their past lives, has the potential to dominate their own and others' perceptions of their role in the GDR. This is particularly the case when informers appear to seek a justification for their collaboration in their own past lives, identifying and often exaggerating a recurring biographical motif which led to their agreeing to work as an informer.

The homogenisation, in the post-unification climate, of what were actually very varied biographies of former GDR citizens is indeed widespread. The emergence in the early 1990s of so-called *Ostalgie* (nostalgia for the GDR) was an indication that many former East Germans felt that they shared a common fate as the losers from unification and the underdogs in the new Germany. In a period of social and political upheaval, a repositioning has been taking place where previous categorisations are no longer applicable and must be re-evaluated, and for many redefined.

There are a decreasing number of people who are interested in seeing that the crimes of the past are openly confronted. The majority of East Germans acted on the whole as opportunistic conformists, and while they are still struggling to come to terms with the social and material strains of unification they may wish to indulge in a form of nostalgia for the pre-1989 past. They are therefore reluctant to be reminded of those who were more directly involved in the former system, either as the agents or the targets of Stasi surveillance measures. Many of this large group of non-perpetrators and yet non-victims are unwilling to confront the fact of their own compliance, since it may be at odds with their preferred image – with, in Timothy Garton Ash's words, 'the mental autobiography with which and by which we all live' (Garton Ash, 1997, p. 20).

The active resistance of these minority groups to the former system or, in the case of former Stasi informers, their active compliance with it threatens to destroy the existing perception of individual and collective history held by the previously largely silent and passive majority. The real or potential stigma associated with having collaborated as a Stasi informer means that the past lives of members of this group may begin to be defined solely by this one aspect of their biography. That is to say, this one facet of past life becomes the defining biographical pole, around which all other events, both before and after the present time threshold, are 're/constructed'. This interpretation of past life may in turn affect behaviour in the present; and this, combined with the possible social and material repercussions of previous collaboration, means that, at least within the turbulent interim period following unification, former informers have felt alienated from their own past life stories and, in some cases, marginalised within and excluded from the new Germany.

Notes

1 'Vierter Tätigkeitsbericht des Bundesbeauftragten für die Unterlagen des Staatssicherheitsdienstes der ehemaligen Deutschen Demokratischen Republik' (Berlin: BStU, 1999), p. 104.
2 Christa Wolf, 'Eine Auskunft', *Berliner Zeitung*, 21 January 1993, p. 2.
3 Interview with the author, 22 March 1995.
4 Letter to the author, 29 March 1995.
5 Some of those who belong to this group may have lived their lives believing that they were in fact under active observation and, at least initially, 40 per cent of those who applied to the BStU to see their files had to be told that no such file existed: 'Erster Tätigkeitsbericht des Bundesbeauftragten für die Unterlagen des Staatssicherheitsdienstes der ehemaligen Deutschen Demokratischen Republik' (Berlin: BStU, 1993), pp. 52–3.
6 Interview with the author, 19 December 1994.
7 ibid.
8 Interview with the author, 8 November 1994.
9 ibid.
10 BStU, ZA, AIM 5665/85, Arbeitsakte, I, p. 141.
11 Interview with the author, 8 November 1994.
12 ibid.
13 Letter to the author, 29 March 1995.
14 Interview with the author, 8 November 1994.
15 Interview with the author, 19 January 1995.
16 BStU, ASt. Potsdam, Reg.-Nr. IV 1709/85, Personalakte, p. 7.
17 ibid.
18 Interview with the author, 19 January 1995.
19 ibid.
20 ibid.
21 ibid.

References

Fischer-Rosenthal, W. (1995), 'Biographische Arbeit im Umgang mit deutschen Vergangenheiten', in W. Fischer-Rosenthal and P. Alheit (eds), *Biographien in Deutschland: Soziologische Rekonstruktionen gelebter Gesellschaftsgeschichte*, Westdeutscher Verlag, Wiesbaden.

Garton Ash, T. (1997), *The File: A Personal History*, HarperCollins, London.

Schröder, H. (1990), 'Identität, Individualität und psychische Befindlichkeit des DDR-Bürgers im Umbruch', *Zeitschrift für Sozialisationsforschung und Erziehungssoziologie*, Special Edition, pp. 163–76.

7 Czech Dissidents: A Classically Modern Community

VLADIMIR ANDRLE
Department of Sociology,
University of York, UK

Introduction

During 1994–5, I conducted 67 life-story interviews in the Czech Republic.[1] Sample selection in that project was guided by the aim of compiling a database of the personal testimonies, concerning developments since the revolution, of people from contrasting 'historical player' networks. In addition to senior functionaries of the fallen Communist state and its ordinary career employees, and the budding entrepreneurial classes of the new era, the sample included a sizeable representation of those people who had chosen to risk the consequences of challenging the Communist authorities by public acts asserting the individual citizen's spiritual freedom and rights. Seventeen interviewees belonged to this category, four of whom pursued the vocation of creative artist outside the institutional framework of state-sponsored arts; and 13 were members of the dissident circles that made up *Charta 77*, the internationally renowned face of Czechoslovak dissent. One of the four freelance artists differed from the other three in that his public performances had outspoken political content, and he was consequently regarded by *Charta 77* leaders as one of their own, although he was not a *Charta 77* signatory and came into frequent personal contact with the Chartists only in the last two years of the Communist regime, when such contact was becoming less dangerous. In this chapter, the focus is on outspoken dissent rather than on the apolitical, independent art scene: that is, on the 13 life-narratives of members of Chartist circles, plus the marginal case, the politically outspoken performance artist who refrained from joining the political dissident networks.[2] Besides the obvious fact of their having had the courage to stand up and be counted for their moral convictions, what do these people have in common, that can be discerned from a shared pattern in the contents and construction of their self-accounts? Of what has the life-world of the dissident been constructed?

I shall seek an answer to these questions by: (a) listing the activities of dissidents *qua* dissidents that have been mentioned in the narratives at least in passing; (b) examining the facts contained in, and the stance adopted by, the accounts of victimisation under the old regime and the reverses of fate brought by the revolution; and (c) examining overall narrative construction and its dominant themes.

Dissident Activities

The activities that were mentioned in the dissident narratives can be listed as follows.

(A) Production and Circulation of Reading Matter

This involved the importation of books and periodicals from *émigrés* and other supporters in the West, and their copying and further distribution. Some of these materials were already in the Czech or Slovak language, and some of the foreign-language ones were translated and reproduced. In addition, a considerable amount of reading matter was printed and distributed from the manuscripts of indigenous authors. The printing technology in use underwent a thoroughgoing transformation, from typewriters, carbon paper and duplicators in the early 1970s to real printing press and computer publishing in the later years of the 1980s. By that time, a number of the dissident circles were capable of printing books in bound volumes, producing dozens of titles in editions of about 200 copies each. Underground publishing and imports by no means involved only political and social science literature. They also involved natural science, philosophy and the humanities, fiction and poetry.

(B) Political Protest Action

This involved the distribution of leaflets advising the population to boycott elections,[3] the public commemoration of historical anniversaries that the authorities would prefer the population to forget, the signing of petitions to the authorities, and the supplying of Western media with information about such events, which was then broadcast back into the country by Radio Free Europe, the BBC World Service and other broadcasters. These actions often concerned the victimisation of individuals by the authorities, highlighting the ways in which the regime broke its own laws to repress dissent. *Charta 77* itself started as a petition in response to the trial of an underground rock group for publishing a record, which took place only months after the Government had put human rights laws on the statute book as required by the international agreement it had signed in Helsinki. Subsequent information bulletins issued by *Charta 77* often detailed repressive or discriminatory actions which the regime took against *Charta 77* signatories. In the later 1980s, some leaders of *Charta 77* also founded additional organisations, which proclaimed (non-violent) political opposition to be their central purpose.

(C) Exerting Influence on Personal Contact

Individual members of dissident circles clearly had their own outside contacts, people who were not yet trusted with information about the clandestine activities, but who were, for example, avid readers glad to be able to borrow interesting books. They were thus open to personal influence and could, for example, be dissuaded from joining the Communist Party when career considerations tempted them to do so.

(D) Speaking Up in Workplace Meetings and Other Officially-organised Forums

The Communist regime appeared to have a need to stage public occasions vaunting participatory democracy, in which 'the working masses' could show their unanimous consent with various government policies or, at a more mundane and practical level, in which they could discuss everyday problems with local managers. This, however, naturally also provided opportunities for individuals to demonstrate an independent cast of mind. It was not always necessary to make explicitly political speeches to make an impact. In a context where a ritual show of conformity was the general expectation, even an unostentatious show of moral backbone sufficed. At an altogether different level, there were also the public spaces created by officially-registered organisations based on personal interests. Thus the screening of a film by an official film club could be followed by a discussion of the film, which could then be 'concluded' by a performance artist coming on stage. It usually took the authorities some time (about two years, according to the freelance artist in our dissident sample) to realise exactly what went on during these additions to the film show, which were the real reason people attended in the first place. The performance artist then found another setting in which he was able to continue his freelance trade.

(E) Insisting on One's Own and One's Children's Legal Rights

Dissidents spent a large amount of time writing letters and seeking personal meetings with officials, in an effort to get the authorities to reverse discriminatory decisions. The issues they pursued in this way sometimes concerned their own employment, but mostly they concerned access to higher education for their children, to whom the school authorities frequently denied the necessary recommendation regardless of academic results. The outcome of these tussles with bureaucracy tended to be a compromise, where the children eventually secured a university place, but not in the subject they most wanted to study and for which they usually had excellent academic qualifications. The ethics of engaging in these personal struggles with the bureaucracy on behalf of one's own children were the subject of some debate in dissident circles, with the view that it was no less honourable than standing up for strangers' rights prevailing. One interviewee indicated that it was his struggles with the authorities over his children's educational rights that drew him back into dissident activism after several years of keeping a low profile.

(F) Sustaining One's Own Community

Dissidents spent and sought to spend a great deal of their time in each other's company. They gathered in each other's apartments to attend seminars, which sometimes featured visiting lecturers from abroad, hear the reading of freshly-written poems and plays, discuss current affairs and politics, hold business meetings, and have a good time. They went on countryside outings together and organised summer camps for their children: whole families were involved in these communal activities. And naturally they were there to support victimised friends, outwitting police checks to attend courtroom proceedings, helping to find reasonable jobs for those whose professional careers were terminated, and giving warm and practical support to those who had just done time in prison.

The timing of these activities, it should be noted, was not confined to the period of the existence of *Charta 77*, from late 1976. The circles and their pattern of engagement with the Communist regime date back to the mid-1960s. At that time, a de-Stalinising movement within the regime gathered momentum, which was the stronger for its having been delayed. In the universities, students produced magazines in which articles appeared that questioned things, the official dogma of the one-party state not excepted. When some of the students were victimised, others made a point of publicly questioning the legitimacy of the punitive act. A pattern of activities that defined a dissident circle and its engagement with the regime was set. Among the older generation, those people who had been students in the immediate post-war period and who in the heady atmosphere of that time had become enthusiastic Marxists were now, in the wake of Khrushchev's de-Stalinisation campaign in the Soviet Union, coming to terms with their disillusionment and guilt about the 1950s. Their Marxism turned into an interest in Kafka and in phenomenology, and into a dialogue with modern Christian theology. Those of that generation who had never been Marxists now gained space for public self-expression, too. When a hardline faction within the Communist Party was defeated in January 1968, the radical elements of both generations supported one another in articulating a radical voice for the Prague Spring. When Warsaw Pact forces invaded the country in August 1968, the wave of public protest, which yet again was especially strong in the universities, brought additional leaders to the fore, who joined the already existing circles of leading activists. Personal networks of anti-regime dissent were thus already in place when the regime clamped down on society with the purge-and-frighten policies it called 'normalisation'. The activists were known to the regime's secret police and dissident actions were soon followed by imprisonments. The organisers of *Charta 77* included people who had already served time in the 'normalisation' regime's prisons.

Living with Victimisation

Being a dissident naturally involved being a target of the Communist state's repressive apparatus. Personal experiences of this, however, were not uniform. Individuals varied regarding the exact extent of their involvement in punishable subversion and in the amount of this that got on to police records; but there were numerous other contingencies in play, including the arbitrary variations in treatment which the police meted out deliberately so as to sow the seeds of mutual suspicion among dissidents. One-half of our sample had to experience prison; and all experienced restrictions on their professional careers, ranging from a bar to any promotion or any travel to conferences to being allowed to find only manual work. Our sample reflected the dissident community in general, in that they were a highly educated group, being all university graduates, four of them on two separate degree courses.[4] Only one or two people in our sample gave the self-account of the professional politician or revolutionary, someone who has not really had a serious commitment to a profession outside the political sphere. The remainder, with one exception, had aspired to success in a professional line of work, which their commitment to the dissident movement jeopardised. This was something they had to grapple with, and it was not easy, as the following makes clear:

> And so I was thrown out of the institute. OK, I didn't have to go down the pits to dig coal, but my professional position became one where I could not do anything, a life with a lid firmly screwed on. You can live. Physically there's nothing wrong – you are not cold or hungry. But you feel life running away, every second. I had nights when I woke in horror, hearing time ticking away, you see. I felt it and heard it, life running away between my fingers. That's the most horrible thing I know, and the only other thing I can compare it with is being in custody in gaol. Not in prison after sentencing – that was not really as bad as the year in custody, there you simply don't live. And this was an identical experience, a horror that is difficult to explain to anyone who has not experienced it. Lost life, and you are experiencing losing it, you see – it's horrible. Today I'm no longer able to relive it as it was then, but I know that it was horror. One kept waking up in sweat, with a feeling that life was flowing, that it was flowing away. (Int. 940910a)

These people's accounts of making a living in other lines of work, however, were not by any means all negative ones. Manual jobs had their compensations, in that their work schedules were often less than tight, allowing periods of time for undisturbed reading. Also, at least in some cases, dissidents enjoyed solicitous treatment at the hands of their foremen, who were respectful of their education and understood their circumstances. Also it was sometimes possible eventually to find a job that gave intrinsic satisfaction. After his release from prison, the interviewee quoted above eventually found work in which he put his scientific mind to good use as a maintenance worker capable of improvising much needed high-tech equipment for a hospital unit. Cruelly, however, the repressive apparatus eventually put an arbitrary end to that career development as well.

The seven interviewees who suffered imprisonment described their predicaments in ways that testify, yet again, to the somewhat variable and contingent manner in which institutions behaved. Spending time in police custody, with its interrogations and uncertainties, was generally worse than serving a sentence. Those who suffered it in the early 'normalisation' period had to put up with some brutal treatment, while in the later 1970s and in the 1980s the interrogators were on the whole quite mindful of keeping their methods within legal limits. The exact conditions under which a prison sentence might be served depended on the prison. One interviewee, who served his sentence in two different prisons, described a contrast between one institution, whose management and personnel used their discretion to add to the punitive content of the standing rules, and the other, which refrained from doing that. In some prisons, political prisoners seemed to be accorded strict treatment as a matter of policy, but seemed also to enjoy the benefit of each other's company, in that they were kept together. Elsewhere, the prison management separated political prisoners from one another and made a point of putting them into the cells designated for hand-picked 'low life'. This was the worst thing that could befall them. It was the general indignity of the prison regime and the unspeakably brutal hierarchy and mores of the criminal habitués, who in some prisons were allowed to rule the roost, that our interviewees still recalled with a shudder. The dissidents' way of coping was, as always, to hold the authorities to the letter of their own law, and to use all possible channels for complaining about abuses. Amid the general grimness of prison life there were also flickerings of good fortune that were still recalled with warm gratitude: the books that the 'normalisation' regime had banned which were still in busy circulation among prisoners; or the screw who always made sure that a daily letter to a prisoner from his wife got delivered without any delay.

1989 and After

The revolution offered dissidents the possibility of high political office. Not all took the opportunity of that personal rise in status, some having already advanced arguments against it.[5] Unsurprisingly, however, many did, including 10 out of the 14 in our sample. The freelance performance artist included in our sample as a marginal case gave an account witnessing to the historic moment:

> My experience of 1989 was very comical because, when I went to perform [in one of the big rallies], the stairs leading up to the stage were crowded with people who had crowded in for reasons unknown, because they were not in

the programme. There were about fifteen people in the programme and here there were some 250 or 300 wanting to be seen there. At that moment I realised that it was not just a struggle against Communism that was going on here, but also a struggle to become part of the new power. I was shocked, because never in my life had I seen so many rulers of the republic at the same time [laughter]. Naturally I felt good to have been called upon that stage, and so I made progress from number 300 in the stairs queue right to number 1. There they checked me out[6] and I was allowed on stage – that was my experience of the benefit that power gives to man.

VA. Did you gain further opportunities to get to power, or to become some big TV figure or something?

No. What played a role was that, for instance, when the Civic Forum was founded, I was called upon to perform before the speeches, and I actually did not realise that I belonged to the future Civic Forum. I simply did my bit and went to sit among the people in the auditorium. But everyone who took the stage after me remained on stage – they took chairs and sat there, and so the first contingent of the Civic Forum came into being. Then there were even people who arrived late and climbed straight on to the stage to stand there, and at that moment I knew that if I didn't get up there and ask for my little chair there to sit on, history would cut me out. But I didn't, because (a) I'd be terribly ashamed to bid for power when I had ignored the opposition, and (b) I was telling myself that there'd be a need for people with a sort of indirect relation to power, without direct responsibility for it, a sort of inner opposition, you see – that suited me because it was in line with what I had been doing. (Int. 940716a)

Those who did take the opportunity did not describe the moment of their ascent to office in terms of crowding the stairs leading to a stage and making sure of staying onstage. They usually referred to it via a formula such as 'I was asked by friends to help with [this or that necessary task]'. Memorable moments with chairs, however, featured in the narratives of two of our interviewees, both of whom recalled the pithy satisfaction they had had of sitting down in the Parliament for the first time, in chairs still bearing the names of the former Communist bosses of their home regions. In all cases, the ascent meant a break from an active, but thoughtful and on the whole evenly-paced, lifestyle and immersion in a heady whirl of long and hectic political workdays with no respite. The break brought a period of euphoria of six or twelve months, along with longer-lasting historic achievements to recall with satisfaction and pride.

It brought traumas, too. Legislators who made 400 important new laws in the first year of government had to make them in full awareness of their lack of legal expertise, to say nothing of the lack of any time to make sure of their quality. Heads of important government institutions had to do their historic institution-building at the same time as they encountered daily the consequences of their lack of expertise in managing large work collectives and complex organisations. These new public figures were unused to being the recipients of correspondence in volumes that far exceeded the amounts they could read, consider and answer; to being constantly surrounded by hundreds of expectant strangers; to having to pay attention to the media; and to finding that, even off-camera and after office hours, they remained 'onstage' because they had lost the normal human 'right' to anonymity often associated with urban life.

All the socially-ascending dissidents in our sample were married men with children. Remarkably, perhaps, only one reported that his new lifestyle had had a major destabilising effect on his family. This man was reproaching himself for having forgotten to ask his wife and children for permission before throwing himself into the whirl. That is exactly what some of the others had done, to good effect. Children complained of their absent dads, but in most accounts families remained, on the whole, supportive and together. The pleasures of friendship, however, which had been so important a part of the dissident lifestyle, were in many accounts placed under strain. Divisive revelations from old-regime police archives, political disagreements and differences of view regarding the ethics of taking or passing up new opportunities took their toll, as did lack of time and, according to one account, the sheer inhibiting power that political office exerted on personal conversation:

> People from dissent who got elevated to high functions – they have difficulty when meeting friends, like they don't have things to say to one another. They are different all of a sudden – preoccupied, unable to focus attention on anything other than what is currently in the centre of their interests. I first noticed it when a friend got a high function. Then I got into my function, and it affected me just the same. He lost his, and it's interesting that he was able quite quickly to find the old ties, and everything sort of settled back with him into how it used to be before. And I still have mine, and it's getting no better. I dread going out. I feel tired and isolated in company. I'm so swallowed up by the work problems, but I can't talk about them really. (Int. 940418b)

The acquiring of office was followed by loss of office. Only three of our interviewees still held office at the time of the interviews,[7] the rest having lost it either in the 1992 election or through the splitting up of Czechoslovakia and the shutdown of its federal institutions in the following year. The experience of reverting back to normal life meant, in addition to coming to terms with political defeat, having to find bearings in a world that had changed:

> When I finished in the Government, I knew that in a way it would be like when I had come back from prison, in that I knew that, with the 6 a.m. to midnight workdays, it was its own world … normal life was going on sort of elsewhere. The mass privatisation happened, and when I came back I found that I was a stranger in my own town. I wasn't capable of even buying myself a bread roll because the shop, which I had used for 40 years, all of a sudden was not there [laughter]. It took me a while to learn the everyday matters of civilisation [laughter] again. (Int. 940428a)

Revelations stemming from Communist police archives caused a great deal of trauma during the years 1990–92. A significant minority of the dissidents, including a number of leading figures, were shown to have been registered as informants. The nature of the trauma was, however, more complicated than a simple need to come to terms with the sense of betrayal brought by the knowledge that a trusted friend had been a police spy. The problem was that no one could be sure how to interpret the information. Many dissidents sensed or knew that it might be possible to get listed by the police as an informant without actually ever giving away any information that might be of any use to the police. In addition, some of the 'informants'' records dated from the 1960s, when it had been standard police practice to file all dissidents as 'candidates for cooperation', and treat them accordingly, before eventually giving up on them and transferring their files definitively into the 'enemy person' category. The common knowledge that the *Stb* had shredded some of its files before leaving its archival legacy was another source of the uncertainty as to what to make of the revelations. The 'lustration law' of 1991 barred former Communist Party officials and secret police officers, agents and informants from public office. But what should one make of a case where it also barred a dissident on whom the Communist regime imposed victim status throughout 1969–89, including a term in prison, because his police record included a moment of at-most-trivial cooperation in the mid-1960s? Our interviews show an uneasy division of opinion on these matters, and a preference perhaps for letting them recede into the past – except, that is, for the interviewee for whom they were still personally acute, because he had been branded under the 'lustration law' and was still in the process of trying to clear his name.[8]

Dominant Themes of Narrative Construction

Each life-narrative in our dissident sample was, of course, different from the rest; it was a construction of an individual subject. But the narratives were all told in the knowledge that the telling was occasioned by the narrator's participation in a shared social identity, that of the dissident. That membership was a prominent feature of the person's constructed self-identity in every case, and the ways in which they spoke about it had three characteristics in common.

First, the dissidents identified themselves with intellectuals rather than with politicians or revolutionaries. The boundary case in our sample – the freelance artist – criticised *Charta 77* leaders for being too interested in political power. But all the life-narratives in our dissident sample in fact shared with his the dominant regard they gave to the vocation of the intellectual, not excluding those of the four interviewees whose dissident activities included a substantial amount of dealing with organisational and political issues. In the dissident life-world and lexicon, the term 'intellectual', of course, does not have just the bland sense of an educated person who reads good books, and is not overlaid with the bashfulness and irony of Anglo-Saxon usage. Being an intellectual means, in addition to a taste for reflection, morally-committed engagement with public issues. Intellectuals make history by speaking truths that undermine orthodoxies and awaken societies to the possibilities of progress. Being an intellectual means living by an effort to achieve truthfulness, a value that is generally liable to fall victim to self-interest and self-delusion. It also means a strong preference for observing the moral principles of civilised conduct in mundane affairs. Intellectuals have an uneasy, somewhat suspicious attitude towards the meaning of the term 'pragmatism', because they sense in its usage a possible intent to cover up a short-sighted disregard for moral principle.[9]

Secondly, the dissidents very much identified themselves with belonging to their dissident circles and the larger community that these circles made up. In this respect, the marginal boundary case (the freelance artist) differed from the rest. Like most people, this man had his network of friends and acquaintances, but it was not clear from his narrative what kind of people they were or what role they played in his life. In the rest of our dissident sample, by contrast, membership of the dissident community meant strong friendship ties with other dissidents and their families, along with unquestioning commitment of time and effort to its activities – those oriented towards the life of the community *per se* as well as those devoted to the cause. The word 'friends' was frequently used in the narratives, and it was invariably clear from the context that it meant fellow dissidents. Sometimes it meant close personal friends (and no one in the sample appeared to have close friends outside dissident circles), and at others it meant the people one recognised as friends because they were members of the dissident circle, the community in which one felt free and at ease, at home. The impact the events of 1989–90 had on these communal ties is an issue that the dissidents considered keenly in assessing the biographical break the events occasioned.

Thirdly, the dissident narratives implicitly or explicitly argued against the currently fashionable axiom that the Communist regime was totalitarian to the extent of effectively denying the individual any space for freedom. Their narratives feature characters whom they referred to as 'decent [*slušný*] people', who were neither intellectuals nor friends, and who clearly were outsiders to dissident circles, but who showed kindness towards prosecuted dissidents and in various ways retained their moral backbone even when it would have been more opportune to bend and look another way. They did not do anything thereby for which the regime prosecuted them; they merely ran a slight risk of incurring some zealous or cowardly official's displeasure. But their acts are recalled with great warmth in the dissidents' narratives, for they defied the popular tendency to petty opportunism on which the normalisation regime relied for its sustenance.[10] The dissidents saw the tendency they observed of exaggerating the old regime's repressiveness as an alibi used by the petty opportunists.

Conclusion

The Czech dissidents' life-world may be characterised as a union of two theoretical opposites. On the one hand, its intellectualism, with its vision of a world unified by deep-lying but knowable principles, its commitment to the values of personal integrity and social progress and its aspirations to professional self-realisation, was a cultural practice of the classically modern (rather than the late-modern or postmodern) type. On the other hand, it was a lifestyle incorporating strong personal and emotional ties to a concrete community: a phenomenon which tends to be theoretically associated with 'tradition' rather than with 'modernity', and the coexistence of which with otherwise patently modern forms of living remains sociologically under-researched. The biographical break which the revolution represents is, therefore, for the former dissident largely a matter of the strains of the late-modern cultural shift that contemporary capitalism brings with it, and of the strains that new-era circumstances have put on the communal bonds.

Acknowledgement

I am grateful to Tomáš Holeček of Charles University, Prague for his incisive comments on an earlier draft.

Notes

1 In the first 17 interviews, the interviewee was initially asked to recount his or her experiences since November 1989. This set of interviewees tended spontaneously to recount parts of their earlier biographies in order to explain their fates and attitudes since the revolution. I therefore conducted the remaining 50 interviews as life-narrative ones, in which the interviewee was asked to mark, on a chronological life-line starting with birth, time periods and events which they saw as being, for whatever reason, especially significant in their life, and then to describe what happened in these selected times and explain why it was significant.

2 Of these 14 interviews, 3 were conducted in the early stage of the project (among the first 17 interviews) and 11 were conducted by the life-narrative method proper – see the previous footnote.

3 Only one candidate, a Communist Party appointee, could stand for each constituency, and the balloting was arranged in such a way as to make votes against visible to the officials who were present. Besides, there were no safeguards with which to restrain the authorities from counting votes against and spoiled papers as votes for.

4 It was (and still is) possible, in the Czech university system, to be a full-time student in two different faculties at the same time. In all three cases, one of the two degrees was in a scientific-technical subject and the other in the humanities.

5 The argument was that the new era would need activist creators of civil society as much as new politicians. See e.g. Jiřina Šiklová (1990), 'Šedá zóna a budoucnost disentu' [The Grey Zone and the Future of Dissent], *Social Research*, vol. 57, no. 2, pp. 348–63 [first published in *Samizdat* and broadcast in Radio Free Europe in Sept. 1989].

6 The narrator used the verb *prokádrovali*, which was the popular as well as the official term for the activities of character checking and personal profiling engaged in by personnel officers and other authorities of the Communist regime.

7 Some of the others, however, were to succeed in making a comeback at the time of the next elections, in 1996.

8 He succeeded soon after the interviews.

9 This was one of the points of clear contrast between our dissident and former-Communist samples. The former-Communist functionaries used the term 'pragmatic' and its derivatives frequently, and always in a taken-for-granted, unreservedly positive sense.

10 The difference between this usage of 'decent people' and the usage current in the St Petersburg dissident bohemia (see E. Zdravomyslova in this volume) may be noted. Bohemian lifestyle and values did not feature in the Czech dissidents' (nor indeed the independent artists') narratives.

8 Anti-Soviet Biographies: The Dissident Milieu and its Neighbouring Milieux

SOFIA TCHOUIKINA
Centre for Independent Social Research,
St Petersburg, Russia

Introduction

This chapter is about participants in the dissident movement that existed in the USSR from 1956 to 1985. From a biographical research perspective, analysis of the life paths of dissidents is particularly interesting since it offers an opportunity to analyse and to describe the 'anti-Soviet biography'. 'Anti-Soviet' was a label which the state in the late-Soviet period gave to people whom it considered to be political enemies of the regime – a label which did not always correspond with these people's self-definition. A typical 'anti-Soviet' biography is characterised by discontinuities caused or stimulated by state interference. In describing the specificity of the 'anti-Soviet' biography in relation to an ordinary Soviet life path, I would like to mention the concepts '*social career*' and '*career break*' introduced by Robin Humphrey (1993). According to Humphrey, a *social career* is a 'combination of interrelated careers' (ibid., p. 169), for example professional, moral, familial. A *career break* is a decisive biographical moment, a turning point, that 'leaves marks on people's lives by altering their fundamental meaning structures' and 'has such a powerful impact that the social career is knocked completely off trajectory and sometimes seemingly put into reverse'. A *career break* is evident in a life story when a single event changes both the form and the extent of a social career. An integral feature of a career break, then, is 'discontinuity in a social career' (ibid., pp. 172–3). A typical 'anti-Soviet' biography is characterised by two career breaks, and is therefore divided into three different 'lives'. The subject lives the first life as an ordinary Soviet citizen, the second life as a dissident and a pariah in Soviet society, and the third life either as an 'ex-dissident' in a post-Soviet society or as an emigrant to another country. In this chapter I seek to provide an answer to the question, how were the boundaries of the dissident milieu constructed by insiders and outsiders,[1] and how was this social construction of difference connected with discontinuities in the dissidents' biographies? The research on which this chapter is based consisted of in-depth biographical interviews with Leningrad participants in the dissident movement.[2]

A clandestine political, cultural, social opposition has always existed in the Soviet Union, even during the harsh Stalinist times (Iofe, 1982). Only with the beginning of the so-called 'thaw' of the mid-1950s to mid-1960s, however, did social life in general become more vigorous, and protest actions more numerous. The most characteristic form of protest during the initial stages of the dissident movement (from 1956 to the late 1960s) was revisionist Marxist criticism of the Soviet regime conducted by oppositional loners or participants of underground groups which were not connected with each other and whose actions were therefore not coordinated or synchronised. A more or less consolidated dissident movement came into being after 1968. The formation of this consolidated milieu in place of the scattered underground groups was related to the emergence of the periodically-issued information bulletin of the dissident movement, the *Chronicle of Current Events* (Alexeeva, 1984; Vaissié, 1999; Voronkov, 1993).

The majority of dissidents in the 1960s and 1970s belonged to the intelligentsia and had received higher education. After the late 1970s they were joined by others, who were in the course of receiving higher education when they became involved in protest actions and consequently were expelled from university. Sociological research shows that the intelligentsia formed the social base of the dissident movement and its main referent (Vaissié, 1999; Voronkov, 1993). In this sense dissidents in Russia were rather remote from 'the people' in comparison with dissidents in some other socialist countries (e.g. Poland) and in the national republics of the Soviet Union. Individual involvement in the dissident movement was usually motivated by one of the following: (1) a wish to protest against certain drawbacks of Soviet society or political events, or to spread one's own political ideas or programme; (2) 'relative deprivation' and a striving for self-realisation; (3) solidarity with other dissidents; or (4) a desire to emigrate (Tchouikina, 1996, 2000; Vaissié, 1999). The history, role and significance of the dissident movement are defined by its ultimate goal (freedom of expression and the breaking of a state monopoly on ideology), by its repertory of protest actions, and by its participants' agreement in terms of methods of struggle (non-violence, transparency of actions, legacy). From the biographical perspective, however, it was mainly the *punishments dissidents received for their protests*, and not social background, education and ideas, which defined the specificity of the dissident biography as against an ordinary Soviet biography.

From 'First' to 'Second' Life: Entry into the Dissident Milieu

An event which marked the first career break was the loss of the status of ordinary Soviet citizen owing to voluntary or unplanned involvement in protest actions. This loss was usually marked by state interference in the person's life and their subsequent punishment (the issuing of a search warrant, dismissal, arrest, condemnation to exile or to a prison term) and ultimate stigmatisation of themselves and their family as politically alien. A punished and stigmatised person could often not continue to live as before, and as a consequence more and more of their significant activities and contacts would take place in a dissident milieu. One woman I interviewed, a participant in the 'Red Cross' dissident social work movement in the 1970s, said the following:

> When my husband was arrested – it is worth describing ... Because when a woman stays alone with children, and she is stepmotherly [badly] treated at her workplace ... And I must admit, one's circle of friends narrows as well. I can't say that all my friends disappeared, but the number of them decreased. Some stayed friends, but nevertheless, I suppose that everyone feels alone in his sorrow. And then, if some of my girlfriends, who do not know what it is to be the wife of an arrested person, if they did not pass through it themselves it is more difficult for them to understand it. It is very hard to live in one town with your husband knowing that he is in prison. Certainly, there were people who tried to encourage me, but I had a feeling that nobody could share my pain for him and my anxiety. They could only feel sorry for me. But the only people who could understand it and share it were those who passed through it themselves.

This woman gave three main reasons for feeling different after the punishment she received: 'stepmotherly [bad] treatment' by some colleagues at work, the narrowing of her circle of friends, and the need for the advice and encouragement of people who had had the same experience.

Those belonging to the dissident milieu divided into 'defenders' and 'defended', the latter being those who had been arrested, exiled or dismissed and the former their relatives (usually wives) and friends who tried to help them. Every 'defender' could, after a time, become a 'defended' himself and vice versa. Thus the experience of political persecution – especially of one's own arrest or of the arrest of a close relative – marked the initial difference between dissidents and others.

Mutual trust played a very powerful role in dissident activities, and so it was very important to distinguish between one's own and strangers, and between 'faithful' and 'faithless'. The 'initiation' represented by being persecuted for anti-Soviet activities or by attempts to defend a punished person was important for a person's being considered 'one of us' in the dissident milieu. But the final sign of fidelity was conformity to certain unwritten rules of behaviour, the only 'evidence' for this being the dissident's life as it was lived (Daniel, 1998). What made a dissident was a 'harmony of one's words with one's life' (Vaissié, 1999, p. 11). As Daniel shows, the life path of a dissident reflected the different stages of his or her dialogue with the state. In this dialogue, a dissident followed the 'paradigm of protest' and the state a 'paradigm of repression'. Actually, the two sides never hoped to persuade each other, and the dialogue was in reality oriented towards the third, silent participant, public opinion (Daniel, 1998, pp. 117–18). The role of 'public opinion' was enacted not by the majority of the population, which in general considered dissidents to be either alien or insane, but only by the sympathetic social milieux sympathetic to the goals of the movement.

The Dissident Milieu and its 'Neighbours'

The boundaries of the dissident milieu can be defined in relation to 'co-terminous' social milieux: that is, milieux that were akin in terms of lifestyles and practices, but whose representatives at the same time identified themselves as being different from their 'neighbours'. In the social layout of Soviet society the dissidents' neighbouring social milieux were, on the one hand, the dissenting intelligentsia and, on the other, hippies and the people of the cultural underground, and the habitués of the Cafés Saigon, Rim, Malaia Sadovaia, Sfinks, Abbey Road: a marginal bohemia, thoroughly described in the chapter by Elena Zdravomyslova in this book. One participant in the dissident movement since the early 1980s, T. Andrey (b. 1961), commented in his interview as follows:

> … dissident ideas found support in two strata. One of these strata was, first of all, the intelligentsia, namely a technical intelligentsia which occupied itself with humanitarian questions, not so much a humanitarian intelligentsia. And on the other hand, as in the song, the 'janitors' and porters' generation', i.e. an underground humanitarian intelligentsia – those who became janitors, porters and stokers and who in these steamshops occupied themselves with humanitarian creative work.

For the most part, members of the intelligentsia did not have direct, regular contact with dissidents, and may be considered 'free riders' in the dissident movement: groups sharing the goals of the movement, but not ready to take the risks involved in participation. In fact, only certain circles of these broad strata communicated closely with dissidents. Both dissidents and representatives of the dissenting intelligentsia pointed out in interviews (often without being asked) the differences between their circles. One of these was the attitude towards professional self-realisation that corresponded with self-identity. As Michael B., a person closely connected with dissident circles since the late 1960s, remarked:

> I don't call myself a dissident, because for me it was not a profession. That is why I don't have the moral right to call myself that. They were professional revolutionaries. Although I was well-acquainted with many of them and kept company with them, I did not become this profession myself. I was standing next to dissent in that sense.

Dissidents themselves stress the predominance of their protest activities over their official professional duties and their importance in terms of self-realisation. One man (b. 1951) who was responsible for helping the families of political prisoners in Leningrad in the late 1970s recalls:

> These activities – this was my life … I occupied myself with all that for 80 per cent of my time, and occasionally 100 per cent. That was, so to say, my work. And on my basic work I, so to say, boiled the pot – made money.

The sacrifice of professional career in favour of the alternative lifestyle was a common trait in the biographies of dissidents and of 'non-conformist' artists (unacknowledged painters, poets and musicians). The lifestyles of the latter were in many ways different from normal Soviet lifestyles. For this reason some groups of dissidents, feeling these 'non-conformists' to be kindred spirits and allies, tried, at the beginning of the

1980s, to persuade them to take part in protest actions. These attempts to commend to them dissident struggle were, however, for the most part not successful. Denying the validity of all social activities officially sanctioned by the state, the non-conformists claimed that 'politics is a dirty affair', that 'politics and art are incompatible', that the dissidents were 'bolsheviks in reverse', and so on. Unlike the dissidents, the people of the cultural underground did not intend to conduct a dialogue with the state: they wished to neglect the state and be neglected by it. Thus, the boundary between the dissidents and the marginal bohemian public was constructed on the basis of differential attitudes towards self-realisation through social/political activity.

Dissidents, then, were described by their neighbouring milieux as 'professionals', and this description accorded with their self-identity. From a sociological point of view, a profession can be defined as a lasting activity bringing an income to and defining the social status of an individual (Radaev and Shkaratan, 1996). So the question is, from a sociological point of view, can dissident activities be considered as representing a kind of profession?

Dissident Activities as a Quasi-profession

In their 'first life' as ordinary Soviet citizens, many future dissidents were successful in their profession. The most outstanding examples are the famous physicist and holder of the Nobel Prize in 1975, the academician Andrei Sakharov, and General Petr Grigorenko. Less famous, but still prominent in their fields, are the doctors of sciences, physicist Yuri Orlov, linguist Larissa Bororaz and biologist Sergei Kovalev, and the members of the Soviet Writers Union Aleksandr Solzhenitsyn and Alexei Kosterin, to mention just a few. For many such people, involvement in protest actions led to dismissal: thus participation in the movement could even put an end to work in one's own professional sphere, or at least to hopes of professional promotion. Professional career had to be, and was, sacrificed to dissident activity – this was one of the contexts of the dialogue these dissidents conducted with the Soviet authorities. The perspective which our interviews with these dissidents opened up on their everyday activities reveals what their routines were, and what were their main occupations and the qualities these required. These routines consisted mainly of two types of activity: work with information, and 'social work'.

Activities of the first type included creative writing (of essays, ideological programmes, pamphlets, analytical articles, leaflets, collective protest letters, information bulletins, translations from foreign languages), along with the editing and typing of these texts, the spreading of them in circles which would disseminate them further, and communication of the new information to the West. Among the dissidents there were many professional writers and linguists (Vaissié, 1999). In fact, the dissidents' main goal was to remedy the 'information gaps' in their society and to influence that society's memory of its past and present. Presentation to the public of unknown facts about Stalin's time, and the recalling of 'repressed' names, was considered especially important. Researchers regard the creation of an 'independent information field' as being the main goal uniting dissident groups of different ideological orientations (Daniel, 1998). The multi-faceted role played by unpublished Russian and Western literature in the process of creating this independent information field and of forming independent public opinion was considerable (Vaissié, 1999). As Aucouturier (1996) argues, the originality of Russian political dissent as a movement lies in its roots in literary activity. If we turn now to the problem of the boundaries of the dissident milieu, we can view the boundaries constructed between dissidents and neighbouring social milieux, no less than those between 'professionals' and 'non-professionals', as similar to those constructed between, on the one hand, writers, journalists, editors and booksellers and, on the other, readers. Indeed, both the dissenting intelligentsia and the non-conformists were interested consumers of the information spread by dissidents.

'Red Cross' social work in a dissident milieu consisted of assisting political prisoners along with their elderly parents and their wives and children – sending parcels to camps, collecting second-hand items and giving them to those in need, providing other practical help, and collecting money and distributing it among the families of political prisoners. Material help often came from friendly milieux: for example, in some cases the colleagues of an arrested person collected money in the workplace and gave it to the family of a political prisoner. There were also a certain number of anonymous donors among the intelligentsia. Only after 1974 did the dissident milieu have its own money to distribute among political prisoners, as a result of the foundations created separately in the West by Sakharov and Solzhenitsyn (Vaissié, 1999). Again, the difference between the dissidents and the friendly milieux lay in the regularity of help. If, for dissidents, helping political prisoners and their families was an everyday routine, for the other milieux it was a mainly episodic and highly underground activity.

I turn next to quasi-professional dissident activities and the social space in which they occurred. This space has been described via the terms 'quasi-public sphere' (Zdravomyslova, 2002), 'private-public sphere' (Voronkov and Chikadze, 2002), 'alternative public sphere' (Hankiss, 1988), 'alternative sphere of socio-political interaction' (Hankiss, 1988). Other terms have also been employed, describing the same phenomenon from different standpoints (Rotkirch, 2000). All these concepts relate to the same characteristic of a socialist society – that the official public sphere was under state control, and that all informal/unsanctioned social activities had therefore to take place in 'locales of quasi-public communication': cafés, literary salons, dissident 'open houses', exhibitions (Zdravomyslova, 2002). The alternative, or quasi-public, sphere was part of a *second society* (Hankiss, 1988). This latter concept defines all those economic, social, cultural and political activities which for different reasons were not subject to state management. All those living in socialist countries were to some extent involved in *shadow* activities in a *second society*, which included a *quasi-public sphere* (Hankiss, 1988; Voronkov and Chikadze, 2002). In this sense, dissidents were different from those inhabiting the neighbouring milieux, and indeed from all their contemporaries, in two respects. First, they were consciously breaking the informal code (cf. Voronkov and Chikadze, 2002) – the unwritten knowledge all Soviet people shared of what could and could not be said or done in the public and private-public spheres. That is why the discussions of the intelligentsia in their 'kitchens', as well as gatherings of hippies, artists, 'non-conformists' and shadowy small businessmen in city cafés, were tolerated by the regime, whereas dissident activities, which aimed at the dissemination of suppressed information, were prohibited. The breaking of the informal code of Soviet behaviour was the only thing that could reveal the 'mystical' nature of Soviet power, the rigidity of the regime and its imperviousness to change. In this, Vaissié (1999) argues, it was successful.

Secondly, dissidents' activities in the 'second society' predominated over their activities in the first. They sought self-realisation mainly in the second society and were publicly banned and punished in the first. Because the second society was, as Hankiss (1988) points out, characterised by 'diffuseness instead of differentiation and integration', and because it was 'not governed by a consistent set of organisational principles', the quasi-professional actitivies of dissidents in the 'second society' were characterised by a weak division of labour and the dissidents were subject to interference in their private lives regarding these activities. Loose and diffuse as they were, journalistic and Red Cross dissident activities still seem more 'professional' than amateur occupations, since they defined the dissidents' social status both in the first and in the second society, were enduring, required special skills, and created capital which made possible a way of life. The money and material goods received by the wives of political prisoners via the help networks represented only a small addition to their modest official salaries, but they still helped mothers with small children to make ends meet. Even more important than material help was the 'capital' represented by ties of friendship. Mutual trust, and mutual aid and support, were in the dissident milieu the only counter-force the dissidents possessed against the repressive force of the state, and so these comrades-in-arms were used to helping each other with everything, including with the problems of everyday life (Tchouikina, 1996, 2000).

In their 'third life', after their exit from the dissident movement on account of emigration or the arrival of *perestroika*, some dissidents returned to or continued with their first profession. Others used their participation in protest actions as political capital and went into politics; many others again used the skills they had acquired in the dissident movement as professional knowledge. There is a certain continuity between the type of a dissident's actitivies and that of their professional occupation afterwards. But what disappeared or diminished with the end of the movement was that 'diffuseness' typical of the second society, along with the overlapping of professional and family roles. Exits from the dissident movement not infrequently led to the breakup of families. The interviewees themselves explained this by the fact that their family lives prior to the breakup had been centred on their dissident activities, which called for different relationships between spouses from those that applied in ordinary everyday life (Tchouikina, 1996). As a result many families did not survive the transition, where professional and social activities were not so tightly bound, and not focused so sharply on defence against hostile external surroundings.

Conclusion

Research investigating the dissident movement in Soviet society has contributed to our knowledge of that society's 'underlife' (Zdravomyslova, 2002). In this chapter I have attempted to analyse the biographies of participants in the dissident movement with a particular focus on: (1) their specific life courses, which are characterised by *career breaks* (Humphrey, 1993); and (2) the socio-structural consequences for late-Soviet society of the persecution and stigmatisation of oppositionists. My research has shown that, in the context of late-Soviet society, breaks in their social careers caused by state interference forced persecuted oppositionists to seek self-realisation in the second society (Hankiss, 1988). Adapting to their marginal official status, they developed their own subculture, their own status symbols, and their own ideas of suitable behaviour. This group of people had, by the beginning of the 1970s, formed a distinct milieu inside Soviet society, for which the 'open homes' of the participants in the movement served as 'public places' (Tchouikina, 1996, 1997, 2000). In the broad structure of Soviet society the social milieux adjoining the dissident milieu were the milieu of the dissenting intelligentsia and the marginal bohemian milieu. Analysis of the dissident milieu in relation to its neighbours not only sheds light on anti-Soviet biographies, but also illustrates the limits of the possible involvement by an ordinary Soviet citizen in activities unsanctioned by the state.

Notes

---

1 For my language of description of the everyday life of dissidents (e.g. the terms 'milieu insiders', 'milieu outsiders', 'neighbourhood') I am indebted to Richard Grathoff. In his 'methodological note' (Grathoff, 1989, pp. 433–40) Grathoff describes the possible stages and methods of phenomenological investigation of a social milieu which addresses the following problems: the boundaries of a milieu; the biographical situation of its inhabitants and the duration of their residency; its 'spatial order' (i.e. private and public spheres in the milieu); the discourse characteristic of the milieu; and political and economic relations between the milieu and wider society.

2 The interviews with participants in the dissident movement from Leningrad were conducted by me in 1995–6 as part of the project 'Women in the Dissident Movement' sponsored by the Heinrich Böll Foundation, Germany. I also used interviews from the archive of the Centre for Independent Social Research, conducted by Victor Voronkov and Elena Zdravomyslova in 1993–5 for the project 'Dissent in the USSR as a Social Movement', interviews from the archive of the SIC 'Memorial' conducted by Tatiana Kosinova and myself in 1992–4, and the interviews of Christina Leiser (FU Berlin) conducted in 1994–5. Full information about the history of the dissident movement in Moscow and the biographies of its participants is given in Vaissié, 1999, and a general history of the dissident movement in the USSR may be found in Alexeeva (1992).

References

Alexeeva, L. (1984), *History of Dissent in the USSR* (Istoriia inakomysliia v SSSR), Khronika Press, Benson, VT.

Aucouturier, M. (1996), *La Dissidence et la revanche de la littérature. De la dissidence à la democratie.* Actes du colloque consacré à la mémoire de Vladimir Maximov, ed. G. Ackerman, Editions du Rocher, Paris.

Daniel, A. (1998), *Dissidentstvo: uskolzajushaja kultura?*, vol. 1, no. 9, OGI, Moscow, pp. 111–24.

Grathoff, R. (1989), *Milieu und Lebenswelt: Einführung in die sozialphänomenologische Forschung*, Suhrkamp, Frankfurt am Main.

Hankiss, E. (1988), 'The "Second Society": Is There an Alternative Social Model Emerging in Contemporary Hungary?', *Social Research*, vol. 55, nos 1–2, pp. 13–42.

Humphrey, R. (1993), 'Life Stories and Social Careers: Ageing and Social Life in an Ex-Mining Town', *Sociology*, vol. 27, no.1, pp. 166–78.

Iofe, V. [pseud. Rozhdestvenskii, S.] (1982), *Materialy k istorii samodeiatelnyh politicheskih ob'edinenii v SSSR posle 1945 goda. Pamiat. Istoricheskii almanakh*, Vol. 5, Editions la Presse Libre, Paris.

Radaev, V. and Shkaratan, O. (1996), *Sozialnaia stratifikaziia*, Aspekt, Moscow.

Rotkirch, A. (2000), *The Man Question: Loves and Lives in Late 20th Century Russia*, Research Report No. 1, Department of Social Policy, University of Helsinki, Helsinki.

Tchouikina, S. (1996), 'The Role of Women Dissidents in Creating the Milieu', in A. Rotkirch and E. Haavio-Mannila (eds), *Women's Voices in Russia Today*, Dartmouth, London, pp. 189–206.

Tchouikina, S. (1997), *The Open House and its Hostess: From the History of the Participants of the Dissident Movement: Feminist Theory and Practice: East–West*, Centre for Gender Issues, St Petersburg, pp. 201–7.

Tchouikina, S. (2000), '"Ich war keine Dissidentin": Politische Biografien der antisowjetischen Dissidentenbewegung (1956–1985)', in I. Miethe and S. Roth (eds), *Politische Biographien und Sozialer Wandel*, Psychosozial Verlag, Giessen, pp. 205–24.

Vaissié, C. (1999), *Pour votre liberté et pour la nôtre: le combat des dissidents de Russie*, Robert Laffont, Paris.

Voronkov, V. (1993), 'Die Protestbewegung des "Sechziger"-Generation: Der Widerstand gegen das sowjetische Regime 1956–1985', *Osteuropa*, vol. 10, pp. 939–48.

9 The Café Saigon *Tusovka*: One Segment of the Informal-public Sphere of Late-Soviet Society

ELENA ZDRAVOMYSLOVA
Centre for Independent Social Research and European University, St Petersburg, Russia

Introduction

The purpose of this chapter is to conceptualise the public sphere of late-Soviet society of the 1970s and 1980s, and to consider its spatial arrangement and the communication patterns that characterised it. It arises out of the fact that certain arrangements and practices of everyday life in the Soviet Union are quickly vanishing from the collective memory. Biographical research, however, is able to stimulate people to offer narratives relating to these things before they disappear completely.

Discussion and conceptualisation of the late-Soviet public sphere has not only a historical but also a political dimension. However vague the concepts 'public' and 'private' are, social scientists use them to reinforce the argument that, despite its lack of democratic traditions, Russian society has an opportunity to modernise politically and to develop public and civil institutions of the Western kind.

I elaborate here upon the construct of the late-Soviet public sphere – the realm of state-independent activities and communication – and its functioning in the large Soviet city. Segments of an informal-public sphere separate from the official public one began to develop in Soviet Russia from the end of the 1950s. Unlike previous decades in Soviet history, when communication had either been totally officially controlled or else had taken place in a private 'kitchen' setting, the 'Brezhnev era of stagnation' provided public space (in the form of legal public places) for communication that escaped such total control. One example of such a public place was a city café that had regular visitors of a particular kind, and where certain communication patterns were maintained: the Café Saigon in Leningrad. This café represented a focus for communication between people opposed to the mainstream Soviet way of life.

The logic I employ to integrate my study of this café with discussion of the division between private and public realms in Soviet society is as follows. I argue that late-Soviet modernity formed a specific set of conditions for the flourishing of spontaneous collective activities and modes of communication not controlled by the state. To describe the specificity of this realm of informal Soviet activities I use the term 'informal-public'. This term is employed to emphasise the well-known fact that opportunities for state-independent activities and communication in Soviet society were limited. This term serves to capture the lack of political, ideological, economic and religious freedoms on the one hand and, on the other, the opportunities that existed for a certain degree of spontaneous activity.[1] What was this informal-public sphere of late socialism? How can it be reconstructed from the vanishing memories of city residents? What were the rules of the game in this communication setting, and what were the milieux that maintained these rules of interaction and communication?

This study may also be important for an understanding of the social structure of late socialism, an area which is still unclear and which requires empirical research. Each social group has its own particular locales. Social groups and groupings occupy distinct places and mark them with their activities, types of interaction and symbolism. These places provide arrangements for communication, interaction and life-practices for those who 'occupy' them. As a result, if we consider the images and practices of a particular locale, we can see how the particular segment of the Soviet public sphere known as the informal-public was organised and which milieux appropriated that place.

There existed in Leningrad particular well-known locales for spontaneous or 'initiative' activities. These places were: alternative art exhibitions, home literary salons, dissident open houses, and certain city cafés. These city cafés were the meeting places and symbolic locales for people whose everyday practices were identified as representing an alternative to those accepted by the official public. Such cafés were the settings for social occasions which allowed 'alternative' persons to gather – those gravitating towards a certain lifestyle which was marginal in respect of officially-sanctioned public life. This is why I name settings of this kind 'informal-public', and the whole realm of activities that took place in such settings the 'informal-public sphere'. The individuals inhabiting this realm, being socially marginal, were not sufficiently integrated into the Soviet way of life. This marginality of the café visitors expressed itself in their values, attitudes, political orientations and everyday life-practices (in the spheres of employment, leisure and family), as well as in their body idiom.

The Café Saigon, in Leningrad, was one such café. It was known both throughout the city and beyond its borders. It was the refuge of 'alternative' people for more than twenty years (from 1964 up until autumn 1991). It has become a symbol for that generation of the urban intelligentsia alive during the late-Soviet period. Today, we can see continuous attempts to commemorate this café in the Russian media, and in art, poetry, folklore and literature. Even in Jerusalem there is a Café Saigon, established by a Soviet émigré.

When we discuss the Café Saigon, we are discussing a form of 'street life' in the city, the existence of which had become known to the city's inhabitants and which they still remember. The Café Saigon is a good research subject, because the café has been extensively discussed in the local media since the end of the 1980s. This popularity and constant attention is shown by the fact that a memorial plaque has been attached to the wall to commemorate the place. All these commemorative actions can be understood in terms of the popular recognised meaning and significance of this café as a symbol of freedom: in terms, that is, of the informal-public life of socialism. In examining this particular case, then, I am aiming to reconstruct one specific milieu of pre-reform Soviet society.

Although the Café Saigon existed for several decades, I focus here mainly on the second half of the 1960s and the 1970s. This was when the café flourished most strongly. The later Café Saigon of the 1980s and its own specific rock-culture have been described elsewhere (Cushman, 1995; Pilkington, 1994; Shchepanskaya, 1993).

This micro-sociological approach will facilitate an exploration of how individual activities combined to make possible a collective identity. The research focuses on those interactive and communicative practices, and those rules and conventions, which constituted the lifestyle of the Café Saigon community.

The *Tusovka* as a Segment of the Soviet Public Sphere

I argue here that the 'public' element of late-Soviet modernity is 'informal-public' according to Habermas's concept of a bourgeois public (Habermas, 1989). Here I concentrate on one particular segment of the Soviet informal-public sphere for which an original term has been developed. This term is *tusovka*. The word is properly untranslatable, like the bulk of those names which form the core of cultural and societal specificity (Boym, 1994). Like such words as *sputnik*, *glasnost* and *perestroika*, *babushka* and *dacha*, which are essential for an understanding of everyday life in Soviet Russia, *tusovka* has become part of an international vocabulary. It is used by Russian and Eastern European researchers to signify particular patterns of interaction. The Café Saigon was a *tusovka* setting.

The etymology of the term *tusovka* is unclear. It began to be widely used in the second half of 1970s although it originated in the 1960s. The generation which made up the original core of the Café Saigon in the 1970s did not call themselves *tusovshchiki*. The word became popular later on, in the 1980s, whereon the first Saigonee generation took it over from their followers.

Tusovka is founded on face-to-face communication between those who enact it. Such actors are united by shared practices, attitudes and styles of individual conduct and interaction. The practices under discussion here consisted of creative work, shadow-economy activities, and various self-destructive behaviours. *Tusovka* presumes a certain type of individual: a liberal individual from the Soviet period, integrated to a minor extent into the life of Soviet officialdom and its *kollektivy*. A particular social contract allowed for the existence of the Saigon *tusovka* as the site of a counter-Soviet efflorescence in the heart of the Soviet city.

I wish to give the slang term *tusovka* the status of a sociological category embracing particular segments of the informal-public sphere of late-Soviet modernity. It represents a specific type of communication and interaction, characterised by a coherent amalgam of body idiom, place, activities and style of conduct.[2] In my view, the essence of *tusovka* can be captured by Bourdieu's conception of the interpersonal *habitus* as *incorporated class*. I argue here that conceptualisation of the public sphere as a communication realm should embrace not only certain organisational forms and forms of face-to-face or mediated interaction, but moral, psychological and even bodily-expressed aspects of individual conduct and interpersonal communication. Public communication presumes a certain individual and interpersonal conduct: the *habitus* of an individual, in whose very posture a knowledge of his or her place in society is embodied. This posture – 'body idiom' in Goffman's terms – manifests in such forms as dress style, gait, tastes and practices, and the vocabulary of communication. *Tusovka* is characterised by a specific *habitus*.

What was the Saigon *tusovka habitus*? I am attempting to find this out from memoirs and interviews, using a phenomenological frame. I consider the micro-approach to be especially relevant for the theorising of communication in *tusovka,* and apply here Goffman's theory of 'communication places' (Goffman, 1963). Goffman argues that social arrangements and institutions in the everyday-life sense are those places – buildings, rooms, plants – where certain regular actions take place. These places constitute the architecture of everyday life. They provide communication space and opportunities for certain types of action. The type of communication appropriate to the place forms the *habitus* of the social milieux of that place. Goffman distinguishes between exclusive and open places. An exclusive place is one which is open only to a particular type of habitué. This *tusovka* was one segment of the underworld of the wider Soviet society, the exclusive place that was appropriated by this specific brand of habitué. My task here is to ascertain which activities constituted the life of the Café Saigon *tusovka* and its people in the 1970s, what the bonds were that connected the people of the *tusovka*, what the nature was of their attachments, and how they were maintained.

The chapter is organised as follows. First, I describe the Café Saigon as the location of *tusovka*, and present its regime, rules, common practices and symbols in the words both of those who frequented it and of ordinary city residents (insider and outsider views). I then turn to the individual life stories of the café habitués in order to show whence they were recruited, what their *tusovka* experiences were *vis-à-vis* everyday life in the Soviet Union, and what the meanings were that they attached to the *tusovka habitus*.

The Café Saigon and its Tusovka

Café Saigon operated in Leningrad from autumn 1964 until December 1991. One famous habitué of the café in the 1970s, a poet and literary critic, recollects:

> The Saigon opened on the very day that I entered the University – on the first of September 1964. These days coincided. Before the Saigon there was a (coffee) place at Malaya Sadovaya Street. We had all been in a whirl there

> and then moved to the Saigon. Since then I've come to the Saigon nearly every day for around twelve years.

Many artists and students of literature and art first came to Café Saigon when they were quite young, in their late teens or early 20s. The café became a hangout for bohemian youth. The core group of habitués had formed and consolidated earlier, in another small café, an earlier version of the Saigon, which somehow lost its popularity. The period 1964–76 represented the years of the first Saigon generation, the people of the 1970s who are the focus of this chapter.

Political Context of the Café Saigon Story

It is timely to mention here that in Soviet political history 1964 was the last year of Khrushchev's rule and four years prior to the Russian invasion of Czechoslovakia. The period when the Saigon began and came to full flowering was the end of the 'political thaw' and long period of stagnation that lasted from 1964 up until the 1980s. This was the time when a certain opening up of the political climate explained the existence of the alternative art, dissident groups, shadow-economy and alternative lifestyles that were officially condemned as marginal to the Soviet mainstream. It was also the period of the maximum development of corruption and of the Soviet double standard – Soviet schizophrenia, a divergence between the word and the deed (Levada, 1993).

Café Saigon people refer to this period in their life as 'a timeless period where one day is similar to another and nothing happen for centuries …' (GG). They perceived Soviet life at this time as 'a corridor … which you enter and which slowly is leading you in a very senseless and ugly direction' (VT). In their memories, this stagnation is marked by the following political events: the intervention of Russian troops in Czechoslovakia (August 1968), the exile of Solzhenitsyn (1974), and the arrests of Soviet dissidents (1965, 1968, 1980).

During these years, certain Soviet citizens learnt to live quite autonomously from the state, ethically, aesthetically, economically and politically. From the second half of the 1960s, the octopus of communication sites – cafés and clubs – 'privatised' by such people began to spread its tentacles over the city. A map for such places in Leningrad can be drawn up, and Café Saigon was the major such place.

The Topography of the Café Saigon Tusovka

Café Saigon was situated on the crossroads of two main streets of Leningrad: the Nevsky and Vladimirsky Prospects. Its location on the corner of two main streets in the city centre made it the most attractive meeting place for many, but especially for those who occupied and 'privatised' this territory. One respondent recalled:

> I knew for sure that if I went there at a certain time (7 p.m.) I would meet the person I needed to see without a special appointment … You could meet your friends and acquaintances.

The place was tightly embedded in the culture of the city. It is often described in interviews as a specifically Leningrad phenomenon, which one could never encounter in any other Russian town or city – neither in Moscow nor in any provincial town. It was known among the intelligentsia far beyond the city borders. People came from Moscow to visit it; it was known abroad, and was part of the cultural mythology of Leningrad/St Petersburg. In the consciousness of its residents and among the Soviet population more generally there existed a myth concerning Leningrad/St Petersburg. It was a city with a mysterious soul and a tragic fate, an antithesis of the orthodox Soviet Slavic merchant capital, Moscow. The history of the city, founded by the first Russian emperor as 'a window into Europe', as well as its recognisably European architecture and air have engendered in public consciousness a stable image of a European city inhabited by a specifically democratically-oriented population which was victimised by Soviet rule and which came to embody cultural protest. The non-official poetry' of the late-socialist period (Brodsky is the most distinguished figure here), underground art (Belkin, Gennadjev) and Leningrad rock (Leningrad Rock Club, the rock groups Kino, Alisa, Akvarium, etc.) are just a few examples of this cultural protest. All this informal Leningrad counterculture of the late-socialist era was made up of *tusovki*. These multiple *tusovki* had their territories in the town and their well-known addresses. Café Saigon was at the centre of the territory of the counterculture.

A whole number of small cafés and ice-cream shops in the Café Saigon area were appropriated for group frequenting. When Café Saigon came to prominence it spread like a spider and took over several public places surrounding it, such as the ice-cream café which was named 'Adjunct' by its habitués. The city toilets, as well as Central Moscow railway station, were nearby. Liquor stores were also around, open until 7 p.m. and later 9 p.m. This city area was the habitat of bohemians and of literary and theatre people, and Saigon was at its crossroads. It was a comfortable meeting place to begin an evening that might consist of communicative meetings including group drinking sessions and informal humorous discussion and the arranging of events and performances. It was the site of face-to-face communication between people who knew each other, trusted one another and now shared the same lifestyle. The café was situated near the artistic Houses of Journalists and Actors and Leningrad Rock Club, which also had their more exclusive comfortable cafés and restaurants.

Symbolism of the café name The naming of places by local residents tells us a great deal about the informal-public sphere, especially in the light of the official names that were given to monuments in the city, which either commemorated historical and cultural persons and events belonging to Soviet mythology or else had no specific connotations. The officially-named cafés at that time were the Landysh, the Nevskoe and the Metropol. There were also places without any names. Initially, Café Saigon had no name.

Since the end of the 1960s folk toponymics had become a part of urban culture. The naming by residents of city monuments, and especially cafés, became common. These symbolic actions were the signs of a slightly liberalised climate. The counterculturalists marked their territory by giving names to and labelling the places they inhabited. They thus symbolically defined the territory as belonging to them. These informal names never appeared as street signs although they were known throughout the city. Certain collective sentiments were articulated in the folklore and symbolism of folk-naming. The café names were indicative: 'Ulster', 'Rome', 'Abbey Road', 'Saigon', 'Bombay'. The 'Ulster' and 'Abbey Road' were situated downtown; 'Rome' and 'Bombay' were situated in other parts of the city. Each café attracted a different kind of habitué.

What might be the significance of such namings? There can be several theories about this. Basically, these informal names alluded to the West. The chosen and maintained names demonstrated an intention of sustaining certain associations – of expressing the fact that the atmosphere of these places was radically different from the Soviet one. For Soviet bohemians, the West was associated with non-authoritarian, uncontrolled protest, sometimes violent ('Ulster'), and a youth culture ('Abbey Road') which had nothing in common with 'official' Soviet public life. Habitués started to call the central café the 'Saigon'. Why this name was chosen and sustained for decades was a question I put to my informants.[3]

Local legend provides the following story of the Café Saigon's origins, one of many. In this café, smoking was forbidden. This official rule was, however, regularly violated by habitués. Once, a militiaman tried to re-establish order. He approached the smokers and said: 'Why are you smoking here? It's absolutely disgraceful. It's so smoky here – you've made a real Saigon of the place.' This was the time of the Vietnam War, and Saigon was perceived as a place where chemical weapons were used. After this, people adopted the name as a label for cultural disorder.

Value and Significance of the Café Saigon for its Habitués

In discussing the attractiveness of this particular public place, its habitués focused on its role in their lives. They gave different explanations as to why they regularly visited the café in the 1970s–80s. First, there existed a need for an informal meeting-place where people could gather spontaneously:

> The very existence of the Saigon was caused by the fact that people strove to unite with each other. It may be that we had been socialised in such a way that it was necessary for us to come together … But this gathering needed to be quite informal, because Komsomol, TU, job, college – these are not what people wanted. (NG)

The need for informal communication and spontaneous gathering demanded public places. For young people, this was a period of intellectual ferment and there was an urgent need to share and to talk. These people badly needed a site where they could communicate and they chose this café from the available urban settings. The place was obviously under the control of the authorities. It was the state-owned catering enterprise affiliated to the 'Moskva' restaurant, and there were police stations and police posts in the area. This control, however, was not rigid. Modes of communication between the 'Saigonees', as I shall term them, ran strongly counter to all those practices that were approved by the state. Simply frequenting this place marked people out. It meant their acceptance in one milieu along with disconnection from their official milieu. This was the main boundary which separated the Saigonees from wider society – the informal-public from the official public.

Secondly, there was a perceived need to escape the 'controlled' privacy of Soviet homes:

> And who had rooms of their own? When you described a person, his main merit was his apartment ... Mother, father and I occupied a room of 30 square metres in an apartment occupied by four families. While the slow repair-work was going on my father fenced off a corner for me made out of timber sheeting that did not reach the ceiling. When I was reading in bed I heard, from my parents' bed, 'Turn off the light. You're stopping us sleeping!' ... I not only slept and ate there when I came home very late, but sometimes, when my parents were away, I had female visitors ... I hung out in the Saigon practically every day from 1970 till 1984 ... until 1979, because then I got a room and so I could spent part of the day there ... (EV)

Young people felt a need to get away from the apartments which they shared with their neighbours (in the communal flat), either with their parents' family or with their spouse and children. In these overcrowded apartments their life was under constant surveillance and control.[4] Those who had the luxury of living away from them held salons and open houses. Everyday guests were typical in such 'open houses' (Tchouikina, 1996). Individuals belonging to this milieu also distanced themselves from the Soviet style of control of marital relations.

Finally, people were looking for adventure. 'Life was interesting there – that was the main thing' (VT). Café Saigon was appreciated as a site for adventures – its habitués felt the demand for adventure strongly. The surprise nature of the happenings that took place there was extremely important for the *tusovka* – for those people who considered Soviet reality unbearably boring in its false seriousness. This sense of boredom, or spleen (*toska*), was a feeling expressed by almost all my informants, who were suffocating in the airless atmosphere of officially-sanctioned public life in the 1970s. Café Saigon became the symbol of an 'air vent' for those who felt alien elsewhere – at home with their families and in official institutions. There was no other place in the city except this one in the centre of the *tusovka* area where one could kill time and show oneself off. Here one could meet friends and, inspired by conversation fuelled by alcohol, begin some adventure or other. One such adventure was the military-archaeological trip to the countryside, where young people dug out Second World War artefacts. Another might be a love affair ...

One informant remarked:

> I've always hated having guests at home or visiting people, because it was easy to predict what would happen. I knew the play from the very beginning to the end. But at the Saigon the situation was open. When I went there I couldn't say whether the night would be crazily boring or intensely happy. I couldn't say who I might meet – whether we'd end the night at the militia

> station or at the Hotel Europe bar. The night could be unpredictable, and all the worries and adventures of the drunken night streets were there for you to experience. (VT)

In addition, Café Saigon held an attraction as the centre of bohemian life in Leningrad. It was the meeting place for those who practised the alternative art of the late-Soviet period. Not without reason was this territory occupied by all the different clubs of the official professional arts associations. The *tusovka* of the 1970s was of an extremely bohemian blend. The cultural and educational attractiveness of meetings in Café Saigon is well-attested by the café's former visitors. It 'created' the writer and the poet who was read by everybody in the milieu – the film everybody had to see, the exhibition everyone attended. The charisma of the 'alternative' artist was strongly felt there:

> This company … was an extremely prestigious one in our eyes. It was a reference group that we looked up to. I had to develop the skill of quick verbal reaction; I had to develop my poetic skills to be accepted there. (NG)

Summing up all the arguments in favour of the place one informant concluded: 'Thank God we had this *tusovka*. It is always good, it educates a person … If it weren't for the Saigon I don't know what would become of me. Probably I would kill myself' (VT).

Regime and Atmosphere of the Café Saigon Tusovka

The term 'regime' is used here to signify official and unofficial rules of behaviour. The official regulations governing café life were as follows. Working hours were from 9 a.m. until 9 p.m., with a break for dinner from 3 till 4 p.m. Café Saigon was a self-service café. The café area was divided into three sections. The first was a bar, where one could buy spirits and other drinks. This area was not crowded; not many people used this bar. The second section was the main one. It was a coffee shop with five or six espresso machines. It was overcrowded: there were regular queues for the coffee, which was known to be among the best in Leningrad. The third section consisted of a buffet, where one could by cheap hot meals. The interior was poorly decorated. There was only one table for sitting down at; customers were supposed to drink their coffee standing at the high coffee tables. Despite this, the coffee was regarded as the best in the city.

Neither smoking nor the consumption of alcohol was allowed in the café: these prohibitions were set out on notices attached to the walls. There were no toilets in the café, a situation which was typical of all small public catering venues with the exception of restaurants.

Nearby was the 'Café Gastrit'. (It was named after the stomach ailment which the cheap and badly cooked meals could cause.) Its official name was Café Automat. There, hungry Saigonees could eat very cheaply, for just 40 copecks.

Basically, the Café Saigon was quite uncomfortable. The interior was not conducive to long talking sessions or relaxation. Nevertheless, the place was popular. People would spend hours there, standing in the entrance or in groups around the tables, or else sitting on the window-sills. (This was also forbidden, though official regulations were widely disregarded.)

The real regulations attaching to café life were often contrary to the official ones. Café Saigon had a different character during different periods of the day. In the morning it functioned as a normal coffee shop, while in the afternoons and evenings it provided a space for the meetings of several *tusovki*. After 7 p.m. people from a whole number of social groups met there: bohemians (poets, actors, artists and rock musicians formed separate groups), people involved in the shadow economy, deaf-mutes. One frequent visitor to the café recalled:

> In the morning there were few visitors – they were either occasional visitors or people such as I, suffering from an awful hangover, withdrawing from early drinking, going there to kill time, who had coffee there ... This was one Saigon. It was quite clean ... At that time it was a quiet place where you could calmly discuss something with a friend. After twelve, from the beginning of the 1970s, the Saigon was full of book dealers, who had their modest breakfast there, spending, I reckoned, about three roubles on it[5] – two sandwiches with red caviar, one sandwich with something else and adding a cake to this, drinking this coffee or even taking a glass of juice. They were the richest until a certain moment ... Between 12 and 1 p.m. they crowded into the Saigon and discussed something and then they went to stand somewhere near the Old Book [an antique bookshop] or somewhere else – they had their work-places there. After that, the Saigon was willy-nilly filled by the casual public who naturally had their coffee there until around 4 p.m. (EV)

The real crowds came a little later, during the staff dinner-and-cleaning break after 5 p.m., when the regular visitors added to the 'occasional' public and changed the character of the place by their styles of behaviour. In fact, there were two different crowds there: 'normal', occasional visitors and the regulars, or locals. These latter considered it their right to be served coffee without queuing, and this caused indignation. There were minor wrangles that ended inconclusively. The waitresses whom the regulars knew by name always served them first.

Smoking was commonplace in the café, as was the consumption of cheap, low-quality wine which the regulars brought with them. Sometimes they shared their bottle with a well-known invalid nicknamed 'Koleso' ('Wheel') who worked there as a cleaner. Cheap, low-quality Moldavian port was the hallmark of the place, though many people preferred dry wine.

A meeting at the café was regarded as the starting-point for a night of conviviality. The standard charge for sharing wine in a group was 70 copecks per person. Someone needed only this much to participate. Group leaders usually paid double the standard charge. At this time, this amount of money could provide drinks for a company of five. Women were not obliged to contribute: usually they were paid for by men. A moneyless habitué could beg for funds in some artistic fashion. One informant recollected that he used to approach good-looking young women in the queue, addressing them in an over-polite way like this: 'Could you kindly afford to lend money without any hope of getting it back?' Startled young women would give him up to 25 roubles. Sometimes he paid them back, sometimes not.

One further advantage of the Café Saigon was that it offered a solution to the problem of where to urinate. Street-life in Leningrad was not comfortable as regards physical needs. One regular recalled:

> Polite People solved this problem [of urination] by not pissing on the staircases. First, it was disgusting. Secondly, it was frightful. By giving 10 or 20 copecks to the doormen one could use the rather dirty WC at the Moskva restaurant. Then I found the restaurant at the Actors House, which is much more decent and which one didn't have to pay for. There you could even wash your hands with soap, and even though there were no towels, there was paper to wipe yourself with – newspaper in the cubicles, sometimes it could be toilet paper – once in half a year it appeared there. (V)

The atmosphere[6] of the Café Saigon *tusovka* was determined by the rules of conduct that applied in the place, along with the practices of the people who made up its milieu. These behaviour patterns were decidedly 'symbolic'. This symbolism signified cultural protest against the normative Soviet way of life. The Café Saigon underground compensated for the negative aspects of Soviet existence. Among those which the café regulars felt particularly acutely were: the lack of any possibility for personal and artistic expression; a shortage of information and books; and a dearth of individuation. Generally speaking, this lack of liberal public discourse was something that was acutely felt by talented people first. The core of the Saigon's visitors consisted of underground poets, artists and musicians. Cultural text, evolved by a Soviet 'bohemia', was the 'capital' which gave one authority in this milieu. This cultural text included not only works of alternative art, but also the violation of official rules of conduct. The language-codes were also partly different.

Many places used *nicknames*, designed to demonstrate 'difference'. ('In our place, we use names that we give to ourselves, not those given by the "oldies", our parents', commented one informant.) Many such names were styled in the Western way (Kol, Bol, Molly, Kit, Marianna, Sandy). Many of them originated in the milieux from which the Saigonees were recruited, for example in the language schools where teenagers learnt English or in youth clubs.

In the 1970s, so linguists maintain, *hippie slang* emerged, and it was widely used in the Café Saigon milieu. According to professional estimates the dictionary of Russian hippie slang includes 600 words (Rozhanski, 1996). Hippie slang was based on borrowings from various sociolects. Researchers identify as the sources for such borrowings the English language (sometimes with a change of meaning), musicians' jargon; *fartsa* slang, youth jargon, drug addicts' jargon. Counterculturalists would, in their casual conversations, combine slang, vulgar obscenities and sophisticated quotations from philosophers and poets. Such communication codes were valued and recognised.

The *symbolism of poverty* was important for the bohemian core of the Café Saigon. Most of those attending the café were not well-off. The place symbolised contempt for Soviet consumerism as an expression of a 'Soviet' career path. According to one informant:

> The Saigon was a very uncomfortable place ... But it was cheap. One could of course go to the restaurant for the same purposes. It was not that expensive, but restaurants were not for Saigonees, they were for *mazhors*.

It was the countercultural milieu that, in the 1980s, introduced the term *mazhor* as a label for consumption-oriented Soviet young men. People visiting the Café Saigon symbolically rejected material prosperity. The demonstrative poverty indicated by their dress may be deciphered as a symbol of generational protest.

A *humorous, light, casual style* typified Café Saigon communication. Seriousness, the grand style, was inappropriate in this milieu. Nothing was taken seriously: neither life nor death; neither duties nor beliefs; not family, nor politics, nor careers. I take this emphatic unseriousness as one more sign of alienation from the false seriousness of the life of the common Soviet man and its collectives, a life whose 'rights' and 'duties' were regulated by the party-state and the credentials it required: state holidays, collective meetings, reports on activities, registered marriages, passports, labour books, housing registration, official street decorations in the form of portraits of party-state officials, and endless restrictions. This bitter, absurdist humour can, along with other practices, be read also as a disguise for the quasi-suicidal orientation of these people, their wish for self-destruction – as a kind of gallows humour. The forms this humour took were various: they were apparent in the oral story-telling (in *telegi*, in the slang of the later hippie generation, and in the culture of anecdotes) that was imbued with absurd, occasional epigrams, as well as in the happenings that took place and in the extravagant garbs that were worn. References to unpublished texts of the Leningrad absurdist literary school the OBEREU of the 1920–30s (Daniel Kharms and Alexander Vvedensky) were respected in this milieu. I see this specific humour as an essential practice that gave charm to Café Saigon discourse. This humour was a means of ignoring and escaping from the wider society and from one's personal life with all its troubles and insufficiencies.

People's broad perceptions of this *tusovka* were ambivalent. On the one hand it had the flavour of human detritus, of the bottom and margins of society. This is how it was understood by lay people. This view was partly shared by the habitués themselves. On the other hand the *tusovka* provided an atmosphere of individuation, of creative work, artistic improvisation, and the expression of cultural freedom. This ambiguity is probably typical of bohemian places elsewhere. One informant gave me a clue as to how the totality of the Café Saigon atmosphere might be grasped. 'The main idea here', he observed, 'was the idea of pose.' *Pose* here is a metaphor used to describe a style, including body idiom, attitudes, behaviour-patterns and modes of interaction. The 'pose' of a Saigonee was that of a lonely, single, independent individual confirmed in his or her appearance, facial looks and smile, mode of talking, dress and gait, and essential practices. All these small behavioural features distinguished the conduct of a Saigonee from that accepted in the wider society. Informants still claim that they could recognise a Saigonee by their appearance. The symbolism of the pose has major importance for an understanding of the late-Soviet informal-public sphere. The Saigonee, like the Saigon itself, is conceived of by former habitués as representing an *embodied* protest. This protest was not an open taking up of arms, but a mode of comprehensive cultural opposition.

Social Structure of the Café Saigon Tusovka

The informal-public realm of *tusovka* activities and the official public realm of late-Soviet society were mutually supportive, because Café Saigon functioned as an ecological niche and as a channelling opportunity for the Soviet underground. Here, individuals were allowed to express themselves with a certain amount of freedom, experiencing only minor repression while being well-observed and -controlled by officialdom. On the one hand, here one could be oneself – this was a so-called 'free place'. On the other, the ecological density of the marginals in the café area made it easier for the authorities to control them. 'Mutual blindness' characterised the contract that operated between the Café Saigon and the wider society. The Café Saigon milieu was silenced in the official-public sphere; it was voiced in the Western or *samizdat* media and in countercultural performances.

The café can also be considered as a setting for the alternative *youth* culture of late-socialist society in the 1970s and 1980s. The bohemian intelligentsia spent their formative years in this environment. It is possible to differentiate the Café Saigon generations: the core group of bohemians dominated until the end of the 1970s, and was then gradually replaced by the rock generation of the 1980s. As regards the official public realm, however, both generations shared the same sense of alienation and rejection.

The *tusovka* was not homogeneous. Informants distinguish the following groupings: poets, 'academics' (people from Café Academichka in the university area), artists, book dealers and shadow-economy people, the group of deaf-mutes. Everybody knew each other on the level of 'Hi' and 'Bye'. The place was large enough to include several groupings. Newcomers were mainly recruited elsewhere and later introduced to the *tusovka*. Every group was engaged in its own activities, and the groups were not contiguous. The core Café Saigon milieu was made up of bohemians and their admirers, fans and supporters. The bohemians – or 'unrecognised geniuses' – were united by the same experience: these talented people were not accepted in the official professional milieu, because its restrictions were unbelievably rigid. Soviet officialdom squeezed out many talented people who did not conform to Soviet standards of loyalty. For several decades, only underground settings for performance were available for the Café Saigon's artists, poets and actors. *Samizdat* publications, salon (flat) exhibitions and home performances were the main settings for Soviet bohemians. The social network of the bohemians did not resemble that of the Soviet collectives. It was based on the solidarity of independent singulars – individuals who negated the Soviet way of life and were involved in alternative art.

Many of these people were not accepted in their professional associations for ideological reasons. Their art was considered 'ideologically unhealthy': it did not fit with the patterns of socialist realism, the official mainstream of Soviet art; it did not fit with the dogmas of orthodox Marxism-Leninism; it did not fit with the *habitus* of *Homo Sovieticus*. In the late-Soviet period, however, such people got their opportunity to create niches for professional artistic communication between artistic creators and their audience. The *tusovka* was united by deliberate negation of the wider society, but it also developed its own rules of professionalism, its own rules of the game and of taste: its own public sphere. These people themselves chose the way, which led them to the margins of 'official' society.

Bohemian artists attracted a specific audience. This public included people with diverse marginal life experiences. There were people who had been released from prison and did not have a place to live. There were people of brutal psychology who could beat and kill. There were homosexuals and invalids. Around Café Saigon, lay people felt the air of criminality. Several Saigonees involved in the shadow economy were arrested, and there were those who were persecuted as hooligans or spongers. Café Saigon offered a space for all kinds of marginality that were considered to be an expression of freedom. The boundaries of Soviet 'normality' were expanded there. A certain undemanding humanism was flourishing there, a certain openness and support for the marginal – it was a performance of compassion and complicity.

Alhough there was no hierarchy among the *tusovka*'s groupings, each company was strictly stratified.[7] Discussing this internal hierarchy one informant observed:

> At the Saigon the sense of status was extremely important – this was part of Saigon socialisation ... One always had a sense of one's place, an understanding of who is lower, who is higher – are you a lieutenant or a colonel? It was a horrible male 'horn-fight', which compensated for something else.

Thus, EV called himself a 'commander' of the Saigon, and the local invalid, K, was humorously called a 'commissar'. Both were always present there, and are remembered as personified symbols of the place. K worked as a cleaner and always had a chance to get his free drink in this or that group. The system of rank functioned there as elsewhere. One visitor observed: 'I was just the Sancho Panza of T, whom I accompanied everywhere.'

The main principle of stratification in the *tusovka*, however, was not physical force, nor appearance or financial assets, but officially-neglected talent and particular social skills. Each group had a recognised male leader. One of the stratification criteria in this bohemian milieu was so-called 'word capital'. A knowledge of literature, of word play, a talent for story telling were highly appreciated and became pivotal for communication in the Saigon *tusovka*. Both female and male habitués from the younger generation recall those group leaders as irresistibly charming and attractive because of their beauty, knowledge, talent, artistic demeanour and aura of autonomy, independence and superiority. One of the younger Saigonees observed:

> I remember this generation of 1969 as a generation of titans. I had never seen such beautiful people, seriously I had never seen [such people] before. They were free people; I was a mother's boy and they were absolutely free guys, who disported themselves in a very different way. (LL)

However different they were from each other, the Saigonees were unified by the common marginality of their practices, which I describe more fully below.

Practices of the Café Saigon *Tusovka*

Doing 'Otherwise'

I use the term 'practice' here to describe the conduct that people of the Saigon *tusovka* considered 'decent'. I shall focus on the habitual practices that made a Saigonee acceptable in the *tusovka*. Among these practices are activities in the public and informal-public spheres of official employment, politics and leisure.

The idea of decent behaviour is important for every community. This concept has different meanings for different milieux and generations. People use this category to describe the appropriateness of certain conduct and its acceptability. So my question here is: which activities were considered decent and indecent in the Café Saigon *tusovka*?

The answer to this question can be summed up in the following generalisation. Among the Saigonees, it was considered indecent to follow the norms of the official public sphere – in work, in politics, in family life and leisure. *Doing otherwise* was the uniting principle of the diverse *tusovka* practices. Countercultural artistic work produced and performed by Saigonees was supplemented by their marginal positions in official society and their self-destructive practices of heavy drinking and (later) drug-taking. There were professional qualifications and statuses that were incompatible with the *tusovka*. Obviously, CPSU members, military officers, mothers with many children and people who did not drink could hardly be accepted there. Of course there were exceptions, but they only served to maintain the rule. Thus for example, one informant explained the shared hatred felt towards a former Saigonee as follows:

> The hatred felt towards MY by the Saigonees was caused by the fact that he started to be published in the official editions and became co-opted [by the establishment]. A Saigon person should on principle not publish his works and should not exhibit his pieces in official galleries. Because they were not published they came to the conclusion that it was indecent to be published. And indeed it was. (KG)

For its habitués Café Saigon was at the heart of their lifestyle. They spent their lives in this place – this was their job and their leisure, their public and their private. What were those marginal activities that were possible for the Café Saigon *tusovka*? For many, the venue was one they frequented for no other purpose than to obtain time and find a place away from the long arm of the state. It was a site for informal conversation, information exchange, drinking; a meeting place from which to set out for the underground concert, flat exhibition or philosophical seminar. In describing activities at the Saigon, one informant remarked:

> What were we doing there? We drank, but not only that. We exchanged information, we read books, visited home exhibitions, we shared information which had a limited circulation. Saigon activity was communication, it was a *tusovka*, which was useful for one's intellectual development – for sure, because discussion of literature and the arts in general issued there on a high level, which was quite unknown for me at the time. Besides, it was a place where speed of intellectual reaction was valued – mental sharpness was

> refined though this communication … The Saigon offered gymnastics for the intellect. But it was also hard drinking and ugliness. (NG)

This combination of freedom and self-destruction, excitement and disgust is typical of the ambiguous nature of the bohemian Saigon *tusovka*:

> But what is Bohemia if one thinks about it? It is a certain way of spending time … I am partly a bohemian myself, but when I see a so-called bohemian person I feel disgust and I shudder and I feel horror. You understand? Imagine some … I don't know – M. Glinka would spent his time in this way and not write his opera *Ruslan i Ludmila*. He would be simply a composer Glinka, a drunkard.

Information Exchange

One of the main modes of interaction in the *tusovka* was the exchange of information (both oral and printed), which functioned as a glue in the milieu. Information about underground events of an intellectual or artistic nature was disseminated through face-to-face contact. Such events included flat and club exhibitions by the vanguard artists, philosophical and poetic seminars, and underground poetry readings. The addresses of the open houses were given out in the café, and people met there to go to these private-public places.

During this period the information deficit was something intellectuals felt keenly. Literature- or word-centred communication was at the core of the Saigon *tusovka*. One informant (VU) remarked: 'One could never understand the cultural idiom of the Saigon if one could not understand what a book shortage meant for cultured people.'

The books and manuscripts that circulated in the *tusovka* came from different sources. One of these was family libraries. Many Saigonees came from the families of the intelligentsia, with large home libraries, some of them built up over several generations and containing editions that were not available publicly. In the state libraries, these books were preserved in special collections and were not available to ordinary readers.

Samizdat (self-made) production and exchange were common among all the generations of the Soviet intelligentsia owing to the book shortage and to rigid Soviet censorship. Even politically loyal citizens collected in their home libraries hundreds of printed or hand-written pages of poetry and prose (from Pushkin and Lermontov, certain passages of whose writings were officially considered pornographic, to Brodsky and Galich, who were considered anti-Soviet). This meant that almost every family could be persecuted for the dissemination of illegal (unpublished by Soviet publishing houses) literature. *Samizdat* literature circulated in the milieu mainly not in book form, but in the form of manuscripts retyped on private typewriters from books published abroad. There were also so-called *tamizdat* books (books published abroad), mainly obtained via foreign visitors to the city: tourists, students, researchers and diplomats.

Another source of illegal literature was the dissident milieu, with which the Saigonees were loosely connected. One informant recalled how in 1977 he read for the first time Solzhenitsyn's novel *Gulag Archipelago*. A couple brought him a book which they had borrowed for one night from another friend. Four friends – two couples – spent the night sitting round the dinner table and passing printed pages (in the form of a difficult-to-read fourth carbon copy) among themselves.

Many habitués of the Saigon had connections with the 'second' economy. They were engaged in the book or art business. They would first sell family libraries or their own books in order to obtain money, and then later buy the books again to fill their libraries. They did this via book-dealers who had their meeting-place also in the Café Saigon. Then there were those who were involved in the illegal trade of icons and pictures. Several of them could not escape arrest and spent time in prison for counterfeiting icons and selling them, for violating currency regulations, or for speculation.

Saigonees' employment Employment is one of the main indicators of one's social position. As for the Café Saigon people, their socio-economic status was low and unprestigious. This was mainly their deliberate decision – they wanted to have as few connections with the Soviet ranking system as possible. Involvement in the Saigon *tusovka* demanded a considerable amount of time, which was available to the jobless and to those with flexible working hours as well as to single people. Explaining why he wasn't able to visit the Café more often one informant remarked:

> … I worked because I had three kids. I had to work at my trade as a locksmith. Students, people of free professions or those who belonged to the so-called generation of watchmen and gas-boiler mechanics were regulars there.

Similarly, one female habitué observed:

> I stopped going to the Saigon when I started a regular job. Fixed working hours and duties prevented me from being at the Saigon at night – in the morning I had to be at my workplace strictly on time.

The café regulars were mainly people who were not employed permanently or full-time in the Soviet economy, and thus were not fully integrated into the major patterns of Soviet living. Moreover, their attitude towards normative Soviet career patterns was one of total rejection. Thus, for example, one Saigonee who worked as a librarian stated:

> I did not want to work there. There was no way to force me. I did not want to work anywhere, but at this place I categorically did not want to work. (NG, a writer)

In this case, in order to avoid a compulsory three-year work-term at the library as a young specialist the informant escaped to a mental hospital, hoping to get a medical certificate which would later help him to be discharged.

The Saigonees' earnings were not permanent ones, and they were obviously small and irregular. Students often lived on stipends, which many got on a daily basis from their parents. Actually, however, everything that was available at that time was cheap and their material needs were trifling.

Turning to the official job positions held by the Café Saigon people, among their occupations we find the following: librarians, guides, watchmen of all kinds, students. The phenomenon of the 'philosopher at the stoke-hole' is well-known in late-Soviet counterculture. The 'generation of watchmen and street cleaners' is commemorated in the songs of the famous Russian rock musician Grebenshchikov, the leader of the group Akvarium.

The job of watchman was considered the best available in the milieu. The following account describes this work:

> … this was the greatest of all Soviet sinecures … This was actually leisure for which one was paid 70 roubles a month. The schedule was one shift every four days. One just had to put up with some bosses and visitors, and after 6 p.m. one's own life started and lasted until morning, and one could do whatever one wanted – study, drink, have guests or just sleep. (EV)

The following is an extract from a personal diary in which one Saigonee describes his working life:

> I've worked since the age of 17, with breaks. I've worked in many places, where I was called a stevedore, a plumber's mate, a supervisor of watchmen, a boat-watchman, an assistant at the research centre, a typist. The main problem was getting to the workplace, if possible, on time … There were several explanations for such difficulty. The first was that I came home late and hadn't had enough sleep, the second was the fact that I didn't feel any material need to work until my mum died, since she had maintained me. The third reason was more specific: I refer to the night vigils with friends, wives and girlfriends, who had flexible work schedules and were not strictly tied to the beginning of the working day. By the mid-1970s many of them had graduated from college … many worked as watchmen or had settled in the gas boilers after finishing training courses … (EV)

Soviet law prosecuted people for sponging. Not working was a sufficient reason to get arrested. Every person had to be at some fixed workplace. At the end of the 1970s the KGB launched a campaign against sponging, and this bore on the life of the Café Saigon *tusovka*. Everyone was duly required to get a job for reasons of personal safety. The same café regular describes how he managed to find a job with the help of friends. Social networks, as ever, proved helpful from the point of view of survival:

> Half a year after being dismissed from my previous work I was taken to the militia station from the café where I was drinking. After I'd spent the night there a strict officer checked my labour book (I didn't have either a passport or a military pass, because the first was lost at another militia station and the second was taken from me by a major after we'd had a fight in the Metro) and made me sign an official declaration that I'd get a job in two weeks. It was the beginning of Andropov's anti-sponging campaign … Everything led to imprisonment under Article 191 of the Criminal Code … My acquaintance – the son of the famous NTS[8] member – helped me to find a job as nightwatchman at the Research Institute …

The job of watchman was a common one for Soviet pensioners and for bohemians. It was not demanding, did not require a qualification, and did not involve responsibility. It did, however, confer a great deal of autonomy. Saigonees used their working hours for reading and for writing their poetry and prose – they took typewriters there and worked at night. Saigon people were often dismissed from their jobs. There were numerous reasons for this: they missed the beginning of the working day, turned up drunk at the workplace, ruined the equipment, or just disappeared. But according to their own reports their supervisors were often understanding and tolerant towards young people. One informant (KT) confessed how he left his job:

'It is not that I was fired. I just got a feeling that it was time to leave the job so as not to test the patience of my boss.'

Thus we can see that for the bohemians their 'true' occupation was their creative work and the task of sociability in the Café Saigon milieu. Their official employment was only a disguise for the activities that allowed them to escape the article of the Soviet criminal code that condemned sponging.

Self-destruction, heavy drinking and drug use were commonplace in the Café Saigon *tusovka*. There are many possible explanations for these practices. Here, I conceive them as being a consequence of the lack of adequate perspectives for these people in Soviet society. The available strategies for self-expression were self-realisation in countercultural salons, and self-destruction through heavy drinking. Another was emigration; in the 1970s and afterwards many Saigonees emigrated on the basis of Jewish origins or other pretexts:

> At the Saigon we met, had the first drink and then went to someone's place – some salon or open house. So this was a meeting-place, where ZV always stood at the entrance smoking. It was 19.30 exactly. We didn't have money, but there was only a small fixed charge – it was 70 copecks. If you had 70 copecks you had a right to go to the Saigon. This was the price of a half-litre bottle of wine. And then things depended on how the situation unfolded.

Describing their habitual heavy drinking, Saigon habitués recalled how they had had their first drink when teenagers, and how pleasant it was for them to be drunk and how drinking was an essential element of communication patterns in the milieu. Intense heavy drinking served to differentiate Saigon people from the pro-dissident circle: 'My world view and interests were in a way continuous with theirs [dissidents'], but we differed in our attitude to alcohol. We drank, they did not' (KV). The alcohol was usually cheap and low-quality, and was consumed in large amounts with small snacks.

Drugs could easily be bought in the environment of the café – they were part of the everyday life of the place. The core group of bohemians in the 1970s, however, were not on hard drugs. Almost all of them tried drugs, but the majority preferred wine. Mass drug use came later, in the 1980s, with the last generation of Saigonees who were closely connected with rock culture (Cushman, 1995). Speaking about her attitude to drugs, KV observed:

> There were people in the circle who were on drugs. But I was not among them. It was politically wrong to be a drug-addict. One could be very dependent and used by the authorities for information if one needed a drug badly. And I knew from my childhood that they [people from the 'official' society] must not know anything about this [unofficial world].

One story about the circulation of drugs may serve to illustrate the regular routine. Once, two friends were looking round an empty apartment because the municipal authorities wanted them to move there. They found three ampoules of heroin there and decided to sell them immediately to their regular barman for three pints of beer each. They took the heroin to the bar, and when the other barmen asked 'What are you selling?', they answered that they were selling books. The deal was done. They obtained wine for the drugs.

The Saigonees' life stories contain plenty of cases of suicide attempts. Nowadays they recall these with amusement, as juvenile conduct that had been accompanied by feelings of 'general unhappiness, without real reason', reinforced by regular heavy drinking.

Sexual practices The Saigon is spoken of as being the site of a revolution in sexual behaviour (Rotkirch, 2000). In such milieux, the sexual ignorance of the wider society, which Kon (1995) has called 'sexophobia', was rejected in favour of the practising of sexual freedom. Partners were easily changed and exchanged there; marital or procreative sex was not the norm. The 'scripts' of sexuality were various: Temkina (*q.v.*, in this collection) characterises them as – *inter alia* – *romantic*, *communication-related* or *market-related*. One informant observed:

> There were no constant partners there. The whole atmosphere became erotic when women appeared. But no serious romances took place there.

Another informant offered another picture of his sexual youth as he experienced it in the Café Saigon:

> We were young and we impatiently looked for a sweetheart. Many of the serious affairs of my life started at the Saigon.

Promiscuous sex is regularly spoken of in connection with the milieu. But for many, sex was not an isolated pleasure – it was the culmination, so to speak, of communication between the sexes, which complemented drinking, the reading of poetry, the singing of songs. Sexual practices were combined with the consumption of alcohol, admiration for underground art, involvement in the illegal information exchange.

One Saigonee recalled how he visited the student dormitory to meet a well-known loose young woman, who told him: 'Excuse me, I am extremely busy now. I have a book here – they gave it to me just for a night. It is *Doctor Zhivago* by Pasternak.' At the time this Nobel Prize-winning novel was on the list of proscribed books. The man waited until she had finished reading and afterwards they made love.

Competition over women was part of the intra-group dynamics of the Café Saigon men, and the 'horn-fight' (as one informant called it) provided potential compensation for a lack of other achievements and for anxieties bound up with unfulfilled masculinity. For women, sex provided access to this basically male *tusovka*, which they appreciated as the setting for liberated sexual practices.

The Saigon *tusovka* included homosexuals. They were largely disliked in the Saigon as being too 'marginal' even for this place, although levels of sexual tolerance were gradually increasing. KV observed:

> I had a couple of gay friends. People from my circle always wondered why I communicated with them. They did not treat them badly – they just avoided them. Now it is different – now my friends and the homosexuals and gays are mutually supportive. Heterosexuals became more tolerant after that period.

Liberated sexual practices in the Saigon milieu also represented one dimension of the cultural protest taking place against Soviet public life, and Soviet norms of family life.

Politics and the Saigonees

There was no articulated political dissent among the habitués of the Saigon:

> There was no special political outlook … it was just a protest … a demonstration of being different from – were *are* different, not the same as those belonging to the formal Soviet structures. We do not want to have anything in common with them, neither in work, nor in leisure and consumption, nor in sexuality. (OL)

Nevertheless, the everyday practices of the Saigonees were clearly anti-Soviet. They were constructed as a negation of normative Soviet practices. The people of the Café Saigon had links with late-Soviet dissident groups, were involved in networks which disseminated anti-Soviet literature, and several times attempted collective street actions. One informant characterised his attitudes and conduct as pro-dissident. There was, however, a mutually-felt barrier separating the café people from the dissidents. One of the café regulars observed:

> There was a mutual rejection on the part of two groups belonging to the same generation. The traditional dissident was not a habitué of the Café Saigon. He considered this place disgusting. For the dissidents, Café Saigon people were dirty drunken idlers, though sometimes outstanding persons. Dissidents treated Saigonees with contempt as being bohemians – they thought it was necessary to do something [i.e. to be socially active] …

Despite this negative perception, almost every Saigonee could be charged with disloyalty towards the regime. Cultural protest too can be conceived of as political in a closed polity.

There were several stories relating to the political involvement of the Saigonees. One informant recalled how he wrote anti-Soviet leaflets with an older friend from the Saigon in his final year at school (1968). His father – a history professor – found this out and stopped it, by telling him that his friend could be a KGB *agent provocateur*. A Polish sociologist told another story. When he came to Russia for the first time at the end of the 1970s he was supposed to bring and disseminate religious literature, which was also forbidden at that time as being *tamizdat*. He did not have any acquaintances in Leningrad, but in Poland he was advised to go directly to the Café Saigon, where he would find the appropriate people, and this is what he did. Another story tells of how a family affiliated to the Café Saigon *tusovka* hid away a copy of the Dissident Archive (literature, self-published or published abroad, denouncing Soviet rule), but did not actually see this as a dissident act. The informant recalled how he had found out that the family had had the Archive under their sofa – the cat urinated on it, and his wife was comically shouting at this wretched cat which had destroyed the Archive. Still one more story reports the attempted public demonstration on the anniversary of the Decembrists' uprising of 1825. The Decembrists (the revolutionaries of noble origin) had a symbolic meaning for those who protested against Soviet authoritarianism. On 14 December 1975 a group of Saigonees went to Decembrists Square for a rally. On their way, many of them were arrested for being drunk or on a similar pretext.

One of my informants, K, recalled that he had had a photo of Solzhenitsyn on the wall of his room in the 1970s. His mother was afraid that visitors would recognise the famous dissident writer. The lady argued: 'It's OK with you. You will just be imprisoned for doing this, but I will be fired – it is much worse.' She relaxed when one of her distant relatives, looking at the photo, remarked: 'K is very like his grandfather, isn't he?'

As regards political attitudes in this milieu, I wish to emphasise that among the core Café Saigon *tusovka* there were no Communist Party members – or if there were, they preferred to conceal the fact. One informant summed up this attitude as follows: 'A simple feeling of prudence made me avoid membership of the CPSU.'

Saigonees report that they did not conceive their anti-Communist stand and their dissemination of anti-Soviet and illegal literature as political protest, for two reasons. One was the fact that, unlike the dissidents, they were not involved in open political action. The second reason was the general *unseriousness* of the *tusovka*, which rejected any kind of public demonstration of feeling and pretended to be distanced from vulgar politics. It was this lack of public political involvement which, they reflected, made it impossible for them to identify themselves with the laconic arguments of the earnest fighters for human rights:

> I was not afraid of any imprisonment, because I was a stupid, naïve and infantile man and never thought of such things. And I still think, just as I thought at that time, that I never participated in dissent. Well, there *were* cases – Jakir, Krasin, Sinyavskii, Daniel – but those people really did something. They disseminated literature, wrote something. I was loyal to the regime because I was not involved in any protest action and I wrote scripts for the mass performances. (K)

> I was not even arrested. And I think that was because they don't arrest chatterboxes such as we were. They knew that it was not serious. (G)

In spite of what they said, many Saigonees were considered political dissidents by the authorities. There are several accounts of the interrogation of Saigonees by the KGB. It was usual for the KGB to charge them with dissemination of illegal literature and to demand that they would inform on people from the Café Saigon milieu or on other suspicious contacts.

Café Saigon and the Public

In this section, I focus on perceptions about the Café Saigon *tusovka* held by residents of the city – ordinary Soviet people. Outsiders' attitudes clearly demonstrated the boundaries that existed between countercultural milieux and wider Soviet society. Most Leningrad citizens considered the Saigon dirty and ugly, even dangerous, and obviously unfriendly. The rules of decent behaviour in the Café Saigon *tusovka* can be reduced to one main principle: to have as few bonds with the wider society as possible, to be separated from it in as many ways as possible. On the other hand, ordinary Soviet people considered it indecent to visit the Saigon or to have contacts with the marginal *tusovka*:

> 'Decent' was [for EV's family and its milieu] quite a broad concept, including not only moral image. The charge of indecent behaviour, or the phrase itself, was quite heavy. It alienated the person and put them among a crowd which included all indecent people, who did not know either limits or tact, who did not have serious concepts of real life, who were ignorant and badly educated. In his youth [EV here speaks of himself, in the third person], V. was often on the border between decent and indecent in the opinion of his parents. (EV; unemployed poet, b. 1945)

Thus we can conclude that, for ordinary Soviet people, decent behaviour was incompatible with Café Saigon affiliation. One female informant vividly expressed popular attitudes towards the Café Saigon *tusovka*:

> I did not like to go to the Saigon – all my life, I don't know why. I got to know about the place quite early, when still at school ... Everybody knew that the other youth met up there – weird people, different people. I can't say in what sense ... Maybe my negative perception of the place was in the tradition of our upbringing, the upbringing of the positive kids living in this neighbourhood – that it is not a really a den, but something horrible, that something bad is coming together at this place. No, I don't mean anti-Soviet, not at all ... How to explain? ... It was something not good, not very clean. Now we use words such as drug-addict, drunkard, prostitute, God knows, something like that ... I was afraid of getting dirty there. (IT)

For this woman as for many others, the café was an indecent place, occupied by those on the margins of society.

Many informants recall how their relatives tried to isolate them from the bad influence of the Café Saigon milieu, that was addicting them to an immoral, dangerous lifestyle. Spouses and parents, militia and Komsomol tried to normalise the lifestyle of the people of this *tusovka*. All in vain: they were already marginal, and official sanctions did not work for them. Thus, NG recollects how his misbehaviour (absenting himself from lectures, drinking in the university, keeping bad company) was discussed and condemned at the Komsomol bureau. The bureau officials voted to fire him from the Komsomol, and were greatly surprised when they found out that he had never been a member of the Communist Youth Organisation.

Parents tried to prevent their children from going to Café Saigon; affiliation to the *tusovka* could cause family conflicts. One informant (KV) recalled: 'I brought my new friends home occasionally, but I never told my parents where I had picked them up. And I was afraid of my mamma. I always told her lies.'

The Café Saigon generation demonstrated their distance from their parents, the sixties generation. Informants described to me their complex attitude towards the older generation, who on the one hand were critical of Soviet officialdom but on the other were well integrated into Soviet society and often held official posts within it. Many Saigonees belonged to the well-established, high-status families of the Soviet intelligentsia, who were involved in leading hypocritical 'double lives'. On the one hand, they were well integrated into Soviet public life as university professors, lawyers, engineers, teachers, doctors. On the other, many of the parents were involved in the 'shadow-life' of this society: they read and disseminated *samizdat*, visited underground exhibitions, seminars and poetry events, and used the strategy of informal favours to get scarce goods.

One informant recalled that when she had entered school at the age of seven, her mother had warned her never to tell in school what she had heard at home, or else the whole family would be in trouble. The burden of hypocrisy lay heavily on future Saigonees. From 'family knowledge' and from *samizdat* they learnt the truth about the regime, and did not want to follow the hypocritical path of their parents. The double lives of the Soviet intelligentsia – the discrepancy between official-public and private-public spheres (Voronkov and Chikadze, in this volume) – were condemned by their children. Thus the younger generation constituted an 'alternative' segment of the public sphere, and 'lived by passion' (Rotkirch, 2000). Indicative in this respect is the confession of one informant, NG, whose family had belonged to the Soviet intelligentsia for three generations: 'To tell the truth I've always been ashamed of my family. I couldn't see how they could manage to live safely through the entire Soviet period and never suffer repression. It was strange and unbelievable. It meant that something was wrong about them.'

The research shows that the informal-public sphere, and the Saigon *tusovka* as a segment of it, had a strong influence on the wider society, and gradually penetrated it. The rock culture of the later generation of Saigonees was especially important here. By the end of the 1980s this had become an urban mass culture. One informant reflected:

> Komsomol leaders of the 1970s and '80s listened to Viktor Zoi and Boris Grebenshchikov, and gradually the second culture imposed its values on the first. It was a total offensive of the second culture on the first, which led to its overthrow. I would say that all the evils and virtues of Café Saigon are reflected in contemporary life. (OL)

Encounters with the Militia

Habitués of the Café Saigon often had encounters with the militia. Regular militia raids searched for drunks and drug-addicts – this was a common practice, a regular part of Saigon life. There were two main reasons for the Saigonees' conflicts with the militia: their sponging (joblessness), and their drinking and hooliganism. When they were threatened on the charge of sponging they managed to find a job in a couple of days. Regular raids in the Café Saigon area searched for speculators and drug-dealers. In recalling these encounters, however, respondents report that militia officers were often quite friendly towards drunkards, often letting them go and even helping them to reach their apartments. The fines were pretty low: official information about detention at the sobering-up stations was sent to the workplace and was supposed to bring about such sanctions as public condemnation by the work collective, or a cut in monthly bonuses. Such a record could be bad for one's career. The Saigonees did not care much about the latter, however. They were not oriented towards upward mobility; they tried to avoid work in the Soviet collectives, and their record of drunkenness and hooliganism in public places did not influence their lowly occupational status.

The Demise of Café Saigon: The Saigonees Today

> The Café still functioned, but fewer and fewer people of my age visited it. By the end of the 1970s there were a great many young people of a younger generation whom we regarded with contempt, and they probably reacted in the same way. (VT)

Café Saigon enjoyed almost three decades of history, and there were both similarities and certain differences between the *tusovka* generations. The similarities were structural: the people of the café belonged to the margins of society, both in the 1970s and the '80s. They can be looked upon as members of an underclass in late-Soviet society which had been consolidated by a common marginality and by the opportunities offered by the *tusovka* life.

The exodus from the Café Saigon had different causes. First, the first generation of café dwellers was forced out by the new Saigonees. These were the hippies and the young people of the Soviet rock generation. (They called themselves 'the people of the System'.) The 'Silver Age' poetry, the dissident literature, were outside their field of interest. They created their own urban art, which was not appreciated by the Saigonees of the 1970s, who considered it unprofessional, provincial and insufficiently refined.

As for the Saigonees of the 1970s who are the focus of this chapter, we can observe how, with the passage of years and the social changes it brought, they flew away from the Café Saigon territory. Some of them died; others emigrated; others again became integrated into the wider society, leaving their youthful protest behind. In certain cases their occupational status did not allow them to hold to a marginal *tusovka* – they became 'decent' people. Still others maintained their lifestyle, but more privately, without visiting this group territory any more. By the mid-1980s, the *tusovka* of the 1970s had finally dissolved.

When we consider the untimely demise of the notable Saigonees we have to recall Sergei Charnyj, who died in 1995 at the age of 39 from a drug overdose; Leon Karamyan, who died in 1990 in a car accident in the Crimea aged 34; and 'Kit', who was killed in a street fight in 1981 at the age of 32.

The democratic protests of *perestroika* brought many Saigonees back on to the city streets, which focused their minds better than any sobering-up station. Their future in post-Soviet times was different from their past. One informant quipped that it depended very much on the 'influence long-term vodka consumption and promiscuous sex had on one's organism'. Many managed to escape final self-destruction – more or less successfully, they developed coping strategies during the chaos of transformation. During the reforms, those Saigonees who had survived and had not emigrated followed different careers from before. Some of them became professionally successful, since the previously unsaleable alternative art now appeared to be marketable. Nevertheless many others remained part of a bohemian underclass. Those people who had been involved in the Soviet shadow economy later created their own small businesses. One such, for example, is now head of the Business Corporation of St Petersburg. Another famous Saigon figure, K, became completely marginal, though he had been expected to gain a new lease of life during the transition. Among the former

Saigonees we may mention EV, who felt so uncomfortable in the new climate that he did not step over the threshold of his apartment for almost ten years, although during those same years he had two collections of his poetry published. His best friend, KB, meanwhile, organised political theatre in the late 1980s and became a theatre director supported by the new democratic authorities of Leningrad. During the same period, former underground artists opened galleries and studios.

The life course of a Saigonee in transition depends on the capital resources they have left after their years of shadow-practices in the *tusovka*, which had presumed heavy self-destruction with only partial opportunities for self-realisation. These people had the experience of being autonomous from the state protection afforded the members of the Soviet collectives, and they knew that they had to rely exclusively on their own initiative as regards their achievements. When they had enough energy, and were not destroyed by habitual heavy drinking or by psychological self-destruction, they managed to find their place in the emerging post-Soviet order of the unsubsidised market and democratic openings. At the end of the 1980s they entered the emerging public sphere and stopped frequenting the Café Saigon.

By the end of 1991 the coffee shop had closed down and had been converted into a store selling toilets made in Italy, which the Café Saigon public saw as a symbol of the drastic social change taking place and of the vanishing of the Soviet underground. In the early 1990s there was much discussion in the mass media about the fate of the Café Saigon as a symbol of late-Soviet cultural protest: people wanted to commemorate their *tusovka*.

The story is not finished. In general, the stories of communities never come to an end. In this case, they live in the memories and destinies of the Saigonees. New stories will, I believe, be told about other places in the city that formed the sites of whatever freedom was enjoyed during the Soviet period. But the charm of the bohemian ambience, the joyful absurdity of bohemian practices, will never be as strong as they were in the *habitus* of the Café Saigon. Let me end this chapter with one of the last stories told about the Saigonees. What its moral may be I do not know. There is a true story told about EK, who at one time seemed to have become utterly lost. The last time (1994) I met him, near the central market-place, he was unrecognisable in comparison with how he had looked in his young years: he was drinking with the beggars and street-vendors at the church gate.

Now, rumour has it that he has won the LOTTO-bingo lottery and has changed his lifestyle completely.

Conclusion

The Café Saigon *tusovka* has been considered in this chapter as a segment of the informal-public sphere of late-Soviet society. The Saigon *tusovka* is characterised by ambiguous practices of, on the one hand, creative artistic production and, on the other, self-destruction. The key feature of the Saigon style is an absurdist humour, which symbolised the distance between the *tusovka* and the 'official' public life of Soviet society. The network of Saigonees did not constitute a Soviet collective. They were an ephemeral community of individuals united by everyday cultural protest against the officially-approved Soviet way of life. Opportunities for the *tusovka* opened out in the late 1960s. On the one hand, without a certain degree of political liberalisation, a bohemia is not possible. The *tusovka* as a social milieu presumed exclusionary communication in the informal-public sphere, either via face-to-face encounters or else mediated by the exchange of information in the form of books, *samizdat*, *tamizdat*, *magnitizdat*, gossip and anecdotes.

Representing as it did the cultural idiom of the late-Soviet public realm, the Café Saigon *tusovka* has no possibility of existence in today's Russia. Political liberalisation and market reforms drastically change social arrangements. With *glasnost*, it became possible to articulate one's political views, to fulfil oneself via creative art. As people now say: 'If you want to say that your President is stupid, just do it, wherever. You don't need a special place to do this.' Former Saigonees now have differing political orientations: the spectrum ranges from radical right to social-democratic. The marketisation and monetarisation of everyday life are not conducive to the Saigon lifestyle:

> In this society, people of the underclass and artists affiliated to them cannot survive, because even the cheapest coffee is pretty costly. If you don't have a regular salary then you either whirl about, which means that you don't have time for meditation and philosophy, or you are totally lost – you go to the bottom, psychologically and in psychiatric terms. (TK)

The character of bohemia is rapidly changing in the post-Soviet conditions, and these people are now dependent on sponsors.

Why was the Saigon, being a site of cultural protest, not suppressed by the Soviet authorities? Why was this informal-public sphere of *tusovki* allowed to exist? I have here tried to show that the Saigon *tusovka* was an essential part of the division of late-Soviet society, which included official and non-official (or informal-public) spheres. One informant put it as follows:

> The Saigon was not destroyed by the authorities, because you could show it off as the bride shows to the folk of the village the bloody sheet after the first marriage-night. It was meant to convince people that we also had freedom. It was part of the institutionalised double standard and hypocrisy. It was a telling demonstration of the Soviet type of freedom which said to the outside world, 'Look – there is a gang of dirty anti-Soviets who run their club in the very centre of town, just two steps from the Big House [the KGB building], and we are tolerant. We consider it normal.' (GG)

All the attitudes and practices that have been described above served to distance the Saigon *tusovka* from the 'official' Soviet public. The life-story analysis shows that the Saigonees did not develop any upward mobility strategies. They did not earn money, conform to ideological patterns, undertake family responsibilities; their lives were wasted, useless and self-destructive in the eyes of the wider society – they did not have any normative perspectives. The freedom they enjoyed was the freedom of marginal existence, marginal activities. This was the freedom of cultural protest against the Soviet way of life, freedom for partial self-realisation via underground art, freedom for psychological self-destruction. The people of the Café Saigon *tusovka* did not adhere to the usual schizophrenic 'double standard' upheld by regular Soviet citizens: their life was a comprehensive social protest, and there was no divergence between their lifestyle and their values of negation. Their group practices and their individual conduct united incompatibles. On the one hand, we can see here the first signs of the emergence of the independent individual who opposes the system in every possible way – especially at the symbolic level, and even at the level of body idiom. A Saigonee was an autonomous individual who rejected the normative social bonds of the Soviet collectives. On the other hand, this protest was combined with long-term experience of marginality and self-destruction. The longer a person of the Saigon *tusovka* was engaged in their marginal lifestyle, the more complete was their self-destruction, and the fewer the opportunities they had to exploit the new opportunities opened up by the reforms.

Notes

1 Viktor Voronkov and Elena Chikadze, in this volume, claim that late-Soviet society was characterised by a split between official-public and private-public spheres, which were arranged according to two different sets of rules: written law regulating behaviour in official-public settings, and common law regulating non-official settings. The informal-public sphere which I discuss here represents the same phenomenon as the private-public sphere so named by Voronkov and Chikadze. I focus here mainly on the spaces and rules of a particular version of this sphere – the life of the *tusovka*. A similar realm of shadowy non-official activities carried on in late-Soviet societies despite party-state control is discussed by Shlyapentokh, Ionin, Yanitskii and others using different terminology (Ionin, 1997; Ledeneva, 1998; Rotkirch, 2000; Shlyapentokh, 1989; Yanitskii, 1993).

2 Richard Stites, Thomas Cushman and Hilary Pilkington have already introduced the term '*tusovka*' to the Western reader. Cushman offers the following description: 'Common-sense interpretations trace the word tusovka from the verb "tasovat" meaning "to shuffle" as in "to shuffle cards". The slang usage of tusovatt'sia is "to gather", "to get together"' (Cushman, 1995, p. 226). Stites (in Cushman) defines *tusovka* as 'a hangout, crash pad or happening among hippies and rock fans'. This definition captures the essence of the *tusovka* as either 'a happening' or a specific place where those engaged in a similar type of collective action 'hang out' (Cushman, 1995, p. 365). Cushman writes: 'The word is used to describe a number of phenomena. First, it describes a group of people who are simply united by the common interest in something. The second sense of the word tusovka describes a discrete happening, event, or gathering ... I would like to argue that the idea of tusovka best describes the sense of collectivity which musicians feel as a result of their common activity as counterculturalists' (Cushman, 1995, p. 168). He continues: 'The very idea of tusovka connotes an alternative collective, a meeting of individuals who are united by common interest in something which is not part of the official Soviet world.' Pilkington (1994) applies this term to the youth culture of the 1970s and 1980s, relating it to such groups as the *stylyagi*, the *gopniki* and the *panki*.

3 Soviet toponymics, including the names of theatres, streets, plants, shops, restaurants and cafés, were not given arbitrarily, but had to be affirmed by the party-state bodies. The café I am discussing here was affiliated to the restaurant Moskva.

4 Housing conditions in Russia, in Leningrad in particular, have been very spartan for the majority of the population. At the beginning of the 1980s, 40 per cent of families lived in communal flats. The presence of multi-generational families brought about a literal absence of private space. One should add that there were very few sites for informal public communication either (Gerasimova, 1999).

5 In calling this breakfast 'modest' the narrator is here being ironic: three roubles is a large sum in this context.

6 The term 'atmosphere' is used here to signify the *habitus* of this place, which is difficult to categorise but which can easily be felt, smelt and recognised, both by insiders and outsiders.

7 I aim to explore the gender structure of the Saigon community in a future publication.

8 NTS: an anti-Soviet organisation with headquarters in the USA.

References

Boym, S. (1994), *Common Places: Mythology of Everyday Life in Russia*, Harvard University Press, Harvard, CT.

Cushman, T. (1995), *Notes from the Underground: Rock Music Counter-culture in Russia*, State University of New York Press, New York.

Gerasimova, K. (1999), 'Soviet Communal Apartments', in J. Smith (ed.), *The Concept of Space in Russian History and Culture, Studia Historica*, Helsinki, pp. 207–31.

Goffman, E. (1963), *Behaviour in Public Places: Notes on Social Organisation of Gatherings*, Macmillan, London.

Habermas, J. (trans. T. Burger) (1989), *The Structural Transformation of the Public Sphere: An Inquiry into the Category of Bourgeois Society*, Polity Press, Cambridge.

Ionin, L. (1997), *Svoboda v SSSR* [Freedom in the USSR], Fond Universitetskaya kniga, St Petersburg. [In Russian.]

Kon, I. (1995), *The Sexual Revolution in Russia: From the Age of the Czars to Today*, The Free Press, New York.

Ledeneva, A. (1998), *Russia's Economy of Favours: Blat, Networking and Informal Exchange*, Cambridge University Press, Cambridge.

Levada, J. (ed.) (1931), *Prostoj Sovetskij Chelovek* [The Simple Soviet Man].

Pilkington, H. (1994), *Russia's Youth and its Culture*, Routledge, London and New York.

Rotkirch, A. (2000), *The Man Question: Loves and Lives in Late 20th Century Russia*, Research Report No. 1, Department of Social Policy, University of Helsinki, Helsinki.

Rozhanski, F. (1996), *Hippy Slang: Materials for the Dictionary*, European House, St Petersburg/Paris. [In Russian.]

Shchepanskaya, T. (1993), *Simvolika molodezhnoj kultury* [Symbolism of Youth Culture], Nauka, St Petersburg. [In Russian.]

Shlyapentokh, V. (1989), *Public and Private Life of the Soviet People: Changing Values in Post-Stalin Russia*, Oxford University Press, New York.

Stites, R. (1992), *Popular Culture: Entertainment and Society since 1900*, Cambridge University Press, Cambridge.

Yanitskii, O. (1993), *Russian Environmentalism: Figures, Facts, Opinions*, Mezhdunarodnye otnoshenija Publishing House.

PART 3

Exile, Migration and Adapting to Social Change

10 Living the Life: Exile in the Experience of the Polish Intelligentsia

JOHN A. JACKSON
*Trinity College Dublin,
Ireland*

Introduction

Political disturbance, invasion, repression, deportation and war are the occasions for interrupted life trajectories in which the experience of separation from family, friends and homeland are common. In looking at the lives of a segment of the Polish intelligentsia interviewed by the author in 1994, one sees that exile appears as a frequent component of the experience over three generations. The interviews with this group of people, most of whom reached adulthood during or shortly after the Second World War, explore their grandparents' and parents' experiences and the effect these had in shaping the lives of the respondents, who were all now moving towards the end of their own lives. The life-history analysis reveals the significance of exile and separation in the lives of those Poles who were interviewed, and also the burden of family history relating to the experiences of their forebears carried by the succeeding generations. The chapter explores the sense of exile in relation to nationalism and the maintenance of national identity, and the relationship to an image of the nation that may contrast with the particular situation of the state at any particular time. Drawing on some of the ideas developed by Benedict Anderson in his book *Imagined Communities*, the chapter develops the theme of identity as a social construct and elaborates its significance for an understanding of ethnicity and nationalism.

Exile

The experience of three generations of the Polish intelligentsia suggests that as a result of exile and dispersal this population, more than most, had to develop the 'imagined community' of the lost Polish nation and homeland. Thus Poland, the nation and the home place, is invested with salience in the ethnic identity of Polish people and in the meaning of Polishness as it is constructed by exiles from a homeland which they may never have seen or from which they have been separated for many years. The condition of exile gives a particular salience to the homeland and the home place. Clearly, political exile was a not uncommon fate of intellectual Poles in the past, and the experience touches in some way all of these biographies.

The experience of exile challenges the ascriptive basis for personal identity that rests in belonging to a particular place where a sense of membership in family and community gives external and objective markers for the definition of the self. The exile is in a true sense a person 'without qualities' unless others are found who can recognise the distinctive location and milieu to which the person belongs or to which they owe their allegiance. Where boundaries have been redefined, as frequently occurred in Europe as the result of invasions and treaties and partitions, many found themselves geographically and politically alienated from their original identity and national affiliation. As Poland moved eastwards after the First World War many Poles were stranded in the newly German territory in former western Poland, and equally after the Second World War the movement of Poland westwards left former Polish territory in Lithuania once again part of a new national definition.

The exile may be a voluntary migrant who has left home for economic or other reasons and is living abroad. Their exile is self-imposed and they can return if, and when, they wish. The political exile, by contrast, is a forced migrant deliberately exported and sent to a place of exile. Within Russia the place of exile for dissidents frequently was Siberia and many Poles subject to Russian rule experienced this destination. Equally, Poles might be sent to other parts of Russia during either the Imperial or the Soviet period at the whim of the authorities at the time. It was Lord Acton who wrote that 'exile is the nursery of nationality' (Acton, 1967), and certainly the history of Poland supports this sense that absence, particularly enforced absence, encourages the nationalist sentiment.

One should in any case be cautious in linking the concepts of nation and state too closely together. Territorial boundaries may correspond at one point in time to the nation, but frequently they do not and if they change it does not mean that the nation disappears also. It may be maintained by the diaspora. Hugh Seton-Watson underlines this point in his definitions:

> A state is a legal and political organisation, with the power to require obedience and loyalty from its citizens. A nation is a community of people, whose members are bound together by a sense of solidarity, a common culture, a national consciousness. (Seton-Watson, 1977, p. 1)

In an interesting discussion of nationalism, Bernhard Giesen has suggested that the nations of central and eastern Europe are better thought of as 'cultural nations' in contrast with the 'state nations' of Western Europe and the new 'territorial nations' of Africa which do not have even their ethnic and cultural sense of homogeneity (Giesen, 1998, p. 6).

Poland offers a good example of a shift from a civic-territorial model of the nation to an ethnic one, though in its case the periods when Poland could be considered an autonomous territory were few enough. The earlier, loosely-defined Polish Commonwealth and the gentry democracy of the sixteenth century which enfranchised every member of the gentry (*szlachta*) was the basis for the concept of a nation with a shared consciousness among this group of large and small landholders. However, it excluded the peasants who, as Millard indicates, 'remained heterogeneous in language and religion, while their economic lot was one of virtual enslavement in conditions of serfdom' (Millard, 1995, p. 1). Torn by conflicting interests among the aristocracy and the *szlachta* who courted support alternately from Prussia and Russia, the Polish state ceased to exist in 1795 following the Confederation of Targowica which was seen as a final sell-out by the now-discredited aristocracy. The Partition of 1792 and the abortive Kościuszko Uprising of 1794 forced many to go into exile, where they continued to foster their work for the resurrection of the state inspired by the general patriotic fervour that had characterised the last days of the Republic (ibid., p. 108). Some of these nationalists from among the petty gentry and emerging Polish intelligentsia had hoped for Napoleon's help in establishing the Polish state, but the failure of his campaign was to be the last hope for the maintenance of an independent Polish state for the next 100 years. Thus began the long period of exiled Poles, or Poles existing within the territorial space controlled by other nationalities, still carrying forward the idea of a Polish state. The seeds of a strong sense of nation were nurtured after the further defeat of the 1863 uprising. Inspired by the European romantic tradition and a community of language, it became a spiritual movement closely identified with the church that justified the continued struggle for independence.

As Weclawowicz notes:

> Between 1795 and 1919 the development of Poland experienced three different conflicting traditions. Prussian absolutism overlapped with an increasing Germanisation tendency and with economic integration of connected territories to the rest of Prussia. In the Austrian monarchy, Poles adapted to the relatively liberalised parliamentary monarchy, and in the Russian part, people were the subject of Tsarist autocracy with the eastern style of executive power. (Weclawowicz, 1996, p. 8)

However, as a result of the historical causes that accounted for the rise of the intellectual tradition, the Polish state was based on the values of individualism together with the glories of an aristocratic past. As the distinguished sociologist Jan Szczepanski wrote in 1963:

> It must be stressed that the Polish way of life is that of gentry and of the gentry related intelligentsia, and that both the upper and lower middle classes of entrepreneurs nourished another set of values which were closer to those of the Western middle class but were not recognised in Poland as dominant. The peasantry and the working class, living more within the 'folk culture' than within the 'representative culture', had still different sets of values and 'patterns of concerns'. (Szczepanski, 1963, pp. 150–1)

As Szczepanski indicates, the values of the Polish intelligentsia built on such values as 'faith, honour, freedom and intellectual or artistic excellence' were 'more valued than the set of middle class values such as the prestige of work and work achievement'. Somewhat like the people of the Irish diaspora, Polish emigrants 'have shown that, given the setting of Western cultures, they are capable of the same achievements and excellence [as] any other ethnic group but the ethos of tradition made such success very difficult at home' (ibid., p. 150).

Case Studies

This chapter draws on transcripts from a set of interviews that took place with members of the Polish intelligentsia in December 1993. Those interviewed included a former political leader, a doctor, two engineers, two former ambassadors, a teacher of languages, a journalist and an editor. Three of the nine were women. The selection of those interviewed was necessarily limited by the need to find people who could speak English, since I do not have sufficient Polish and was very limited in the time available to me. Through the help of Polish research colleagues a selection was made of those who had been adult or were coming to adulthood during the Second World War. It turned out that they represented two distinct groups: those who came from the families of intellectuals which had remained part of the intelligentsia whatever vicissitudes life threw at them, and secondly, those who in their own lives had been drawn into the intelligentsia from a peasant background as a result of a combination of experiences: the Army, the Communist Party, education.

These interviews were intended to allow a typification of this group in Polish society and to set the transitions in the society against the background of the experience of these individuals. In addition to their own lives the interviews explored the lives of their parents and grandparents in order to situate their experience solidly within the framework of their own public and private social formation in Polish society. These three-generational life histories therefore represent a strand in biographical methods different from and complementary to the well-established tradition of autobiographical competitions in Poland and elsewhere. The life stories and intergenerational accounts allow one to see at an individual level the effect of some of the transitions, structural changes and transformations that are taking place in the wider society. It is precisely because we know quite a lot about the social structure at a macro level that we can with confidence attempt to fit the experience of individual lives into this matrix. These individual lives are lived out against a background which gives salience to their field of action and serves both to constrain and to enable the strategies that can be adopted in given times and places. Whatever may now be rejected of Marx, he was surely right in his assertion that '[m]en make their own history, but they do not make it as they please; they do not make it under circumstances chosen by themselves ...' (Marx, 1979, p. 103).

In an earlier article I have considered the significance of nationalism and education as part of the experience and formation of this group (Jackson, 1996). In this chapter I want to begin to focus on the question of exile and the importance it had in the lives of this group. It is not uncommon in descriptions of the intellectual milieu to find that they are the group of people in society who have a wide range of international contacts and are conversant with foreign languages and with travel. However, rather less stress is placed on the extent to which this is made necessary by their choice and circumstance of making public issues part of their private lives (see e.g. Kennedy, 1990). In this small sample, not only in their own lives but in those of the preceding generations, exile and forced and voluntary absence feature strongly as part of their experience.

The three oldest people in my sample show how pervasive these experiences can be. The first is an engineer who was born in 1913 in Kiev. His mother's father had been exiled to Siberia and had eventually been able to establish himself in the Ukraine, where he had set up a sugar factory. At the end of the Second World War the new Communist regime demanded that the factory be reactivated, but his mother was unable to do this, since her husband had left to join the Polish Army and her brother was unwilling to take on this responsibility. Forced to escape this situation she left with my respondent, then a boy of four, for Kiev, where they stayed until 1922, during which time she managed a shop. They were then able to travel to Poland, where he eventually joined the Polish Air Force and became qualified as an aircraft engineer. He had then fought in the 18-day war against the German invasion of Poland in 1939 and had managed to escape with his crew to Romania, where they were imprisoned in a camp. After a few months he managed to escape and, through the help of the Polish embassy in Bucharest, get on a ship to Beirut and then Marseilles, from where he eventually got first to Casablanca and then to Gibraltar and eventually Liverpool. There he became the only Polish officer in a group of about forty Polish airforce personnel and spent the remainder of the war involved in the maintenance of aircraft engines. After the war he came back to Poland, landing in Gydnia with a number of other returnees. However, as a member of the Polish Air Force in exile his status was rather uncertain in Poland at that time and he tended to be treated with some suspicion, especially when several attempts to get him to join the Communist Party had failed. After a period working at an aircraft factory in the south of Poland he came back to Warsaw, where he worked for the electric company as a manager and then was put in charge of the first district heating scheme:

> I was in charge of district heating plans and distribution and the first job was to put in a line from the power station to the Palace of Culture. I had no pass. I could only get as far as the gate, no further. It was a new industry. I knew I could be imprisoned any moment if anything went wrong.

Eventually, after retirement, he spent a period of five years as an engineering consultant in India before returning to Warsaw where he now acted as a consultant to an American company.

The second case is of a woman from a Jewish family whose grandfather had been sent to Siberia after the 1864 uprising in Poland. When telling me the story she showed me a picture of her grandmother 'who is in a black dress because Polish women in 1864 after the fall of the uprising always wore black dresses'. After describing her father, who was a political cartoonist, she went on to describe her mother who was, she claimed, the first woman with a medical diploma in Russia. She had obtained the qualification in Switzerland because women were not allowed to study medicine in Russia. After sitting second diploma examinations in St Petersburg she moved to Vilna (Vilnius), where my respondent was born. In her own life, in 1940, after she was married to a journalist and pregnant with her first child, she travelled with her husband and a small group of Jews to Sweden. From there they then went across the Soviet Union to Vladivostok and eventually to the United States, where they were helped by a group of Polish socialists and an American Jewish organisation. She trained there as a social worker and finally returned to Poland in 1947.

A third example is of a woman who was active in the insurrection in Warsaw near the end of the war and was imprisoned for much of 1945 in SS camps. As a military prisoner she was in Lansdorf camp for women near the Belgian border, from which she was transferred to a camp at Verona in Italy, and after the fall of Italy she was released by the Allies to a displacement camp in England. After returning to Poland at the end of the war she became a writer and editor.

Dislocation

Exile, however, takes many forms. All the people in the sample had suffered some form of dislocation in relation to their homeland as the result of the two World Wars. In some cases the movement made by individuals involved not physical separation but social transformation. In three cases, one could describe the individuals as among the 'achieved' intelligentsia because they had moved socially from the peasant class to the intelligentsia, often with the assistance and support for education of the Communist Party and the military in which they served. What is of greater interest, however, is that they all came from backgrounds in the peasantry that were in some respects atypical, in that they carried elements either of aristocratic values or of those of nationalistic independence and resistance. In one case there was an association with a local estate and the landlord class that ran it. In another the possession of a small landholding had given the family some status in the area. In another instance the informant's mother had been involved as a child in the school strike of 1906 in the western part of Poland in an attempt to have the Polish language restored to the school system. These all suggest links, however tenuous, with the national tradition and with the larger society in which it was carried by the intelligentsia. The most striking features of the three-generational histories covered by the sample were, on the one hand, the constant exposure of each generation to invasion, danger, enforced exile and risk of death and, on the other, the way in which nationalism informs the history of their own, their parents' and their grandparents' lives.

These cases illustrate the theme of exile caused particularly by the events of the Second World War but in fact replicating experiences of the preceding generations. This theme is a common feature of many Polish autobiographies as a result of occupation and repression by one or other of the invading powers from West or East. It was rare for it to be entirely voluntary, but it was more often the consequence of arbitrary circumstance: being in the wrong place at the wrong time, belonging to the group or persuasion that was currently opposed to or repressed by the occupying regime. The grandfather of another of my informants, having qualified in law at Warsaw University, was as result of his political activity given the option of working either in Siberia or in the Caucasus Mountains among the Tartars. The latter was considered to be especially dangerous because Russians used to be killed by Tartars. The first lesson he learnt was to say 'I am Polish, not Russian' in Tartar. 'My grandfather', the informant recalled, 'went through a real paradigm shift because he survived Tsarist exile in the Caucasus, full freedom in the state of Azerbaijan and was then imprisoned by the Red Army after the Revolution.' However, as this informant shows, there may well be advantages to be gained from being an outsider. After her husband had been imprisoned and the Communist Republic of Azerbaijan had been formed, her grandmother was defined as 'the enemy of the nation':

> She and her children might have been killed but because she was a member of the Polish intelligentsia she could type and speak French, English, Russian and German. So a month after the main executions she was employed at the

first Ministry of Foreign Affairs because there was no one else who could do the secretarial job.

In some cases accident plays a part in defining the exile, and for those born as children away from home, identity with the nation is a legacy from parents or grandparents. Clearly, the homeland that is projected may no longer remain or may no longer readily recognise the romanticised or ideologically unpalatable past. Return from exile may therefore be hazardous when it is a return to a homeland that the individual has not known and experienced him- or herself. Even when such an individual belongs to the generation that properly can make a return, the national consciousness and identity to which they aspire may have been transformed by successive rewritings and rationalisations of past events, including the causes of their own exile.

Benedict Anderson (1991) has suggested that the homeland becomes, during periods of exile, an 'imagined community' that is part of the survival and reconstitution of the individuals' identity. Within the three generations I have been considering, the homeland has been subjected to invasion and possession by foreign powers. Indeed, it was only in the period between the two World Wars that Poland became an autonomous state, and even this was constrained by boundary issues to the West and to the East. Such a situation is a reminder of the fact that exile, as separation from a desired sense of homeland, can also occur when it is caused by the occupation of territorial boundaries by others rather than by the physical relocation of exiled individuals and families.

Conclusion

These examples of exile among a group of Polish intellectuals illustrate the significant part that may be played in the construction of nationalism by the factor of forced or voluntary exile and absence. Poland was, throughout the late nineteenth and early twentieth century, a source country for the great transatlantic migrations to North America. Although Thomas and Znaniecki's famous work (1918–20) was a consideration of Polish peasant experiences in Europe and America, some of the same features affect those who represented themselves as the intellectual conscience of Polish society. The potential and the reality of separation from the homeland come to be a more or less permanent marker on those who remain to claim and guard the national heritage, culture and history. In a long history of periods of occupation or control by an external power, the preservation of the idea of the nation against the existence of the state has often necessitated what one respondent called a 'constant ambiguity' in the position of the intellectual in Polish society. This corresponds closely to the sense and reality exile had for those who for greater or shorter periods were excluded altogether.

References

Acton, J.E.E.D. (1967), *Essays in the Liberal Interpretation of History*, University of Chicago Press, London.

Anderson, B. (1991), *Imagined Communities: Reflections on the Origin and Spread of Nationalism*, Verso, London.

Giesen, B. (1998), *Intellectuals and the German Nation*, Cambridge University Press, Cambridge.

Jackson, J.A. (1996), 'Nationalism and Education in the Experience of Polish Intellectuals', in L. O'Dowd (ed.), *On Intellectuals and Intellectual Life in Ireland: International, National and Comparative Contexts*, Institute of Irish Studies and the Royal Irish Academy, Belfast and Dublin.

Kennedy, M. (1990), 'The Constitution of Critical Intellectuals', *Studies in Comparative Communism*, vol. 23, pp. 281–303.

Marx, K. (1979), 'The Eighteenth Brumaire of Napoleon Bonaparte', in K. Marx and F. Engels, *Collected Works*, Vol. 11, Lawrence & Wishart, London.

Millard, F. (1995), 'Nationalism in Poland', in P. Latawski (ed.), *Contemporary Nationalism in East Central Europe*, Macmillan, London.

Seton-Watson, H. (1977), *Nations and States: An Enquiry into the Origins of Nations and the Politics of Nationalism*, Methuen, London.

Szczepanski, J. (1963), *Polish Society*, Random House, New York.

Thomas, W.I. and Znaniecki, F. (1918–20), *The Polish Peasant in Europe and America*, 5 Vols, University of Chicago Press, Chicago, IL.

Weclawowicz, G. (1996), *Contemporary Poland: Space and Society*, UCL Press, London.

11 Biographical Continuities and Discontinuities in East–West Migration before and after 1989. Two Case Studies of Migration from Romania to West Germany

ROSWITHA BRECKNER
Vienna University of Economics and Business Administration, Austria

Introduction

In general, migration is considered to be an experience of discontinuity which, on a biographical level, is expected to have a relatively deep impact on the subject's sense of life-continuity. In any event, it appears to represent a challenge to the continuation of 'life as usual' on the basis that things can be taken for granted and that they will work in the way one is used to (Schütz, 1972). From a postmodern perspective, this characteristic of the experience of migration and its biographical impact is unexceptional (Bauman, 1996). According to this line of thinking, every member of a postmodern society is experiencing radical changes all their life, particularly nowadays following the historical upheavals of the last fifteen years. Migration is no longer considered to represent an outstanding experience of discontinuity in life. Rather, it seems to have become part of the normality of (post)modern biographies (Fischer-Rosenthal, 1995, 2000) such that there is no longer a relevant distinction to be made between biographies with a migration background and those without. Hardly anybody, so the argument goes, is 'fixed' any longer in one milieu, social stratum or culture all their life. All of us undergo, during the course of our lives, more or less dramatic changes *vis-à-vis* our positions within changing family and work systems, the professional sphere, social strata, generational systems and, in the case of major societal upheavals, the whole institutional system and organisation of a society. In other words, the experience of biographical change has, even in its radical forms, become common. On the other hand – and this will be the main assumption of this chapter[1] – different experiences of biographical discontinuity are shaped differently, and retain their specific characteristics and impact on the processes of constructing biographical continuity. In this respect, migration can still be regarded and described as a particular experience occurring on a biographical level, even though migrants share, in a very general sense, the experience of radical change, and the effort to construct continuity, with all those undergoing different forms of biographical discontinuity.

But what is it that makes migration a specific experience? First of all, the actual process of migration affects different life-spheres at the same time. These have to be rearranged synchronically in an actual present and near future: finding a new job; undergoing a re-evaluation of one's achieved professional competence and experience; rearranging one's connections with the social security systems in the different countries; finding a new flat with new neighbours; listening to and speaking a different language; rearranging relations with relatives and with old and new friends owing to them living either nearer or further away than before; adapting to different climatic conditions and new local cultures while reshaping one's relationship to the old ones left behind; and so on. The list could be extended. These changes are usually interrelated and require immediate (re)action and restructuration.

The migration process does not, however, end with the accomplishing of these changes. Rather, they are supplemented by biographical transformations affecting the extended past and future in diachronic time, which generally become visible only in a long-term perspective. They relate, in most cases, to more implicit or latent levels of the structuration of biographies. As we shall see later from the case studies, in these East–West migration biographies it was mainly the embeddedness of the biographies in historical time, connected to the more generational family history as well as to the history of the collective or milieu to which the subjects were related, which was at stake at the time the interviews were conducted in the early 1990s – in some cases twenty years after the actual move had taken place.

Finally, for the *biographical* meaning of a migration, the interrelation between all these changes occurring in different time perspectives is of specific interest. A present-oriented restructuration, for example the restructuring of a professional career owing to migration, can be connected with a restructuring of those parts of one's life which relate to the distant past, for example by the reconstruction of one's place in a generational family history in an attempt to construct new 'life-messages'.[2] Conversely, a structural change in the biographical construction changes also the immediate orientations with which discontinuities brought about by the migration process are handled. In this perspective, the experience of discontinuity in the actual and immediate process of migration is, generally speaking, embedded in biographical structures developed in a long-term perspective. The opposite is also true: the long-term biographical structures are moulded by present experiences of continuity or discontinuity. Thus, the question of what in a biography is continued and what is changed in the course of a migration process has to be reconstructed on different levels and as interrelated processes of discontinuity and continuity.

In migration processes, however, 'continuity' of everyday life is no longer something to be taken for granted as it has been before. As a result, the experience of migration can, in general, be considered as challenging the sense of continuity. At the same time, every migration is embedded also in processes of continuation. Thus, the question is not so much whether a migration *is* a discontinuing or a continuing life event, but in what way the continuity and discontinuity of biographically relevant aspects, practices and patterns *interact* within a migration process by reference to an actual situation as well as to a long-term perspective. Furthermore, this question seems to be an empirical one, in the sense that, in most cases, the relationship between biographical continuity and discontinuity in migration processes cannot be derived from the type of migration (e.g. work migration, forced migration, marriage migration). In every one of these migration types, the meaning of migration as a biographically continuous or discontinuous event and context of experience can vary greatly, and also change over time.

In presenting the cases of two people who have moved from Romania, as country of departure, to the Federal Republic of Germany, as the country of residence at the time of the interview,[3] I would like to show two similar, but at the same time structurally different, patterns of experiencing and constructing biographical discontinuity and continuity in connection with migration. In both cases, the meaning of the migration as a discontinuous or continuous biographical event has changed after 1989, when the respective biographies were restructured in the context of changing societal and historical scenarios. First, however, in order to establish more clearly the (changing) contexts of the two biographies to be presented, I shall briefly characterise the conditions for East–West migration during the Cold War and after 1989, focusing in particular on Romania and West Germany.

The Context: Migration from the 'East' to the 'West' of Europe before and after 1989

Migrants coming from Eastern European countries to West Germany before 1989 had to cope, in their everyday lives, with the crossing of a polarised system-border. This border not only divided countries, but had drawn a historically new boundary between the 'East' and the 'West' of Europe, quite impermeable following the events of 1956 in Hungary, 1961 in the GDR, 1968 in Czechoslovakia and 1980–81 in Poland. This new boundary manifested itself in a number of specific aspects of East–West migration, especially in the last two decades before 1989. In most cases, there was no possibility of reversing the migration and returning to the home country (Poland and the former Yugoslavia were exceptions). Even tourist visits were complicated, and in many cases impossible. Abrupt discontinuation of the contexts left behind is, then, a typical aspect of these migration processes. The actual discontinuities brought about by the specific circumstances of the migrations were, nevertheless, experienced differently, and could, as we shall see from the case studies, have different biographical functions.

Another characteristic of migration from a 'communist' to a 'capitalist' society, from one polarised system to another, can be seen in the ambiguous status of Eastern European migrants in the country of arrival, specifically in West Germany. In the public sphere in West Germany, these migrations were perceived as indicative of a refusal to live under 'communism', and Eastern European migrants were used as a welcome political instrument in the ideological battlefield of the Cold War. It was possible for these migrants to ask for political asylum and to receive German citizenship if it was wanted. On the other hand, they were regarded as 'aliens', even as suspicious persons who might have been 'infiltrated' by communism. For them to have articulated anything positive in connection with their life before migration, or to have expressed feelings of mourning and loss, would have increased this suspicion. Eastern European migrants were expected to be happy to live in the 'free' part of the world. They were not encouraged to communicate the complex social and biographical contexts in which the migration took place.[4]

Since there were only a limited number of migrants to West Germany from the different East European countries before 1989 (except, again, from Poland and Yugoslavia), these migrants found only very small and scarce ethnic networks or communities.[5] As a result, in everyday life they had to cope individually with emerging questions of group identity or belonging and, furthermore, had to construct for themselves a meaningful context for understanding their past in the light of their new experiences, while at the same time developing new orientations regarding the future.

With the fall of the Iron Curtain in 1989 the migratory situation changed almost overnight, creating new possibilities for East–West migrants. The enhanced possibility of their restoring regular contact with their countries of origin, even the theoretical possibility of their relocating there, shaped new points of reference for biographical orientations, especially for those who had arranged their lives around the perception of an impermeable and unchangeable border between the places where they lived before and after migration. Concomitantly, new constellations arose for the (re)interpreting of past experiences and periods of life in a changing present and future.

At the same time, migrants from Romania especially were confronted in West Germany with a changing image of their nationality. They were no longer perceived as political refugees, living proof of an inhuman system from which they had escaped. After 1989 they were instead perceived increasingly as 'foreigners', and even discriminatorily labelled 'the gypsies of Europe'. At the minimum, they were confronted with the question of whether, as Romanians, they belonged to Europe, or instead represented the 'Balkans' as the negative 'other side' (Todorova, 1997), with all its connotations in the Western part of Germany and Europe of being 'uncivilised' and even 'barbaric'.[6] Negative pictures of 'the East' appeared again in public life. Now, however, they were no longer formulated, as they had been during the Cold War, through metaphors of dichotomy between two economic and political systems but, increasingly, in terms of differences based on cultural, ethnic and national categories. The pictures used now referred to historical contexts, indicating that, along with the changes of 1989, historical images of and preconceptions about 'the East' had reappeared. The division of Europe therefore remained a relevant context of experience, but after 1989 was expressed in a different way.

Now, cultural and ethnic rather than political and economic differences were stressed. In nearly every biographical interview which I conducted, unprompted self-location in conflictual historical and national contexts, especially those involving the two World Wars, was a relevant issue. Even though the reference to 'history' has different meanings and functions in the biographical constructions (Breckner, 1997), it is remarkable that in most cases it related to the present perspective of (re)constructing the biography, whereas contradictions and conflicts between the societal systems of 'capitalism' and 'communism' were mentioned only in narratives which referred to past perspectives. They were no longer a point of reference or frame for the present organisation of biographical self-presentations. I shall now examine two different migration biographies in order to show how these conditions operate concretely.

The Changing Meaning of Migration in Two Case Studies

In both of the presented cases, who left Romania in 1970 at the ages, respectively, of 17 and 19 and whom I interviewed in 1993–4, the migration experience was a relevant point of reference for the presentation of the whole biography. The meaning of that experience, however – the connected biographical contexts, the historical and family backgrounds, as well as the strategies employed to construct biographical continuity – differed between the two cases. In the first case, the migration constituted a turning point which severed former life-strands on the manifest biographical level, but, on the other hand, created a previously-disrupted continuity with hidden aspects of the family history. In the second case, the migration had served to reinforce the subject's professional career as the main biographical strand at the time it had actually occurred, but at the time of the interview it represented for him its interruption and even a plunge towards existential discontinuity, in connection with a now-conscious perception of his family and collective history, whose continuity was endangered by war, persecution and extermination.

Romica Brasovean: Discontinuity as an Opportunity for Working on Hidden Continuities[7]

Romica Brasovean was born in 1953, the eldest son of Romanian parents living in a multicultural Transylvanian town.[8] After participating, as a 17-year-old adolescent, in a sporting event in West Germany in 1970 he refused to return to Romania, leaving his country in a risky and dramatic act of flight, in the knowledge that he would not for a long time have face-to-face contact with his parents or see again everything that he had left behind. At that time, migration for him meant an act of liberation, an escape from a family conflict, which had taken the form of fighting between an adolescent son and his father. The nub of this conflict was Romica's objection to being forced to go to a Romanian boarding school in a small Romanian town. This would have cut him off from the sports club in his native town, which was dominated by the German minority and to which he had been admitted as the only Romanian. His main biographical aim at that time had been to become a 'German', an aim which his father's decision endangered.

By fleeing to the other side of the Iron Curtain Romica appeared to have escaped the conflictual situation, including the obligation for him to be a Romanian. This part of his life belonged now to a past which was separated from his present by an impermeable border. His family of origin, as a frame of reference for his building biographical continuity, even disappeared. He felt 'like an orphan', as he put it in the interview. The way for him to 'become a German' seemed now to be set clear before him. But it was a group of Romanian exiles who came to be a substitute for his family, in particular a Greek Catholic priest who took the place of his father. Furthermore, the group offered Romica a context of positive identification as a Romanian, taught him folkloric dancing, religion, and 'another' Romanian history. Romica became a Romanian nationalist, even though in Romania he had strongly rejected everything 'Romanian'. Now, he started to rebuild his biography in the context of this extreme-right group of exiles. In terms of his education, he left the track his father had tried to push him along and followed the advice of the priest, who offered him the opportunity of attending a religious boarding school after two years of casual jobs. Thus, the initial period following his migration was marked by manifest discontinuation, first of his aspiration to become a 'German', and secondly of his course of education.

Four years after his arrival in Germany, however, Romica entered a hippie commune, thus putting into practice his wish to 'belong to the Germans'. This, however, resulted in him losing contact with the group of exiles. His reorientation towards left-wing youth culture was not accepted by the right-wing group. The pattern that was manifesting itself implied that every attempt to create continuity via biographical aspirations or former embeddedness was accompanied by an abrupt discontinuity in terms of belonging to a contradictory milieu, which also had become biographically relevant. In terms of Romica's pattern of action, we can assume that it was his objective (albeit an unconscious one) to connect socially with contradictory milieux in order to free himself from identification with, and embeddedness in, all of them via acts of rebellion. This pattern of activity was, however, limited to a period of about seven years following the move, after which Romica consolidated his life as a freelance cameraman in a local broadcasting company, where he worked for more than ten years until 1989.

The period of radical acts of discontinuation connected with Romica's move, which in the long-term perspective created a separation between his life in Romania and his life in Germany, may be explained initially by the circumstances of the migration itself, and especially by the fact that he could not return (Breckner, 2000a). Such a phenomenon can be shown to operate in a number of cases.[9] In Romica's case, however, on a latent level and in the context of his family and collective history it is clear that, through his acts of discontinuation, he reinforced the hidden continuity of his family history, which was shaped by its connections with the collective history of Romania, in particular its relations with Germany and German people during World War II. These links between Romica's pattern of action and the (hidden) connectivities between German and Romanian collective history, in which, as we shall see, his family was typically involved, were not visible for Romica in the period after his move. For him, these links became apparent, and part of the conscious construction of his biography, only after 1989, when he began to restructure his biography again during a roughly two-year period of repeated and intense visits to Romania. During this process of reconnecting disjunct life-periods spent in Germany and Romania, the connections between his family history and the collective history of Romania, especially during World War II, came to seem to him relevant biographical background, especially in terms of his understanding and explaining his flight. This became clear, for instance, in his response to an open question asking him to say more about his family. The question did not focus on a specific aspect of family life, not least because 'family' had hardly been mentioned in the interview up until then. Romica began his response by mentioning his mother's hope that he would return to Romania now that things have changed, pointing out that she is always implicitly asking why he went away, thus separating himself from her and from his father for a very long time. He then turned to his father's life history, seeking for an answer to this question there:

> My father was, that's also interesting, an admirer of the Germans, he had, erm, (4) he had been a pilot, in the Second World War. (2) He had studied mechanics, and he was, therefore, erm, he always admired the Germans, it was his, erm, so, when he told stories, they related to aeroplanes, Messerschmidts, the M104 or suchlike, which were famous [German] aeroplanes in the Second World War, and (2) for, for him the Germans were the big masters. (I: 106)[10]

Starting from here, Romica went on to tell the story of his father from the perspective of his being the son of a peasant who had returned from working in the USA and had helped the family upward in the traditional farming milieu, as well as in the industrial sphere by sending his eldest son to study mechanics in the 1940s during the fascist regime. The second son, Romica's uncle, inherited the land. This can all be seen as part of a family strategy, during the 1930s and '40s, of catching up with industrial development in the country while at the same time retaining the farm as a traditional resource. After 1945, the period of the family's strong upward mobility came to an end. As the son of a 'big farmer', Romica's father did not enjoy stable employment until 1964, even though he was an engineer, which at that time was the qualification most strongly sought after in the state-fostered extension of the industrial sphere. After Ceauşescu came to power in 1964 a liberalisation occurred in terms of the evaluation of class origins. It was then that Romica's father got his chance as the 'son of a farmer', and was asked to join the Communist Party. Shortly after he had been admitted to the Party he became second-in-command of a big factory. He thereby finally managed to move up in the technical-administrative élite of the country, and as first-born son to continue the upward-oriented family pattern, despite the break in 1945. He nevertheless remained bound to his agricultural and farming background, as Romica stressed in the interview. This, for Romica, explains why his father tried to send him to an agricultural boarding school, which was at the heart of the conflict with his father that had led to his fleeing. At that time, of course, this background was not spoken about, and probably not understood, not even by Romica's father.

Notwithstanding his own perceptions and aspirations, Romica represented a strong part of the (unspoken) family tradition probably from the very beginning of his life. Also an eldest son, he was given the same first name as his father and grandfather. He was probably expected to continue the family's upward mobility in the industrial sphere, but at the same time to remain loyal to his family's farming background. Owing to the expropriation of the land and the transformation of agriculture into a collective 'agro-industry', the traditional farm communities had in fact already been destroyed in many parts of the country.[11] At the same time, from the beginning of the Ceauşescu era in the mid-1960s, rural life was ideologised, in Communist rhetoric, as being the main source of popular culture, and became basic to Romania's national self-definition. Romica therefore experienced the farming community mainly in an ideological dimension, and not in terms of an attractive or realistic possibility of continuing his family traditions of rural living. Faced with this incoherent and conflictual historical situation, he rejected all commitments to a traditional nationalist model of society. He instead developed an admiration for the Germans, along with an orientation towards Western youth culture of the '60s, and a fascination for its music and fashion which he perceived as a more attractive and explicitly 'Western' alternative to the 'Romanian' way of life:

> That was always so, I felt the Romanians are underdeveloped, and then the Germans in T. [his home town] were different, er, it was such (1) a specific community, and it was not so easy for a Romanian, to gain access to it. But for me, because I was in this sports club, it was easier. There were these parties, also a German institution – at that time music was very important, the Beatles and the Rolling Stones, and the Germans were those who had the best music, they always got discs from Germany. But until you got access to Germans that took a long time, that was not so easy. And the main thing that fascinated me was the opening to the West. (I: 90–1)

Identification with 'the Germans' turned out to be part of the conflict between Romica and his father as well. Among Romica's father's generation admiration for the Germans was widespread too, but in the context of a different political regime and thus connected with different political orientations. After 1944 the Germans, even though they were generally labelled 'Nazis' by the new regime's propaganda, were still viewed in accordance with a general cliché that they were representatives of 'modernity'. The fascist political connotation receded into the background. The collaboration between Romania and Germany during World War II, including in the Holocaust, was hidden, in post-war Romanian society, as a taboo, thus creating an unresolved ambivalence towards the 'Germans'. On the one hand, they were still admired as representing riches and power; on the other, in the perspectives of the Romanian Communist Party and state, they represented the Nazis and were to be kept at a distance. To identify with the Germans in the context of Romanian society thus entailed different and even contradictory orientations: on the one hand, an affirmative connection with the fascist period before 1944 in which Romica's father's generation was deeply involved; and, on the other, enjoyment by Romica's generation of a post-war liberal hippie culture. In Romica's father's eyes this historical involvement with 'Germans' had somehow proven to have become a problem, and he therefore probably tried to prevent his son from getting too close to 'Germans'. On the other hand, his admiration for the 'Germans' had already been part of his transmission to his son, who had probably not been able to understand why his father had tried to cut him off from his own contacts with Germans of which he had been so proud.

Today, Romica embeds his answer to his mother's question as to why he had fled from his family in this complex that is his collective and family history, striving to make biographical sense of it. Against this background, his aspiration to become a 'German' in Romania, his flight to West Germany and his willingness to become a Romanian nationalist there seem by no means a mere adolescent caprice. The factors which had led to his abrupt emigration and its consequences, which have marked his biography up until today, appear, in this perspective and also to Romica today, as an arena in which hidden, contradictory continuities in the collective national history in which his family was typically involved were acted out and, finally, integrated one by one. One of the 'global' evaluations structuring Romica's self-presentation in the interview was his comment 'You are constantly confronted with fascism, no matter whether you are Romanian or German'. He seems to have accepted that a particular kind of continuity, namely, 'to be confronted with fascism all the time', has affected his life also, even though he has tried hard to escape from it. An attempt to discontinue these traditions in his biography, however, is also apparent from his concluding biographical statement:

> I often thought, basically I always was an uprooted person, but I'm happy to be an 'uprooted', because you look at things differently. Although you sometimes feel lonely and have your doubts, I am, I always was happy to be an uprooted person. (I: 37)

In this perspective, his move to the other side of the Iron Curtain represented for him the main tool or means whereby he distanced himself from any involvement with unpleasant and contradictory 'traditions' constituted by the interrelationship between Romanian and German collective history. At the same time, it represented a means of maintaining an ostensibly broken, but actually still present, connection with the fascist period of the collective and family history.

Stefan Georgescu: The Changing Meaning of Continuity and Discontinuity in the Context of a Professional Career

Stefan Georgescu was born in 1950 in Bucharest, the son of an Armenian mother and an assimilated Armenian-Romanian father. Together with his father and mother he moved to the USA via the Lebanon following seven years' attempts on the part of his parents to emigrate. These had caused considerable problems within the family owing to the pressure the Romanian state put on those who tried to emigrate. Stefan dealt with these sometimes dramatic events by concentrating on his education as an artist in a special grammar and high school, thus creating the educational, and later on the professional, sphere as the main element in his life representing continuity and security. In this context his migration, at the time the actual move took place, opened up for him new possibilities of continuing a professional career at a very high level, even though in order to do this he interrupted a professional training course which he had just commenced at the most prestigious state institution of its kind in Romania. Throughout the period of his migration his career remained in the foreground, even in the light of his experiencing the immigrant situation in the USA as one 'cut off' from the European cultural context. After completing a degree in New York, he returned to Europe in 1974 without his family, living first in Germany and then in France, with some years spent commuting between Berlin and Paris. These migrations were exclusively connected with his professional career, and were constitutive in terms of his continuing life as an artist, in which permanent movement was regarded as a normal condition.

Surprisingly given this background, in his self-presentation Stefan did not refer to this continuous and very successful career. Instead, he began by connecting his biography with the impact that World Wars I and II had had on his family history. He stressed the discontinuities and uncertainties that these periods had meant for his Armenian family, reconstructing the history of his grandparents and parents in the context of war, refuge, genocide and 'accidental' survival.

Afterwards, Stefan referred to his own life in six lines only, focusing on his admission to the Academy of Arts in Romania at the age of 19 and his subsequent emigration. Then he stops, thus creating, in textual terms, a biographical turning point in relation to his emigration from Romania. In other words, his 'successful' emigration from Romania has now become – representing as it does discontinuity – *the* structuring event of his present biographical self-presentation. During analysis of the case, it became apparent that the present meaning that this event has for Stefan was strongly connected with changes which took place in his life after 1989. After 1989, he could not continue his professional career on the same level as before, and was forced to earn his living as a teacher in a public school. His professional life, as a basis for constructing biographical continuity, was seriously vitiated, especially with regard to its future. Stefan started to travel to Romania, sometimes with the aim of putting himself forward as an artist. His identification with the country where he had obtained an education that was strongly oriented towards the European cultural context came to the surface again. His education in Romania had been connected with a systematic building up of his career as an artist, a member of the cultural élite and avant-garde not only of his own country but of the whole of Europe. Seen from this perspective, and in the context of his present experience of professional discontinuity, his emigration from Romania had come to represent the loss of this option, since he was now living in the professionally unstable 'West'. Furthermore, he found a country that was economically and culturally almost destroyed, and realised that he could not re-establish continuity with his former life there. The cultural state of 'his' country shook even his identification as a Romanian:

> Now I am in conflict, I always think, it was a bad joke of nature to be born in Romania [...] and I told my mother, 'You are Armenian. There are Armenians all over the world, why did you have to give birth to me in Romania?' [...] Now, at this moment I really wished I had not been born in Romania.

In trying to free himself from 'being a Romanian' (Inowlocki, 2000), Stefan turned now to his Armenian family background. It is in this context that his family history became relevant in his construction of his biography. But as well as finding a stabilising context for building up new biographical continuities in the Armenian part of his family history, he was confronted with the problematic and discontinuous background of his life there.

Stefan discovered a family history which was hidden until 1989, and which is still partly unclear. The threat posed to his family by persecution, flight and the death of a grandfather during World War I represented a new dimension in his perception of his family history in the context of Armenian history. In this context, he came also to realise that he was now, in Germany, living in a country inhabited also by people who had been involved in the Armenian Genocide (Ohandjanian, 1989), which rendered his presence in the place where he had hoped to establish himself for a longer period questionable. In other words, in the context of his family history a historical and existential dimension was added to the biographical uncertainty that had been provoked initially by discontinuity in his professional career. Furthermore, his emigration from Romania now represented a general loss of certainty, and the beginning of permanent exile:

> I was very tied to my place [in Bucharest] and suddenly I was forced to become a 'professional emigrant' in my life, involuntarily, I have no talent for that [laughs] ... I would have liked not to have been an emigrant any longer.

Stefan's construction of his own life had now become paradoxical. In a climate of uncertainty regarding his professional career he turned, after the fall of the Iron Curtain, to his homeland and his family history as a new field for constructing biographical continuities and certainties. But now he discovered the impact that two World Wars had had on his family history, the disturbances, threats and discontinuities connected with these historical events and their relevance for his own biography. During Communist times in Romania this background had remained hidden, and he had not discovered it after his emigration to the 'West'. In this context, Stefan's own life, a situation of permanent migration in a professional context, now appeared even more fragile than it used to be. Even though he was reluctant to accept this as the 'normal condition' of his biography which connected him with his family's history and Armenian background, in the permanent migratory context of his life he had developed the potential for dealing with discontinuity, even if it had been created unwillingly, a potential on which he could rely in a situation of professional crisis, the main basis for him of biographical continuity.

Conclusion

In the two cases that have been presented, emigration from the 'East' of Europe to the 'West' has created both continuity and discontinuity in terms of the different life-spheres and life-periods, and the different time-perspectives, in which each emigration had become a relevant biographical experience. Nevertheless, the pattern of continuation and discontinuation are different in the two cases. Romica Brasovean used his emigration and its discontinuities to construct a biography which he perceived as being autonomous, free from family traditions and focused on his own life, especially his life in the 'free West'. Stefan Georgescu, by contrast, first experienced emigration as part of a continuous professional career, but by the time of the interview it had come to represent a turning point which has diverted his career from its secured and successful path and rendered it unstable and fragile.

In terms of family and national history as contexts for the reconstruction of biographical continuity, especially after 1989, both men were confronted with breaks and discontinuities rather than with a common past which could be shared. For both, therefore, family and national history have – for different reasons – become problematic as points of reference for constructing biographical continuity. Nevertheless, both are attempting to approach and to understand the biographical meaning these past contexts have for their present situation and the impact they have on it. For the 'Cold War' generation represented by the cases described here, the problematic aspects of interrelations between 'East' and 'West', which mainly concerned the two World Wars, became apparent only after the fall of the Iron Curtain. The historical context, from which this generation was cut off by the reconstruction of Romania as a Communist state after 1945, and which did not become clear either after the migration to the 'other side' of the Iron Curtain, came to the fore after 1989. For Romica, this meant dealing with the imagined involvement of his father with the fascist regime, trying to maintain distance, but also to reconcile himself with his own simultaneous involvement with an extreme right-wing group of Romanian exiles. For Stefan, it meant being confronted with persecution and a discontinuation of the collective history of the Armenians, something which posed a particular challenge to his feelings about his own biographical continuity in a context of biographical crisis.

Against this background, and in this type of biography, the construction of biographical continuity in the context of family, culture and history has to be based on strategies for normalising discontinuity. Romica Brasovean was attempting to do this from the perspective of an 'uprooted' person with positive life-perspectives, Stefan Georgescu from that of a 'professional' migrant. Both men integrated their experiences of discontinuity brought about by the migration into a meaningful continuation of their biographies by regarding them as a 'normal' condition, even if this process occurred somewhat unwillingly and was sometimes experienced more as a challenge than as an opportunity. Moreover, the meaning the migration had for them as an event constituting biographical continuity or discontinuity has changed, according to the temporal context and their experiences in the different life-spheres to which it was and is connected. In both cases, the concrete challenge to integrate the discontinuity they experienced in the process of migration was related to their restructuring of the whole historical context in which their biographies were embedded through their family history (Breckner *et al.*, 2000). In this context it became apparent that their biographies and family histories were already attached to different collective histories, specifically to the Romanian, Armenian and German. But defining to which history they might connect their own biographies and in what respect was not the only challenge they faced. The (problematic) conjunction of these collective histories had become visible for the generation represented by these two cases after 1989, and it was mainly this which created the need for them to restructure their own position *vis-à-vis* the tangle of interrelated collective histories which had been separated for forty years.

Notes

1 For a detailed discussion of this assumption see Breckner (2001).

2 For a more detailed reconstruction of the new meaning of 'messages from the past' in times of radical social change see Semenova (2000).

3 The empirical research from which these two cases come is based on the analyses of biographies of, primarily, Romanians from different cultural and national backgrounds (e.g. Romanian, Armenian, Jewish, Hungarian, Swabian, etc.) and different ages (17 to 53) at the time of departure between 1969 and 1989. I chose these two cases because their age and generational contexts are quite similar, but the dynamics and biographical impact of their migration processes are rather different. Apart from these two cases, I conducted and analysed 20 narrative biographical interviews between 1991 and 1995, following the methods of Gabriele Rosenthal which in turn are based on the structural hermeneutics of Ulrich Oevermann and the techniques of narrative interviewing and text analyses of Fritz Schütze (1983) and the thematical field analyses of Wolfram Fischer and Fischer-Rosenthal. For a more detailed description of the principles and procedures of these methods see Schütze, 1983; Oevermann, 1983; Rosenthal, 1993, 1995; Fischer-Rosenthal and Rosenthal, 1997; Breckner, 1998; and, concerning the biographical approach in general, Kohli, 1986.

4 This is demonstrated also by the fact that nearly no sociological research existed on the biographical impact of migration between East and West Europe until 1989.

5 Statistics for migrants from Eastern Europe which allow us to reconstruct a precise and detailed picture of the different groups in West Germany hardly exist. Most statistics represent figures concerning the countries of departure, or on Western Europe as a whole as the context of reception (e.g. Münz and Fassmann, 1994). In the case of Romanian migrants living in West Germany, on whom my research focused, the number of 20,000 was hardly exceeded in the whole period between 1944 and 1989. The main implication of this is not that there were only a very small number of Romanian migrants in general; it only indicates that Germany was not the main target country of Romanian emigrants. In the context of Romanian emigration the picture looks different. The first serious wave of emigration arose mainly in Jewish and Armenian communities in the late 1950s. From the figures published by Trond Gilberg (1973, pp. 58ff) it is apparent that between 1956 and 1966 the Jewish community diminished from 146,200 to 42,800, and the Armenian from 6,400 to 3,400. The main target countries in this period were Israel and the USA. A second period of slight 'opening' began in the late 1960s, when Ceauşescu was seeking contact with the West. Sporting, cultural and scientific exchanges were organised, and negotiations were begun also with the Federal Republic of Germany, particularly concerning the emigration of an increasing number of ethnic Germans. To the extent that statistics provide a reliable picture, we can say that between 1974 and 1989 around 130,000 ethnic Romanians, 160,000 ethnic Germans, 46,000 ethnic Hungarians and 19,700 Jews left Romania to go to the West (Poledna and Poledna, 1994). The main countries of reception in this period were France, the USA and, from the 1970s on, also the Federal Republic of Germany, Hungary and Israel.

6 See e.g. the findings of Wodak and Matouschek (1993) for Austria, where, especially after 1990, Romania was no longer regarded as part of a Habsburg monarchy idealised as 'harmonious'. Romanians were now described as 'alien' and 'dangerous'. Comparable phenomena were investigated in Germany by Bohn, Hamburger and Rock (1993), who pointed out the function of this xenophobic discourse. On the history of the dissociation between 'the West' and 'the East' see Stölting (2000).

7 The structure of this 'lived life' and its presentation as a 'life story' (Rosenthal, 1993) were evolved on the basis of two narrative biographical interviews each lasting four hours.

8 The biggest ethnic minorities consisted of ethnic Germans (25 per cent) and Hungarians (17 per cent); see *Recesămîntul Populaţiei din* (1956), Vol. 2, p. 216.

9 See e.g. the discussion of the meaning of re-identification with one's nation immediately following emigration in Breckner, 2000b.

10 ',' = a short break; '(2)' = break of 2 seconds, '(3)' = break of 3 seconds, etc.; 'I' = first interview; '106' (e.g.) = page of transcript.

11 The so-called 'systematisation' of villages that has been going on since the 1980s (i.e. the complete dismantling of old village structures and the building of new apartment blocks) is only the most recent manifestation of the Romanian state's strategy of reconstructing agricultural land as industrial land.

References

Bauman, Z. (1996), 'From Pilgrim to Tourist – or a Short History of Identity', in S. Hall (ed.), *Questions of Cultural Identity*, Sage, London, pp. 18–36.

Bohn, I., Hamburger, F. and Rock, K. (1993), 'Die neue Ost–West Migration', in H. Meulemann and A. Elting-Camus (eds), *Lebensverhältnisse und soziale Konflikte im neuen Europa*, Westdeutscher Verlag, Opladen, pp. 424–7.

Breckner, R. (1997), 'The Use of "History" in European East–West Migration Biographies', paper given at the ESA Conference, Essex, August.

Breckner, R. (1998), 'The Biographical-Interpretative Method – Principles and Procedures', in Sostris Working Paper No. 2, *Case Study Materials: The Early Retired*, Centre for Biography in Social Policy (BISP), University of East London, pp. 91–104.

Breckner, R. (2000a), 'Processes of Re-constructing Migration Biographies. The Experience of "Return" from the West to the East of Europe after 1989', in B. Agozino (ed.), *Theoretical and Methodological Issues in Migration Research: Interdisciplinary, Intergenerational and International Perspectives*, Ashgate, Aldershot, pp. 91–106.

Breckner, R. (2000b), 'The Meaning of the "Iron Curtain" in East–West Migration Biographies', in R. Breckner *et al.* (eds), *op. cit.*, pp. 367–87.

Breckner, R. (2001), *Leben in polarisierten Welten. Zum Verhältnis von Migration und Biographie im Ost–West Europäischen Migrationsfeld*, dissertation thesis, Berlin Technical University.

Breckner, R., Kalekin-Fishman, D. and Miethe, I. (eds) (2000), *Biographies and the Division of Europe: Experience, Action and Change on the 'Eastern Side'*, Leske & Budrich, Opladen.

Fischer-Rosenthal, W. (1995), 'The Problem with Identity: Biography as Solution to Some (Post-)Modernist Dilemmas', *Comenius*, vol. 15, pp. 250–65.

Fischer-Rosenthal, W. (2000), 'Address Lost: How To Fix Lives. Biographical Structuring in the European Modern Age', in R. Breckner *et al.* (eds), *op. cit.*, pp. 55–75.

Fischer-Rosenthal, W. and Rosenthal, G. (1997), 'Narrationsanalyse biographischer Selbstpräsentation', in R. Hitzler and A. Honer (eds), *Sozialwissenschaftliche Hermeneutik*, Leske & Budrich, Opladen, pp. 133–64.

Gilberg, T. (1973), 'Ethnic Minorities in Romania under Socialism', in *East European Quarterly*, vol. 7, no. 4, pp. 435–58.

Inowlocki, L. (2000), 'Doing "Being Jewish": Constitution of "Normality" in Families of Jewish Displaced Persons in Germany', in R. Breckner *et al.* (eds), *op. cit.*, pp. 159–78.

Kohli, M. (1986), 'Biographical Research in the German Language Area', in Z. Dulczewski (ed.), *A Commemorative Book in Honor of Florian Znaniecki on the Centenary of his Birth*, Naukowe, Poznan/Poland, pp. 91–110.

Münz, R. and Fassmann, H. (1994), 'Geschichte und Gegenwart europäischer Ost-West-Wanderung', in R. Münz, H. Korte and G. Wagner (eds), *Internationale Wanderungen*, Demographie aktuell, Vol. 5, Humboldt University, Berlin.

Oevermann, U. (1983), 'Zur Sache. Die Bedeutung von Adornos methodologischem Selbstverständnis für die Begründung einer materialen soziologischen Strukturanalyse', in W. Friedeburg and J. Habermas (eds), *Adorno Conferenz 1983*, Suhrkamp, Frankfurt am Main, pp. 234–92.

Ohandjanian, A. (1989), *Armenien: Der verschwiegene Völkermord*, Böhlau, Vienna.

Poledna, R. and Poledna, S. (1994) 'Vorbemerkungen zu einem Forschungsprojekt', University of Babes-Bolyai/Cluj, manuscript.

Recesământul Populației din (1956), Vol. 2, Bucharest [Romanian Census from 1956].

Rosenthal, G. (1993), 'Reconstruction of Life Stories: Principles of Selection in Generating Stories for Narrative Biographical Interviews', in *Narrative Study of Lives*, Vol. 1, pp. 59–91.

Rosenthal, G. (1995), *Erlebte und erzählte Lebensgeschichte. Gestalt und Struktur biographischer Selbstbeschreibungen*, Campus, Frankfurt am Main and New York.

Schütz, A. (1972), 'Der Fremde', in *Gesammelte Aufsätze*, Vol. 2, Martinus Nijhoff, The Hague, pp. 53–69.

Schütze, F. (1983), 'Biographieforschung und narratives Interview', *Neue Praxis*, vol. 3, pp. 283–94.

Semenova, V. (2000), 'The Message from the Past: Experience of Suffering Transmitted through Generations', in R. Breckner *et al.* (eds), *op. cit.*, pp. 93–113.

Stölting, E. (2000), 'The East of Europe: A Historical Construction', in R. Breckner *et al.* (eds), *op. cit.*, pp. 23–38.

Todorova, M. (1997), *Imagining the Balkans*, Oxford University Press, New York.

Wodak, R. and Matouschek, B. (1993), 'Wir und die anderen: Diskurse über Fremde', *Journal für Sozialforschung*, vol. 33, no. 3, pp. 293–302.

12 Trajectories of Coping Strategies in Eastern Germany

OLAF STRUCK
Institute for Sociology,
University of Leipzig, Germany

Introduction

The incorporation, after 1989, of the GDR into the FRG's existing system of institutions (Mayer, 1993, p. 39) has led to a dynamic process of change in the living arrangements of East Germans. In this chapter, I shall examine stability and change as they operate in various dimensions of individual coping strategies. To do this, I analytically distinguish four elements: frames, habits, utilisation of available resources, and framing. It is stability and change in these elements that determine biographical decisions which are theoretically and practically relevant in everyday situations. In the theoretical sphere, Goffman's studies using frame analysis, Schütz's studies of relevant structures and the unfamiliar and Esser's use of rational choice and frames in his analyses, as well as the investigations of Bourdieu, Berger and Luckmann, and of Elias on *habitus*, have all been incapable of providing a clear explanation of how, and under what conditions, change occurs in structures relating to relevance and habits. Clarification is needed here if we are to arrive at a satisfactory analysis of everyday practical problems. With respect to social integration, for example, it is important to know whether and to what extent mentalities and habits endure social and socio-cultural changes. Indeed, in many studies of societal transformation, deficiencies in socialisation are considered by reference to the cause of the subjects' dissatisfaction and to obstacles to the process of societal modernisation.

In the following, I show that the actions which constitute the coping strategies of nearly all the East Germans we interviewed are directed towards their achieving a stable career trajectory. Their actions can be characterised as pragmatic, and in most cases are successful. Despite their orientation towards the social inclusion mode and the fact that they have become part of mainstream society, the interviewees showed specific signs of desolidarisation. Their actions were mainly directed against state intervention and collective bodies, and contain a high potential for disappointment with respect to the development of society.

Sample and Method

The research project investigated decision-making processes within the individual life course, paying particular regard to career and family formation under the new conditions brought about by the transformation from the centrally-planned economy of the GDR to an individualised market economy.[1] We interviewed skilled workers and academics, who graduated from vocational schools and universities respectively in 1985, 1990 or 1995. Three sets of data were collected: a macro and a micro panel, and case analysis of companies (meso-perspective). The macro panel is a quantitative retrospective survey (n = 2,130) designed to analyse life-course event-history data. These data were gathered in 1994 and in 1999. The survey of company data was designed to help identify the cohort-specific effect of company personnel policies (Struck and Simonson, 2000). The data were gathered in 1998 from companies in the manufacturing sector and the public and the private services sectors (n = 53). The micro panel consists of 63 qualitative interviews, involving two sets of biographical interviews, conducted in 1992 and 1996 (Struck-Möbbeck *et al.*, 1996), and case analysis of companies in the manufacturing sector and the public and private services sectors (n = 30). A summary of the study's findings is presented in Sackmann *et al.* (2000). The following analysis employs findings drawn from the biographical interviews of the 1985 and the 1990 cohort only.

Theoretical and methodological considerations for systematically integrating temporal variations in the data into the overall analysis were a significant aspect of the methodology applied in the study and the panel design. This design allowed for the comparison of the stability and discontinuity of elements in coping activities on the basis of comments made by the interviewees at two separate points in time. It also enabled us to analyse expectations and goals in conjunction with actual events and, subsequently, to investigate the time-dependent, interactive process of individual and structural causes of trajectories.

Common methods used for the analysis of narratives permit the researcher to draw conclusions about authenticity and consistency only by using the criterion of degree of detail (in the case of group discussions it would be the criterion of density of event description and processing) (Schütze, 1981). In the evaluation phase, it is only possible to identify discrepancies between an event and its description. Even at the higher reflective level of the shaping of the biography as a whole, where self-defining and -repressing functions are interpreted, discrepancies can only be identified as inconsistencies (Schütze, 1983, p. 286). The method cannot elucidate the content of the discrepancy between an event and its description or between individual motives and actions heavily influenced by social structures.

The panel design we chose allows us, however, to determine the content, that is, to identify in a controlled way the position of the individual in his or her social environment. The method minimises the danger of succumbing to respondents' potential tendency towards rationalised and desired responses. In the first interview we asked about prospective occupational aspirations, desires, fears and the relationship between individual frames and resources. In the second wave the interviewees were asked to reflect retrospectively about events that had occurred during the time between the two interviews. As a result we obtained data about actual expectations and aspirations at the time of the first interview. By contrasting statements from the first interview with statements from the second we also gained information about the interviewees' plans and strategies for achieving goals, as well as information about the causes of changes in perspectives and the structural conditions on which actions were based. This method made it possible, on the one hand, to incorporate the significant expectation structures into the analysis and, on the other, to control for biographical consequences, such as adaptation to socially desirable behaviour.

Theoretical Framework

A glance at the available literature reveals that there is a problem of clarity in distinguishing the concepts of frames, framing and *habitus*. Thus there is a need for theoretical and methodological precision before we proceed to our central question: when and to what extent individual adaptation of frames and habits occurs.

Goffman describes frames as structures that are capable of recognising 'what is actually going on' (Goffman, 1977, p. 16). For Goffman, frames are socially predetermined structures. Similarly, Schütz (1971; 1972a;

1972b) speaks of 'structures of relevance'. This needs to be contrasted with framing as an individual's understanding of meaning in a decision-making situation. The distinction between the definition of a situation and that of an individual decision in connection with an action aimed towards a specific end is sadly neglected. An example of this is when the 'rational choice' theoretician Esser disregards relevant imposing externalities, and instead confines himself to frames or framing as 'a simplification of situations in relation to a dominant goal' (Esser, 1990b, p. 242 [in relation to the definition on p. 238]; 1990b; 1991).

If one accepts Goffman's distinction between 'frame as structure' and 'frame in use' (Crook and Taylor, 1980, p. 247), the frame is 'a potential world that answers all questions about what it is that shall be taken by participants as real, and how it is that they should be involved in this reality' (Gonos, 1977, p. 860). The concept thereby points to biographical disposition, that is to an intermediary 'relay station' (Elias, 1980, Vol. 2) between frame as structure and framing or frame in use. This disposition is to be referred to as *habitus*.

Habitus constitutes, out of all potential worlds of frames, the vital, specific and appropriate worlds of framing. If frames determine what constitutes the situation, so then do habits determine how a situation is reacted to. Bourdieu elaborates: 'The conditioning which is connected to a certain class of conditions of subsistence [e.g. the secure living situation of a generation or a social class] generates forms of *habitus* as systems of longer lasting and transmittable dispositions' (Bourdieu, 1987, p. 98). Gehlen (and, following him, Berger and Luckmann (1969)) had already much earlier written of 'systems of stereotypical and more stabilised habits' (Gehlen, 1986, p. 19). Elias speaks of 'apparatuses of habit' (1980, Vol. 2, p. 320ff.). Gehlen (1957) and Berger and Luckmann (1969), much more than Bourdieu and Elias, see in the capability to change a socially-adapted habit a gain in the capability to act in unpredictable and unfamiliar decision-making situations. Here routine creates room for innovation. On the other hand, Gehlen and Berger and Luckmann stress, as do Elias and Bourdieu, that *habitus* creates restrictions whose generation is predisposed to limits (Bourdieu, 1987).

Framing as the actual generator of ends and means thus has a social and biographical history which can be expressed in terms of frames and habits. Moreover it is related to individual usable resources. We find this mediating relationship expressed chiefly by Bourdieu. His analysis of different understandings of capital, such as economic, social, and cultural (Bourdieu, 1982, 1983), is similar to that outlined by Elias in his description of court society, 'Höfische Gesellschaft' (Elias, 1980, Vol. 2, pp. 370ff.; 1983). Along with material economic conditions, social capital determines specific contexts of interaction. Furthermore, the possibility of developing cultural capital is associated with the different levels of ability to build strategies and to reflect upon one's own actions and those of others.

These theoretical considerations constituted the basis of our model of biographical action. In this model, against the background of their respective frames (i.e. the structure of relevance which was generated in the process of interaction), actors perceive the range of options with respect to their occupational and private lives. They then choose a dominant goal, and a means to this end, in the form of framing on the basis of their frames and habits as well as on the basis of their social, economic and cultural resources. Thus, they make decisions on the basis of related experiences and transmit them into action.

Following on from these theoretical considerations and taking into account the dynamic process of societal change, the following concrete questions were formulated:

1. How have the structures of resources available to East Germans for everyday life changed?
2. Have frames (i.e. the interactively-gained cognition of a situation) changed?
3. Have habitual dispositions changed or have they remained stable over time?
4. How are individual action strategies and the social system related?

Stability and Change

Owing to the limitations of space, the discussion of the findings on stability and change will be confined to the presentation of an illustrative case. This will show how the model of biographical action can be used to elucidate and interpret coping strategies. This interview, however, can be taken as representative in terms of the conclusion drawn within the presented theoretical framework.

Frau Einser, born in 1969, completed her education as a technical chemist in 1985. After the birth of her first child in 1986 and her first marriage that followed she had continuous health problems and consequently took parental leave for a year. Subsequently, she wished to return to the job market but could not find a free space for childcare for her infant. Angered, she refused to participate in the obligatory national elections of the delegates to the GDR legislative body, the People's Chamber. She elaborated:

> I refused the ballots in the first place. I was angry that I did not get a place at a nursery ... Then I was visited by a delegate who made me an offer ... I was then an assistant at an infant care centre.

Once a member of the staff, she managed to assert herself, despite the tremendous opposition she faced since she was not formally qualified to work in childcare. Directly following the political changes in 1989–90, she began, parallel to her job, to attend a vocational training programme in business financing. Her parents, who by then had become unemployed, took on responsibility for caring for her child. During this period her husband also was subject to repeated bouts of unemployment. In 1993, she became self-employed as a financial consultant through the help of a government programme. During the second interview, she told us that she had become the victim of fraud, which had serious financial consequences. The lack of emotional support in this matter by her husband motivated her to file for divorce:

> He said: 'Give it up and find yourself a real job.' And I could just not see it that way after having invested so much effort and everything. And I was of the opinion that I would make it ... and I did.

She looked for emotional support from another partner. She soon became self-confident again and was able to expand her business. Today she employs three workers. Her daughter, who has now reached the age of eight, is still taken care of by her grandparents and her uncle when her mother is occupied with business.

Coming back to the central question of stability and change in elements of biographical actions, the following assumptions can be made. Continuity and change in an actor's biography is shaped by their cognition and knowledge of institutional conditions and society's risks. If the living situation of East Germans had been characterised by stability and security (as long as one met with political approval), the situation after the political changes in 1989 can best be characterised as flexible and uncertain.

Changes in social and economic circumstances were accompanied by changes in accessible individual resources. In the respondent's view:

> there was a general increase in prices ... joblessness, my husband had already been laid off before ... Also the situation for women who had a career, for instance – I was told from the very beginning that I could not be placed since I had two children.

She found the situation threatening, realising:

> A lot can go sour just because of being afraid of not having a job.

In saying this, Frau Einser has identified the main frame of her biography: the holding or regaining of occupational security. While, under the GDR regime, developing an occupational career, starting a family and keeping up friendships were viewed as being equally important for the process of framing, as soon as the political climate and conditions changed it was only securing one's position in an occupation that was discussed as a central frame.

Resources and frames changed significantly for East Germans. By contrast, the *habitus* remained stable. This offers room for innovative solutions such as those suggested by Berger and Luckmann and Gehlen. With her goal in sight, Frau Einser courageously pressed on, before and after the transition to the free-market economy, towards realising her interests despite all opposition. Her self-confidence remained intact and she confidently used her support system of family and friends – which she had built up before the political and economic transition – to seek childcare and emotional support. If certain individuals did not provide the necessary support required to advance her career, they were replaced.

The following generalisations can be made. Regardless of general and personal insecurities, the *habitus* remained stable over and beyond the major social transformation. At the same time, in spite of the stability of the *habitus* the cognition of situations was able to change. Framing by East Germans was characterised by a high degree of pragmatism, although consequently, after reunification occupational security quickly became a dominant frame among the structures of relevance.

The investigation into stability and change in biographies gave us cause to differentiate analytically between the levels of frames, habits and framing. Only then was it possible to understand human actions under conditions of social change. In our study, this meant, for example, that it was not the deficiencies in socialisation attributed to a pre-modern society (Gaus, 1987; Geissler, 1992; Pollack, 1990; Srubar, 1991) and custodial state (Henrich, 1989) as propounded by modernisation theorists (Mayntz,

1992, p. 23) which evoked a nostalgic wave of criticism from East Germans after the reunification. Habits, indeed, remained stable, but this stability did not an hinder an individual's realistic cognition of the situation or pragmatic goal-oriented behaviour in response to a new living situation.

What, then, is the reason for the critical perspective adopted by East Germans concerning the transformation process? Why did the majority of those interviewed, who managed to alter their paths successfully, nevertheless express disappointment? In the last section I summarise the main findings and how our model can be used to interpret coping strategies in biographical research.

Hopes and Disappointments

Frau Einser said, in the first interview:

> Right now I am retraining to be a financial advisor. At the moment it's damn hard. Not so much because of school and the exams, which I actually quite enjoy, but because of the travelling and my child.

In response to the question of what she wanted to do once she had finished the course, she replied:

> I'll probably start my own firm, in property and insurance. There are state-funded programmes and assistance from the chamber of commerce for people wanting to becoming self-employed. I've already spoken to a lot of people about this.

These two passages highlight two points: first, that the rapid retraining from laboratory assistant to financial advisor was a heavy burden; and secondly, that state assistance (i.e. state aid in becoming self-employed) was called upon (i.e. for retraining) and was expected.

Four years later, we found that her marriage had not withstood the strain placed upon both her and her partner. She had, however, become a property and insurance broker after having received start-up assistance, and her firm was operating successfully.

Despite the fact that she could successfully call upon state assistance, she described the actions of the state as ineffective:

> Ah, the state. I'll give you an example. Look at the new roads being built here with the state's money. OK the road is redone, finished. Then Telecom comes along and digs it up again and it has to be closed again. Then the electricity

> and gas people come along, and in the end the road was dug up three times. It's just the same with all the qualifications and stuff. The state should be a sort of supervising authority that coordinates everything. Everyone has to put their cables in before the road is finished. The state should have a duty to control and support. But in reality companies earn money with everyone digging up the road, and the organisers of educational programmes earn money with providing useless qualifications.

Our interview partner, who did not share the experiences Frau Einser described and who had managed to fulfil the goals and aspirations she had announced in the first interview, called upon and received state support as a matter of course. She took a pragmatic approach: 'Assistance is offered, so I take it.'

A typical feature of transformation societies is expressed here. The individual's high hopes and aspirations in relation to the reform of the state and the economy were not fulfilled. This, however, is not mainly a question of the objective actions of collective actors, but instead primarily a phenomenon at the level of the individual. After the collapse of the GDR in the autumn of 1989 aspiration levels in general rose, but not in concert with a perceived need for a change in occupational self-image. With monetary union and reunification in 1990 the usefulness of existing personal resources decreased. Initial high-flying life plans were downsized. In time, either it was possible to adapt resources to the new demands at work and to life in general, or else some resources, such as wages and job security, increased. A more controlled and realistic balance was struck between desires, concepts and self-images on the one hand and resources on the other. The high level of personal performance which is expected in times of dynamic change overshadows the performance of collective actors. Disappointment was highest when expectations were greatest. In the words of Frau Eisner: 'What happened at that time and what we achieved was amazing.'

The former GDR citizens had low expectations as far as businesses and the economy as a whole were concerned. They had learnt in school and from Western television that capitalism produced unemployment. They did, however, have high expectations with respect to politics and the state's responsibilities for its citizens' welfare. In the former GDR the state was, for many people, highly relevant in terms of their individual lives: in a negative sense in terms of control, but mainly positively in terms of direct negotiations between them and the state.

Politics was everywhere in the GDR, and at the time of the transformation it was the political actions of Mikhail Gorbachev, Helmut Kohl and other major political actors which dominated perceptions of events. Moreover, it was the West German politicians who promised 'blooming landscapes'. Biographical experiences during the transformation created, therefore – with good reason – high expectations of competent, political actions on the part of the state.

The will to succeed, and the experience of having brought together personal aspirations and expectations with available resources, encouraged a feeling of self-efficiency. Although the expectations for an efficient state continued to exist, however, hopes and aspirations for the future of society were disappointed. A final remark of Frau Eisner on this topic is pertinent: 'As I said, the state shouldn't produce so much bureaucratic rubbish, but do its job of controlling, and supporting the weak.'

It is apparent in this statement that the pragmatic and instrumentalist approach towards one's own life and the performance of the state does not go hand in hand with consciously chosen egotistical actions or a desire for desolidarisation. Nevertheless, such a desolidarisation occurred. The purposeful, pragmatic behaviour that we observed both at work and in relationships with friends had the effect that efforts to establish collective goods were not activated. Collective efforts were not even perceived. In spite of individual successes the problem of the lack of communal effort, or the reluctance to pay for this, becomes more and more apparent. Organisations (e.g. trade unions and charities) and state-run institutions, both of whose actions were judged to be inefficient, were under heavy pressure to justify themselves. In view of the fact that the collective achievements looked pale when compared with the successes of individual achievements, collective actors, even if they worked successfully, could not alter the spread of these individualistic perceptions in the short and medium term. New lines of social conflict have emerged as a result. At the time of the interviews people were not willing to work to establish a collective good if this collective good was not visible or if it was perceived as a waste. During this process, social mechanisms of marginalisation gradually affected parts of the population profoundly, even though justice and participation are values still prevalent among East Germans.

Conclusions

The results can be summarised in six theses:

1. An analysis of stability and change in biographies gave us cause to differentiate analytically between the levels of frames, framing, habits and resources.
2. The successful inclusion in the new social structure of large numbers of individuals who pushed and developed transformed relevance structures and changed useful resources was based on pragmatic, instrumentalist framing. This framing was occupationally-oriented.
3. Combining aspirations and goals with personal resources creates, at the level of the individual, a feeling of self-efficiency. On the other hand, combining expectations about the future of society with resources, even where it was successful, left behind a feeling of bitterness.
4. It is not nostalgia for the old state of affairs, an explanation much discussed with regard to attitudes in transformation societies and therefore in Germany as well, that is the reason for the disappointment among East Germans. Instead, the cause is individuals' realisations that a willingness to succeed and self-efficiency do not have counterparts at the level of the social system, something which has been neglected.
5. Under this constellation of circumstances, pragmatic, instrumentalist action does not lead to a consciously egotistical attitude. The ideal of a community is still very much alive, and the interviewees regretted the exclusion of many social groups. There are, however, no active efforts being made to build new solidarities or communal and state support. This finding incorporates a paradox. It is precisely because of the high expectations of the state as a fair arbiter that the necessary personal, solidaristic contribution is not made.
6. When analysing fragility and stability at the level of the individual actor above all, we have to observe the extent of the framing of aspirations in addition to the extent of socio-structural representation inside and outside different areas of society. As the narratives show, a story of successful inclusion does not mean that it was perceived as such at the time. That a biographical perspective helps to establish micro–macro links is already well-known. But further, only the biographical perspective is (especially if a panel design is used) able to incorporate the different levels of expectations, real trajectories and stock-takings that characterise the parallel and interdependent processes in operation here. This approach opens the researchers' eyes

to surprises. Supposed paradoxes become lucid, and not only the consequences but also the causes of inconsistencies can be explained.

Note

1 The research project 'Occupational Trajectories in Social Change' is part of the Special Collaborative Centre 186 (Sonderforschungsbereich 186) in Bremen. The members of the project are Susanne Falk, Matthias Rasztar, Reinhold Sackmann, Olaf Struck, Ansgar Weymann, Michael Windzio and Matthais Wingens.

References

Berger, P.L. and Luckmann, T. (1969), *Die gesellschaftliche Konstruktion der Wirklichkeit* [The Social Construction of Reality], Suhrkamp, Frankfurt.

Bourdieu, P. (1982), *Die feinen Unterschiede. Kritik der gesellschaftlichen Urteilskraft* [Fine Distinctions: A Critique of Social Judgement], Suhrkamp, Frankfurt.

Bourdieu, P. (1983), 'Ökonomisches Kapital, kulturelles Kapital, soziales Kapital' [Economic Capital, Cultural Capital, Social Capital], in R. Kreckel (ed.), *Soziale Ungleichheit* [Social Inequality] (Sonderband 2; Soziale Welt), Schwartz, Göttingen, pp. 183–98.

Bourdieu, P. (1987), *Sozialer Sinn. Kritik der theoretischen Vernunft* [Social Meaning: A Critique of Theoretical Reasoning], Suhrkamp, Frankfurt.

Crook, S. and Taylor, L. (1980), 'Goffman's Version of Reality', in J. Ditton (ed.), *The View from Goffman*, Macmillan, New York, pp. 233–51.

Elias, N. (1980), *Über den Prozeß der Zivilisation: soziogenetische und psychogenetische Untersuchungen* [On the Process of Civilisation: Sociogenetic and Psychogenetic Investigations], 2 Vols, Suhrkamp, Frankfurt.

Elias, N. (1983), *Die höfische Gesellschaft. Unterzuchungen zur Socologie des Königtums und der höfischen Aristokratie* [Courtly Society: Studies on the Sociology of the Monarchy and the Courtly Aristocracy], Luchterhand, Darmstadt/Neuwied.

Esser, H. (1990a), *Alltagshandeln und Verstehen. Zum Verhältnis von erklärender und verstehender Soziologie am Beispiel von Alfred Schütz und 'Rational Choice'* [Action and Understanding in Everyday Life: On the Relationship between Explanatory and Interpretative Sociology with Special Reference to Alfred Schütz and 'Rational Choice'], Mohr, Tübingen.

Esser, H. (1990b), '"Habits", "Frames" and Rational Choice. Die Reichweite von Theorien der rationalen Wahl' ['Habits', 'Frames' and Rational Choice: The Scope of Theories of Rational Choice], *Zeitschrift für Soziologie*, vol. 19, pp. 231–47.

Esser, H. (1991), 'Die Rationalität des Alltagshandelns. Alfred Schütz und "Rational Choice"' [The Rationality of Everyday Action: Alfred Schütz and 'Rational Choice'], in K. Troitzsch (ed.), *Modellierung sozialer Prozesse* [Modelling of Social Processes], Informationszentrum Sozialwissenschaften, Bonn, pp. 235–79.

Gaus, G. (1987), *Wo Deutschland liegt. Eine Ortsbestimmung* [Where Germany Is: A Determination of Place], Hoffman & Campe, Hamburg.

Gehlen, A. (1957), *Die Seele im technische Zeitalter. Sozialpsychologische Probleme in der industriellen Gesellschaft* [The Soul in the Age of Technology: Psycho-sociological Problems in Industrial Society], Rowohlt, Reinbek bei Hamburg.

Gehlen, A. (1986), *Urmensch und Spätkultur. Philosophische Ergebnisse und Aussagen* [Ancient Man and Late Culture: Philosophical Deductions and Statements], Aula Verlag, Wiesbaden.

Geissler, R. (1992), *Die Sozialstruktur Deutschlands. Ein Studienbuch zur Entwicklung im geteilten und vereinten Deutschland* [The Social Structure of Germany: A Textbook on Development in the Divided and Reunited Germany], Westdeutscher Verlag, Opladen.

Goffman, E. (1977), *Rahmen-Analyse. Ein Versuch über die Organisation von Alltagserfahrungen* [Frame Analysis: An Essay on the Organisation of Everyday Experiences], Suhrkamp, Frankfurt.

Gonos, G. (1977), '"Situation" versus "Frame": The "Interactionist" and the "Structuralist" Analysis of Everyday Life', *American Sociological Review*, vol. 42, pp. 854–67.

Henrich, R. (1989), *Der vormundschaftliche Staat. Vom Versagen des real existierenden Sozialismus* [The Guardian State: On the Failure of 'Real Existing Socialism'], Rowohlt, Reinbek bei Hamburg.

Mayer, K.U. (1993), 'Die soziale Ordnung der DDR und einige Folgen für die Inkorporation in die BRD' [The Social Order of the GDR and Some Consequences for its Incorporation into the FRG], in *BISS Public*, Vol. 11, No. 3, pp. 39–55.

Mayntz, R. (1992), 'Modernisierung und die Logik von interorganisatorischen Netzwerken' [Modernisation and the Logic of Interorganisational Networks], *Journal für Sozialforschung*, vol. 32, pp. 19–32.

Pollack, D. (1990), 'Das Ende einer Organisationsgesellschaft. Systemtheoretische Überlegungen zum gesellschaftlichen Umbruch in der DDR' [The End of an Organisational Society: System-theoretical Reflections on Social Upheaval in the GDR], *Zeitschrift für Soziologie*, vol. 19, pp. 292–307.

Sackmann, R., Weymann, A. and Wingens, M. (eds) (2000), *Die Generation der Wende* [The 'Wende' Generation], Opladen, Westdeutscher Verlag.

Schütz, A. (1971), 'Struckturen der Lebenswelt' [Structures of the Lived World], in *Collected Essays, Vol. 3: Studien zur phänomenologischen Philosophie*, Martinus Nijhoff, The Hague, pp. 153–70.

Schütz, A. (1972a), 'Der Fremde. Ein sozialpsychologischer Versuch' [The Stranger: A Sociological Essay], in *Collected Essays, Vol. 2: Studien zur soziologischen Theorie*, Martinus Nijhoff, The Hague, pp. 53–69.

Schütz, A. (1972b), 'Die soziale Welt und die Theorie der Handlung' [The Social World and the Theory of Action], in *Collected Essays, Vol. 2: Studien zur soziologischen Theorie*, Martinus Nijhoff, The Hague, pp. 3–21.

Schütze, F. (1981), 'Prozeßstrukturen des Lebenslaufs' [Process Structures in Biography], in J. Matthes *et al.* (eds), *Biographie in handlungswissenschaftlicher Perspektive* [Biography in a Behavioural Science Perspective], Verlag der Nürnberger Forschungsvereinigung, Erlangen/Nürnberg, pp. 67–156.

Schütze, F. (1983), 'Biographieforschung und narratives Interview' [Biographical Research and Narrative Interview], *Neue Praxis*, vol. 3, pp. 283–93.

Srubar, I. (1991), 'War der reale Sozialismus modern? Versuch einer strukturellen Bestimmung' [Was 'Real Socialism' Modern?: Attempt at a Structural Determination], *Kölner Zeitschrift für Soziologie und Sozialpsychologie*, vol. 43, pp. 415–32.

Struck, O. and Simonson, J. (2000), 'Übergänge im Erwerbsleben. Theoretische Konzepte und empirische Befunde zur betrieblichen Lebenslaufpolitik' [Transitions in Working Life: Theoretical Concepts and Empirical Results in the Field of Operational Biography Policy], in R. George and O. Struck (eds), *Generationenaustausch im Unternehmen* [Generational Exchange in Business Enterprise], pp. 21–54.

Struck-Möbbeck, O. *et. al.* (1996), *Gestaltung berufsbiographischer Diskontinuität* [Structuring of Discontinuity in Professional Biography]. University of Bremen, Sonderforschungbereich 186, working paper No. 38.

13 Inequality and Exclusion in the History of Poor Slovak Families

ZUZANA KUSÁ
Institute of Sociology,
Bratislava, Slovakia

Introduction

The family-history project *The Social History of Poverty in Slovakia*[1] terminated in 1997, more as a result of lack of funding than of the topic being exhausted. It had originated as part of the international project designed by Julia Szalai, and was based on the provocative idea that unemployment and poverty in many post-Communist countries represented the outcomes not so much of the current economic transformation as of the (under socialism uneven) structural opportunities that existed for escaping dependence on a feudal state and developing new entrepreneurial competencies (Szalai, 1995). A recognition of the importance of family transmission, and of the transmissibility of various kinds of capital, for social mobility in modern societies (Bertaux, 1993, p. 512) resulted in the family-history approach being adopted as being that most suited to the study of structural opportunities for upward mobility under Communism.

In this research, the family-history approach took the form of collecting and interpreting the narratives of family members of the three 'non-advancing' generations. This meant that we had to construct the ideal type of 'non-advancing' family,[2] and then to look for families that would fit our model. As usual, it was less difficult to obtain family addresses[3] than it was to obtain families' agreement to take part in the research. We had in the end to relinquish our aim of obtaining family histories from six family members – two per generation – as well as that of eliciting narratives told without other family members being present. Those families who were coping with shortages were not willing to 'attract the attention of the responsible authorities' to shared problems regarding their livelihood. The high refusal rate stemmed partly from a disbelief in the direction of the research and partly from family disunity; families themselves involved in conflict could hardly take a united view of the three-generation agreement to be interviewed (Kusá, 1999). The participating families also remained cautious about sharing their histories.[4] Despite the promise of anonymity, many narrators suspected that other family members would somehow come to know what they revealed about them.

History and Politics

Like numerous other life-history researchers, we were interested in how the subjects described political and historical events in their narratives. To avoid the artificial eliciting of information and composition of narratives, we avoided direct questions about history or politics. This non-intervention bore fruit: contrary to what might have been expected, numerous political regimes, their leaders and the changes they underwent scarcely appeared in the collected narratives. This suggests that political and historical events took place far from the narrators' lives.

In the grandparents' narratives, political regimes are identified only via narrators mentioning the nationality of people (Hungarians, Czechs, Jews) entering or leaving their place of residence, or via the changed names of their workplaces. The grandparents did not attempt to explain the poverty of their childhood. They remarked only that 'there was a lack of work', that 'they only paid in kind' and that 'life was very poor in those days', without giving even the name of the country.[5]

It looks as if the state has embraced their life-realities and started to frame their everyday experiences only recently. The grandparents, like the parents, use political terms only in describing their present problems bound up with criminality, the securing of a family livelihood, price increases, or the costs of healthcare and their children's education. For example:

> ... all that talk that the Government will help – I don't know anybody who was helped. Neither Government, nor the national council. If someone starved him[self], or went on strike, that would not help today. All their talk is only about *macro-economics*, they will not change their tune ... (Ladislav, b. 1944; Nitra, 1996, p. 33)

Ladislav here points to the gap between the concerns, and the language and experiences, of politicians and those of ordinary people. Politicians take comfort from the upward movement of macroeconomic indicators. These, however, are things outside the direct experience of ordinary people. On the one hand, Ladislav's ironic use of political language suggests a recognition of the functions and responsibilities of the state. On the other hand, the exercising of political power is still seen as being distant from ordinary people and beyond their control.

According to Ladislav, it is impossible to exert any influence on the exercise of state power. Why is he so pessimistic? Did he forget the events of 1989 as evidence of the 'power of the powerless'? How could he believe that strikes and other actions would not help? He mentions very individualistic forms of protest – self-starvation – along with the collective one: striking. He indirectly equates them. This puzzling logic is not accidental. The Slovak media of the early 1990s retreated sharply from civil optimism, and did not represent strikes or self-starvation as legitimate or effective political tools.[6]

'Invisible' history and a poorly adumbrated relationship between the worlds of politics and everyday life can also be explained by the simple fact that narrators avoided political topics because we asked them to speak about their lives and the life of their family. They might exclude politics just as they might all other places and persons of which they had no direct experience and which they did not meet face to face.

Food

In a comparison of the past with the present, food plays a crucial role. Food was apparently among the key items of the household economy under socialism, although a considerable amount of food was home-produced. The period of its greatest abundance represented the Golden Age of the family. It was mainly those narrators who lived in towns who recalled nostalgically the food they had enjoyed in the past owing to their small garden or allotment or their breeding of poultry. They viewed restrictions placed upon eating with malevolence. It is unjust, they asserted, to deny to their children what they themselves had had in their younger days:

> Shall we really eat only garlic soup all the time? Was there someone who planned it this way? Let him eat it then, if he did so. However, those who work hard, they have to eat properly ... However, they do not mind! Garlic soup will not make you strong enough for manual work! Only those who sit

> at desks and work with papers can afford it! (Izabela, b. 1948; Galanta, 1996, p. 15)

Working-class Identity

Izabela's distinction between manual workers and 'planners' is among the strongest expressions of class-consciousness in our collection of narratives. It is surprising that forty years of insistent framing of Marxist ideology have not left deeper traces. The narrators do not use words like 'capitalism', 'exploitation' or even 'working class'. That their class-consciousness is underdeveloped is, however, no great surprise. The Communist system focused, first, on the ideological control of people in managerial positions. Although its complex system of lifelong ideological education covered everybody except retired persons, people in marginal positions could avoid the else-obligatory cultivation of class-consciousness without great pains. In addition, in the present Slovakia, there is no political interest in raising the class-consciousness of poor people or in disconnecting the issue of exploitation from the Communist agenda.

The narratives suggest a belief that ordinary people cannot influence politics. The narrators do not mention any politicians by name, and do not distinguish between 'better' and 'worse' political parties. Why, then, do they speak about politics at all? It seems that they do so in order to give vent to frustration. Given that it is awkward to criticise one's relatives in public, politics has become the generally accepted target of people's spleen. This was the case for Izabela. The new era humiliated her – it made her not only unemployed for a period, but also a debtor. She was unable to pay the rent on her apartment for almost a year. Izabela constructed her narrative so as to explain the origin of her debts and to prove that she and her family were not guilty in respect of them. (Her son was doing military service, and so she had to send him money and parcels otherwise he would have stood out from the others. She was simply behaving as any good mother should.)

Moreover, by venting their spleen on politics people could protect their sense of personal integrity. By stripping the realm of civil society and politics of any credibility and worth, they were able to avoid perceiving their marginal and insignificant position in society as a humiliating one.

Work and Dignity

The middle generation of the families under study were social benefit claimants. Many of them had been unemployed for more than a year. The long-term-unemployed of the middle generation spoke about their search for work in the past tense. They and their unemployed children (three families) spontaneously compared the financial costs and advantages of having a job and being on benefit, and explained their not working on the grounds that there was almost no financial difference, and that they might even be poorer after entering minimally-waged employment. Though their reasoning is sound, this middle generation do not feel comfortable in accepting the social identity of benefit claimants. Like the grandparents, who unanimously reject the strategy of being 'looked after', they do not show any solidarity with people from the same group. Themselves long-term-unemployed, they talked harshly of 'persons unworthy of social benefit':

> That wasn't in the past. Then, if someone was not working, they put him in jail. Now all these leeches – I need to call them that. They have big support and are still doing *bad things*. When someone has money for drink, he can also work. Today, all those vagabonds going from one jail to another, they have big disability support. They are even giving them more money for social support. Where is this written? The honest person doesn't get anything! (Alžbeta, b. 1944; Nitra, 1996, pp. 46–7)

Such a distancing from the *category* of unemployed (Silverman, 1998) provides a defence against, and a dissociation from, the social identity of persons whose unemployment might be taken as behaviour disruptive of social standards. The negative categorisation of the unemployed is accentuated by the strict view of grandparents that ignoring the duty to 'toil' constitutes a moral offence, and by the neo-liberal discourse of the 'undeserving' poor. An unemployed family member, however, is not criticised directly. 'Laziness' is criticised, but only on a general level, or else indirectly, for instance by emphasising the older generation's hard work in the past and how their grandparents had managed to make ends meet without receiving benefit.

The generations' views on living on benefit differ. Let us compare a mother, Jolana (b. 1948; Martin, 1996), and her daughter Helena (b. 1973; ibid.). Jolana has basic education and worked as a cleaner for twenty years. She appreciated this job because it was 'much easier than a job on the building sites'. Helena completed a two-year technical school course for sanitary staff. She could then have obtained a cleaning job, but she turned this offer down, reasoning 'it was not a qualified job and I would not enjoy it'. Her mother honoured her decision, saying, 'No one has ever wanted to do the job of a cleaner ... These days, everybody chooses delicate jobs.' According to Helena and other unemployed young people in our sample, being unemployed has more dignity than doing *any* job. Parents (mothers in Rimavská Sobota and Martin) accept the younger generation's views.

Although hard work is seen as *the* important measure of human character, the narratives suggest that the official labour market and personal income have never been seen as the main arena for the testing of this quality. Rather, evidence for it – along with a source of personal dignity – has taken the form of household labour utilising a variety of skills, and the ability to be self-sufficient and to restore income that is always lacking. Provided that they are involved in such domestic self-supplying production, the family still considers its unemployed members hard-working. This explains also why our narrators do not experience loss of employment as social exclusion.

Childhood and Work

All the narrators of the grandparents' and parents' generation, whether they grew up before the War or under socialism, recall the work they were required to do when they came home from school or during summer holidays. None of them considered hard work an injustice. They do not stress side-effects. They value highly the ability of their parents to care for the family. They were all proud of having become accustomed to working. 'Father taught us to do many things. When we didn't want to work, he said that we should not be ashamed of hard work' (Hana, b. 1950; Likavka); 'My father told me not to be afraid of work – he said that hard work made real men' (Ján, b. 1952; Levice, 1996, p. 49).

Lýdia's family lived in a mountain area, where land collectivisation had been delayed:

> My parents had their farm on distant land; in winter my father helped doing woodwork. My grandparents also lived on [such] land, this was the only way of living in those days ... there was no time for me to learn – just to have something to eat after I came home from school and to graze cows. Even if we had been willing to learn there was no time for that. We were not really interested in going to school – I don't know, we probably thought it was all

> right … and [that] we should live in that way. (Lýdia, b. 1952; Rimavská Sobota, 1996, p. 25)

She could not recall if her teachers had impelled her or her siblings to undertake further studies:

> Well, I don't really know – maybe. However, we usually answered the same: 'We can't afford that, we don't have enough money for that.' That was all, nothing else. Our father has never encouraged us to go. Our parents needed our help in the farm, to make hay, dig potatoes … And they had no money for educating us, so why should they even mention this subject? (Lýdia, b. 1952; ibid., pp. 23–4)

Júlia now regrets having passed up the opportunity she had of obtaining the General Certificate of Education:

> It was *my fault*, and that of my parents, because they did not teach me to try hard to achieve higher goals … I was clever enough to learn and I was at a good age, too, but I did not see any reason why I should do so … I had no other idea. Even during my schooldays, my mother and my mother-in-law were preparing everything for my wedding. I knew I would get married ten days after I left school. I would stay at home, take care of my family. I was prepared to be another one of those generations whose lives would be filled with constant working in the fields, domestic animals and [staying] at home with children. However, I was brought up in such a way that what my mum told me I had taken for granted. And this was: 'It is important to learn a trade and then work properly.' (Júlia, b. 1962; Prešov, 1996, pp. 34–40)

Sharing Resources

The hard-and-fast rule of sharing household resources is represented in all the narratives of the older or middle generations. These narratives show that there was a basic duty to hand resources over to the 'household treasury' that was kept by the mother or the father:

> When I brought money home, I did not see it any more. It was not as it is today, that is, 'I earned the money, it is mine' – that was impossible. My father took it from me. I can remember, when I was 14 years old, I got my first wage. I bought myself a checked coat for winter. It cost only 80 crowns. It was not very expensive in those days. My father wanted to punish me: 'And who told you to do so? You've got a coat, haven't you?' 'Yes, I have,

> but I wanted a new one, and the old one is too small for me.' My father beat me with his belt ... No, I was not allowed to do what I wanted with the money. (Izabela, b. 1948; Galanta, 1996, p. 28)

This capacity to function as a household unit is bolstered by a pattern of authority that requires children to be obedient. Izabela's disobedience was severely punished. Izabela acknowledges she was punished for behaviour that is nowadays considered quite normal. She appears to be recalling this episode not to complain, but to transmit a moral message from the past.

It was probably not only our research that had revived these extensive memories of sharing resources and of personal demands being refused, factors that used to dominate family lives. Such memories might function as yardsticks for a younger generation's behaviour, a pattern to follow. The moralising nature of the reminiscences of the older generation indicates that opinions about the sharing of family resources were different in their families.

A Shop-window

Family histories suggest that the 'common' household economy is now in decline. There are at least two reasons for this. First, children have ceased to be a working force. They have become instead a family 'shop-window', an advertisement, so to speak, of the status and wealth of the family as a whole. The second reason is the disintegration of 'local' definitions of happiness and material wealth. Happy village children spending their summer playing near a stream in worn-out tracksuits, without dreams of beautiful beaches and CD Walkmans, seem to belong to a forgotten past. Universal norms of consumption feed the feeling of inferiority. The remark 'At present children are more demanding' appears in every family history:

> I try to do the same as my parents did – to give my children everything they need. However, there is a huge difference between those days and the present day. We appreciated those things much more than they do now! They take it for granted, as if we were obliged to do that. (Jozef, b. 1951; Levice, 1996, p. 39)

This shifting of children towards the family centre and the idea of their being a 'shop-window' exposes families to the universal pressures of consumer demands. Júlia decided to 'ensure my children would have everything', and strictly adapted her housekeeping to that aim. She bases her home cooking on private-plot-grown products and only buys essential foodstuffs. The only exception to this rule concerns elevenses, the meal her children take to school:

> As far as school is concerned, this is something they *must* have, OK? Only at school. Every day some food, every day some sweets. Or some fruit. They must not suffer … from the remarks of other children …

Thanks to her cost-cutting measures (Júlia also makes dresses for her children, and her husband made most of their furniture) the family were able to buy electronic equipment which makes them feel up to the prevailing standard. When Júlia applied for social security because her family income was at roughly the minimum level, Social Security staff inspected her flat:

> They visited us and looked around and they told us we were 'above-standard' – that we lived at a high standard and could not be granted benefit. Our household was [ironically] 'equipped for these days in an above-standard way'. I do not know what they found above-standard, but you know – this is what they wrote. On that paper, we are [bitterly] 'an above-standard family'. (Júlia, b. 1962; Prešov, p. 16)

The family histories suggest that children's needs are privileged and, at the same time, feared. In order to ensure the welfare of their children, and that they do not appear to be different from others, parents are prone to fail in their rent payments, to fail to keep their children on their diet when they are seriously ill, or to agree to spending an entire sum of benefit on one pair of shoes. These families experience social inclusion mainly via consumption opportunities. As a form of psychological defence, they sometimes try to reinterpret the humiliating dichotomy between rich and poor by associating the rich with crime. This, however, offers no lasting comfort to them when they are up against their children's inevitable demands regarding 'consumption standards' and the reduced market value of unskilled physical labour.

Conclusions

There is a temptation to frame the analysis of family histories with an (implicit) path-dependency hypothesis. Such framing is not sensitive to the fact that family histories and life stories tend to be related in such a way as to help their narrators deal with their present problems. In our research, the narrators' substantial need was to sustain family collaboration.

I have tried to show how poor families perceive social differences. They complain of a neglectful government, but their critique appears to be a more-or-less-ritual form of swearing. I also suggest that their lethargy stems from a lack of awareness of other reasonable alternatives, both of means of protest and of ways of securing a family livelihood. Formally speaking, we may hardly consider the families under study to be socially excluded. Despite their exclusion from the labour market they are included in the system of political rights and the social security system, as well as in their families (Atkinson, 2000). A number of fears regarding exclusion, however, are expressed in the narratives. There is a fear of moral exclusion bound up with the identification of a category of 'undeserving' benefit claimants. There is also a fear of exclusion from consumption opportunities – a fear, that is, of not being able to demonstrate one's similarity to others.

The 'over-cautious' form that the family narratives take suggests that the most essential, and also fragile, medium of social inclusion is the narrator's family. Despite their lack of a fine education, the narrators appear to know that storytelling can both break and strengthen the fragile ties of family cooperation. As a rule, they structure their narratives around their efforts to maintain and enhance a commitment to family solidarity. The family histories suggest that this mode of family cooperation and mutual assistance represents a time-tested instrument for securing family livelihoods and, at the same time, testifies to the narrators' will to continue the process. The histories should, therefore, be studied and appreciated as a form of investment in a common family future.

Notes

1 The project was carried out under the auspices of the Social Costs of Economic Transformation in Central Europe, initiated by the Institute of Human Sciences, Vienna, in 1996.

2 In the Slovak case, the three generations had the following characteristics. The grandparents had to be born in the country prior to World War II; they had only basic education, and either their parents or they themselves worked as agricultural day labourers or petty peasants. The middle generation was represented by the couple made up of skilled or semi-skilled workers in agriculture and industry, one of whom is now unemployed. People of this generation had two or more children, and lived in villages or smaller towns (with fewer than 50,000 inhabitants) in regions with a higher-than-average rate of unemployment. The young generation were persons aged over sixteen who finished or intended to finish their education via apprentice school without

obtaining a GCE. For further information about the resources of the theoretical ideal type and about the sampling strategies see Feglová, Kusá and Radičová (1995).

3 We obtained the addresses thanks to Social Department officials, who were (in 1995) eager to defy the personal data protection law.

4 The first, 'unrestricted' part of the narrative interview (based on Schütze, 1977) took about 3 per cent of the total length in more than a half of cases. It followed the pattern of an official CV, with data about birth, education, marriage, or loss of employment. This conventional form could serve as a safe 'refuge' during interaction with troublesome strangers. Another noteworthy feature was a strong focus on the positive aspects of family life, and the avoidance of strict judgements about other people in general (see Kusá, 1999).

5 This may have been Czechoslovakia (1918–39) or Slovakia (1939–45). Nobody mentioned Slovakian independence (neither that of 1939 nor that of 1993).

6 In my study of the Slovak economic privatisation discourse (Kusá, 1995) I argue that civic powerlessness was deepened by being framed by the 'law of the jungle' metaphor, widely used by the leftist Slovak press.

References

Atkinson, R. (2000), 'Combating Social Exclusion in Europe: The New Urban Policy Challenge', *Urban Studies*, vol. 37, nos 5–6, pp. 1,037–55.

Bertaux, D. (1993), 'Sociálne genealógie komentované a porovnávané', *Sociológia*, vol. 25, no. 6, pp. 507–26.

Feglová, V., Kusá, Z. and Radičová, I. (1995), 'Conceptualisation of Poverty in Slovakia', in *The Social History of Poverty in Central Europe*, Max Weber Foundation, Budapest, pp. 291–302.

Galanta (1996), Family history recorded in the town Galanta. Transcript. Institute for Sociology of the Slovak Academy of Sciences, Bratislava.

Kusá, Z. (1995), 'Public Discourse and Civil Powerlessness', *Slovak Sociological Review/Sociológia*, vol. 27, nos 7–8, pp. 47–58.

Kusá, Z. (1999), 'Poor People – Poor Stories? Ordinary and Extraordinary in Life History Narratives', *Sociológia*, vol. 31, no. 3, pp. 263–90.

Levice (1996), Family history recorded in the town Levice. Transcript. Institute for Sociology of the Slovak Academy of Sciences, Bratislava.

Likavka (1996), Family history recorded in the town Likavka. Transcript. Institute for Sociology of the Slovak Academy of Sciences, Bratislava.

Martin (1996), Family history recorded in the town Martin. Transcript. Institute for Sociology of the Slovak Academy of Sciences, Bratislava.

Nitra (1996), Family history recorded in the town Nitra. Transcript. Institute for Sociology of the Slovak Academy of Sciences, Bratislava.

Prešov (1996), Family history recorded in the town Prešov. Transcript. Institute for Sociology of the Slovak Academy of Sciences, Bratislava.

Rimavská Sobota (1996), Family history recorded in the town Rimavská Sobota. Transcript. Institute for Sociology of the Slovak Academy of Sciences, Bratislava.

Schütze, F. (1977), *Die Technik des narrativen Interviews in Interaktion-feldstudien dargestellt an einem Projekt zur Erforschung von kommunalen Machtstruturen*, University of Bielefeld.

Silverman, D. (1998), *Harvey Sacks: Social Science and Conversation Analysis*, Polity Press, Cambridge.

Szalai, J. (1995), 'Power and Poverty', in *The Social History of Poverty in Central Europe*, Max Weber Foundation, Budapest, pp. 203–18.

PART 4

Ethnicity and Sexuality

14 Different Generations of Leningrad Jews in the Context of Public/Private Division: Paradoxes of Ethnicity

VIKTOR VORONKOV AND ELENA CHIKADZE
Centre for Independent Social Research,
St Petersburg, Russia

Introduction

The purpose of this chapter is to explore the construction of the ethnic identity of several different generations of Leningrad Jews, as a microcosm of the changes that have taken place in Russian society in terms of the private/public division of social life. Our reflections on this subject are based on biographical narratives we collected during a research project carried out in 1993–6 by the Centre for Independent Social Research.[1]

Biographical research represents an excellent means of demonstrating that different generations of Soviet people were socialised in substantially different ways. Different generations' experiences resulted in different types of ethnic identity. Thus, the Jewish identity of migrants from the Pale was succeeded, in the subsequent generation, by a quasi-ethnic Soviet identity. Generations of people who lived their lives under late socialism, and who witnessed the dissolution of the Soviet Union, have attempted a revalorisation of Jewish ethnic identity, but only a limited proportion of assimilated Jews have redefined the meaning of their ethnicity. Over the whole course of the Soviet period, reflections on ethnicity were closely bound up with the changes that took place in the relationship between the public and private spheres. The public/private division in the Soviet Union was formative in terms of social structures and played a crucial role in the determination of Soviet life-practices.

This chapter also represents a response to the debate in Russian sociology about the 'borrowing' and applying of Western concepts and theoretical models in studies of Russian (Soviet) society. We argue that the usefulness of (Western) sociological models and concepts for Russian studies can only be tested empirically. Moreover, we believe it is necessary to reflect on our own experience of cross-cultural research, since doing this will help us to understand better the problems that exist in comparative studies.

Key Concepts of the Study

We see ethnicity as a social construction that is formed in the border situations of the encounter with others, when certain social agents ascribe definite properties to themselves and to others.[2] The elements of this construction are not rigid, but indeterminate and open to change. In nomadic contexts ethnic identity may undergo change, and may disappear from the public arena, subject to the particular conjunction of circumstances. In this study, therefore, we use the word 'Jew' to signify not only individuals who have Jewish identity, but also those whose ancestors considered themselves Jewish.

A 'generation' is a community of individuals of approximately the same age who have similar cultural and societal orientations, follow similar behavioural patterns, and are involved in the same practices. These orientations and patterns are formed through a socialisation process involving shared experiences. In modern societies (including Russia), the formative age for the character of a generation (the inter-subjective *habitus*) is 16–24: in other words, experiences gained during this period of the life cycle serve as a foundation for basic social beliefs.[3]

In the context of the present chapter, it is important to note that we consider generation not as a biological entity but as a sociological category. The problems associated with the concept of generation lie in the social arena; and, though the concept rests upon the idea of the life cycle of a group, it cannot be reduced to it. We might not, therefore, assign to a certain generation everyone who might be assigned to it by age. It seems reasonable, for example, to include in a generation those individuals who are younger, but who were socialised under the powerful influence of cultural and social experience that was relevant for the previous generation. Generations thus defined may sometimes even include biological fathers and children.

The dynamics of Soviet modernity make it possible to establish boundaries between the generations, each of which was socialised under different conditions. These resulted in different types of self-consciousness, different value systems, different attitudes towards social memory, and different life-practices.

The Public/Private Division in Soviet Society

The concept of public and private spheres of social life is crucial for this study, and the distinction needs to be explained here, because our interpretation of the two spheres does not accord with the tradition operating in the Western social-scientific community.[4] The public/private distinction in the Soviet Union involved a rigid boundary. The rules of the game in the two spheres, and the corresponding life-practices, were different from those operating in Western societies.

Before we specify this distinction, however, we need to clarify those rules or codes that regulated human behaviour in Soviet society. We make a distinction between habitual (informal) and written (formal) codes. By the former, we mean those non-legal, informal, conventional regulations that were objectified in the practices of everyday life. In the late-socialist period, this informal code evidently played a dominant role in the regulations governing everyday life.

Every modern society, in fact, is characterised by an analogous distinction between a written and a habitual code. But the dominance of the informal code in the USSR during the final socialist decades implied fundamental shifts in social life. The development of the private sphere, and of the informal household economy as well as of entrepreneurship, was mostly regulated by the habitual code.

The Russian researcher Oleg Witte notes that both codes were considered legitimate by people in the Soviet Union, whatever inconsistencies they embodied. Legitimation of the habitual code was necessary, since otherwise the written code would have had to have been revised, and this revision would have led to the failure of the regulating system. Strict demands that the written code should be observed could have led to the failure of the regime. This is why the initiatives of citizens in breaking the written code and thereby installing the informal code were used to promote and reinforce the efficiency of written-code activities. It also explains how this very specific duality in terms of inconsistent codes was accepted by the community as normative.[5]

Legitimation of the coexistence of the two inconsistent codes *per se*, however, was not sufficient to give the system stability: reinforcement of the legitimacy of the habitual code was ruining the legitimacy of the written code. This is why a mechanism existed for combating social destruction: the deforming of the legal sphere was 'balanced' by a parallel deforming of the communication sphere. Thus the public (official) realm was constructed so that discussion about the habitual code was taboo there. As Witte notes, 'the practical priority of the habitual code was compensated for by the placing of a taboo on discussion about its operation'. The immense growth in the diversity of informally-regulated practices was admitted into the public realm under the banner of a 'fight with the relics of capitalism'.[6]

Life in Soviet society was officially represented in terms of a utopia completely at odds with everyday experience: it was a world of outstanding construction projects, heroic labour, great cultural achievements, high moral standards, humanistic slogans, etc. The day-to-day reality of social life-practices, however, contrasted sharply with what was publicly admitted and discussed. Thus, the official-public sphere represented only written-code practices, and single cases where these were broken. Beyond the official-public realm, by contrast, everything was submitted to discussion. What was this 'beyond'? It was the private sphere, which underwent change over the course of Soviet history.

The Stalinist system was characterised by a lack of privacy. This was the period when the borderline between private and public was unclear and indeterminate. Beginning in the 1920s, the private realm was reduced to a minimum: it is as if it were absorbed by the public realm. Such an absorption resulted from a collectivist ideology, from the practice of overall party-state control, from new everyday life-practices. The housing policy adopted in towns led to the mass destruction of apartments for individual families. Local governments practised what was called a 'density housing strategy', according to which tenants who previously had occupied individual apartments were forced to reduce their living space to one or two rooms. The remaining rooms were distributed among workers who were resettled from the basements, and among numerous migrant peasants.

Living conditions in the so-called *kommunalkas* (shared apartments) left almost no space for privacy. The climate of mutual suspicion and bad relations among tenants led to total social control being exercised at the level of social interaction. Thus private space was reduced to a minimum, and the public/private division became subject to a purely conventional understanding. A motto was coined: 'A true Soviet citizen has nothing to hide.' In other words, there could be no subject closed to public discussion.

Nevertheless, parallel with the official-public sphere there came into being another public sphere. The latter was separated from the former by a rigid demarcation. This new public sphere started to develop with the end of Stalinism. The XXth Party Congress, along with the official critiquing of Stalinism and new opennesses in the political regime, resulted in critical reflections being undertaken on the nature of social reality. This was the period of the 'double message'. On the one hand, real life still could not be discussed in the official-public sphere; on the other, the risks associated with involvement in reflective criticism diminished with the Khruschev thaw. Such an ambivalence brought into being a new conception of the 'public'. We shall call this new dimension of social life the private-public sphere. This was a social space where almost any issue of interest could be discussed. In our view, this sphere is much more comprehensive than the '*demi-privée*' sphere discussed by Ariès (visiting, invariant theatre-boxes, limited access clubs, etc. – i.e. public realm, though closed).

We have already mentioned that the latent functions of housing policy were the construction of social space, and the promotion of an appropriate private/public distinction. The massive house-building programme that began in the 1950s provided a solid space for the private sphere, involving as it did the construction of separate flats, or flats containing only one household. With these changes in housing and living conditions, the boundary between official-public and private-public spaces became clearer. By contrast, that between the private sphere proper and the private-public sphere was rather unclear. The former, in Soviet society, was rather ill-defined. One example of this is the famous 'intelligentsia kitchen', the home as a 'yard with a through-passage', etc.

The relevant concept here is not that of a 'second society', as discussed in some studies of dissident groups and of the informal economy in Eastern Europe (Hankiss, 1988). One need not assume that the private-public sphere was associated only with the practices of identifiable social groupings (which might possibly offer opposition to the authorities). We assume that every Soviet individual, including those constituting the nomenclature, lived and acted in both spheres, respected the invisible but effective boundary between them, and did not confuse the different rules regulating the official-public and private-public realms. This is the essence of that social schizophrenia which is justly attributed to the 'common Soviet man'.

Methodological Implications of the Public/Private Division

What are the implications of the dynamics of the public/private distinction for the sociological interpretation of narrative interviews (not to mention that of data gathered via survey questionnaires, where the interpretation of answers is always uncertain)? We would argue that social arrangements in the Soviet Union gave a new meaning to the issue of the reliability of information drawn from narratives and problem-oriented interviews. In analysing narratives, sociologists should take into account the rigid division between the rules of the game applying in the public-private and official-public realms of Soviet life. Lack of awareness of this division results in distorted explanations of social actions, and a distorted construction of biographical realities.

For an interview respondent, communication with a sociologist is a fact of the official-public sphere. As a result, the respondent's behaviour is regulated, perhaps even non-consciously, by the rules relevant in this sphere. These rules define what may be discussed (or else hushed up), and in what way. And this applies not only to the taboo on the verbalising of certain themes (i.e. sexuality, social origin, military service, etc.). As we mentioned above, it was 'wrong' (inappropriate) to discuss 'real life' in the official-public sphere. Therefore, the issue of 'inappropriateness' represented part of the accountability (as an aspect of communication) of the interviewer and the narrator. The style and substance of official-public interaction differed drastically from those of private-public interaction. Thus a Soviet individual had at his or her disposal two differently constructed biographies, which as a set of biographical facts differed in terms of their interpretation and of their presentation within a narrative structure.

A typical example of such a double biography is the tale of the poverty career. A sociologist who has been granted permission to conduct an interview gains detailed information about low wages at an official place of employment, about the irregularity of payments, and about official allowances and pensions. The matter of unofficial incomes gained in the shadow economy (and in contemporary Russia most people gain the majority of their income in the shadow economy!), however, does not appear in the narrative. This is not only because the informant may be afraid of being seen to be involved in racketeering, or of being investigated by the tax police, but mainly because of the incongruity of discussing real-life strategies in official-public interaction. Attempts to stimulate discussion of these strategies threaten communication in general. The real, relatively well-off lifestyle of the informant observed by the sociologist contradicts the narrative of poverty created specifically for the official-public sphere.

On the other hand, in cases where the informant is well-acquainted with the sociologist and trusts the sociologist, he or she can probably elicit quite a different presentation of the biography, one designed for a circle of confidential friends and relatives. Although its conditions and life-rules are undergoing serious change, Soviet socialisation exercises a lasting grip on informants. Our research experience demonstrates that there is a cultural continuity in habitual notions of what can be discussed in the public realm, and how.

The interviews we conducted with representatives of the younger generation (those under 25) whose secondary socialisation took place in the post-Soviet period affirm this statement. In these interviews, we encounter the phenomenon of double biography less often. More and more topics become open for discussion. The very refusal on the part of an individual to be interviewed shows that he or she is trying to escape from a situation where double biography is unavoidable. We hypothesise that in interviews with younger narrators, the official-public and the private-public versions of the life stories do not differ markedly (although admittedly we have insufficient evidence for such an assertion).

The misconceptions we encounter in the literature on the Soviet Union can be explained by a failure to recognise this phenomenon of the double biography. For example, there are numerous publications which give a somewhat myth-based representation of the everyday lives and problems of Soviet Jews or Soviet Germans who emigrated to Germany. It is quite easy to understand the origins of these myths. One of the authors of this chapter took part in some research examining a Russian community in Berlin. At one point, a recent immigrant, describing to him how he had been interviewed by a German sociologist, said the following: 'Don't worry – I told him absolutely everything that I thought it was necessary to tell.'

Thus we consider that the stories presented by a Soviet informant in the official-public sphere (i.e. those presented to sociologists) are not of great value for an understanding of everyday life (or 'real life', as we conventionally call it). It is clear that under such conditions a great deal of attention should be paid to the technique of participant observation. A version of biography presented by an informant who does not trust the sociologist can scarcely be interpreted properly. An atmosphere of trust and confidence is critical in field research. Without this trust, the sociologist will not be able to reconstruct the reality of the informant, and will attribute to the informant's actions his or her own meanings. These are the specific difficulties involved in sociological investigation of Soviet Russian society which employs traditional methods.

Below, we consider the reconstruction of a typical ethnic biography of several generations of a Leningrad Jewish family.[7] We identify four generations of Leningrad Jews, which we reconstruct on the basis of participant observation and narrative biographical interviews. We use our conceptualisation of the dynamics of the private/public division in Soviet society to distinguish between these generations, which have different ethnic identities. We turn first to the analysis of the ethnic identity of the first generation.

The Generation of the Internationalist Period

The first generation of Leningrad Jews (our respondents' parents or grandparents) were the teenagers and young people who came to the city from the former Pale of Settlement regions.[8] Many of them, as well as a considerable number of Russian Jews, welcomed the Revolution, which promised to abolish discrimination against Jews. The Revolution abolished the prohibition that had hitherto existed on Jews living in Russia's big cities. As a result, Jewish young people from the former Pale of Settlement moved to these cities in order to realise their new life-strategies. According to census data, in 1910, 35,000 Jews were living in St Petersburg. As a consequence of the disastrous events associated with the Revolution and Civil War the population of the city was reduced by two-thirds. The majority of Jews either died or left the city. In 1926, however, the Jewish population totalled 84,000, which was two and a half times greater than it had been before the War.

The secondary socialisation of this generation took place in an already-Soviet environment, and gave rise to an internationally-oriented Soviet world view where ethnic values, attitudes and practices were losing their significance. Thus one young informant told us, with a certain amount of surprise, of letters which his grandmother, a Komsomol member, had written in 1925, in which she described events that had taken place some 70 years before the interview:

> It was rather funny to read the lines where my granny tells of a delegation of Austrian young people that visited Kharkov. And she describes their clothes and says that she was dressed in a red headscarf and in a leather double-breasted jacket. I mean, I understand now that it was exactly like she wrote, that these were not symbols or an image invented later. And she writes: 'as our Russian Komsomol member'. Thus in these letters – there are not many of them – you will not find any emphasis on Jewish origin, no mention at all, so, exactly like this: this is our Russian Komsomol member. This was such an epoch. (Leonid G., b. 1973)

It seemed strange to the informant, who constructed his Jewish identity on the basis of two 'Russian' generations of his family, that his 'Jewish' grandmother did not think of herself as a Jew, as it would have been 'natural' for her (in her grandson's eyes) to have done, but instead called herself Russian. Ethnicity, however, was probably not something his grandmother at that time problematised, and the signifier 'Russian' did not seem to contain any ethnic meaning for her.

Despite the fact that the primary socialisation of this generation had occurred within a traditional Jewish environment of *mestechkos*, the young people who had moved to Leningrad were rapidly adapting to the new conditions and were successfully forging their 'Soviet' careers. The overwhelming majority of young Jewish migrants graduated from universities and colleges:

> My father was a Komsomol member in the '20s, then he became a Red Professor. That is to say he was an absolutely Russian person.[9] He remembered his childhood in Byelorussia, he comes from there. But then he became a European, a Russian scientist in the broad sense. (Elena L., b. 1939)

> My grandparents came from a small borough called Konotop: it is located in the Eastern Ukraine, and my grandfather belongs to exactly this generation – the people who got their first education at a *haeder* [a Jewish religious school]. Then he entered the Young Communist League, later he entered the Party, and soon he arrived in Leningrad, went to work at the plant, then the Army, where he acquired a military rank, then during the war he became a colonel. Well, he is a military professional, he graduated from the Military Academy. (Alexander F., b. 1961)

The parents of the young people who had settled in Leningrad moved to the city from *mestechkos* to join their children. Jewish values, attitudes and practices usually remained important for the older generation. The young people did not interfere with their parents' upholding of Jewish religious traditions. But their elders did not constitute a reference group for them, and their Jewish identity remained simply a fact of their private life linking them with their parents' family:

> However, none of my relatives, children, nephews and nieces, nobody can speak the language in our family, nobody. My father [the Komsomol member of the '20s who had arrived from the *mestechko*] could speak a little, my grandfather and grandmother spoke fluently, my mother did not speak at all. ... My grandfather and grandmother sometimes spoke Jewish (Yiddish), when they wanted to conceal something from us ... (Elena L., b. 1939)

> My aunts and grandmother, when the Jewish Easter came, made something in line with the rites, and my father took it calmly. This attitude came from a general standpoint existing in society, from an urge towards atheism.[10] Jewish traditionalism burst under the pressure of socialist ideas. (Boris M., b. 1938)

The reunion of Jewish families in Leningrad did not prevent the ongoing Sovietisation of the younger generation, who continued to lose their former ethnic identity. One informant remarked: '... my mother ... was, generally speaking, Russian, though she was entirely Jewish by birth.' She went on:

> My mother's parents were politicised people, they were sort of engaged by the Soviet power. That is, my mother's father was even a member of the Communist Party, and his wife – my grandmother – in the '20s took part in the Young Pioneers movement ... Jewishness – it has always been associated with religion. And as they were such people – those who loved the Soviet system – I mean my mother's parents, big patriots of the Soviet state, true Leninists, true Stalinists, I would say, then, quite naturally, everything that was related to religion had to be swept aside. Therefore my mother did not have it [Jewish identity]. Though, naturally, when they (my mother's parents) were a boy and a girl, they got this Jewishness from their parents, because my grandfather, before he became a Communist and a military·man, had studied in a yeshiva – this is a Jewish school – and my grandmother – my mother's mother – she also was sort of the same ... Well, all this was on the level of grandmothers and grandfathers – this is something that is inherent in every Jew, because they all had to live there ... (in Jewish *mestechkos*), therefore it could not be otherwise. (Elena L., b. 1939)

> My father was a typical Leningrad child. His parents attended only a primary school, so they were completely uneducated people. And after they had arrived in Leningrad, the maximum they did in their homes was circumcision,

> which they did to their children – boys, of course. But my parents – neither my father nor my mother – had anything else of this kind. All this had stopped at the level of grandfathers and grandmothers, and moreover – both grandfathers and grandmothers only had it in their early years. And nothing more than that. (Irina I., b. 1960)

Along with this Sovietisation, the number of mixed marriages increased, which in the opinion of one informant is '... inevitable. If the grandmother and the grandfather come from one and the same *mestechko*, [then] already her youngest daughter marries a Russian, and almost all her grandchildren enter into [ethnically] mixed marriages' (Irina B., b. 1952). Jewish customs, religious practices and language disappeared with the dying out of the older generation. 'Our family almost did not follow the traditions. Only my grandfather and grandmother spoke Yiddish. They spoke fluently. But they died when I was three years old. And I did not need the language' (Osip M., b. 1933).

Jewish culture at that time still existed, both in the private sphere and in the public realm, as the culture of the older generation (in Jewish organisations and cultural institutions, and in the mass media, and so on). Ethnic issues were still subjected to public discussion, although they were losing their topicality. Ethnic discrimination, which later conditioned the problematisation of Jewish identity, did not exist at that time. The large-scale repressions which took place in the late 1930s did not involve the systematic persecution of definite ethnic groups. Any event in a life story (including ethnic origin, of course) that set a person apart from the great mass of others could serve as a reason for repression. The NKVD invented cases of 'nationalists' (e.g. Poles, Finns, Estonians) who had their 'ethnic native land' outside the USSR. At the same time, its repressions were not aimed directly against ethnic groups.[11]

Even the subsequent repressions that took place on ethnic grounds did not, up until a certain point, concern the Jews. (None of the parents, grandparents or relatives of our respondents suffered seriously during this period.) As a result, there are clear reasons for defining the first generation of Leningrad Jews, and perhaps all Jews who lived in urbanised Russia, as those who originated from Jewish families, later abandoned Jewish practices, and finally stopped being *homines ethnici*. Most of these people were born during the first two decades of the twentieth century, and so their secondary socialisation occurred during the period described. This predetermined their future assertion of 'internationalist' Soviet values above ethnic values whatever their life-circumstances.

The Generations of the Anti-Semitic Era

The following two generations of Leningrad Jews were socialised under fundamentally new conditions. They had much in common, and for the most part we do not observe any great intergenerational differences between them. The first of the two generations came to adulthood at a time when the policy of anti-Semitism was being established.[12]

By the end of the 1940s, even formal ethnic status (either as registered on a passport or as conferred by a 'Jewish' surname) served to jeopardise effective life-strategies (' ... as for my mother [b. 1925], I guess she has always been afraid of the fact that she was Jewish, and she tried to think about it as seldom as possible' (Nikolai G., b. 1952)). At that time a campaign was launched to fight 'Jewish nationalism' and cosmopolitanism, and everyday manifestations of anti-Semitism increased sharply. This resulted in a striving on the part of 'formal' Jews to get rid of the stigma: whenever possible, they tried to obtain passport registration as ethnic Russians both for themselves and their children.[13] Families' previous Jewish heritages were hushed up. All these strategies led to the deliberate destruction of social (ethnic) memory, and to the ousting of references to Jewish ethnicity not only from public but also from private life. These 'survival' strategies resemble those of the upper strata of Russian society after the 1917 Revolution, when in order to survive physically parents concealed their social origin and family history from their children.[14] Children of the anti-Semitic generations recalled these parental strategies as follows:

> I got to know about it [his nationality] I guess at the age of 8 or 10 ... Before that I believed that a Jew was sort of a military rank, and I confused it with a 'corporal' ['Jew' in Russian is *yevrei*, and 'corporal' is *yefreitor*]. And even when the gypsy children – when we lived at our dacha – cried 'Hey, you Jew, Jew!' – I remember it well now – I could not understand why they called me a kind of soldier. I thought that the word 'Jew' meant a corporal, a soldier. And only later, when somebody started to throw stones on to our roof and to break windows, at this point I started to understand something ... and once, after the next stone was thrown into the kitchen window of our *dacha*, I did not understand why exactly our windows were broken, so I asked my grandfather about it. And then my grandfather explained to me ... that's because we were Jews ... He said: 'This is a nationality.' And my grandfather told me that many great people were Jews as well. This is how I got to know that we also belonged to this thing. (Alexander K., b. 1962)

> And when [I was] in kindergarten, there was a girl, and once she called me a *zhidovka* (a Yid) [an offensive, scornful name for a Jew in Russian]. I remember that I came up to my mum and asked what a *zhidovka* was, as I did not understand it at all. She told me that in tsarist times there were such ... such a word was thought up, well, something like this. There was always such an unpleasant feeling – I felt that this was so bad, that it was really an obscene word. Then my father started to tell me about something – you see, I think he was always telling me, well, something ... historical facts, some scanty information from [the] Old Testament. (Elena Sh., b. 1974)

These two excerpts illustrate how children encountered their Jewish origins in the standard occasions of early socialisation – at the *dacha* or in the kindergarten. The family left these children secure, and ignorant about their Jewishness. Under external pressure, parents were forced to provide certain explanations regarding ethnicity in the form of a justification, because these first encounters with their ethnicity were harmful for Jewish children. Even in these interviews, they can hardly find a fitting word to describe their Jewishness.

If, on the part of the first generation of Leningrad Jews, we can observe a rapid and unquestioning formation of Soviet Russian identity, among the second and third generations a sense of Jewish identity had already become a rare exception:

> I belong to the Russian culture, and I can't find anything stronger [than Russian culture] in the Jewish culture. (Boris M., b. 1938)

> ... Assimilated, to a great extent assimilated [her parents], yes. In principle, I believe that if it hadn't been for the passport, for some recent events, maybe we would never have thought of the fact that ... (Elena Sh., b. 1974)

Even when some remnants of Jewish identity have been preserved, Soviet identity is nevertheless much more important for these Jews:

> My mother [b. 1927] was such a ... sort of a Soviet woman, simply a human being, ordinary, very nice. The fact that she was a Jew – in general, she never concealed it, she was never ashamed of it, but for her it was never a very essential feature, and actually this is not a very essential feature anyway. I mean, one did not try to forget about it, but at the same time – there were times when this was also not needed. Look at me – I am Jewish. And so what? I am an engineer, I am working at the research institute. What of it that I am Jewish – does it make any difference? (Leonid G., b. 1973)

One informant recalled that in 1980 she was not allowed to work as a guide with foreigners. Striving to overturn this decision her mother went to the dean of the university where her daughter studied and said the following:

> If necessary, I can bring recommendations from my work, from my husband's work, from our Party committees, that we never ... the very best characteristics, that we are not connected ... that is, we are good workers, we are active participants in all Party meetings, political seminars – that nobody is tangled up with anything suspicious ... and my husband also attends all these ideological seminars. I am doing Marxist-Leninist courses ... (Irina I., b. 1960)

Outside the family, Jewish children more and more often felt that 'Jewishness was already something indecent' (Boris, b. 1959). The categories 'decent' and 'indecent' are often used to describe the discomfort caused by Jewish ethnic identity. 'Indecent' meant abnormal, not good, dangerous, suspicious: in other words, marginal to the Soviet mainstream. Thus a child had to face the problematisation of ethnicity in the public sphere. For instance, if somebody called him a 'Jew', he already perceived this as an obscene word. This problematisation of Jewish ethnicity represented a public challenge, demanding of Jews ethnic self-identification as 'indecent' people. On the part of the second 'anti-Semitic' generation, the response in the private sphere to this public challenge was a jettisoning of ethnic identity.

After the XXth Congress of the CPSU, however, when Stalinism was exposed, and with society becoming more and more open, a new type of reaction to the public challenge gradually began to develop in the private sphere. Relations started to tell children the ancient history of the Jewish people, citing the names of famous Jews of the past (usually the list of names was the same: Karl Marx, Einstein, Eisenstein, Charlie Chaplin ...). One of our informants remembered the feelings of surprise, happiness and pride that seized him when he learnt that a favourite poet of all Soviet children – Samuil Marshak – was a Jew like himself. As a result, his simply formally being a Jew led to an ambivalent feeling: '... from one side, a pride that came from nowhere, and from the other – a terrible humiliation' (Yuri P., b. 1951). Such a humiliation registers as discomfort, and creates a desire, if not to conceal, then at least not to overemphasise the shameful fact of the life story: 'I knew that it is shameful, an awkward position – decent people – and being Jews ...' (Elena Z., b. 1961).[15]

Thus, 'ethnic pride' was cultivated in the private sphere of family and friendships, and 'ethnic humiliation' was mainly a public phenomenon. The gulf between personal, private dignity and public humiliation deepened. At the same time, in the public sphere distinct 'rules of the game' regarding the contact of Jews with the state were upheld by mutual, silent consent. Violation of these rules was considered importunate and indecent. As an example, one of our informants told us how she, then an active Komsomol member, was not allowed to go abroad in 1962. When she submitted her papers a second time, she did something which was considered absolutely unacceptable in the public sphere. She went to the official who was dealing with the matter, and asked her bluntly whether she would be allowed to go abroad given the data regarding nationality that were on her passport. The official was completely taken aback. The girl won permission for the planned trip, though the outcome might well have been different and rather unpleasant for her (Elena L., b. 1939).

We consider the Arab–Israeli Six Day War of 1967 as marking the borderline between the two ethnic generations, which were in many ways similar to each other. The Israeli victory in this war created a new public challenge to the identity of Soviet Jews and brought about changes in Soviet policy regarding Jews. On the one hand, a strengthened state policy of anti-Semitism seriously trammelled the life-strategies of Soviet Jews. A campaign against 'Israeli Zionists' was launched in the mass media:

> Every paper wrote only about Israeli aggressors. But of course they could not write that Jews were just bastards. It could not be said: I do not like Jews. But one could well say: I do not like Zionists, they do great harm to poor Arabs. It was clear that Zionism meant Jews. (Boris S., b. 1959)

At the beginning of the 1970s a special 'Jewish' KGB department was created. As a consequence, the education and employment of Jews were rigidly regulated. Jews could not choose any college or university they wished: both written and unwritten rules specified those colleges they were allowed to enter and the relevant quotas. The same was true of employment, as the majority of our informants attest.

On the other hand, the appearance of the Israeli theme in the official-public sphere (in the mass media) created new opportunities for the constructing of Jewish identities. It became possible for Jews to reconstruct their Jewish identity in a new symbolic space:

> Israel gave us some pride, of course. There had been such a strong feeling of humiliation all the time, that they [Jews] could neither fight nor work, neither in agriculture, nor anywhere, and then it appeared that the most productive cows were there in Israel, that they gathered God knows how big harvests, and the main thing was that they knew how to fight. (Lyubov' D., b. 1948)

Thus, private ethnic pride was justified by a publicly-avowed military victory. At the end of the 1960s, the legal opportunity to emigrate from the USSR on the basis of Jewish origin was re-established. This conjunction of political and social-psychological circumstances incited differentiation among Soviet Jews, including, first of all, differentation between the two generations of the anti-Semitic period. The first of these generations was homogeneous enough in terms of its Soviet Russian identity. These Jews, who were the majority, had long considered themselves 'Russian' (in the sense of 'Soviet'), and the above-mentioned conjunction did not really affect this. By contrast, in the next generation we can observe the growth of a minority which for various reasons opted for the ethnic identity of their grandparents who had come to Leningrad from the *mestechkos*.

We can mention one example of intergenerational conflict in the family centring on the issue of Jewish identity. One informant described to us his father, who had been such a 'decent' man that he had even not attempted to enter the CPSU, as he had never considered himself worthy to be a party member. This man visited his cousin who was leaving for Israel, and told him that 'everyone who was leaving our state was his personal enemy' (Yuri P., b. 1951). The first generation of the anti-Semitic period and the Soviet Russian majority of the second are essentially similar. In the following, we focus on the formation of a minority (new groups of Soviet Jews) who developed a new ethnic identity and new ethnic strategies.

It was at the end of the 1960s that a number of those Soviet Jews who had long been assimilated started to assume for themselves Jewish values, which they attempted to reconstruct from the scant information they had about Israel.[16] From this time on, one can speak of the formation of a specifically Jewish environment in the private-public sphere. However, the characteristic practices of this environment did not so much replicate those of these people's great-grandparents from the *mestechkos* as relate to contemporary images of the Israeli hero.

The 'New Jews' violated the established rules of the game, forcing a transfer of the discussion to the public sphere. Society became open enough for some forms of protest to manifest themselves. The protest against anti-Semitism took the simplest possible form: a desire to emigrate. The majority of potential emigrants did not get permission to leave the country (they were unofficially called *otkazniki*, i.e. those whose right to emigrate had been refused). In any case, if a person applied for permission to leave they were stigmatised and encountered powerful discrimination. Since the state prohibited free migration, a movement emerged upholding the right to emigrate. In public, a Jew who intended to emigrate resembled a dissident engaged in anti-Soviet activities. In the official-public sphere such Jews found themselves isolated, and this contributed to the construction of Jewish self-identity and a Jewish ethnic milieu in the private-public realm.

How was Jewish identity constructed in this period? Here is a typical story presented by one of our informants (Boris S., born 1959). Boris's grandfather (born in 1902) took part in the Civil War on the side of the Red Army, then graduated from the Red Professors Institute, and later worked at the Komintern. His grandmother (born 1904) was a pious woman, but, as Boris himself puts it: 'I think that she had not had much influence on my upbringing or on anything else: the family was absolutely assimilated.' However, although his grandparents knew Yiddish, his parents (who were born in 1927 and 1933) did not know their mothers' language. 'No traditions were kept', observed Boris. His father was a communist. At school, both secondary and high, 'I tried to be like others. I tried to avoid any confusion.' He started to reflect upon his ethnicity: 'Well, I am a Jew, and what does this mean? Who are these Jews, and where did they come from? You couldn't read anything about that anywhere.' He also started to read some available (i.e. anti-Zionist) literature, then he became acquainted with an *otkaznik*, an active member of an illegal Jewish group. He took the process of constructing a Jewish identity further, and his life became separated into two spheres: the official-public, lived out at the plant where he kept working, and the private-public, lived out at Jewish seminars and lectures where all his interests were concentrated and where his 'personal milieu' was being formed.

On the one hand, then, analysis of the ethnic identity of the generations of the anti-Semitic period reveals the almost complete assimilation of Leningrad Jews, which was additionally stimulated by state discrimination. On the other, examples may be found of a new response to the changed conditions that led to the formation of the new Jewish identity. The numbers of those attending illegal Jewish associations in the 1970s (circles, seminars) were not great, because participation in such activities was risky and could lead to persecution. Nevertheless, by the end of the 1970s, in the private-public sphere a non-formal Jewish community was emerging made up of ethnic social networks. Although more and more 'New Jews' were recruited into this milieu the community was unstable, since the losses to it were high: many people emigrated (i.e. succeeded in realising their life-strategies), for the sake of which they 'became Jews'.

In the public sphere, discussion of 'the Jewish theme' was somewhat polarised: there existed aggressive 'Israeli Zionists' and Soviet 'persons of Jewish nationality', the latter protesting against the activities of the former and thus supporting the decisions of the CPSU. Life as it was lived was echoed in the public condemnation of 'non-typical' cases of disloyal conduct on the part of 'certain derelicts' – the traitors to the motherland who were willing to leave the country.

The Generation of the Transformation Period

The reforms that commenced in the second half of the 1980s resulted in the gradual attenuation of the Soviet private-public sphere. Ethnic discourse underwent crucial change. Awareness and discussion of ethnicity passed from the private-public sphere into the public as restrictions on the content of public discussion disappeared completely.

Further reforms led to the aggravation of an identity crisis in Soviet society. At the same time, these reforms created further new opportunities for the development of strategies based on new identifications. In Leningrad (which in September 1991 reverted to its historical name St Petersburg), this meant that achieved Jewish status provided opportunities both for emigration and for successful survival strategies based on the advantage of belonging to the ethnic community. The very fact of belonging to the Jewish community presumed participation in the ethnic networks relating to foreign support, jobs within the community, education, humanitarian aid, etc. With support from abroad, the community expanded and developed rapidly and came to include a number of Jewish organisations.

How did this transformation influence the ethnic identity of the younger generation? The early socialisation of some of our young informants took place in what was still the pre-*perestroika* period, and thus a bifurcation of consciousness was intrinsic to them just as it had been to many from the 'anti-Semitic' generations. One informant remarked:

> It seemed to me that, on the one hand, this was ... sort of my misfortune. I always suffered because I had this bad luck – to be a Jew ... Then, on the

> other hand, I was sort of proud of it. I thought: the token people ... It was sort of a struggle inside me. I would have been happy – earlier – if I had not been a Jew. (Elena Sh., b. 1974)

Now that the issue of ethnicity has entered public discourse, however, those young Jews who have been involved in community activities (camps for Jewish youth, a Jewish college, Jewish theatre, etc.) have discovered that Jews are 'absolutely normal people' (Elena Sh., b. 1974). As they have eliminated the 'split-personality' complex, so they have discovered many opportunities for self-expression offered by the Jewish community, and have sought to become Jews and convert to Judaism.

It was in the narratives of the younger generation that we encountered once more descriptions of those grandmothers who had come to Leningrad long ago from the small regions. These *babushkas* and their Jewish practices are the focus for a myth that forms the basis for the construction of a new identity. In many interviews, reminiscences about these *babushkas* or grandmothers occupy a lot of space; the role of these grandmothers in their socialisation seems to be very important for these young respondents:

> My grandmother [b. 1896] always stayed with us, she always celebrated Jewish feasts – until the age of 95 she always went to synagogue. Her native language was Yiddish. So it was no revelation to me that I was a Jew – I was soaked in it somehow. (Leonid G., b. 1973)

> For me it [Jewish nationality] has always been important ... perhaps because I was mainly brought up by my grandfather. He told me a quite a lot. I remember, they brought me in my childhood to the synagogue. I liked being there! I lived with my parents, separately from my grandparents, but quite a lot of time I spent at my grandparents'. Saturdays there was cooked something fantastically delicious – I remember that most of all I liked eating something tasty on Saturdays ... (Natalia G., b. 1974)

For comparative purposes we can quote from our interviews with informants belonging to previous generations that demonstrate the different attitudes such people had towards the Jewish traditions of their grandparents: 'My grandfather [born 1809] attended [synagogue], prayed mornings, and also he read prayers. At that time it looked, of course, grim' (Lubov D., b. 1948). And: 'From my mother's side my grandfather was very religious. All the devotions and customs we knew from our childhood, but we definitely did not keep all that up ... It brought about disgust which lasted all my life' (Lilia L., b. 1949).

Thus our research shows that, in the transformation period, a number of Leningrad Jews of the younger generation are constructing their ethnicity by re-forming the intergenerational bond with their grandparents through memories of their customs and practices.

Conclusion

Our analysis of the biographies of typical Leningrad Jewish families (the descendants of the migrants of 1920s and 1930s from the *mestechkos*) has shown that the construction of ethnicity (in this case, Jewish ethnicity) is embedded in the local historical context. Changes taking place in this context may be conceptualised as changes in terms of the private/public division, and also as a modification of the 'rules of the game' operating within the two spheres. Ethnic discourse may be viewed as changing correspondingly. We can distinguish, in terms of the private/public division and the specific rules of the game in these spheres, several generations of Leningrad Jews, characterised by specific kinds of ethnic consciousness. We may name these generations according to the local historical context which was formative for Jewish ethnic consciousness. Thus we may distinguish four generations: the internationalist generation, and two generations of the anti-Semitic period and one of the period of transformation.

We wish to emphasise once again that we are discussing here sociological generations. Although the core of such generations is made up of people of approximately the same age, in reality they include younger and older people who have gone through the same formative social experiences of a milieu.

Thus the first Soviet generation of Leningrad Jews, formed in the internationalist period, was one for whom ethnicity ceased being a major dimension of identity. The second generation, whose secondary socialisation coincided with the period of anti-Semitism, had already ceased practising their Jewishness and gradually forced out every memory of Jewish traditions, not only in their public presentation but in their private life as well (they may be termed 'assimilated' Jews). The third generation (i.e. the second of the anti-Semitic period) became split, along lines of ethnic consciousness, into two: an absolute majority of assimilated Jews, and an emerging minority of those who attempted a new construction of their Jewish identity in the private and private-public spheres. Finally, in the transformation period, Jews of the new, fourth generation discuss issues of ethnic identity both in the public and in the private spheres, and are to a great extent polarised. Along with the 'Russian' majority in the public sphere one can distinguish a quite noticeable Jewish community, which involves in our estimation about ten per cent of those whose ancestors were among the first generation of Leningrad Jews.

Gradually, as the old Soviet social structures cease to exist, social space is acquiring a shape more or less familiar to the Western observer. The rigid restrictions of the Soviet public sphere are gradually being weakened; the private sphere is becoming autonomous. This redisposing of social life resolves into a dissolution of the Soviet private-public sphere, which is becoming meaningless. As a consequence of these structural changes, Jewish ethnic identity throws off its disguise and serves as a foundation for individuals' life-strategies.

The ancient Hegelian law of dialectics – that of the 'negation of negation' – may serve as a metaphor for the history of the ethnic identity of Soviet Jews: first Jews converted to Russians, then Russians converted to Jews.

Notes

1 The project 'The Formation of Ethnic Communities in St Petersburg and Berlin' was supported by the Volkswagen Foundation, led by Ingrid Oswald and Viktor Voronkov. The aim of the research was the analysis of the formation of the ethnic identities of Soviet citizens and the creation of ethnic communities during the process of disintegration of the Soviet Union. In the course of the research more than 30 biographical interviews with Jews in St Petersburg were conducted.

2 Here we use the definition of ethnic identity offered by Barth (1969).

3 Karl Mannheim (1952) was the first to formulate the idea of sociological generations. Most researchers now subscribe to this view.

4 One can distinguish at least four approaches to the public/private division. The liberal-economic model presumes a distinction between state administration and the market economy (Hirschman, 1982; Olson, 1971). The Republican-virtue (and classical) approach of Habermas (1982) and Arendt (1958) treats the public as political (the sphere of private individuals who come together in public against the state to debate problems of common concern). In the 'dramaturgic' approach (Ariès, 1962), the public sphere is equivalent to the sphere of fluid and polymorphous sociability. Finally, the feminist critique considers the public as non-private (where the private sphere is reduced to family; see e.g. Weintraub (1997)).

5 So far as we are aware, Oleg Witte (1996) is the only researcher to have noticed and analysed this phenomenon.

6 ibid.

7 Among the random sample of our informants the majority were descendants of those Jews who migrated from the Pale of Settlement soon after the 1917 Revolution. It is they who represent the dominant contemporary type of St Petersburg Jew. Reconstruction of families' ethnic biographies was done on the basis of the narratives provided by informants born in the 1930s or later. The aims of the project did not include interviewing older people, but Leningrad Jews of the 1920s and 1930s as an ethnic group have been studied elsewhere (Bayzer, 1999).

8 Here, the word 'Russian' is for the narrator a synonym for 'Soviet'. The loss of their ethnic identity did not convert Jews into ethnic Russians, but rather made them Soviet, along with the majority of the population in the USSR. In this case, the concept 'Russian' was not linked to ethnicity, but rather implied the notion 'Soviet' (and 'Russian-speaking').

9 The 1920s and 1930s represented a period of atheist ideological propaganda. The destruction of religious values undermined ethnic identity, for which religion served as an ideological basis.

10 Ethnic repression in the USSR started at the very end of the 1930s (the war with Finland) and then broadened with the USSR's participation in World War II. The formal ground of such repressions was 'nationality' (ethnic origin) as stated on a passport. Hitherto, this article in a passport had been filled in on the basis of a citizen's statement. However, following an NKVD instruction issued in 1938 this article was filled in only according to the documents identifying the ethnic origin of the applicant's parents. The absence of such documents created a lacuna in the passport, which caused suspicion on the part of the authorities. Such a procedure made it impossible to conceal a 'wrong' ethnic origin and facilitated ethnic repression. In broad terms, the 'passportisation' of the Soviet population started in 1932, initially in large towns. One of the social control functions of the passport system was the selection of population along lines of class, ethnicity, age, marital status, residence, etc. Residence was legal only if confirmed by the military authorities, on the basis of both passport data and NKVD files. The passport fulfilled the same selective and discriminative functions in terms of gaining employment or entering educational institutions.

11 We chose 1947 as the cut-off year for the second Soviet-Jewish ethnic generation because, in spite of the importance of World War II experiences for this cohort, we do not consider the major changes in ethnic practices that occurred in Russia during the war. Although the relatives of many Leningrad Jews perished in the Holocaust, the Soviet ideological machine hushed up the Jewish genocide. As late as 1996, when the truth about the Holocaust was publicly debated, 50 per cent of Russian citizens reported total ignorance of this fact (as against 8 per cent of German, 9 per cent of Polish, 10 per cent of French, 24 per cent of British and 33 per cent of American citizens). The politics of state anti-Semitism are usually associated with the sublimation of the failures of domestic and foreign policy, the difficulties of the post-war period and the personal anti-Semitism of Stalin. The beginnings of political discrimination against Jews can be dated back to 1947.

12 Statistics for the age-distribution of Leningrad Jews in 1989 (when the massive emigration of Jews from Russia began) shows that the proportion of Jews in different age groups differs. This is not on account of a longer life expectancy for Jews or differences in the birth rate (over the last few decades these differences have been statistically insignificant). The chief reason for these differences is a change in the

strategy for choosing the nationality in the case of mixed families. According to micro-census data for the city's population, fewer than 10 per cent of children born in Russian-Jewish families were registered as Jews; the others were registered as Russians (O natsionalnom sostave naselenija Sankt-Peterburga. Peterburgkomstat, St Peterburg, 1995, s.17).

13 Bertaux (1966).

14 On the other hand, in one of our interviews an informant remarked: 'I never considered my Jewishness as something shameful' (Osip M., b. 1933). This case is essentially different from the typical ethnic biography of a Leningrad Jew. We interpret this difference in terms of the specific social experience of the informant. He is the only one of our interviewees not to have belonged to the middle class and to have held the post of industrial worker at the plant. For people of Jewish origin this is quite a rare case. The majority of Jews in large Russian towns belong to the middle class (bearing in mind the conventionality of such a designation in the Soviet context) in terms of education and social status. According to the 1989 census, 70–5 per cent of Leningrad Jews in the 25–55 age range had received or were receiving the highest level of education (by the 1970s this indicator falls to 60 per cent). By comparison, among the non-Jewish population the percentage of those who had received higher education was almost three times lower (Kogan, 1994). Differences in social experience (in particular in work experiences) result in different perceptions of ethnicity. Our research confirms the theory that experiential differences accumulate to create different meanings, different 'rules of the game' and different ethnic practices for people belonging to different social classes. Our interlocutor did not encounter state anti-Semitism, but often came across everyday offensiveness typical of the working-class mileu: 'Of course, they insulted me – "Yid!". I took it easily and if they start insulting me they know I'll beat them back right away...'

15 It is important to emphasise that a demonstration of Jewishness does not imply self-identification as a Jew. Sometimes such demonstration has been the only way of confirming one's right to emigrate. Instrumental usage of ethnicity did not, however, distinguish these Jews from non-Jews who bought false 'Jewish' documents that would enable them to emigrate. (This was the context in which the proverb emerged 'Jewishness is not ethnicity, but a means of transportation'.)

16 Those grandparents who, according to our informants, were influential in the reconstruction of Jewish identity had grown up in *mestechkos*. Although they might be younger than the core age group of this generation, their socialisation in the *mestechkos* milieu and their experience of migration to industrialising central towns make it possible to apportion them to the first Soviet-Jewish generation. On the other hand, in the case of Leonid G. we have the phenomenon of the so-called late child with its implications for identity formation: in the case of a child born to parents over 45, the grandparents belong to the first generation of Leningrad Jews and the second generation is 'missing'.

References

Arendt, H. (1958), *The Human Condition*, University of Chicago Press, Chicago, IL.

Ariès, P. (1962), *The Centuries of Childhood: A Social History of Family Life*, Vintage Books, New York.

Barth, F. (1969), 'Introduction', in F. Barth (ed.), *Ethnic Groups and Boundaries: The Social Organisation of Culture Difference*, Universities Forlaget/Allen & Unwin, Bergen-Oslo/London, pp. 9–38.

Bayzer, M. (1999), *Evrjei Leningrada. Natsionaknaya zhizn I sovetizatsija 1917–1939* [Leningrad Jews: National Life and Sovietisation], Mosty kultury, Moscow.

Bertaux, D. (1966), 'Transmissija sotsialnogo statusa v extremalnoi situatsii' [Transmission of Social Status in the Extreme Situation], in V. Semenova, E. Foteeva and D. Bertaux (eds), *Sudby ljudej: Rossija, XX vek* (The Fate of Individuals: Russia, the Twentieth Century), Institute of Sociology, Moscow, pp. 207–39.

Current Russian Attitudes toward Jews and the Holocaust: A Public-opinion Survey (1996),The America Jewish Committee, New York.

Habermas, J. (1982), *The Structural Transformation of the Public Sphere: An Inquiry into a Category of Bourgeois Society*, MIT Press, Cambridge, MA.

Hankiss, E. (1988), 'The "Second Society": Is There An Alternative Social Model Emerging in Contemporary Hungary?', *Social Research*, vol. 55, nos 1–2, pp. 13–42.

Hirschmann, A. (1982), *Shifting Involvements: Private Interest and Public Action*, Princeton University Press, Princeton, NJ.

Kogan, M. (1994), 'The Jews of Leningrad according to the Census of 1989', *Jews in Eastern Europe*, Winter, pp. 50–1.

Mannheim, K. (1952), *Essays on the Sociology of Knowledge*, Oxford University Press, London and New York.

Olson, M. (1971), *The Logic of Collective Action: Public Goods and the Theory of Groups*, Harvard University Press, Cambridge, MA.

Weintraub, J. (1997), 'The Theory and Politics of the Public/Private Distinction', in J. Weintraub and K. Kumar (eds), *Public and Private in Thought and Practice*, University of Chicago Press, Chicago, IL and London.

Witte, O. (1996), Izbirateli – vragi naroda? Razmyshleniya ob adekvatnosti elektoral'nogo povedenija i faktorakh na ee uroven vlijaiushchikh' (Voters: Enemies of the People? Reflections on the Adequacy of Electoral Behaviour and the Factors Influencing its Level), *Etika uspekha*, pp. 58–71.

*****

The authors wish to express their sincere thanks to Daniel Bertaux and Elena Zdravomyslova for their assistance.

15 Shame, Promiscuity and Social Mobility in Russian Autobiographies from Poor Working-class Milieux

ANNA ROTKIRCH
Department of Social Policy,
University of Helsinki, Finland

Introduction

This chapter will examine two descriptions of poor and socially marginal milieux written by two men from different Soviet Russian generations.[1] 'Mikhail Ivanov' (born 1935) talks about incest and about promiscuous milieux of the 1950s, and 'Aleksei Lukashin' (born *c.* 1960) about Leningrad suburban gang and rock subcultures of the 1970s and 1980s. I am interested in the links between *private and public selves*, and in the conflicting *ideals of masculinity* exhibited in these autobiographies. The first autobiography, also, created doubts as to its authenticity. I conclude with a discussion of whether it is possible to extrapolate a certain way of life from only a couple of autobiographies, and propose a conceptual distinction between *milieux* and *subcultures*.

The autobiographies belong to a corpus of 47 items, collected in an autobiographical competition about love and sexuality organised in St Petersburg in 1996.[2] They clearly differed from the rest of the material, and were for me personally among the most unexpected and shocking to read. Ivanov's life story paints a fairly classical picture of the Soviet class journey from poor, marginalised worker to well-to-do upper-working-class citizen. Just as in workers' autobiographies from a century earlier, male self-control, including sexual self-control, is seen as an intrinsic component of upward social mobility (Maynes, 1995). Ivanov depicts an amoral world, from which he eventually succeeds in distancing himself. Parallels between middle-class morality and social ascent are made by Ivanov himself throughout the text.

Lukashin, by contrast, has had to let go of his initial dreams of becoming a doctor. He has worked in show business and as a masseur. Like Ivanov, Lukashin describes relations of sexual corruption and prostitution. In the beginning, such affairs added to his status in the working collective, but they were not integral to them. But in the late 1980s his sexual affairs moved to the centre of the picture and promiscuity became a central feature of his professional life.

Ivanov's life story evolved away from an acultural setting towards established Soviet middle-class life, while Lukashin's social mobility is horizontal. The evolution from Ivanov's *blat* relations to Lukashin's semi-open prostitution are evidence of recent economic and structural dynamics in Russia. The typical Soviet path of social ascent through education has become blurred. In parallel with this, behaviour that used to be 'underground' or 'semi-official' has come to be a part of public and professional life. That these developments also affected men is not to say that they were gender-symmetrical. On the contrary, Lukashin's deliberate misogyny is a good example of attitudes that entered the Russian public sphere with the generation of the 1970s.

Discussing the Margins: Workers, *Lumpen* and the Rest

A silenced phenomenon in official Soviet discourse,[3] the working poor often represented, for urban-educated Soviet citizens, suspect and rejected 'others'. In the rhetoric of *perestroika*, they were often disdainfully referred to as the *lyumpeny*, or the lumpenproletariat, while the supposedly lacking, or at least vanishing, civilisation and education in Russia were referred to as the *lyumpenizatsija* of the country.

As in many other cases, the 'otherness' of poorly-qualified workers is here characterised by two traits: demonisation and trivialisation. On the one hand, such people are called *nekul'turnye lyudi*: the uncivilised, drinking, violent, animal-like, amoral and sexually promiscuous, who often are pictured as having (too) many children. Many autobiographies of children from educated families are 'implicitly contrasting their own behaviour with that which they believed to be characteristic of the popular milieux surrounding them' (Maynes, 1995, p. 148). For instance, the autobiography of one woman (born in 1946 and professionally educated) describes her learning at an early age about sexual things from other children on the street, and playing advanced and consciously daring doctor games. She stopped when a girl from a cultured family disapproved of her behaviour.

On the other hand, ways of life in these popular milieux are seen as so embarrassingly simple as to be uninteresting. For instance, when Alexandra Chistyakova's life story was published and then nominated for the Russian Booker Prize in 1998, the major part of the Russian mass media questioned the relevance of her testimony. Although comprehensive life stories about Russian peasant and working women had scarcely been published in Russia before, Chistyakova's testimony of famine, social struggle, illegal abortions, alcoholism and family violence was discarded as something that 'everybody knows' and that would 'interest only Western feminists'.[4]

Neither have Russian or Western scholars had much interest in, or adequate access to, the poor and marginal groups of the population. It is still utterly unclear who belonged to such 'groups' and how extensive they were.[5]

The conceptual vagueness of the term 'the masses' persists in today's Russia. While sociologists of the 1990s struggled to determine the scope and criteria of the new middle class, the categorisation of the 'rest' – the classes under them – was at least as problematic. In the model of Russian society put forward by Tatyana Zaslavskaya (1998, p. 12), one of Russia's leading sociologists, over half of the population belongs to the 'basic stratum', with one tenth as the bottom (the 'underclass' and the 'social bottom' – presumably the homeless, criminals, and so on). In Timo Piirainen's (1997) classification, the lower segment is called the 'proletariat' and amounts to 40 per cent.

For lack of better concepts, then, I will here refer to the 'working poor' or the 'lower social classes'. In the two cases below, much-needed information (e.g. about the education and occupations of parents or partners) is absent. These testimonies belong to what Mary Jo Maynes has described as the seemingly patternless stories that defy and question categorisation. Maynes (1995, p. 150) stresses the importance of including such texts, as they 'hint at the many lives that never culminated in autobiography'. In the case of Soviet Russia, we may still add a 'yet'.

Post-war Promiscuity

Ivanov the Taxi Driver

The autobiography of 'Mikhail Ivanov'[6] is lengthy – almost 80 double-spaced pages – and covers his whole life course. Born in 1935, he lost his father in the War in 1942 and grew up with his widowed mother and elder sister. After the seventh grade he started studying at the age of 16 at a vocational training school. His sister finished ten grades and then studied at an agricultural institute. Their mother advised her daughter to content herself with a lower education at *tekhnikum* (professional college) level, but Mikhail's sister refused even to consider that option, showing clear signs of social ambition. The sister left the family and later moved, together with her husband, away from Leningrad. Mikhail served in the Army for three years in the mid-1950s, after which he started working as a chauffeur for a larger enterprise. In 1959, he married 'Raia', his first wife, with whom he had two children in the early 1960s. His mother died of cancer of the uterus during that period.

In the second half of the 1960s, Mikhail divorced Raia and married Ksenya, with whom he was still living at the time of writing in 1996. He also adopted Ksenya's daughter from a previous marriage. Towards the end of his first marriage he changed workplace and became a taxi driver. Although he probably still continues with this in both Soviet and post-Soviet conditions quite lucrative work, he complains of scarce financial resources.

Ivanov's life in his two first homes – that of his childhood and of his first marriage – constitutes the main bulk of his autobiography. Both families represented the milieux of material and cultural poverty, from which the young Mikhail repeatedly tried to escape. His relatives and friends worked as doormen, factory workers, saleswomen and porters. In one family which is described with envy, the wife works as a *dvornik* (caretaker) 'because of the apartment space', while her husband was a doorman at the famous Metropol restaurant. They lived as well as they could by buying 'crystal, gold, silver, everything from drunkards'. These are lower-working-class people, often migrants, and the first generation of Leningraders. They were culturally marginalised, albeit not necessarily any longer materially destitute, during the last decades of the Soviet regime.

Ivanov gives detailed descriptions of various everyday situations, for instance the customary heavy drinking (although he proudly notes rejecting alcohol if he had to drive afterwards: 'If I had to work the next day, I was always in form, and almost always sober'). He also describes his working career, but mostly through his sexual relationships at work. They are, in turn, merely a sub-theme of the main, overshadowing subject of this autobiography: Ivanov's lack of life-control – which is here equated with lack of sexual life-control – and his aspirations towards better living conditions and a 'normal' family life.

Is Ivanov's Story Authentic?

Ivanov talks about having been, throughout his life, seduced, exploited or practically raped by family members, women neighbours, his wife's girlfriends, and female colleagues. From the age of seventeen, Mikhail had various sexual experiences with girls, but his first fulfilled sexual intercourse was with his mother. Their incestuous relationship continued until after he finished his army service and moved away from home. When he married his first wife, it was largely due to the activities of his mother-in-law, who he writes repeatedly tried to seduce him, and with whom he eventually had a sexual relationship towards the end of his first marriage.

This autobiography caused the only serious disagreement between me and the Russian scholars involved in the research project. The three Russians who originally read the text found it an exceptionally rich, interesting and totally believable story.[7] I, on the other hand, was for the first time inclined to suspect the authenticity of the related events. But the Russian readers pointed out that the living milieux, personages, street addresses and work relations were most convincingly described. We agreed to award this autobiography one of the jury's special prizes. After our discussions, and after having repeatedly read the text, I have come to limit my objections to three points, all of them related specifically to the depiction of female sexuality.

First, this autobiography has an unusually large amount of dialogue in the form of direct quotations. This is not a common or an advisable device in autobiographical writing, since one seldom remembers the exact wordings of sentences uttered twenty or thirty years ago (Roos, 1994). But it is especially problematic here since many of the quotations in Ivanov's autobiography are put into the mouths of women, all of whom are sexually uninhibited and actively desiring personalities (only the second wife, Ksenya, modifies the overall picture by being ascribed an indifferent attitude towards sex later in the marriage). The dialogue is also written in the vocabulary of pornographic stories, such as in this excerpt where Ivanov's mother talks to the teenager Mikhail: 'You, my son, have really got a big one. Not all men have such a big one. You'll reach the girls even in the womb, and well, I wouldn't say no to that myself ...'

Second, some sexual events repeat themselves suspiciously often. One is the theme of mother–son (or mother–daughter) incest. Mikhail's best male friend during his teenage years is said to have told him how he 'fucked his mother as well, and she is very content with that, and I don't forget my sister either'; later one woman friend at work told him how she had 'made a man' out of her son. Another key scene is Mikhail seeing a woman he loves and desires making love to another man. Such voyeuristic scenes take place with his mother, his schoolteacher, his first girlfriend Galya and his first wife Raia. The repetitions are psychologically understandable, but difficult to relate to as sociological evidence.

Third, women's sexuality is depicted according to physiological stereotypes common in pornographic literature. In addition to explaining explicitly what they want and how, and commenting aloud on intercourse while it's taking place, practically all Mikhail's partners regularly have multiple orgasms during which they 'let out juices'. These formulations can be interpreted as pure exaggeration or, more diplomatically, as merely an attachment to a certain sexual vocabulary. But similar behaviour has not been confirmed in empirical research on women's sexuality in Russia or elsewhere (e.g. Hite, 1978; Haavio-Mannila and Rotkirch, 1998; Temkina, 2000).

On each of these three counts, the author's way of describing events can be interpreted as more or less phantasmagoric. Even if the events actually took place, which is not impossible, they have been retold according to a (subconscious?) pattern of repetition and in a specific pornographic vocabulary, which make any generalisations about Soviet social sexual practices problematic.

My solution has been to relate the social interactions and their environments depicted by the narrator, assuming they are basically adequately rendered. For example, I render the descriptions of contraceptive devices and domestic abortions described in the autobiography. They do not follow a usual pornographic rhetoric and sound believable. But I have avoided quoting and commenting on Ivanov's representations of what the women surrounding him supposedly said about sex and desire. I cannot exclude the possibility that Soviet women in some milieux may have expressed themselves and behaved like that, but I think it highly improbable. In any case, I would wait until we have at least some kind of similar evidence from women themselves. Only one recurrent theme in Mikhail's sex talk with women, that of breast milk, will be discussed in connection with his views on masculinity – that is, inside the realm of symbolic interpretations to which it undeniably does belong.

Fallen Women and Social Ascent

Ivanov's social mobility follows a path from a suburb of Leningrad to the centre of the city, through successive apartment changes and gradually improving housing conditions. The autobiography opens with a description of the family's deplorable material situation during the war years:

> It is better not to think about how we managed – like everybody else ... we were moved to a small one-storey house, after they had moved the Finns out[8] ... The little house was divided into two parts, and we got one room as before, although this one was smaller, and a kitchen, and two storage rooms. We did not have much furniture – a table, some chairs, two stools, and two single beds which we seldom used. A couple of big and wide barrack-beds were patched together in the room, and we slept on them, all three of us under one big blanket – it was warmer that way. We did not have enough firewood for the winter, but somehow we managed to keep warm – we probably burnt everything that could be burnt.

Mikhail married inside this poor milieu. Along with his first wife, he shared a wooden house without any facilities with her sister, brother and mother. Raia and her mother work at a factory making agricultural machinery. In 1960, a commission checked their living conditions and the family received a room measuring ten square metres in one of the new dwelling-houses associated with the factory in which the women were working. 'This was a real blessing', Mikhail notes: now they had an indoor toilet, although the heating was still by wood fire. Mikhail, Raia and their children moved to this apartment, but they continued to be in geographical and social proximity to Raia's mother. Ivanov describes the mother-in-law as the central and supporting force of the household, especially at the beginning of his marriage. All the family members gave her their salary. When a new wood-shed proved too small, it was she who arranged a tractor-load of old boards, out of which they built a new shed. She was the one who provided the household with firewood, or the young couple with condoms; and when, soon after the wedding, her daughter became pregnant for the first time, she told her how to provoke a miscarriage.

After the second move, the family's material situation became more satisfactory. For instance, Mikhail was not pressuring his (in his view lazy) wife to return to her waged work, as 'we still had enough money'. A few years later, the family received an apartment in the centre of Leningrad. They got two rooms and a kitchen, central heating, hot water, a bathroom and a separate WC: 'My God, what a miracle – you don't need to prepare wood, carry water and carry the waste water out.' Mikhail's mother-in-law and her other two children also received a two-bedroom apartment.

After divorcing his first wife, Mikhail left their apartment to her and their children and moved in with his second wife, Ksenya, her daughter and mother in a three-room apartment, also situated in the city centre. We are not told the occupation of his second wife, but it is clear that the second marriage continued and stabilised his improving social status. It is through Ksenya that Mikhail finally escaped both the material and the moral stigma of his first two families, although the past returned as a dividing issue between the spouses later in their marriage. Parallel with the story of escaping material poverty is the description of escaping moral stigma and sexual promiscuity, condensed in the figures of Mikhail's mother and his first wife.

In the late 1940s, Mikhail's mother started to work in a military unit that occupied his family's previous house. The female neighbour with whom they shared their new dwelling also worked there, and both women received soldiers who 'gave them food products' and were their lovers.

At the age of fourteen, after Mikhail got drunk for the first time, Ivanov describes how his relationship with his mother became explicitly sexual, involving kisses and petting and her giving abundant advice about how to do things with girls 'in the right way'. The boy was highly ambivalent about his whole life situation. On the one hand, Ivanov tells us he trusted and admired his mother. This, for instance, is how he describes his feelings after one of their first sexual encounters: 'In the morning everything was fine. After that I did not taste wine for a long time and started to relate tenderly to my mother – how wise and good she was, after all!' Also their first intercourse, when Mikhail is about seventeen years old, is described as a happy event:

> So my mother got up, took off her nightgown, put in a [contraceptive] pill and lay naked in the bed. I pressed myself against her breasts and started to suck the nipples, squeezing the tits. My mother was swooning ... She was content with me, and I was in high spirits. That is how I was my mother's man for the first time, and neither was it the last ... In the morning I woke up in a good

mood. After breakfast both of us went to do our own business. I did not tell anybody about this event, not even Oleg, and now I am for the first time in many years telling this story.

But both before and after the first seduction Mikhail describes how he was 'unwilling' and 'disgusted' to go to sleep in the same bed with his mother, or even to go near her. He was often depressed and desperate. 'It was all so difficult and disgusting. I became angry with everybody. It is hard for me to describe all my worries.' From the age of seventeen, Mikhail started to detach himself from his mother. He notes that he had then become older and had 'perhaps got more sense in the head'. His studies provided a way out of the intimacy and the drinking into which his mother enticed him:

I started to develop a different attitude towards sexual life, and to life in general. I started to get irritated by the persistent girls and the men that came to our house. As a rule, they all brought vodka with them. My mother was drinking with them, and they offered me drink. I got drunk a few times. But when I woke up I saw the house was a mess. My mother sank morally, and I did not even want to talk with her any more, not only not to go to sleep in her bed. But when there were no men next to her she asked me to lie with her again. She said that she cannot do without men, that she feels want all the time, and she was crying. I felt sorry for her, and the drinking made me feel sick, especially the next morning. I was afraid of the hangovers because I had to study, to work, and I started to run away in order not to take part in the drinking. I dived head-first into my studies.

Mikhail graduated from his vocational school and started to work in a factory. Through his new acquaintances, he further 're-evaluated' (*pereosoznat'*) many things relating to families and morality. The connection between material and moral standards is almost seamless in the following reflection:

After having visited my friends, who lived in the city even if in communal apartments (and some in separate apartments), I understood what kind of hovel I was living in. My friends did not have to think about getting wood, fetching water and emptying buckets with waste water, or running out on the street to the outhouse. And I also saw other kinds of family relations, I got to know many good girls, who were shy about changing clothes in front of me, were shy about showing their precious parts, and who blushed if something awkward happened. Those girls did not offer their kisses and did not let themselves be kissed *too* daringly – they either pushed you away, or ran

> away, and avoided being alone with you after that. This made me feel both more lighthearted, and more gloomy. I did not want to go home at all, and I tried to stay overnight at my friends' place.

He welcomed military service as a means of escape:

> In the factory we had a wonderful sports collective, with our own sports centre, where you could do sports in winter and in summer and occasionally stay overnight. Looking at such families I understood that we had completely abnormal relations with my mother – she was both a mother to me and not a mother, but a mere woman, female and drunkard – and that started to torment me. Now I simply waited for the day when I would go into the Army – everything else was just secondary.

Mikhail obtained a chauffeur's licence while preparing for his military service. He was satisfied with his experiences and says the Army occupied him totally: 'The most important thing was that there were no women.' Also his social ambitions were supported. He entered the sergeant school, and was looked up to: 'I was the only one with a seven-year education and I counted as being from Leningrad.'[9]

But in his second year in the Army his mother came to visit him. 'So mother came, like snow on the head in the middle of summer.' With her, 'women' and sexuality entered his army life, ending it. Ivanov describes his mother having intercourse with two of his superiors on the way to the hotel where mother and son were going to spend his leave together. When he reproached her, she explained that she did it only because it was in his interests. Indeed, only two months after her visit he was prematurely demobilised in 1956, which he thinks was due to his mother's contacts. After that, however, he ended the sexual relationship with his mother:

> I was appalled to look at my mother, my own mother. She started to drink, smoke and lead a whore's life. Soon after my demobilisation [from the Army] she gave birth, but the child died in hospital. I do not know why, and neither was I interested – I had my life and she had hers.

Towards the end of the 1950s Ivanov's mother increasingly became an alcoholic: 'She had stopped hiding [the fact] that different men came to her, brought something to drink, and she paid them with her body.' Ivanov writes that he knew he had to sort out his life. First he started working, and then he soon met his future wife, Raia, at a dance venue in the suburb where he lived. He became infatuated with her, and first perceived her as a suitably nice and decent woman. Raia had an elder brother and younger sisters, who 'characteristically, were all born of different fathers. I learnt that a little later, but at the moment I was not thinking about that, and I did not know.' Raia was not drinking vodka at that time, but her mother liked drinking. She got cross when Raia refused alcohol and objected that it was always all right to take a little at dinner: 'This also made me unhappy, but it became clear only after quite a while.'

The couple dated following the norms of Soviet romantic courtship (Rotkirch, 2000, pp. 58–63). For a long time Mikhail was not allowed to kiss Raia. 'I was not insisting, but in the end she kissed me herself. I had brought her flowers, and then we started kissing all the time, but things did not go further than that.' The couple started disagreeing, but Mikhail remained infatuated: 'We started to quarrel about anything and nothing, but I was still drawn to her like a magnet.'

During this period of 'pure' dating, Mikhail had sex with Raia's friend. While later moralising over his mother's and his wife's behaviour, he is here describing his own pre-marital sexual relations in a neutral and non-judgmental way. Raia's friend told him that Raia was more experienced than she had let him understand, but he refused to believe such rumours. Mikhail also visited his mother's acquaintance, who worked as a porter in a *obshchezhitie* [student dormitory] and could arrange for some girl to come and spend time with him. 'The girl knew why she was brought there, and without words or preludes she either undressed or merely took her trousers off.' We are not told whether Mikhail paid these girls, and the woman arranging the meetings is said to have asked him only for sexual favours 'in exchange', which he refused. Probably, the woman got some kind of material reward for her services.

If Mikhail at first thought well of Raia, Raia's mother is from the start described as the intriguing and the driving force in this period of his life. Ivanov admires her ability to arrange things, but was also repelled by her sexual advances and her determination to get him as an in-law; he would later accuse her of literally using spells in order to bewitch him. One evening during their dating period, she is described as having made Mikhail and Raia drink and having put them to sleep together in the wood-shed. Ivanov says that the mother thus directly encouraged him to take her daughter's virginity, after which he would be obliged to marry her. Another time, he noticed that the cellar was full of wine, vodka and moonshine. Raia's mother explained that it was for the wedding: 'I had not even started to think about marriage, but I was already being married.'

Mikhail eventually married Raia in 1959 and moved in with his wife's family. After the birth of their second child the marriage started falling apart. Like his mother, Raia started smoking, drinking and talking openly about her affairs on the side. 'She knew I did not like [the fact] that women smoked or drank wine, but later Valya [her friend] taught Raia to smoke too, and they started to smoke and drink, the two of them, and that was the beginning of the end of our family life.' Mikhail felt trapped:

> I openly blamed my mother-in-law. There was nothing I could do. I could not leave the children and break up the family, so I had patience for the time being. I said, 'It was you who married me to your daughter. Why did you bewitch me, why?' And there was nothing she could say in reply ... I was fed up with everything – my work, my family – but you have to preserve the family because of the children (*no semju nado hranit radi detej*). But you can change your workplace. So, weighed down by my work ... I quit and started working as a taxi driver.

Once again, a change in Mikhail's public life-circumstances gave him some sense of life-control. Earlier, this sense came to him through his studies and his army service; now it came through a new job. But in the private sphere, his helplessness grew. It culminated when Raia started expecting a third child, about the paternity of which he was uncertain:

> I did not know anything about this pregnancy, and neither did my mother-in-law. We learnt about it when her stomach was visibly big. Everything happened in silence – once again, nobody knew what to do. We started to wait for the third child, and I did not know whose it was.

It was too late for an official abortion, and this time Raia failed in her usual attempts to 'get rid of it herself'. But the child was still-born and evidently was malformed: Mikhail never learnt the details. He was interrogated by the doctor, who eventually refrained from pressing charges, 'although it was obviously a crime. It seems Raia had also confessed to that.' While Raia was still in hospital after the tragic birth, Mikhail was seduced by her mother, and then he engaged in other sexual relationships.

Soon afterwards, Mikhail fell in love with his future second wife (a friend of Raia's sister), moved in with her and eventually applied for a divorce. In this third family setting he finally managed to escape from 'loose living' (*besputnaia zhizn'*), the expression he uses, for instance, when seeking reasons for his mother's premature death from cancer of the uterus. In his thirties, living in the centre of St Petersburg in a family with 'normal' relations and taking pride in handling his work tasks well, Ivanov had established himself as a proper Soviet middle-class person.

Sexual Blat *and Prostitution*

Ivanov's autobiography is full of descriptions or mentions of sexuality as a means of exchange. It appears in two forms: prostitution and sexual *blat*.[10] A specifically Soviet phenomena, *blat* relations were a middle form between gift and exchange, corruption and friendship (Ledeneva, 1998). Thus prostitution here denotes an exchange of sexual favours for money in a somehow organised setting, including pimps, certain specified places, contact persons, etc. (Of course, in many cases the line between sexual *blat* and prostitution is blurred.) *Blat* existed in the form of horizontal ties within circles of friends, and vertical ties between different social classes or hierarchical positions in, notably, the workplace. For instance, Ivanov describes these relations among taxi drivers: 'I never suspected that money decides everything in the taxi – you have to pay to everybody and for everything with money. The result is that you become dependent on everybody.' In this passage, 'money' does not mean overt bribes. This is clear from the ensuing example, where Mikhail, at the end of the working day, went to the central office in order to thank one of the *telefonistka* women, who had provided him with a great many advantageous orders during the day. 'I had bought a cake [tort] and a box of chocolate and [...] was almost knocked over by laughter. Later I understood that I should have brought something to drink and cigarettes, at least Bulgarian ones [if not Western ones].'

Ivanov has not been involved in outright prostitution, of which he describes only indirect knowledge.[11] For instance, he talks about an elderly woman who was his neighbour when they first moved to one of the factory-owned residences in 1960. She was somehow involved in court proceedings against an underground brothel. 'Then it became clear to me that there were many brothels in town. I heard especially much about them while working as a taxi driver. But that happened a long time, ten years, later.'

Working as a taxi driver, Mikhail met women passengers who offered themselves for payment (which he declined), and men who asked him to provide them with alcohol and women:

> When I told them I did not know where to get that [alcohol], they would not believe I did not have any vodka or wine and do not frequent prostitutes. But

> that's how it was. It took me a long time before I came into the know (*pronikat'*) while working as a taxi driver.

An outsider to prostitution in Soviet times,[12] Mikhail was often part of, or a direct witness to, sexual *blat* relations. The visiting soldiers of his childhood, and his mother's way of getting him prematurely released from the Army, are the first examples in the text. Later, after returning from the Army and shortly before meeting his first wife, he worked as a chauffeur in a research institute. Once, he drove food to one *stolovaia* or workplace restaurant and met the director of the place. They agreed to meet after work and eventually spent the night together. After this, Mikhail was soon called to her office:

> There I was unequivocally told [by the director] that if I would, at least sometimes, pay Nina V. attention in a sexual way, I would gain a good position in society and at my workplace. Instead of answering her I put my arms round her shoulders, pressing her against my chest, and our mouths were united in a single passionate kiss.

While Ivanov is not prone to moralising over his own pre- or extra-marital affairs, the *blat* relations are condemned and described in negative ways in his account. This is not related to the relations *per se* – he openly acknowledges the benefits he got from them and did not seem to mind them in the beginning. Rather, he judges negatively the psychological discomfort and social stigma eventually created by such affairs. 'It turned out I was a prostitute', he remarked:

> She was content, and I was also, to a certain extent – I always had enough to eat and did not have to think about my daily bread, and I got a new car, and a better wage, and the director even appointed me as a stand-in in the buffet. So sex had such a good influence on my career and my life. But of course, that could not continue for a long time: I had to arrange my private life …
>
> ... I was content with my work. I had to pay attention to the director, but that was without any future prospects – I will not marry her, she is much older than I am, her daughter is already grown-up. Well, so far she is keeping herself in shape, but for how long can it continue later on? It is not such a pleasure with an old lady, but sexually I continued to satisfy her, and she did not stay indebted to me, so it turns out that I was a prostitute.

The relationship ended when the director got caught for dubious financial transactions and lost her position ('lucky me, and unlucky her').

Mikhail lost his opportunity for extra work and additional income in the workplace restaurant, but he got to do more financially rewarding long-distance driving. Later, a female colleague proposed an affair, to which he first objected on the grounds that 'there was no love between us'. She let him know his position, however – 'if I want good trips and good moonlighting, I have to show her attention once in a while' – and they eventually had a two-year-long relationship.

Ivanov also describes a failed *blat* arrangement. His sister-in-law was supposed to marry a close friend of her boyfriend, a released convict, in order to help him get a *propiska* (set of residency papers) in Leningrad. After they had made an application for a registration of marriage, the boyfriend demanded that she should have sex with his friend. Thus the two men deliberately confounded gender *blat* (marrying the friend of a friend in order to help him) with sexual *blat* (having intercourse with him). She refused, but her boyfriend left the apartment and let her be raped by her 'fiancé'. In revenge, the young woman 'of course did not go anywhere' (i.e. did not report the matter to the police) but withdrew her application for marriage. This was something the two men had evidently not expected, and to manage with it she needed the support of her brother, who warned the two men against attempting any kind of reprisal.

As I have previously stressed, we have no way of knowing whether the women involved in these cases of *blat* really did express themselves as explicitly in reality as in the autobiography. But the relations themselves were not improbable. Neither is it surprising that, although some autobiographies written by women in my material talk about sexual *blat* relations with men (Rotkirch, 1999), there are no other mentions of *blat* where women occupy the higher position and demand sex in exchange for material favours. Ivanov's affair with the director is a clear example of *vertical blat* relations, close to (but not identical with) prostitution. This gender constellation was certainly much more rare than the opposite one, if only for the reason that there were more men in middle and upper managerial positions in the Soviet Union. The secrecy and stigma attached to *blat* relations in general, and to sexual *blat* in particular, would also be highest in the case of a harassing woman. As a man, Ivanov justifies his relations by appealing to valued masculine features such as his great capacities as a lover and the attractiveness of the women who desire him. For a Soviet woman, it would be harder to present (ab)use of power and sexual initiative as part of accepted femininity. Double moral standards were common in all sexual generations of Soviet Russia (Haavio-Mannila and Rotkirch, 1998, 2000).[13] At the same time, Ivanov also conveys his moral ambivalence and feeling of a lack of life-control as the *blat* relationships continued.

The other workplace affair, and the related story about his sister-in-law's failed fictive marriage, are examples of *horizontal blat* relations between work colleagues or friends. In Ivanov's two experiences of sexual *blat* in the workplace, the biggest problem is not the rewards themselves, but the absence of feelings between the partners. Belonging to the silenced generation born in the immediate pre- and post-war years, Ivanov is typical in his emphasis that sex without love is to be condemned. After meeting his second wife, he refused all relationships on the side, emphasising love and fidelity. And when yet another work colleague tried to seduce him, he notes how 'I could no longer trade my consciousness. I had fallen in love with K and could not be unfaithful to her, even with those whom I depended upon. I could no longer have sex without love. It was prostitutes who had sex and got money and presents instead of love.' At the time of writing, he similarly notes that his occasional passionate meetings with younger women are so rewarding, because they give him 'the feeling that you are still needed, which provided an indescribable satisfaction and pride'.

Ivanov's need for moral justification is also felt in his stories of refusing prostitution or other types of casual sex on the road. On long-distance drives, he earned an additional, informal income from taking people along with him (hitchhikers). He notes that many women offered themselves to him, but he usually refused since he was afraid of venereal diseases and since 'sex on the road did not tempt me very much'.

In Ivanov's class journey, social mobility was connected with a rejection of loose living and development of 'normal' family relations. The cultural clashes between poor workers' and middle-class milieux, public Soviet institutions and private complicated chaos, resulted in feelings of loneliness, ambivalence and lack of life-control.

Maynes's (1995) study of nineteenth-century workers found a pattern in men's self-presentation, where sexual restraint was equated with self-control and social mobility. Ivanov's life story follows the same logic It also features more detailed evidence of the tension between two conceptions of masculinity, the crude 'brute' (*muzhik*) and the courteous man, or 'knight'.

From Muzhik *to 'Knight'*

Two more or less mutually exclusive notions of masculinity are present in this story: the local brute, or *muzhik*, and the courteous man, or 'knight'.

The *muzhik* comes from the local milieu within which Mikhail was brought up. It is symbolised by his best childhood friend, Oleg. Ivanov was a lonely child who was tormented by jealousy and he several times remarks that 'nobody loved me when I was a boy'. During the difficult times of his youth, Oleg became the one who 'helped me with everything'. Clearly idealised by Mikhail, it was Oleg who first taught Mikhail how to handle girls, along with the main sexual vocabulary. Oleg has also had the same incestuous experience with his mother (and even his sister) as Mikhail, but talks about it without any shame. He is made to represent the harsh, commanding and highly sexual male, the *muzhik*, who says 'I never let anybody pass whom I could fuck'. This type of man also appears in the already-mentioned story of how Mikhail's sister-in-law was raped. 'She was against it, but as he was a man [*on vse-taki muzhik*], he added: "If you won't undress I'll fuck you nevertheless, and that'd just be worse for you." ... He tormented [*zamuchil*] her, and only when V returned to the apartment did he let her go.'

The second, contrasting masculine ideal of the responsible man belongs to Soviet notions of proper courtship and family life. These ideals were elaborated in the 1930s and 1940s and represented the lifestyle of the emerging Soviet middle class culture (Dunham, 1976). They are condensed in a statement put forward towards the end of Ivanov's autobiography: 'The preservation of the family is one of the big problems of our day.' Quite unexpected and unintentionally comical in this context, this declaration sounds like a direct quotation from a psychological or pedagogical 'expert' or from a headline of the 1970s or 1980s. Earlier, when Mikhail's first marriage was falling apart, he provided similar-sounding arguments for not getting a divorce ('You have to preserve the family because of the children' [*no semju nado khranit' radi detej*]).

Interestingly, Ivanov does not at any point openly condemn the *muzhik* ideal taught to him by Oleg. At one point, Oleg destroyed Mikhail's relations with his first girlfriend by forcing her to perform oral sex with him, an event which Ivanov witnessed and which, he writes, made him want to hang himself. Already in those years Mikhail longed to distance himself from such crude manners, and the text stresses the importance of love and reciprocity in sexual relations. The contradiction between macho manners and romantic ideals jumps into the eye of the reader, but is not at all commented on or elaborated by Ivanov. Mikhail actually behaves like a *muzhik* only on rare occasions. Mostly, as we have seen, he perceives himself as the passive, insecure man being seduced. Once, towards the end of his first marriage, he saw a naked young woman at a party, and 'one thought overwhelmed me: how to fuck her'. But even here his behaviour is justified by a statement by the same girl, who commented on the infidelity with the words 'people don't have a normal family life anyway now – everybody is on his own'. And of a similar wild party, he remarks: 'I did not fall in love with anybody just like that, without love. I did not want to get closer to anybody. I did not even feel aroused by [the naked girls] without their trousers on.'

A similar contradiction appears in Ivanov's relationship with pornographic magazines. At first, he disapproved of his first wife Raia's loose morals. When she took imported condoms and Western pornographic magazines home, Mikhail supposedly said 'Take them away. I don't want to look at naked women, and even if I want to look, I don't want any pictures.' But later in life, he talks about hiding pornographic magazines from their daughter as an example of his efforts to provide a strict moral upbringing.

The 'knight' ideal of the responsible man seems closer to Mikhail's self-understanding than the *muzhik*. Such Soviet middle-class culture is, in the beginning, represented by his student milieu and later on by his second, enduring marriage. In this family, his wife was quite embarrassed about any discussions about sex, and Mikhail was the one who has to explain and teach the curious daughter. The parents took care while making love and avoided appearing naked in front of the child. They carefully hid their erotic literature and journals, and Mikhail explained to her that only husband and wife may watch each other naked in the bathroom. Nowadays, they have discovered erotic books, 'some kind of boulevard sex', and condoms in their student daughter's bag. They asked her about this, but did not reproach her. At 18 she started bringing boyfriends home – 'We decided it was her fiancé, but we were deeply wrong, because she had quite a number of such fiancés' – in sum, for many Western readers a fully recognisable, tolerant approach to teenage sexuality, with minimal control being exerted, even if quite a lot of worry is felt.

The *muzhik* and the 'knight' are exclusive of each other to the point of resembling the classical female dichotomy between whore and madonna. Nevertheless, the contrasting ideals of masculinity have one thing in common: they serve to control the situation. In this particular life story, the ideals provide different reactions to the perceived threat of feminine immorality/material poverty. The 'knight' ideal is the culturally-approved, proper way out, much like the self-restraint advocated by Maynes's (1995) working-class autobiographers. The *muzhik* is the immediate, brutal response: he is the man who does not rise socially, but who does control. The big difference between the young Mikhail and his friend Oleg is that the latter is not ashamed of his incestuous relationship and even brags about it.

Ivanov's self-understanding remains divided. He tells us that, as a young boy, he used to suck his mother's breasts both with tenderness and passion. Later, his wife suggested he should drink her breast-milk (she was breast-feeding their second child for almost two years) since it was healthy and would strengthen his potency. Mikhail retorted: 'I am not such an idiot as to drink women's milk – that's the last thing I need.' Once again, Ivanov does not seem to perceive these kinds of contradictions in his account. Still, he does articulate and reflect on his experiences. Towards the end of the text he describes a quarrel with his wife. She complained about his looking at young girls on the beach. He in turn complained about her refusing to have sex and pointed out (again with clear allusions to popular pedagogical literature) that 'sexual relations are formed in the family – they depend on how you are growing up, and are being brought up, what and how you are seeing in your milieu [*sreda*]'. She retorted that one could, indeed, see from his behaviour where he had been growing up and told him that his former sister-in-law had told her all about his relationships, including those with his mother and step-mother.

After this revelation there follows the 'credo' of Ivanov's autobiography, summarising his pain and powerlessness:

> Saying that, she [his wife] did not understand that I grew up in a milieu where there were women and girls who were unashamed of me, who were naked and who washed with me, or rather I with them, in the sauna, and that I was sleeping with my mother who was young and did not shun men. It was not my fault that she made me lie on her and made me a man, and later, my mother could not and would not refuse herself sexual pleasure, and she did not pay attention to who was beside her at that moment, so I said to her: 'Be content that you had your mother, a grandmother for your daughter, and that she got used to sleeping in her own bed since childhood. It's not clear what would have happened had O. [her daughter] slept with you, what she would have been drawn to – perhaps she would also have become a lesbian, and would have been drawn to others like herself. And about that mother-in-law

> ... you know how she got me married, and you know the rest. So you should not blame me now.' And later, in what followed, all my life went in some kind of sexual dependency, and despite everything I have seldom chased women – the women have chased me – and so what if they succeeded?

Here, finally, the contrasting male ideals merge in order to support Mikhail's explanation. Sexuality appears, like in the *muzhik*'s behaviour, as a wild, raw and potentially destructive and immoral force. Then the cultured knight enters: with proper education and upbringing sexuality can be civilised and the development of perverse habits (incest, lesbianism) can be reversed. Nothing was Mikhail's own fault, because what happened is how things inevitably evolve in that situation. In his view, the naturalisation of sex moves on two levels: it first excuses male *muzhik* behaviour and then blames education for failing to regulate it. Women are only partly embraced by these justifications. Loose women are morally condemned, unlike the *muzhik*, and women are additionally blamed for not providing the social regulation (here symbolised by a separate bed for the children) by which both sexes become civilised.

Suburban Gang Culture of the 1970s

In the Cellar

Aleksei Lukashin, a medical student who has worked as a sound operator in a rock band, a doctor and a masseur, and nowadays works in show business, was born in 1960. Like Ivanov, he was raised by a single mother in a clearly poor district of the city. He was the youngest of three boys. The eldest brother moved out when he was still a toddler, but he spent a lot of time with his middle brother. Aleksei's schoolteachers are said to have lost all hope at an early stage: the only one who really minded him not attending classes was the sports teacher, who is described as having chased him around the building with a basketball, his eyes bloodstained after Aleksei had made a stone hidden in a briefcase fall down on his head ... This anecdote says much about the social setting, as Soviet schools in the 1970s generally had severe discipline.

The young Aleksei and his friends took part in some sports together (especially ice hockey, but also some cross-country skiing) but in the main just 'hung out' together. In this autobiography, there is never any hesitation about which ideal of masculinity should be followed: there is much fighting with fists, knives and occasionally even guns, and much laughing, drinking and dragging people about. 'My brothers were held in esteem in the whole *okruga* [neighbourhood]. They fought very well. I tried not to be worse than they were ... When it became necessary, I took part in the battles. When I could, I went out with them in the company of girls.' These girls, who later in the text are usually called 'beauties', figure only as sexual objects who circulate between the men. It is a *muzhik*'s world, where the word 'love' is mentioned only in quotation marks and there are no attempts at 'knight' discourse, except in order to ridicule or oppose it.

Whether out of straightforwardness or provocation, the text opens with a close-up of a 'meeting' many others would call a gang rape:

> It happened a long time ago. It is over twenty years since. I was about 15 years old. I was a clever, quick little guy. I was physically strong, above my age. I was friends with my classmates, but also with guys who were 3–5 years older than me.
>
> My first close encounter with a woman took place in a cellar. My elder brother had brought some girl or other. Together with his friends we got drunk, and then everybody fucked her. Around the tenth turn was mine. I was very nervous, standing in line. The older friends calmed and encouraged me. 'You won't even have to do anything', they said. 'Just take off your pants' ... When I went in, she was lying on the floor, smoking a cigarette. To hide my anxiety I behaved rudely (like a big boy), and took off my pants without a word. I firmly followed the instructions. I lay down on her. Physically, I felt her body, and some kind of smell that was new to me. Sensing this all so close to me raised my worries to a qualitatively new level. My legs started shaking. But like a bulldozer, without noticing anything around, I acted. It was very wet in there ... After that I quickly left and went home. At home I washed myself and went to bed. I was all trembling with excitement. I lay down for just a short while. Then I jumped up, dressed and ran to the cellar, but, alas, there was already nobody there.

This is the first episode in Lukashin's sexual memoirs. Of the hundreds of other sexual encounters, none is as closely described. Lukashin's first time is recalled with a strong component of tactile sensations and emotions – smells, touching, trembling. Later, he merely describes the appearance of his female partners (giving them grades), the positions used and the general impressions of the conquest in question. But in many respects the style of the cellar-scene description is typical of the whole text. On the one hand, the author makes a strong effort to remember, but on the other, he adopts a half-joking, anecdotal tone which often serves to belittle the events and distances the reader from them.

The frequent mentions of laughter – with the boys, or while first flirting with a girl – are among the most personal and sympathetic features of Lukashin's account. Otherwise, Lukashin clearly expects the reader to want a story of his sexual escapades, very much according to the genre 'readers' letters' in pornographic or erotic journals. The directives provided in the announcement of the autobiographical competition (to begin with early childhood, to write about both sex and love, to talk 'as to a close friend', and to reflect on various phenomena, e.g. homosexuality or prostitution (Rotkirch, 2000)) do not seem to have left any trace. Lukashin clearly enjoys recalling some very successful or unusual affairs, but discards others: 'I have left a great deal out on purpose, and I think there is also much I simply do not remember.' Some experiences, such as his family relations or his religious views, are deemed irrelevant in this context ('That is another story'). Towards the end of the text, he complains of being tired of writing and of having too little time left since his wife (or partner) will soon return and he does not want her to read the text.

The girl in the cellar is not described as having resisted the boys in any way. At the same time, it is hard to imagine that any teenage girl would of her free will participate in such a scene. She may have been threatened in some way, just as Ivanov's sister-in-law was forced to agree with the argument that it would simply be much worse if she did not cooperate. At the very least, the girl in the cellar had for some reason reached a point where she did not or could not care about her own integrity. This is the most striking example of the moral grey area and the ambivalence about sexual norms that were especially pronounced during late socialism (Rotkirch, 2000, pp. 66–76). The Soviet statistics already indicate that sexual violence was frequently committed by young males and that, specifically, group rapes by youth gangs were more frequent than in other countries (Kon, 1995). Yet we may suppose that the events reported to the police must have been among those perceived by all participants as being more or less unequivocal violence. In addition, there were probably many more situations akin to Lukashin's sexual initiation, in which neither the offenders nor the victim seem to have had clear notions about how to name, react to, or later think about what happened. His version represents the other side of what the autobiographies written by women describe as foolishness, fatal innocence, becoming paralysed or fearing to scream (Rotkirch, 1999; Zdravomyslova, 2000).

These practices created intense and contradictory feelings, which evidently found no adequate or stable frames of interpretation. This is obvious when Lukashin relates how he later was recognised by the girl in the cellar. His first reaction was ('naturally') guilt:

> That was my first close encounter with a woman. By the way, she remembered me (although it had been quite dark in the cellar). A month or two later we met each other on the street one evening. I didn't recognise her – two girls just asked for a cigarette and we started to talk. Then one of them left, and the other suggested we go to another place to smoke, which turned out to be an attic, and even a comfortable one – it had a sofa. We sat down, smoked, and that was when she reminded me of the story with the cellar. I naturally denied it at first, but she calmed me, saying that she had no grudges, that it was her own fault and so on – well, and that she had liked me. I looked at her. She was about ten years older [than me].

This time, they had more varied and longer sex. But then this *latter* sexual encounter is in retrospect called (albeit jokingly) a rape – of himself!

> After I had been raped (as I now understand) by my brother's girl in the attic, my life took on different colours. I somehow changed sharply. Something in my head awoke that drove me crazy.

Aleksei invited one girl home and forced her to undress before him by bending her fingers so it hurt. The girl agreed, but on condition they would not have intercourse. After this they often met for mutual petting and without any mention of further persuasion by force. When Aleksei insisted on intercourse, she promised to provide another girl for him. Indeed, after some time a new girl appeared in their circle of friends: 'I do not remember what I told her, but relatively easily I took her to a hut on a construction site', where the new girl 'calmly lay down'. Aleksei got nervous when he discovered she was a virgin, as he did not know how to manage without any help from his partner. Furthermore, the other young men had already formed a line outside the hut. 'It all ended with us just getting dressed and I followed her home, which happened and still happens to me extremely seldom.'

Aleksei obviously rescued his partner from another gang rape like the one in the cellar. His noble behaviour is presented in the rhetoric of 'praising by downgrading', with him stressing that he practically never followed golden rule number one of Soviet romantic courtship: that the man should accompany the woman home. He also provides us with a cynical ending to this relationship. The couple met again and managed to have intercourse. He was confronted by her boyfriend and beat him up, after which they had sex 'a couple of times more, and then she went from hand to hand'.

The list of women, and of kinds of and places for sex during the next fifteen years, continues, until Lukashin in the last page declares, a little surprisingly, that he is actually tired of all this: '... sex has long ago lost its urgency for me'. In his mid-thirties, he has not settled in his family life nor in his professional circles. He was at the time of writing cohabiting, but dreaming about finding a completely 'harmonious woman'. He was employed in show business but finishing his studies on the side, hoping that 'the best is yet to come' in his life. This phase of personal and professional unrest may have created for Lukashin the need for self-reflection, or at least the urge to remember, that prompted him to write.

Although Lukashin's social status is far from settled, his social trajectory represents a very different pattern from that of the previous generation. This is evident in the perceived relation between sexual restraint and social success, as well as in his attitude towards women.

Attempts at Social Ascent

Initially, Aleksei Lukashin's path follows a similar logic to Mikhail Ivanov's: to get away from his childhood milieu by putting order into his life and studying. At the end of the 1970s, Aleksei served two years in the Army, where he used all his spare time 'maximally, in order to develop my intellectual and physical qualities. It produced results. When I returned after the military service everybody found me different. I did not drink or smoke and I talked about important goals in life.' However, the dramatic separation and opposition of spheres – home milieu v. student milieu, chaotic family life v. responsible working life – characteristic of Ivanov's social trajectory is not paralleled in Lukashin's case. For instance, the Army improved Aleksei's intellectual ambitions, but he also notes how 'in the Army my muscles of stone started to weaken and indifference and apathy entered my soul'. Public life and Soviet institutions do not appear in the role of stabilising and saving structures, as was the case, for instance, in Alexandra Chistyakova's (1998) life story.

While Ivanov's lifestyle 'relapsed' into lack of life-control and promiscuity owing to his first marriage, Lukashin interrupted his plan of higher education in order to work for some years with a touring rock band.

The latter also had fewer problems with women than with his own drinking, but the basic logic of women and alcohol versus social improvement and life-control is dominant at the beginning. He represents the work as a way of escaping his lifestyle at home:

> At that time I needed to somehow detach myself from women, and actively looked for some interesting work. An administrator I knew well suggested I could call the administration of one particular regional centre and mention that he'd recommended me. I did so, and was offered work with a rock group that was more or less famous at the time.

Touring life proved even more full of sexual encounters, and Aleksei started to drink and smoke again – blaming for this the meeting with his elder brother in a Siberian town, a celebration which evidently was not conceivable without excessive alcohol. He was also christened 'the specialist on bitches [*spetsialist po babam*]' in the group since he had had so many affairs and also 'seriously helped everybody else to get women'. But life on the road exhausted him: '[I] left a part of my health at the tours and I had a serious need to regain my former strength. I skipped drinking and smoking, and started to go to a body-building gym.' He left the rock band after a couple of years and began his studies. The balanced and healthy lifestyle was not incompatible with several sexual affairs or shadow-market transactions [*fartsovka*] to gain extra money. Aleksei also married one of his girlfriends, who had become pregnant and who also appears to have had immense patience with him, including with his infidelity during the wedding festivities.

But then, times started changing. Lukashin does not once refer to any social or political factors, but it is hardly a coincidence that he quits his education after the mid-1980s. He left the medical institute and the straightforward track into a feminised profession, low-paid in Soviet times and one of the relatively worst-off professions in the 1990s. Instead, he acquires the less demanding qualifications of a masseur. At his first workplace, the succession of affairs started again. 'I had to fuck in the city hall, at the registration office (*ZAGS*) before somebody's marriage, and so on.' At the same time, he divorced his wife, telling us he found her too lethargic. Following the classical script of short first Soviet marriages, she automatically kept the child (if it was ever born – there is no mention of it at all in the text) and the apartment, and he moved to one room in a communal apartment, which was close to his work but far away from his mother and ex-wife.

Through an acquaintance, Aleksei got a temporary assignment as a physician. Once more, he tried to straighten up. He proudly notes being able to save a woman's life, and how he 'did not drink, did not smoke and was in good form ... For about half a year I recovered morally. No sex, no nothing. I was all in my work.' True, the next paragraph describes how 'the most interesting women received complete satisfaction' and only the locals were refused special treatment, although they tried hard to get some.

The same winter, he looked through his telephone notebook and called an acquaintance, who arranged for him to work as a masseur in a newly-established private sauna. Here the old logic – social ascent equals adoption of proper middle-class morals (the normal family life, in Ivanov's terms) – is broken. True, Lukashin underlines how good he was at his new work, getting clients from his already-established colleagues. But he also notes that it was 'a psychologically hard transition from the image of a doctor to the image almost of a bath-house attendant [*banshchik*]. But I had to live and support myself somehow. I couldn't expect help from anywhere.' Soon, he is working a great deal, and this included sex.. 'I had to fuck sometimes several times a day. Naturally with different women. Everything started to spin and swirl ... I started to drink and to smoke. The bacchanal continued for about three years. I actually tried to regulate the process somehow.'

But, clearly, regulation of the 'process' did not succeed. The nature of his sexual relations in the sauna is not clear – Lukashin says most of his female clients were prostitutes, although some were rich married women, but who paid whom and what kind of exchange of sympathies or favours took place remains unclear. Neither does he mention any relations with the male customers that he also received in the beginning. He alludes to propositions also on their part: 'I was surrounded by all sorts of strange people – gays, dykes and so on [*vsyakaya vsyachina – golubaja, rozovaja i t.d.*].'[14]

At this point, Aleksei's professional and personal lives have become completely intertwined. Far from helping him move away from the behaviour he himself perceives as problematic, his job in one of the new post-socialist commercial structures exploited and reinforced it. By trying to improve his life – moving from a medical position in state-owned polyclinics to a professionally inferior but economically better position in the private sector – he made his working life and his sexual life more entangled than before. On the road with the rock group, or as a doctor in a tourist base, he had numerous affairs, but of his own choice and as an addition, a non-obligatory complement, to his working profile. The fact that his own body has been cynically exploited by his employees and their clientele may perhaps explain Aleksei's pronounced cynicism with regard to women.

Misogyny and Male Bonding

Aleksei Lukashin presents himself as an uncaring man, whose only aim is to seduce women. Only once or twice does he note, for instance, that he 'by the way, also held a seriously deep feeling towards her'; or that he was disappointed when one meeting 'satisfied only the lust, but without anything like a more human thing, with proper setting and scope [*rasstanovka i razmakha*]'. Statements such as 'I belong to those who think that the best moment with a woman is closing the door after she has left', or '[The intercourse] could be graded as satisfying, that is, for me – I let off steam, and her opinion did not interest me', are among the mildest. In themselves, they are quite possibly explained by his bachelor lifestyle and resistance to stable love relationships, coupled with a longing to find the perfect woman.

But there are also a few descriptions which indicate a deeper hatred of women. Sexual violence is practised without any regrets, as has already been discussed above. The women's hesitations about or opposition to having sex are always rendered with overt contempt. For instance, one woman picked up after a rock concert was got completely drunk by Aleksei and his friends, who both had sex with her. That she never completely agreed to this is made clear from the summarising statement: 'In the morning we parted with her, not as friends, but not as enemies either.' Another time, he and his friend had picked up a woman in a hotel bar and invited her to their hotel room. When she 'pretended to leave', Aleksei asked her to stay:

> She began [to say] something stupid about being an honest girl and so on. But I understood that she had simply not had enough to drink ... Morally I was already tired, but the lust-devil [*pokhot-zlodeika*] in me surfaced. Finally she started to talk less and react more to my caresses ... It was as if a wind had blown away from the girl all the education, upbringing and manners that she had at first displayed, like a model of upbringing.
>
> It seems really to be so, that when the natural, the core [*estestvo*, *nutro*] of a human being is speaking – which is, according to one theory, animal – then everything that has been artificially adopted disappears without a trace.

This woman is described as having enjoyed the night with Aleksei and his friend, to the extent of inviting her girlfriend for a foursome the following evening. But notwithstanding the woman's feelings, there is in Aleksei's comment much contempt for her way of negotiating[15] and especially for her education and good manners. Sexuality, and especially wild and daring sex (like group sex with strangers), is described as the natural drive that surfaces in both sexes when the surface is a little melted with alcohol. Educated women's opposition is seen as merely artificial and dishonest behaviour. This logic is of course familiar from many pornographic and erotic texts, notably Henry Miller's. It presents a naturalised view of sexuality ('the natural', 'the inner', 'the animal') where women who, through education and ambition, socially compete with men are especially denigrated.

Lukashin's misogyny is matched by strong homosocial ties. Men are the self-evident frame of reference, and Lukashin often notes how he had been respected and feared on account of his physical strength, courage and success with women. In his youth, it was indeed a question of interpersonal violence as a pattern of communication (Zdravomyslova and Chikadze, 2000). A little later, alcohol in itself suffices. Lukashin describes a funny incident of male bonding, when he consoles his boss, who found him in bed with the woman the boss had been courting:

> [The boss] started to scream, wave his arms and spit around him about what kind of trash [*negodiai*] we were. He was a proper, intelligent man, taking her, it appeared, to dinner in restaurants, following her to her [hotel] room, almost reading her a fairy-tale before she fell asleep, but instead she …[dumped him]. I stood calmly, contemplating it all in silence. To fight with him was simply not of any interest to me, and well, the guy had to speak out. When he stopped I immediately offered him drink, although he was not drinking anything at all. But now he accepted. We drank. Our talk gradually turned to the subject of the hardships in his life. In sum, I became almost as dear to him as his own brother after that night.

His male friends are pitied and ridiculed if they suffer on account of unhappy love, like some of his young friends who slashed their wrists or attempted to jump from a ceiling because of women. Lukashin says he was 'spared by God' and merely trembled in front of women, until the age of 25, when he stopped doing even that.

In his autobiography, Lukashin presents himself as a 'straightforward guy'. There are seemingly few conflicts between personal feeling, social practices and their ideological interpretations. He appears a physical, active man who always enjoys sex and more or less successfully combats his drinking. He represents the most complete realisation of a late-Soviet, macho, Don Juan-like *muzhik* ideal. In his few reflections on sexuality, he advocates a naturalised view of sexuality – sex is an inner core, which only artificial education or too-well-behaved women deny. This aggressive, naturalised sexual ideology also seems to compensate for professional and personal instability and failed attempts at social ascent. At the very end of the autobiography, more serious aspirations surface:

> I do not look at the world with wide-open eyes, but I think that the best is yet ahead. Sex has long ago lost its actuality for me. I mean … to fuck somebody is no problem. The problem lies elsewhere. To meet the perfect woman [*garmonichno slozhennaia*] (physically, psychologically and intellectually) is very hard. To keep her, after having met her, is still harder. Usually they have far too high self-esteem, demands, and so on. In my opinion one should trust the will of the divine and [accept that] if something should happen it does and vice versa. But that is the theme of another essay.

Here again, the reader is reminded that Lukashin consciously follows the genre of erotic memoirs, and hides, for example, his possible religious or other more serious opinions. He admits to longing for a stable relationship, although his expectations seem high enough, especially if the perfect woman should not have high self-esteem or 'demands'. Interestingly, Lukashin's final credo absolves him – just as does Ivanov's final justification – from any responsibility or active agency. Where Ivanov blamed his upbringing, in line with the dominant pedagogical ideas of his adult years, Lukashin provides a semi-religious, fatalistic solution characteristic of the Soviet 1970s and 1980s – 'if something should happen it does'.

Concluding Comparisons

From Acculturation to Blurred Mobility

Mikhail Stern, an *émigré* Soviet doctor, has offered the following characterisation of the sexual mores of the Soviet lower social groups: 'Though sex may be a taboo subject among "respectable" people in the Soviet Union, those people who live on the fringes of society, who think of themselves as belonging to "the lower depths", talk about sex very openly and naturally' (Stern, 1979, p. 199). The 'loose behaviour' of the lower working class is a prevalent social stereotype, in Russia just as in the rest of Europe. But, as Mary Jo Maynes has pointed out, even if workers may have a less strict attitude towards some types of sexual behaviour (e.g. virginity) than the middle class, this does not imply that their cultures were more 'natural', without their own specific codes of shame and respectability. Against the kind of simplification of working-class sexuality that Mikhail Stern's statement represents, Maynes argues that the 'links between sex and social identity were not generally the same for workers as they were for their class superiors, but they were equally problematic' (Maynes, 1995, p. 131; see also Steedman, 1991).

This chapter has only looked at male examples of such links in poor working cultures. The few texts I have read by Soviet women workers place a quite different emphasis. None of the working-class men could make the consoling claim made by this working-class woman born in 1925: 'That was life as well, even if [it was] very gloomy, not like normal life. But love is love everywhere, however savage that seems.' For Ivanov, love was not the same everywhere, and for Lukashin there was no love. The links between sexual and social identity seem especially problematic for these two male cases from marginal milieux: the men place a more dramatic gap between local and dominant ideas about sexuality and family life, and they have a harder time reconciling them with each other.

Ivanov's life draws a quite classical picture of the class journey from poor, marginalised worker to well-to-do upper-working-class person. Just as in the workers' autobiographies from a century earlier, male self-control was seen as an intrinsic component of upward social mobility (Maynes, 1995, p. 135). Although Ivanov depicts a seemingly amoral world, the fact remains that he himself was deeply morally affected by it. The parallels between middle-class morality and social ascent are explicitly drawn by Ivanov himself throughout the text. He willingly followed the path of *okulturivanie*, becoming a 'cultured' and civilised person, adopting stricter sexual norms after starting out from a situation with very little 'culture'.

Lukashin, by contrast, has had to let go of his initial (albeit diffuse) dreams of becoming a doctor. Like Ivanov, Lukashin describes sexual *blat* relations, for instance how one of his lovers who worked as an administrator in a hotel always provided him with de luxe rooms. Affairs like those may have added to his status in the working collective, but they were not integral to it. But in the private sauna, Aleksei's affairs moved to the centre of the picture, and the promiscuity appears as a central feature of the establishment itself. He also relates how he worked for a short time in a sports and health institution, where the administration wanted to arrange a 'commercial line' (*kommercheskoe ruslo*). Aleksei helped them organise the new sauna department, and describes the wealthy and criminal clients, billiards played with naked prostitutes, etc. The sexual component of the sauna institutions had moved from occasional meetings between two people in closed rooms to a display in front of the whole clientele in the main room.

Russian women are more often objects of the intertwining of sex and work described in these male autobiographies (Rotkirch, 1999). But the evolution from Ivanov's *blat* relations to Lukashin's semi-open prostitution are evidence of the same economic and structural dynamics. The traditional Russian and Soviet way of social ascent through education was at least momentarily suspended. Ivanov's life story evolved away from an acultural setting to established Soviet middle-class life, while the private and the public in Lukashin's biography are blurred: his social status remains undefined, and his sexuality moves into the centre of his professional life.

Milieux and Subcultures

The two autobiographers belong to different Soviet generations. Ivanov, born in 1935, was part of what I have called the silenced sexual generation, while Lukashin belongs to the generation of personalisation (Rotkirch, 2000). I have claimed to describe a 'way of life', without specifying what that refers to, or how extensive that way of life may have been. What, indeed, can be said about the spread of the sexual cultures and male attitudes described by Ivanov and Lukashin? Were they stable ways of life and how far did they extend?

A way of life has been conceptualised as a specific combination of *generation*, *culture* and *class* expressed through a particular *habitus* (Roos, 1988).[16] Although this definition does not deal with the *temporal* dimension, it approaches ways of life as something long-lasting. However, we can use the examples above to introduce an additional distinction. Both represent specific ways of life, but the first (Ivanov) was more limited and short-lived than the second (Lukashin). I propose to talk about the ways of life of a *milieu* in the first case, and of a *subculture* in the second.

The main distinction is that a milieu is smaller, and does not get culturally transmitted and reproduced. A subculture is, by contrast, transmitted symbolically and through habits. A subculture has the potential for becoming a dominating and hegemonic culture, if it continues to spread. A milieu would thus be more of a random chance, connected with exceptional social and ecological circumstances, while a subculture is a milieu that has become rooted in society. In order of size and cultural visibility, we could imagine the following axis: *circles of friends – milieux – subculture – class culture – dominant culture.*

What in the autobiographies supports such a distinction? I have found evidence on the basis of two criteria: how the author describes *meeting other social milieux*, and what kind of *language* is used.

In Ivanov's text, entering different social milieux is described as a recognition of differences. As a student, and in the Army, Ivanov began to think that his family milieu was abnormal and unusual. By contrast, Lukashin behaves the same way with everybody, although he travels around the country. He notices that middle-class women are 'too innocent' to be approached too harshly, but not once does he depict feeling himself an outsider whose norms do not fit in with the present surroundings. I propose that Ivanov's milieu may be seen as a temporary, literally anomic milieu, created by the social upheavals and war periods in the preceding decades. Lukashin encountered similar morality and behaviour whether he was in his home milieu, in rock groups, or in a tourist base. It was no longer a question of a possibly unique milieu, but of a rooted and extended, if not a dominant, way of life.

My second, linguistic criterion is on more shaky ground, since it is hard to tell whether the language employed was used in the youth of the narrator or has been adopted in more recent years. Still, Ivanov's text is marked by self-made and very local expressions. Lukashin, by contrast, uses special terms (e.g. 'deflowering') as if they were a part of his vocabulary even in the 1970s. This could indicate that the sexual subculture was wide and large enough to include access to a varied popular scientific and pornographic vocabulary.

If this analysis is correct, we may see how a certain attitude towards sexuality and masculinity gradually establishes itself in post-war Soviet history. For instance, while Ivanov was highly ambivalent about a naturalised view of sexuality, Lukashin embraced it totally. He recalls using this argument with women: 'I mumbled something about the elevated and beautiful, about how good sex is for your health, about the beautiful music that was playing and how it is better to listen to it lying down and relaxing, with your eyes closed and so on.' In this seduction talk, some shattered pieces of romanticism remain ('the elevated and the beautiful').

But they are used purely for strategic reasons, and paired with the totally different view of sex as a 'healthy' thing.

This is glaringly different from the case of Ivanov and his generation, who sincerely searched for the elevated and beautiful, and perceived it as being in painful opposition to lust and the sexual. Ivanov emphasises the role of education in prohibiting sexual excess and perversions, while Lukashin understands sex as less problematic, a healthy activity. In both cases, however, the adopted views serve to enhance the men's feelings of control over women, over their own lives, without their blaming themselves for anything in their past experiences. Lukashin's deliberate misogyny is yet another good example of a trait of Soviet subculture that entered the Russian public sphere along with the generation of the 1970s and became one of the most dominant and visible attitudes.

Notes

1 A slightly modified version of this chapter has been published as Chapter 8 in Rotkirch (2000).

2 The competition was organised by Alexandr Klyotzin and Liza Lagunova from the Institute of Sociology in St Petersburg. It was advertised in the weekly newspaper *Chas Pik* and on billboards. The social representativeness of these self-solicited autobiographies has been analysed by comparing the authors with a representative survey of the St Petersburg population (Haavio-Mannila and Rotkirch, 1997). For a description of the social profile of the authors, the genres of their sexual autobiographies, the original text of the competition announcement, etc. see Rotkirch (2000).

3 Soviet social policy defined several 'vulnerable' social groups eligible for monetary assistance and other benefits, such as housing and special discounts in shops. These categories of social aid were not tied to a conception of poverty or the working poor. Instead, they included single mothers, invalids, war veterans, families with three or more children, etc., regardless of social status or level of income (Liborakina and Rotkirch, 1999).

4 The negative reactions to Chistyakova's life were confirmed to me by Irina Savkina from the University of Tampere in February 1998 on the basis of her close following of the Russian media. We can note that in the same historical period, a woman's autobiography about childhood poverty, social struggle, illegal abortions and family violence became a bestseller in Ireland, although this book (O'Faolain, 1996) is also much better written than Alexandra Chistyakova's life story.

5 The difficulty with any discussion of social margins and lower social groups is also connected with the class problem in Soviet society. The Stalinist 'two and one half' formula, which divided Socialist society into workers, peasants and the intelligentsia, remains the dominant one in both vernacular and academic thinking about Soviet Russia, with the addition of the Soviet élite classes or 'nomenclature' as a fourth

stratum. These categories are not so much classes in a socio-economic sense as peculiar forms of quasi- or proto-estate, the adherence to which was decided by the Soviet state (Fitzpatrick, 1993). Furthermore, they superficially united professionally, politically and economically distinct, and in some cases even potentially antagonistic, social groups. Thus Fitzpatrick (ibid., p. 766) underlines how the category of the Soviet 'intelligentsia' merged 'the old "employees" category with both the [pre-Revolutionary] intelligentsia and the Communist administrative élite to form a single white-collar conglomerate'. The same problem overshadows any discussion of Soviet 'workers', and especially the working poor. Soviet categorisations made additional distinctions between high-, semi- and low-skilled workers. But the two lower categories, especially, were actually supposed to cover culturally very different groups: from semi-agrarian communities, migrant *limitchiki* [guest or migrant] workers and ex-convicts to factory workers of the second or third generation with a basically middle-class lifestyle.

6 The names are pseudonyms. I will use the last name to refer to the author of the autobiography, and the first name to refer to the protagonist of the story, i.e. 'Ivanov writes extensively about when Mikhail, as a young boy ...'.

7 In addition to Alexandr Klyotzin and Liza Lagunova, the organisers of the competition in St Petersburg, Anna Temkina also read and commented on this autobiography. I am grateful to all three for their shared insights.

8 The city of P. was on the old border between Finland and Russia. After 1943 it became Soviet, and the Finns were forced to move away or deported.

9 Actually, Ivanov lived only in a suburb of Leningrad, and was probably a migrant of the second or even the first generation – we are not told where his parents were born, or whether the family had moved to P. before Mikhail and his sister were born.

10 I am grateful to Liza Lagunova (1997), who first directed my attention to the many examples of women's sexual harassment or exploitation of men in this corpus of material.

11 The existence of underground brothels is an excellent example of how sexual knowledge varied with class and place. The boy from a poor promiscuous suburb did not know what several Leningrad women of the same generation, but from the educated middle class living closer to the centre, have assured me was general, if silent, knowledge.

12 Today, Ivanov writes that he cannot use the services of prostitutes owing to a lack of money, implying he would not be against buying sex. But I suspect this comment to be rather an expression of macho rhetoric than a deeply-felt possible solution to his present difficulties of finding women. Towards the end of his autobiography, Ivanov emphasises the importance of tenderness and the feeling that he is needed by his sexual partner.

13 In the St Petersburg survey from 1996, 75 per cent of the respondents say they think it is acceptable for a woman to take the sexual initiative, as against 93 per cent of Finnish respondents in 1999 (and 81 per cent of Finnish respondents in 1971). Also, one third of St Petersburg men supported double moral standards for the sexes – they stated that they accepted the infidelity of a husband but not that of a wife. Only 2 per cent of Finnish men gave the same reply (Haavio-Mannila and Rotkirch, 2000, p. 10). In contemporary literature, Maria Arbatova has described the challenge facing a

sexually autonomous Moscow woman in the 1970s in her autobiographical short story 'My Teachers', published in the collection *My Name Is Woman* (Arbatova, 1997).

14 *Goluboj* (light blue) and *rozovaia* (pink) are popular Russian expressions for homosexuals and lesbians (Essig, 1999).

15 What from a man's perspective may be seen as feigned innocence and dishonest coquetry may just as well be explained as a woman's way of negotiating and flirting, no less authentic than the man's supposed straightforwardness. This point is well argued in Toril Moi's close reading of Sartre (Moi, 1994).

16 The interaction between class and generational experiences remains undertheorised. However, it seems unquestionable that the dominating and middle classes are in a position to influence what becomes 'generational' through their presence in schools, mass media, the arts, etc. Even when classes and groups more marginal to the dominating discourse identify themselves with their 'generation', they often show a parallel awareness of their own specificity regarding the 'common experiences' of 'our times'.

References

Arbatova, M. (1997), *Menia zovut zhenshchina* [My Name Is Woman], Alma Mater, Moscow.

Chistyakova, A. (1998), *Ne mnogo li dlia odnoi? Pis'mo iz Kemerovo* [Too Much for One Person? Letter from Kemerovo], life story recorded by V. Shiriaev, *Dinbyl'*, pp. 34–84.

Dunham, V. (1976), *In Stalin's Time: Middleclass Values in Soviet Fiction*, Cambridge University Press, Cambridge.

Essig, L. (1999), *Queer in Russia: A Story of Sex, Self and the Other*, Duke University Press, Durham, NC.

Fitzpatrick, S. (1993), 'Ascribing Class: The Construction of Social Identity in Soviet Russia', *Journal of Modern History*, vol. 4, no. 65, December, pp. 745–70.

Haavio-Mannila, E. and Rotkirch, A. (1998), 'Generational and Gender Differences in Sexual Life in St Petersburg and Urban Finland', *Yearbook of Population Research in Finland*, vol. 34, pp. 133–60.

Haavio-Mannila, E. and Rotkirch, A. (2000), 'Gender Liberalisation and Polarisation: Comparing Sexuality in St Petersburg, Finland and Sweden', *Idäntutkimus, The Finnish Journal of East European Studies*, nos 3–4, pp. 4–25.

Hite, S. (1978), *The Hite Report: A Nationwide Study of Female Sexuality*, Dell, New York.

Kon, I. (1995), *The Sexual Revolution in Russia: From the Age of the Czars to Today*, The Free Press, New York.

Lagunova, E. (1997), 'Sexual Harassment of Men in Autobiographical Stories'. Presentation at the seminar 'Biographical Perspectives on Post-Socialist Societies', Centre for Independent Social Research, St Petersburg, November 1996.

Ledeneva, A.V. (1998), *Russia's Economy of Favours: Blat, Networking and Informal Exchange*, Cambridge University Press, Cambridge.

Liborakina, M. and Rotkirch, A. (1999), 'Social Consequences of the 1998 Crisis in Russia', *Idäntutkimus, The Finnish Journal of Eastern European Studies*, no. 2, pp. 24–48.

Maynes, M.J. (1995), *Taking the Hard Road: Life Course in French and German Workers' Autobiographies in the Era of Industrialisation*, University of North Carolina Press, Chapel Hill, CA and London.

Moi, T. (1994), *Simone de Beauvoir: The Making of an Intellectual Woman*, Blackwell, Oxford.

O'Faolain, N. (1996), *Are You Somebody? The Life and Times of Nuala O'Faolain*, Hodder & Stoughton, London.

Piirainen, T. (1997), *Towards a New Social Order in Russia: Transforming Structures of Everyday Life*, Dartmouth, Aldershot.

Roos, J.P. (1988), *Elämäntavasta elämäkertaan. Elämätapaa etsimässä, Vol. 2*, Tutkijaliitto, Helsinki.

Roos, J.P. (1994) (also *www.valt.helsinki.fi/staff/jproos/truelife.html*), 'The True Life Revisited: Autobiography and Referentiality after the "Posts"', in *Lives and Works: Auto/Biographical Occasions*, special issue of *Auto/Biography*, vol. 3, nos 1–2, pp. 1–16.

Rotkirch, A. (1999), 'The Travelling Maiden and the Man with Parallel Lives', in J. Smith (ed.), *Beyond the Limits: The Concept of Space in Russian History and Culture, Studia Historica* 62, Finnish Historical Society, Helsinki, pp. 131–50.

Rotkirch, A. (2000), *The Man Question: Loves and Lives in Late 20th Century Russia*, Research Report No. 1, Department of Social Policy, University of Helsinki, Helsinki.

Steedman, C. (1991), *Landscape for a Good Woman: The Story of Two Lives*, Rutgers University Press, New Brunswick, CA.

Stern, M. (1979), *Sex in the USSR*, Times Books, New York.

Temkina, A. (2000), 'Sexual Scripts in Women's Biographies and the Construction of Sexual Pleasure', in M. Liljeström, A. Rosenholm and I. Savkina (eds), *Models of Self: Russian Women's Autobiographical Texts*, Kikimora Publications, University of Helsinki, Helsinki, pp. 187–206.

Zaslavskaia, T. (1998), *Sotsial'nye rezul'taty reform i zadachi sotsial'noi politiki* [Social Results of Reforms and Challenges to Social Policy], in T.A. Zaslavskaia (ed.), *Kuda idet Rossiia? Transformatsiia sotsial'noi sfery i sotsial'naia politika* [Where Is Russia Going? Transformation of the Social Sphere and Social Policy], Delo, Moscow, pp. 3–15.

Zdravomyslova, E. (2000), 'A Cultural Paradigm of Sexual Violence Reconstructed from a Woman's Biographical Interview', in M. Liljeström, A. Rosenholm and I. Savkina (eds), *Models of Self: Russian Women's Autobiographical Texts*, Kikimora Publications, University of Helsinki, Helsinki, pp. 229–48.

Zdravomyslova, E. and Chikadze, E. (2000), 'Scripts of Men's Heavy Drinking', *Idäntutkimus*, no. 2, pp. 35–52.

16 The Construction of Sexual Pleasure in Women's Biographies

ANNA TEMKINA
European University,
St Petersburg, Russia

Introduction

The representation of women's sexuality in public academic discourse in Russia differs from its representation in the West. Only a few research projects have been devoted to the analysis of women's sexuality (e.g. Golod, 1999, 2000; Temkina, 1999). Feminist discourse in the field is still poorly developed. The existing academic discourse mainly reproduces traditional gender stereotypes; with only a few exceptions, sexuality in general is considered to be a marginal sphere of research. It is very difficult for the Russian researcher to locate her- or himself within contemporary Western discussion on women's sexuality (feminist and postmodern), owing to the poor development of corresponding discourses in Russia. Moreover, since a number of different forms of sexuality, hierarchy and sexual domination fall outside the frame of such discourse, they do not attract academic attention. This vacuum in the discourse forces the researcher to 'open' phenomena which were effectively closed up until the 1990s and which are still not considered sophisticated topics for academic research. One of the fields in which this operates is the conceptualisation of forced narratives (interviews) about women's sexuality in real everyday life.

This chapter is devoted to one particular issue in women's sexuality, that is, women's sexual pleasure. Approximately 36 per cent of women (5 per cent of men) in St Petersburg (1996) report having sexual satisfaction rarely or not at all (Haavio-Mannila *et al.*, 2000). This gender gap is not specific to Russia (cf. Kontula and Haavio-Mannila, 1995), but narratives of sexual pleasure have, so far as I know, never been the focus of academic research in Russia.

This chapter is devoted to an analysis of how women's sexual pleasure is constructed in the biographical interviews. First, the script approach, as the theoretical base of the research on sexuality, is described. Secondly, ideal types of sexual scripts are reconstructed on the basis of interviews with urban Russian middle-class women. Thirdly, the different meanings of pleasure, corresponding to the different scripts, are reconstructed on the same basis. Different ways of constructing sexual pleasure in women's sexual biographies are illustrated by three concrete life stories.

1 The Script Approach in Research on Women's Sexuality

In this chapter, the concept of the 'script' is applied to the analysis of the construction of sexuality and sexual pleasure in women's sexual biographies. The theory of scripts has been applied to research on sexuality in Western sociology and psychology (Gagnon and Simon, 1973; Gagnon, 1990; Weeks, 1985, 1997; Jackson, 1999), where sexuality is understood as a cultural construct (a set of learnt behavioural patterns). According to Laumann *et al.* (1994), the scripting theory is applied to explanations of how sexual scripts specify with whom people have sex, when and where they should have sex, what they should do sexually, and why they should perform certain sexual activities. Socio-cultural processes play a fundamental role in determining what is perceived to be 'sexual' and how sexuality is constructed and interpreted. Simon and Gagnon distinguish three levels at which scripts operate: cultural, interpersonal and intrapsychic (Gagnon and Simon, 1973; Simon and Gagnon, 1984). Cultural scripts are instructions for sexual and other conducts embedded in cultural narratives. Interpersonal scripts are the scripts of behaviour in a particular (interactional) context. Intrapsychic scripts are the private world of wishes and desires.

I assume that cultural meanings of sexual behaviour (appropriate to a particular milieu, generation, age, status and gender) frame the individual stories about everyday life practices and experiences of sexual life. The script is considered to be the frame,[1] which applies to the description of the sexual situation (a situation which is defined as a sexual one) on the level of interaction. In the definition of sexual scripts I follow the interactionist perspective, with its emphasis on 'the social self, the negotiation of meaning and the social practices whereby the gendered sexual world is produced as an everyday accomplishment' (Jackson 1999, p. 23). Individual scripts presented in the biographies are studied as cases of the negotiation of cultural instructions. The interactionist perspective on the conceptualisation of sexual scripts was developed by Gagnon and Simon (Gagnon, 1990; Gagnon and Simon, 1973, 1987; Laumann *et al.*, 1994; Simon and Gagnon, 1984). Plummer applied this approach to the analysis of sexual stories (Plummer 1982, 1995). Its modern version is proposed by Jackson (1999), who argues that the concept of a sexual script is completed by the analysis of cultural discourses on sexuality and structural inequalities, in particular gender inequality. This last point is crucial for both the critique (Connell and Dowsett, 1992) and the development of the script approach (Jackson, 1999).

Following the interactionist tradition in the script approach, I argue that stories about sexuality can be conceptualised as stories about sexual situations involving interaction, that is, about the social situations of the actors' (sexual) interactions. Different meanings of the 'sexual' are borrowed from the cultural context and are applied to the description of the interaction. Such descriptions include self-identification (does a woman identify herself as wife/mother, or lover, or friend, or a person who sells sex, etc.?), the identification of partners (are they husbands, or lovers, or friends, or clients, or sexual partners, etc.?), and the interpretation and justification of activities which connect the actors.

Different stories are told and written about sexuality, in which different themes prevail. 'Before reconstructing the biographical meaning of single experiences and events, it is necessary to find out how the narrator or biographer has understood the given topic ...' (Rosenthal, 1993, p. 87); the interpretation of a given topic (in this research sexuality) 'must be identify and localised within the framework of the biographer's overall construction' (ibid., p. 87). On the basis of the material from the biographical interviews, I found six main themes around which narratives about sexual life have been organised. The main theme of the story is considered to be the pivot of the script, which frames the interpretation of the actors' interactions and their identifications. Such themes could shape a narrative about the whole life, or else different themes could prevail in the description of different kinds of sexual interaction.

The most important criticism of the script approach (primarily aimed at the Gangon and Simon version) is that it lacks a social account of what links the diverse scripts together, and of how progress is made in moving from one stage to another (Connell and Dowsett, 1992). Here I follow the phenomenological perspective, reconstructing how women produce the 'social self' (i.e. the scripting self according to Simon's (1996) definition) in the stories (Jackson 1999, Plummer 1995) and how they themselves explain any changes in their lives. The social self is constructed through experience, which is constantly 'interpreted, theorised through the narrative form and devices available to us' (Jackson 1999, p. 24).

Different sexual scripts express and construct a gender culture, which respondents present in the narratives in terms of appropriate gender identities, that is, the individual's sense of a gendered self (Lorber, 1994). Following the feminist tradition and the modern script approach I argue that sexual pleasure in women's biographies is a social construction, in which gender identities are determined by the gender structures of inequality.

The issue of 'gender and sexuality' is well-elaborated within feminist frames which focus on homosexuality, power and commercial sex (Jackson and Scott, 1996; Parker and Aggleton, 1999; Zita, 1998), but only more rarely is the discussion aimed at the conceptualisation of heterosexual relationships (Jackson, 1999). In Russia, the situation relating to academic discourse is different: there are comparatively few conceptualisations of homosexuality, power and commercial sex, but at the same time Jackson's thesis is true: 'heterosexuals do not generally expect to be asked to explain themselves ... heterosexuality has usually been unmarked as the unexamined norm which needs no name and no justification for its existence' (Jackson, 1999, pp. 2–3).

My task here is to reconstruct the real stories of women's sexual life, predominantly heterosexual, where different scripts coexist in order to describe the construction of sexual pleasure. I argue that this construction depends on the script(s) which are applied to sexual situations throughout the life course. Sexual pleasure in biographies is presented as dependent upon the characteristics and the activities of partners and their interactions, that is, as dependent upon a certain sexual script. Therefore, I shall first distinguish the ideal types of sexual scripts, then reconstruct how pleasure is described in connection with the scripts and gender identity. I then illustrate this by three concrete sexual biographies.

2 Ideal Types of Sexual Script in Women's Biographies

Ideal types of sexual script are reconstructed according to the themes that are prevalent in the narrative, and according to the different meanings of sexuality that are applied to self-identification and to the description of partners and relationships. The ideal types of script differ in accordance with the meaning ascribed to sex in relation to the following issues:

1. What does the story relate and what categories are used in the sexual vocabulary?
2. How does the individual ego identify herself and her partner(s)?
3. What kinds of sexual relationships and sexual practices are described in the stories?

For the concrete purposes of this research I also look at the location of sexual pleasure in a sexual script.

The empirical data consists of biographical interviews with 20 middle-class women,[2] five of whom are aged 27–34, nine 39–48 and six 57–63. Of these women twelve are divorced, two are widows, three have been married for the second time, one has been married once and two are unmarried. The majority are highly educated.

The interviews included discussion of the following issues: childhood, adolescence, first sexual experience, marriage and divorce, parallel relationships, relationships with steady partners. They also involved questions relating to sex talk with a partner, love and jealousy, adolescent sexual experiences, violent sex, contraception, childbirth, abortion, and sexually-transmitted diseases.

A person describes sexual experience in a biographical narrative by means of available cultural instruments. Biographical data offers the possibility of analysing the categories through which sexuality is constructed in personal narratives. Sacks's method of *membership categorisation* is applied here to text analysis (Sacks 1972a, 1972b; Silverman, 1997). This method of text analysis is based on the identification of categories and category-bounded activities, through which Sacks and Silverman analyse 'the skills (artful practices) through which people come to develop an understanding of each other and of social situations' (Silverman 1997, p. 60). This technique is adopted here for the distinguishing of main themes (categories) around which narratives about sexual life have been organised, and for the analysis of actors (categories) and their activities (category-bounded activities) through which interactions are described in the text.

On the basis on the interviews I distinguish the following ideal types of sexual script: the *pronatal* script, where sexual life is described as reproductive/family life; the *romantic* script, where it is described as an expression of emotions and feelings (above all love); the *sensual* script, where it is described in terms of an orientation towards sexual pleasure; the *communicative* script, where it is described as a means of informal (or intellectual, or friendly) communication; the *market* script, where it is described as oriented towards material benefits; and the *achievement* script, where it is described as a means of self-realisation. Several scripts can be found in the same biography, depending on the stages of a person's life cycle or the context of the sexual relationships involved.

1. Pronatal (Family) Script

> Sexual life was defective, but I got used to it. (woman aged 63)

The story concerns relationships between (mainly) married couples. The actors are husband and wife. The script of the story as follows. The first sexual experience is formed by romantic love. The husband is the first sexual partner, and sexual life takes place within the marriage. Sexual interactions and sexual life are synonymous with marriage and reproduction, which forms the story into a narrative about pregnancies, childbirth and abortions. Sexual life has the trajectory of the relationships with the husband and childbirth. Sexual practices are described as monotonous, routine and unsatisfactory; it is generally difficult for the narrator to discuss sexuality and sexual satisfaction. Women's sexual activities are submitted to men's, and gender identification in sexual interactions is passive and irresponsible.

2. Romantic Script

> Sex is the consequence of feelings and the instrument of love. You have sex if you have an attachment to a person. (woman aged 46)

Sex is described as love, as an attribute of 'love', and as 'amorousness'. 'Love' is the main category in the vocabulary. Actors are lovers. The narrative is constructed as a series of romantic and emotional stories, where sex is a by-product of feelings and does not concern questions of technique. The narratives tell about steady relationships with a lover, and about a series of feelings (including excitable and dramatic ones), and sexual practices are described as embodying some constraints and difficulties.

Women's sexual activities are submitted to men's, and gender identification in sexual interactions is passive and irresponsible.

3. Communicative Script

> We are getting closer to each other not in order to have an orgasm, but in order to talk and communicate. We have sex to talk. (woman aged 32)

In this script, sex is described through the category of 'communication'. 'Understanding', 'language', 'personal relationship' are the main categories of the sexual vocabulary. Actors are friends. The story tells of a friendly relation with a close person, where sex is interpreted as an instrument for showing respect and friendship and for expressing commonality of interests. This is a story about personal relationships, the quality of which constitutes the main reason for having sexual relationships (within or outside marriage), and which are rooted in joint work or a shared milieu. Sexual interactions are described as a series of marital, extramarital or parallel relations, both steady and casual, and sexual pleasure and satisfaction are seen as objects of negotiation. Sexual knowledge may be obtained through the common experience, where a woman locates herself as an equal partner with a man. Sexual practices are extensively described, but mainly in response to questions from the interviewer.

4. Sensual Script

> I decide not to confuse sex and love ... I can have sex with a person for whom I have no feelings. Sex is the greatest pleasure given to human beings by nature. (woman aged 31)

The script describes sex as an autonomous sphere of life; it is distinguished from love, marriage and reproduction, and understood as a natural drive and expression of personality. The main categories in the sexual vocabulary are sexual pleasure and those which directly describe sexual practices. Actors are sexual partners. Detailed descriptions of sexual technique are given in the story. Sexual feelings are described as inborn, and virginity is considered something that one should lose as soon as possible, even with a casual partner. The main reason for having sexual relationships is 'to give pleasure and to take pleasure'; sexual relationships are conceived in terms of the satisfaction of hunger or appetite. A sexual interaction is a 'game' or an 'art', and a subject for discussion. Sexual relationships can also include lesbian sex and group sex. Women's gender identification is active and responsible.

5. Market Script

> I pay with sex for material benefits. (woman aged 34)

Sex in this script is described as a means of receiving material benefits: sex is 'work' to be done, and therefore men should pay for it. The actors are 'clients' or 'sponsors' and 'women who sell sex'. The stories talk about the sale of sex and about prostitution. Sexual life is scripted in terms of 'using', 'consumption' and 'resources'. The main reason for having sex is to receive material support in the form of money and/or other benefits. Relationships can be both casual and steady. Sexual pleasure is usually absent, but sexual practices are described in detail, and contraception is a subject for discussion. Women's gender identification is determined in terms of 'exchange', which may be interpreted as equal or subordinated to men's desire.

6. Achievement Script

> Sex improves my self-evaluation, it proves my value … I am important, I am needed. (woman aged 34)

> It proves that I am attractive. (woman aged 39)

This story is about self-evaluation and self-realisation: the motive behind having sex for the first time and for sexual relationships and marriage is to give proof of self-esteem. The actors are 'true women' and 'true men'. The relationships between them are both casual and steady. In this script, sex speaks of 'recognition' and confirmation of the woman's sexuality and femininity, and thus it is not important to receive sexual satisfaction, which can be faked. Sex is considered as a means for achieving status, and for attaining female competence demonstrated by male desire.

These scripts were reconstructed on the basis of interviews with both married and unmarried women (the data represent only a small number of the latter). The interviews were conducted with heterosexual women, though one case of sexual identity transformation also fitted the above distinct scripts.

The frames reconstructed above do not embrace all the possibilities of interpreting sexual conduct. Other interpretations can also be found in the texts, as for example when sexual interactions are described in the frame of an 'esoteric practice' or orthodox beliefs, but they are rarely presented as integral narratives. Another important theme is 'violence' (Zdravomyslova, 2000), but this could be looked upon as organising the whole life.

There is seldom an ideal type of script in an individual biography, and the frames change during the life course. The communicative and sensitive scripts may be considered more modern than the pronatal and romantic ones. Empirically speaking, the former are more typical for younger women and for the later stages of the life. This coincides with the liberalisation of sexuality in Western countries following the 1970s (Kontula and Haavio-Mannila, 1995; Laumann *et al.*, 1994), as well as with the findings of research on sexuality in post-Soviet Russia (Haavio-Mannila and Rotkirch, 1998; Rotkirch, 2000a; Golod, 1996). The achievement script is the script of modernisation of sexuality, and is widespread among women of the middle generation.

The period represented by the stories told in this research coincides with a rapid change in the nature of academic discourse regarding sexuality in Russia (Kon, 1995; Rotkirch, 2000), which had created new cultural possibilities for the interpretation of sexuality. These include the representation of 'new sexualities', prostitution, AIDS, pornography, sexual violence, sexual techniques and public discourses of sexual pleasure, all of which were totally 'closed' as public issues in the late-Soviet period. Structural possibilities had also changed, contraception became available, abortions became easier, and official control upon intimacy weakened. Such changes created possibilities for redefining a formerly 'silent' sexuality and making discussion of sexuality more open in public and in everyday life. At the same time, gender discourse did not undergo radical transformation during this period. Traditional gender norms were preserved in public discourse, although some new gender representations appeared (homosexual, feminist, etc.). In general, 'open' sexual discourse reproduces traditional gender stereotypes; this discourse is reflected in the biographies, where men are considered to be responsible for women's sexual identification, quality of sexual life and sexual pleasure. At the same time, new identities emerge, and women take responsibility for the quality of their sexual life and pleasure.

Below, I focus on the location of sexual pleasure within different sexual scripts, and then describe how sexual pleasure is constructed in biographies in relation to the characteristics and activities of the partners, the way in which they interact sexually, and the frame through which sexuality is described.

3 Differing Meanings of Pleasure in the Sexual Biographies

Pleasure, in the biographical narratives, is described in different ways. 'Moral', 'erotic' and 'sexual' (bodily) categories are the most common in such descriptions. These categories are opposed to the 'absence' of pleasure in the whole sexual life. The absence of pleasure, at least at the time of the first sexual experience, is something which the majority of the women mentioned. Those women who told their story in the frame of the pronatal script frequently reported the absence of pleasure throughout the whole life course. The contrasting case, which is opposed to the absence of pleasure, is the case of sexual satisfaction in the majority of relationships. This is the ideal type of the sensual script.

Erotic feelings and erotic pleasure are described in the majority of sexual scripts, with the exception of the pronatal and market scripts. Pleasure as a 'moral' feeling is opposed to 'bodily' perception and is often reported in the frame of the 'achievement' script. 'Moral' pleasure is described in terms of pleasure arising from the sexual relation itself.

The representation of pleasure is connected with the representation of gender identity. Pleasure is absent, or depends upon men's activity, in the cases of 'woman as mother' (the pronatal script) and 'beloved woman' (the 'romantic' script). Such women explain the absence of pleasure first in terms of their socialisation – in terms of structural conditions (the absence of private housing and of contraception) and the absence of sexual knowledge during the Soviet period – and secondly in terms of the behaviour of their partner. The partner (husband or lover) is responsible for the quality of sexual life. Women describe themselves as irresponsible and passive and as the object of male action and desire. Sex for them is separated from the body and from feeling. Women perceive themselves as the victims of social conditions and of their partner's behaviour in a frame of traditional stereotypes, which produces feelings of deprivation. This view is shown in the first story in the next section of the chapter.

Love is often described as an alternative to bodily pleasure. 'I felt in love. And this was enough for pleasure ... pleasure is not the same as orgasm' (woman aged 48). When a woman tells a story about love (the 'romantic script') her position is changed. She is active and responsible in her feeling, but she is still passive in the sexual relationship and is waiting for male activity *vis-à-vis* the achievement of sexual satisfaction. These interpretations are found in the second and third stories.

'Moral' pleasure in this type of narrative is intertwined with having sexual relationships. 'Very often I receive moral satisfaction from sexual intercourse' (woman aged 48). Pleasure depends on a claim for her body. 'Sex for me means confirmation, recognition' (woman aged 34). She is sexually desired and pleased. Woman is the object of (heterosexual) desire; her sexual 'recognition' is the base of gender identity in the sphere of sexuality. Her partner feels sexual desire, and this is the main condition for a woman's receiving moral pleasure. The woman's position is passive; she is the object of sexual desire and activity. This is shown in the second story.

Women of this age cohort often talk about the absence of sexual satisfaction, and about particular efforts to hide this absence. They talk about the faking of orgasm during intercourse and about masturbation, about which they feel 'guilty'. The reasons for the absence of sexual satisfaction and bodily pleasure are interpreted in the stories in terms of personal troubles: 'I am very repressed' (woman aged 40). Women of this generation consult professionals (psychotherapists, psychologists and sexologists) in order to solve the problem of the absence of pleasure. The quality of the sexual relationship depends either on the partner or on professional efforts. Such interpretation is also found in the second story.

Bodily pleasure in the frame of the sensual script is described as a 'natural function of the body' or as a 'process of learning'. The woman learns in 'communicative' or 'love' relations, and then begins to act as a free person, who makes her own sexual choice. She represents herself as responsible for the quality of her own sexual life. Her sexual relations presuppose her being sexually experienced and possessing a highly-developed sexual technique. This is illustrated in the third story.

The market script is based on the traditional gender identification of woman as the object of desire. Its ideal type does not include sexual pleasure.

One can find a combination of different scriptings of sexual pleasure in the actual stories. Different kinds of interaction and identity are referred to in the construction of sexual pleasure. In the following, I describe these interactions as they are framed by the different scripts. Three cases will be analysed in detail.

4 The Construction of Sexual Pleasure in Biographical Narratives

Case Study 1. 'Absence of Pleasure in Marital Life' (A, aged 57)

> My trouble is that I never feel orgasm with my husband.

This is a story about marital sex, scripted within the 'romantic' and 'family (pronatal)' frames. This story tells of the absence of bodily pleasure in sexual life. A is a widow, who has had one sexual partner (her husband) in her life. She was married at 32; she has no children; her husband has died.

The informant refers to the absence of sex education and of sexual interest prior to her twenties. She describes herself as having been in adolescence absolutely ignorant about sexuality. Owing to illness she even had no knowledge of human anatomy, which is taught at schools, and had no communication about this topic within her peer group. 'I was intelligent enough, but about this [sexuality] I was in darkness ... When my periods began at the age of sixteen and a half I decided that I must have been pierced through.' At the same time, she characterised the atmosphere in the parental family as one of intimacy, friendship and trust, things which for her were not connected with sexuality. The only source of information about sex she mentioned was classical literature. Her biography is constructed in the frame of sexual ignorance.

The next frame of reference is her first love, in her twenties, which is described in a very detailed way within the romantic frame. This first love was the strongest feeling in her life. She tells a story of dates with her lover and romantic letters, of their visiting each other in different cities and of her refusal to get married at 22 owing to her feeling of 'not being ready to become a woman'. Their bodily interactions were limited to kissing. Her beloved then had his first experience of sexual intercourse with another woman, who became pregnant, and they married. She evaluated the behaviour of her lover as 'treason'. Telling her story, A considers herself 'talented in love', and this talent she evaluates as 'God's gift', but she never 'struggled for her love'. Moreover, she considers that her talent in love 'as a mother, friend, lover and wife' was never realised, owing to the absence of appropriate men. Love was never united with sex in her life.

The next frame of reference is her marriage in her early thirties. The marriage script represents a traditional pronatal script (with the exception of childbearing). Her husband was much older than she was; he had been married twice previously, but this had no bearing on his sexual experience. A felt love for her fiancé, even though 'one half of her heart was burnt down in the previous love affair', but her husband was 'sufficiently intelligent, clever and adult' for her to respect and trust him. The death of her mother, to whom she was very close, forced her to get married.

She was not happy in her sexual life with her husband. 'My problem is that I never had an orgasm with my husband.' She explains this in terms of lack of experience and knowledge, and in terms of her own passivity. 'It was necessary to court me, but my husband was not interested in this … he was satisfied and immediately went to sleep.' Her partner did not take care of her sexual needs and pleasure, while she herself was afraid of revealing her needs. Their sexual interactions never included verbal communication, and served only for the satisfaction of her husband's sexual need. Their living conditions are described as having limited the sexual relationship: for seven years they lived in different cities and visited each other.

She also evaluates her sexual life as unhappy because she 'didn't implement a women's destiny – to give birth to a child'. Her husband was responsible for her not having children. When she became pregnant, in her 40s, her husband reacted very roughly and the pregnancy was spontaneously interrupted. Her husband was also against their adopting a child.

After her husband's death she saw no possibility of a new relationship. 'In my late 50s, I am as inexperienced in a sexual sense as a young woman in her 20s. This is ridiculous … It is not so ridiculous in one's 30s – probably a woman will not have been lucky enough to meet a true man.' An absence of knowledge and experience deprives this woman of possible relationships, although she feels that she still could love.

A man (her husband) was responsible for the quality of her sexual life (the absence of sexual pleasure), as well as for the fulfilment of her destiny as a woman. For a woman, it is necessary to meet a 'true man' who will take care of her sexual life. A describes herself as passive, as the object of male action and desire. Sex in her life is separated from emotions and from the body. She perceives herself as the victims of her partner's behaviour in the frame of traditional stereotypes, which have led to a feeling of deprivation.

Case Study 2. 'Search for Recognition and Benefits' (B, aged 34)

> Sexual relations prove that I am valued … they are sometimes beneficial.

This story illustrates a shift from a dominant frame of 'achievement' to a market frame. The narrative also includes situations which are framed by romantic and sensual scripts. B was married and divorced. She has two children, and before, during and after her marriage she had multiple, steady and casual, relationships. After her 30s she also had a homosexual relationship.

Her first reference was to her first sexual experience. She describes herself being a virgin as follows: 'In my early 20s I felt myself inferior... Everybody had something, and me not, so I should do this.' First sexual relationships were very important: 'They prove that I am valued. It increased my personal self-evaluation ... it was my recognition.' She relates that there was no pleasure in that relationship, except for a moral one. Her first partner educated her, gave her literature, explained what masturbation meant. He was older than her, and was married, but she didn't feel jealousy. She thought his relationships with other women were 'exploitative' both for him and for the women. By contrast, she thought their relationship was better than his other relationships as she did not exploit him (although she felt he exploited her). To him, she was just another woman: 'naïve, ingenuous, innocent ... uncritical. It was secure for him.' Simultaneously, she had sexual relationships with other casual partners. None of these relations was pleasurable in the bodily sense. 'I had little pleasure from this, practically none. Sometimes it was painful, but I feigned [pleasure]. I feigned pleasure and I was successful in that.' But she did receive moral pleasure: 'I was claimed.' She identifies herself, in such relations, as the person who is sexually wanted (the object of men's desire), and her partner as the person who wanted her (the subject of desire). Their sexual interaction proves her self-evaluation and confirms it. Her identification in this frame is as a non-experienced woman who is desired. Her partner is the experienced one; there are no feelings between them; they are connected through the opposition 'desirer and desired'.

The next frame of reference is her marriage, which lasted for ten years. She fell in love with her future husband, but the love was very short-lived ('I fell in love for three days ... It was something unusual, but it's gone') and the love was not her reason for getting married. She wanted to get married: 'I was 22 or 23. Practically everyone around me was married. I felt a spinster, my job didn't satisfy me, it was necessary to do something to improve my self-esteem.' She described her husband as a loving man who was interested in having sex with her and marrying her. She identifies herself as experienced regarding sex, though it does not provide her with sexual satisfaction. This was the reason for her consulting a professional sexologist.

This is the next important interaction to which she refers in her story. She felt deprived of pleasure, which she knew about from 'special literature'. Professionals did not help her; after her visits she felt guilty for not talking about sex with her husband, for her immaturity and for her problems with lack of satisfaction. The end result was that her inferiority complex grew.

She then changed her strategy in the sexual interaction with her husband. 'My husband became for me an object of consumption. I permitted myself to masturbate ... and I had no need for anything else.' Her husband was redefined as the object of (sexual) consumption.

New, parallel partners appeared at this time. She told of feeling shy about masturbating and of faking orgasms with partners outside her marriage. If she had strong feelings, sexual pleasure was not necessary for her. 'I was disappointed in sex ... he wasn't interesting as the sexual partner. I faked it and he didn't mention this – he was very self-confident. But the love was so strong that sex did not make any difference – I could bear it.' This is a typical identification of a romantic relationship, where sex and pleasure are not important. She formulates alternatives: either she uses a man as an object (her husband), or else she is being used as an object of desire herself (by her lover). Feelings of love limit her ability to use a partner. She is passive in the romantic sexual relationship, and is waiting for male activity in the achievement of sexual satisfaction.

She describes some other relationship as having been 'beneficial': 'I received material benefits: presents, books, which I couldn't buy. I was invited ... Sometimes money... I paid by sex.' (This is the period of the late-Soviet shortages.) Her sexual relationships later on include group sex and lesbian sex and relationships where her partners (including her husband) took the initiative. A (foreign) woman insisted on having sex with her. 'My husband asked me, why not try?' She related that her female partner fell in love, and 'I felt sorry about that, and I agreed out of kindness'. 'Sensations were exciting ... It was quite a new experience.' B described this relationship as beneficial in a material sense. Her husband was offered some work owing to the efforts of her female partner.

Then she fell in love with another woman, who insisted that B divorce. B describes her feelings as having been very strong. She explains that there is no difference for her in having sex with a man or a woman; the difference is purely a 'technical one'. 'Sex was very obsessive ... night, day, night. I was exhausted, it was painful. But I wish this woman to be with me and I bear it.' B explained that the main difference for her is that she should 'try not to dissemble'. 'I think that this is the right way, but it costs … It is very difficult … I am too much of a coward and I am afraid to lose the benefits … I am afraid to be poor and [so] I paid for moral and financial benefits.' The alternative still exists: either to be sincere in sexual relationships – that is, to manifest real bodily feelings (including problems achieving satisfaction) – or to dissemble. She explains that it is now not necessary for a man (or woman) to desire her for her to feel self-confirmation, but she is still economically dependent on sexual relationships and wishes to be free from this, to receive money from her own work. She is trying to improve the quality of her sexual life by moving it in the direction of more open and intimate relations and more pleasurable sex, but she is still limited by economic restraints. She manifests a wish to change her gender identity in accordance with her current identification, that is, to be free from structural strains and 'beneficial' sex.

Case Study 3. 'Sexual Pleasure as a Learning Process' (C, aged 46)

> In the course of my life I have had more and more casual sexual encounters.

This story shows the changing of the script from pronatal to romantic and communicative and then to sensual. C spoke of the romantic script in terms of 'true love', 'passion' and a 'mad love affair', and of the sensual script as 'technical', 'simple, good, easy' sex, where it is enough 'to desire each other' and 'to love each other's bodies'. C was married and then divorced, and both during her marriage and afterwards she had parallel steady and casual relationships. Her story is a story of the redefinition of sexual pleasure. In the interview she characterises her orientation as striving for sexual pleasure in multiple relationships.

She refers to sex education in the parental family as having been for her an important context. She connects sexual problems in marriage with a lack of sex education. She often mentions this lack and describes her behaviour as a means of overcoming this problem. C describes how she learnt from her youth two contrary ways of conceiving of sex. On the one hand, she understood sex as something 'indecent', 'unintelligible' and 'dangerous'. 'I had strange views in my youth. When I was 19, after petting I thought about pregnancy.' She explains this as a consequence of her upbringing ('Nobody told me anything'), and underlines her lack of knowledge and understanding. On the other hand, she characterises the atmosphere in the parental home as one of love and intimacy. This formed the basis for her idea that wife and husband are sexually happy. Thus she also expected herself to have a happy sexual life in marriage, and oriented herself towards not having sex before marriage. The main categories – running counter to her interpretation of sex in her later life – are 'lack of knowledge' and 'orientation towards having sex in marriage'. Her biography can be constructed as a process of her improving her own sexual experience and of separating sex from marriage.

The second frame of reference is her marriage in her twenties. The marriage script represents traditional variants of sexuality (the pronatal script). C provided the following descriptions. Her first sexual contact was with her husband. She characterises her husband as having been an 'honest, good person' and 'intelligent'; she respected him, but felt a lack of love and sexual attraction. She was not happy in her sexual life with her husband. She explains this in terms of their attitudes towards sex and their lack of experience and knowledge. Her husband is characterised as a non-experienced person, 'without [a] culture of sexual communication'. He treated sex as 'satisfaction of needs, like hunger, thirst'. 'I felt that sex was indecent, he that it was harmful.' She describes the marriage as lacking in love and in sexual satisfaction.

Another problem, in her story, relates to gender relations in marriage. She describes her husband's feelings as those of a 'typical male', which are oriented towards sexual conquests, of making a wife belong to him and of treating her as property. Throughout her life she has wanted to overcome these gendered attitudes. She repudiates the notion of woman as property and orients herself towards an egalitarian choice, and even towards the task of teaching a 'sexually inexperienced man'.

The next frame of reference is an extramarital relationship with her first lover (which lasted for several years), for whom she had a 'strong passion'. This relationship is evaluated as love, as 'passion', based on common interests, and characterised by powerful sexual attraction, desire, and strong feelings of jealousy. There was not such a good personal, human relationship as she had with her husband. She described this relationship in terms of a process of learning about sex: 'because of him I understood what sex was'.

C describes her life in her thirties (after her divorce) as having been 'strange' or 'different', with both casual and permanent relationships. This period, which she characterised as sexually satisfactory, stands in opposition to the previous one. She described her relationships with two steady lovers. With the first lover the relationship lasted eight years, and consisted of rare dates considered as 'holiday occasions'. The context of this relationship was determined by the status of her partner, who was married without having an intention to divorce, and her own status as a single mother living with her son in conditions (including housing) not conducive to intimacy. The relationship developed from one of love to one of habit in the context of limited choice. Later, when her son was older, she began to have casual relationships.

The relationship with her second lover lasted nearly three years, and she describes it as having contained 'strong love with passion'. She pictures it in terms of 'harmony' and of 'sexual perfection' involving 'mutual sexual abilities and skills'. Her 'sense of inferiority' was 'overcome', and her relationship with her body changed. At that time she 'did not need any other partners'. Her narrative about this partner is very short, and there is no explanation for why the relationship ended. This was the only relationship about which she did not feel like providing any details. 'I know what I did for him, but I don't want to speak about it.' A unity of love and sexual satisfaction is the basic frame of reference for this relationship. In other cases, the absence of love is approved on the basis of an assertion of the possibility of separation of sex from love.

The connection between the different periods is explicitly mentioned. Casual relationships began when 'I recovered from being sick after my divorce' and after being desperate for a love affair. 'I was physically sick, and one of my friends, a psychotherapist, told me that I should immediately have sexual contacts ... And I did ... This happened after I turned forty.'

C's current relationships are distinct from any love-relationship ('Such a love does not happen more than two to three times in a life'). They are distinct from marriage, which she considers as a 'complicated system of financial, material, moral, and kinship relationships, which also includes problems of housing, ageing, health'. They are not based on shared interests and views or shared intimacy. They presuppose experience, abilities, skills, and highly-developed sexual technique. Sexual satisfaction for C derives from her practice and has become a 'mechanical experience'.

She teaches men who lack skills and experience. These men are evaluated as 'helpless in sexual life'; their attitudes towards sex are 'terrible' (they are similar to her husband's and her own when she was young). A man as a teacher (her first lover) turns into a partner in training (her last lover) and then into a pupil. Man – she means all men – needs to be taught, 'has no idea about his abilities', and 'hesitates to speak about sex'. He has 'complexes and fears' and 'feels shy about bodies', his 'sensuality is not developed', he cannot 'enjoy and get pleasure from sex', and he cannot 'give pleasure to a woman'. He is 'shy and vulnerable'.

What kind of woman can teach sex? She does not want to 'own' the man; she feels no jealousy and considers herself sexually superior; she knows her own body well; she expresses respect for wives and mistresses; she has no financial problems (she is currently working in business); she has experiences that younger women usually do not have. She makes her own sexual choices, and she 'teaches all her partners'. Sexual relationships can, however, lead to 'strong feeling and love': 'it is desirable to have love and sex. But this is not what happens every time.'

These features are distinct from those of her early life. Sexual relationships oriented towards sexual pleasure are connected with experience, knowledge (learning), status and age. Her sexuality is described in terms of a learning process, through which her gender identity becomes responsible, active and experienced.

Conclusion

The analysis of the empirical material presented above shows that the construction of women's sexual pleasure depends on the identification of the sexual script. Different gender identities led to different expectations about pleasure and its realisations. The script determines (and is determined by) who is responsible and who is active: the man, the woman, or both partners. In the majority of sexual situations, men are identified by women as dominant and as responsible for women's pleasure. The 'pronatal (family)', 'romantic', 'achievement' and 'market' scripts frame the subordinated identity of women. Hierarchical domination also exists between women where their sexual relations are scripted by the 'market' script. The 'communicative' and 'sensual' scripts create an opportunity to change identities and thus to overcome the hierarchical system in sexual relationships.

Notes

1 R. Connell and G. Dowsett define the script approach as a 'frame theory' of sexuality (Connell and Dowsett, 1992).

2 These interviews were collected in the course of a Finnish-Russian project 'Cultural Intertia and Social Changes in Russia' in 1996–7. One part of this project was devoted

to research on sexuality in St Petersburg. It included a representative survey, the conducting of 25 interviews with women and 25 with men, and a biographical competition (under the supervision of E. Haavio-Mannila, J.P. Roos and A. Rotkirch). Some of the findings of this study are published in English and Russian: Haavio-Mannila and Rotkirch (1997, 2000), Rotkirch (1999a, 1999b, 2000a, 2000b, 2002), Temkina (1999, 2000), Zdravomyslova (2000). This chapter is based on the interview material, collected by a group of researchers under the supervision of Elena Zdravomyslova. Four of the interviews were conducted by me, while others were conducted by my colleagues who were involved in this project. I also conducted two additional interviews with middle-aged women.

References

Connell, R. and Dowsett, G. (1992), 'The Unclean Motion of the Generative Parts: Frameworks in Western Thought on Sexuality', in R. Connell and G. Dowsett (eds), *Rethinking Sex: Social Theory and Sexuality Research*, Melbourne University Press, Melbourne.

Gagnon, J. (1990), 'The Explicit and Implicit Use of the Scripting Perspective in Sex Research', in J. Bancroft (ed.), *Annual Review of Sex Research*, Vol. 1, pp. 1–44.

Gagnon, J.H. and Simon, W. (1973), *Sexual Conduct: The Social Sources of Human Sexuality*, Aldine, Chicago, IL.

Gagnon, J.H. and Simon, W. (1987), 'The Scripting of Oral-Genital Sexual Conduct', *Archives of Sexual Behaviour*, vol. 16, no. 1, pp. 1–25.

Golod, S. (1996), *XX vek i tendentsii seksual'nykh otnoshenij v Rossii* [The 20th Century and Sexual Relations Tendencies in Russia], Aleteja, St Petersburg.

Golod, S. (1999), 'Seksual'naya emansipatsija zhenshchin i problema Drugogo' [Sexual Emancipation of Women and the Problem of the Other], *Zhurnal sotsiologii i sotsial'noj antropologii* [Journal of Sociology and Social Anthropology], no. 2, pp. 105–14.

Golod, S. (2000), 'Rossijskie seksual'nye standarty i ikh transformatsii (vtoraja polovina XX stoletija)' [Russian Sexual Standards and their Transformation (Second Half of the 20th Century)], *Zhurnal sotsiologii i sotsial'noj antropologii* [Journal of Sociology and Social Anthropology], no 2, pp. 139–53.

Haavio-Mannila, E. and Rotkirch, A. (1998), 'Generational and Gender Differences in Sexual Life in St Petersburg and Urban Finland', *Yearbook of Population Research in Finland*, vol. 34, pp. 133–60.

Haavio-Mannila, E. and Rotkirch, A. (2000), 'Gender Liberalisation and Polarisation: Comparing Sexuality in St Petersburg, Finland and Sweden', *Idäntutkimus*, vol. 7, nos 3–4, pp. 4–25.

Haavio-Mannila, E., Kontula, O., Lewin, B., Rotkirch, A., Temkina, A. and Traneen, B. (2000), 'Indicators of Sexual Life', University of Helsinki [manuscript].

Jackson, S. (1999), *Heterosexuality in Question*, Sage, London.

Jackson, S. and Scott, S. (eds) (1996), *Feminism and Sexuality: A Reader*, Edinburgh University Press, Edinburgh.

Kon, I. (1995), *The Sexual Revolution in Russia: From the Age of the Czars to Today*, The Free Press, New York.

Kontula, O. and Haavio-Mannila, E. (1995), *Sexual Pleasure: Enhancement of Sex Life in Finland, 1971–1992*, Dartmouth, Aldershot.

Laumann, E., Gagnon, J., Michael, R.T. and Michael, S. (1994), *The Social Organisation of Sexuality: Sexual Practices in the United States*, University of Chicago Press, Chicago, IL.

Lorber, J. (1994), *Paradoxes of Gender*, Yale University Press, New Haven, CT and London.

Parker, R. and Aggeton, P. (1999), *Culture, Society and Sexuality: A Reader*, UCL Press, London.

Plummer, K. (1982), 'Symbolic Interactionism and Sexual Conduct: An Emergent Perspective', in M. Brake (ed.), *Human Sexual Relations*, Penguin, Harmondsworth, pp. 223–44.

Plummer, K. (1995), *Telling Sexual Stories: Power, Change and Social Worlds*, Routledge, London.

Rosenthal, G. (1993), 'Reconstruction of Life Stories: Principle of Selection in Generating Stories for Narrative Biographical Interviews', in *The Narrative Study of Lives*, Sage, London, vol. 2, no. 1, pp. 59–91.

Rotkirch, A. (1999a), 'Journeys as Sexual Transgression During Late Socialism', in J. Smith (ed.), *Beyond the Limits: The Concept of Space in Russian History and Culture*, Finnish Literary Society, Helsinki.

Rotkirch, A. (1999b), 'Women's Agency and the Sexual Revolution in Russia', in P. Ahponen (ed.), *Women's Active Citizenship*, University of Joensuu Studies in Social Policy, vol. 9, pp. 91–104.

Rotkirch, A. (2000a), *The Man Question: Loves and Lives in Late 20th Century Russia*, Research Report No. 1, Department of Social Policy, University of Helsinki, Helsinki.

Rotkirch, A. (2000b), 'Loving with and without Words: Same-sex Experiences in Women's Autobiographies during Late Socialism', in M. Lijestrom, A. Rosenholm and I. Savkina (eds), *Models of Self: Russian Women's Autobiographical Texts*, Kikimora [Series B: 18], Helsinki, pp. 229–48.

Sacks, H. (1972a), 'On the Analysability of Stories by Children', in J. Gumpertz and D. Hymes (eds), *Directions in Sociolinguistics: The Ethnography of Communication*, Holt, Rinehart & Winston, New York, pp. 329–45.

Sacks, H. (1972b), 'An Initial Investigation of the Usability of Conversational Data for Doing Sociology', in D. Sudnow (ed.), *Studies in Social Interaction*, The Free Press, New York, pp. 31–74.

Silverman, D. (1997), *Interpreting Qualitative Data: Methods for Analysing Talk, Test and Interaction*, Sage, London.

Simon, W. (1996), *Postmodern Sexualities*, Routledge, New York.

Simon, W. and Gagnon, J. (1984), 'Sexual Scripts', *Society*, vol. 22, no. 1.

Temkina, A. (1999), 'Dinamika stsenariev seksual'nosti v avtobiografijakh sovremennykh rossijskikh zhenshchin: opyt konstruktivistskogo issledovanija seksual'nogo udovol'stvija' [Trends of Sexual Scripts in the Autobiographies of Russian Women: The Constructive Analysis of Sexual Pleasure], in A. Kletsin (ed.), *Gendernye tetradi* [Gender Papers], Issue 2, Institute of Sociology, St Petersburg, pp. 20–54.

Temkina, A. (2000), 'Sexual Scripts in Women's Biographies and the Construction of Sexual Pleasure', in M. Lijestrom, A. Rosenholm and I. Savkina (eds), *Models of Self: Russian Women's Autobiographical Texts*, Kikimora [Series B: 18], Helsinki, pp. 187–206.

Weeks, J. (1985), *Sexuality and its Discontents*, Routledge, London and New York.
Weeks, J. (1997), 'Sexual Values Revisited', in L. Segal (ed.), *New Sexual Agendas*, Macmillan, Basingstoke, pp. 43–59.
Zdravomyslova, E. (2000), 'A Cultural Paradigm of Sexual Violence Reconstructed from a Women's Biographical Interview', in M. Lijestrom, A. Rosenholm and I. Savkina (eds), *Models of Self: Russian Women's Autobiographical Texts*, Kikimora [Series B: 18], Helsinki, pp. 207–22.
Zita, J. (1998), *Philosophical Reflections on Sex and Gender*, Columbia University Press, New York.

Index